Armies and Warfare in the Middle Ages

The English Experience

Michael Prestwich

Yale University Press
New Haven and London   1996

Set in Sabon by Best-set Typesetter Ltd, Hong Kong
Printed and bound in China through World Print Ltd

Library of Congress Cataloging-in-Publication Data

Prestwich, Michael.
  English armies in the Middle Ages: the English Experience by Michael Prestwich.
  Includes bibliographical references and index.
  ISBN 0–300–06452–7 (hbk.)
  ISBN 0–300–07663–0 (pbk.)
  1. Great Britain—History, Military—1066–1485. 2. Great Britain—History—Plantagenets, 1154–1399. 3. Military art and science—England—History. 4. Armies—England—History. I. Title.
DA60.P74   1996
355.3′0942′0902—dc20   95–36142
                                                              CIP

A catalogue record for this book is available from the British Library.

Armies and Warfare in the Middle Ages

Contents

Illustration Acknowledgements

By permission of the British Library: x (Stowe 54 f.83), 13 (Add. MS. 42130 f.202v), 14 (Cotton Nero D VI f.61v), 20 (Roy. 2 A XXII f.220), 27 (Stowe Ch. 622), 50 bottom (Stowe 553 61v), 79 (Roy. 2 B vii), 85 (Cotton Julius E IV f.6v), 94 top (Cotton Nero D VI f.4), 94 bottom (Cotton Nero D VII f.7), 114, (Add. MS. 47680 f.40), 132 (all Add. MS. 42130 f.56), 139 (Add. MS. 42130 f.147v), 144 (Cotton Nero E II (2) f.166), 158 (Cotton Nero D VI f.31), 167 (Roy. C VII f.41v), 205 (Cotton Julius E IV art.6), 221 (Cotton Julius D I f.17v), 225 (Harley 4379 f.43), 226 top (Cotton Nero D VII f.105v), 261 (Roy. C. 20 VII f.41v), 264 bottom (Add. MS. 42130 f.161v), 265 (Roy. 10 E f.19), 279 (Roy. 20 C VII f.189v), 283 (Roy. 14 E IV f. 281v), 316 (Arundel 48 f.168v); (c) RMN, Paris: 3; Bibliothèque Nationale, Paris: 4 (MS. fr. 2643 f.18), 102 (MS. fr. 2643 f.77v), 107 (MS. fr. 2643 f.312v), 203 (MS. fr. 2643 f.207), 226 bottom (MS. fr. 2692 f.67v–68), 227 (MS. fr. 343 f.3), 321 (MS. fr. 2643 f. 165v); Courtesy of the Board of Trustees of the Victoria and Albert Museum, London: 8; The Pierpont Morgan Library, New York: 19 bottom (MS. 619), 163 (MS. 804 f.128), 244 (MS. 638 f.27v), 279 (MS. 804 f.44v); Copyright British Museum, London: 21, 23, 18, 236; Courtesy the Monumental Brass Society: 22 (all three); Photo RCHME © Crown copyright: 24, 112; Museum of London: 25; Courtesy Master and Fellows of Trinity College, Cambridge: 29 bottom (MS. O.9.34 f.24); The Dean and Chapter of Durham: 28 bottom, 170, 238; The Bodleian Library, Oxford: 28 top (MS. Douce 180 f. 31), 329 (MS. Arch.Selden B. 26 f.17v); Ashmolean Museum, Oxford: 36 bottom; Leiden University Library: 37 (MS. BPL 20 f. 60); Conway Library, Courtauld Institute of Art, London: 50 top, 99, 162; The Governing Body of Christ Church, Oxford: 82 (MS. 92 f3), 290 bottom (MS. 92 f.67), 292 (MS. 92 f.73v); Burgerbibliothek, Bern: 105 (Cod. 120 II f.129); © The Trustees of the National Museums of Scotland 1996: 108; Photographie Giraudon: 130 top, 140, 241; The Master and Fellows of Corpus Christi College, Cambridge: 130 bottom (MS. 16 f.52), 309 top (MS. 16 f.85); AnitkvariskTopografiska Arkivet, Stockholm: 137; Public Record Office, London: 138 (E101/46/20); Reproduction by permission of the Syndics of the Fitzwilliam Museum, Cambridge: 184 (Marlay. Add. 1 f.2v); Photo the author: 207, 210, 290 top, 291; Suffolk Archaeological Unit © Suffolk County Council: 295; By permission of the Syndics of Cambridge University Library: 309 bottom (MS. Ee 3. 59 f.32v); Glasgow Museums, The Burrell Collection: 316.

Preface

The history of the medieval army is very different from that of more modern forces. The absence of regiments, the fact that there was no career path for army officers, nor indeed anything approaching a standing army, alone makes it distinct. Yet in other respects there were striking similarities, for many of the problems of fighting with cavalry and footsoldiers remained much the same until the advent of mechanisation. Ideas that the middle ages were somehow characterised by something called 'feudal warfare' in which concepts of strategy, military intelligence, and even tactics had no place are the product of prejudice, not of evidence.

Military history is often written, with some considerable success, by military men. I have to confess that as a British citizen in the second half of the twentieth century I have no military experience. I do not count Tuesday afternoons in the school cadet force, for they taught me little. Poking the barrel of a dismantled Bren gun out of a bush while waving a football rattle, bore, I believe, little resemblance to the reality of soldiering. I do not even have experience in the skills which were vital to medieval soldiers; I have not sat on a horse since the age of twelve, and cannot hit a target with bow and arrow at any appreciable range. There is a view that it is only women who should write women's history; I hope that military history can be written by a civilian.

The aim of this book is to examine the ways in which soldiers were recruited, commanded and supplied in medieval England, together with the way they fought. The reasons why men fought were complex. In part, the answer lies in systems of obligation, but the question of the material rewards of pay and plunder was at least as important. There was no simple progression from a world in which men served in return for holding land, to one in which they fought in return for pay. The importance of food to armies hardly needs emphasis, and the means by which men were provided with the very considerable quantities of grain, meat, fish and drink they required need to be investigated. Both strategy and tactics are examined, as are the set-piece military occasions of siege and battle.

The selection of commanders was important, as was the quality of information provided for them. Although this is a book about armies, it would not be complete without some consideration of shipping, for the transport of men and supplies presented its own challenges. It is not easy to reconstruct the mentality of the past, but the question of how far, and in what ways, chivalry affected the reality of warfare is one which cannot be ignored, even if all the questions cannot be fully answered. I hope that by drawing these various elements together a picture may emerge of the way in which medieval English armies functioned.

There are no clear starting and finishing dates for this study, but readers will rapidly discover that there is a concentration on the thirteenth and fourteenth centuries. There is no consideration of the relative obscurity of the centuries before the eleventh, and little of the fifteenth beyond the reign of Henry V. The Wars of the Roses are not within the book's scope. One justification for this chronological emphasis is that the documentation is especially full for the thirteenth and fourteenth centuries; another is that it was then that highly important developments were taking place. If there was a medieval military revolution, it was perhaps in that period that it happened. One of the themes of the study is to determine whether the concept of such a revolution, which has been applied with enthusiasm to their period by historians of the sixteenth and seventeenth centuries, is applicable to an earlier age.

Some disclaimers are needed. This is a study of English armies, and there is therefore little discussion of the armies that the English raised in Gascony to fight during the Hundred Years War. The English contribution to crusading warfare is another element which is not extensively considered. It is not the intention to explore the financial aspects of warfare in any detail. It was of course the case that it was only because the state found ways of extracting substantial sums of money from its subjects that it was possible to recruit large armies and sustain expensive wars. This is a vital part of the background to the themes which are taken forward in the following chapters, but to examine financial policy and administration in detail would be to move too far away from the central subject matter, though these matters are briefly raised in the final chapter.

My thanks are due to various colleagues and friends for their advice and help. John Gillingham and Mark Ormrod read a complete draft of the book; their comments have done much to improve it. Anne Curry has generously provided me with advance copies of her work, as has Matthew Strickland with some of his. I have had fruitful conversations with Robin Frame. Ann Hyland has been generous in her visits to Durham, when she has tried to remedy my ignorance about horses. I have learned much from teaching both undergraduate and graduate students, and should acknowledge in particular Michael Haskell, Ruth Ingamells and Andrew Fisher. My father has of course done much over many years to inspire my interest in matters medieval and military; I hope it will please him that Geoffrey de Mandeville makes an entrance in a small way in this book. I am grateful to him for his constructive comments on draft chapters. Historians always depend on the work of their predecessors, and this is especially the case in a wide-ranging study such as this; I hope that my debts to the many previous scholars who have worked on this field have been sufficiently acknowledged in the notes. The faults in the book are, of course, all my own. My thanks are also due to all those involved in the university administration at Durham, for making it possible for me to continue to write while engaged in other duties. The History department has been generous with its support, both in providing travel grants for work in the Public Record Office and in other ways. Steven Allan of the Geography Department kindly drew the sketch maps. I am very grateful to Robert Baldock and Sheila Lee at Yale University Press for all their assistance, and to my excellent copy-editor, Margaret Wallace. My main thanks naturally go to my wife Maggie, who has read many drafts, corrected proofs and provided invaluable encouragement.

Michael Prestwich
Durham, March 1995

1

The Nature of Medieval Warfare

It is not easy to recapture the reality of medieval war. It is not that there is no direct evidence from participants, for although most chroniclers probably had no practical personal experience of fighting, there were a few who did. William of Poitiers, who described William I's conquest of England, had a military career. In the fourteenth century Thomas Grey, a northern knight, was captured by the Scots and used his period as a prisoner of war to write his *Scalacronica*. Henry V's chaplain, who wrote the *Gesta Henrici Quinti*, was present at Agincourt, though in the rear not the front line. Contemporary authors, however, were not concerned to provide later generations with a sense of what it was like to be in a medieval army. Their interest, understandably, was with the course of events in a wider sense.

In 1233 the young Richard Marshal rebelled. He was the second son of the great William Marshal, a man who had risen from relative youthful poverty and obscurity to the heights of the earldom of Pembroke and the regency of England during Henry III's minority. The account of the rising in the pages of Roger of Wendover's chronicle gives a very traditional impression of medieval warfare. It is a tale of mounted knights, of great feats of arms, bravery and betrayal. At Monmouth in 1233 the Marshal with a small force was attacked by Baldwin de Gynes with a much larger one. During the conflict, Baldwin with a dozen well-armed companions attempted to capture the Marshal. The latter was able to keep his assailants off, swinging his sword to left and right. Eventually his horse was slain by lance thrusts, but the Marshal, trained on the battlefields of France, unhorsed one of Baldwin's knights by pulling at his leg. He then jumped into the saddle, and continued the fight. Baldwin, infuriated by this lengthy resistance, rode up and grabbed the Marshal's helmet, heaving at it so hard that the blood poured from his mouth and nose. In the final conflict in Ireland, when the Marshal was betrayed and captured, he put up a magnificent display. One of his opponents, Richard de Burgh, attempted to grapple with him and pull his helmet off, but as he raised his arms the Marshal with one sword blow cut

An idealised, romantic view of medieval warfare: a battle at the gates of a city, from a late fourteenth-century manuscript.

off his hands. Another knight wishing to avenge Richard was struck a fearsome blow by the Marshal, which split his body in two down to the navel. Not surprisingly, few dared go near him, until at the end of the battle common soldiers surrounded him, unhorsing him by a savage attack on his mount. Fallen to the ground, the exhausted Marshal was not so formidable an enemy, and he was mortally wounded by blows from behind. He died a few days later from a combination of his injuries and the medical treatment he received. There are hints, even in Wendover's highly coloured account of the Marshal's rising, of another aspect of warfare. The region between Shrewsbury and the Welsh border was ravaged, and Shrewsbury itself burned. Corpses lay unburied, and the smell of death lay on the countryside.[1]

A sanitised and glamorised image of war was provided by the poet who accompanied the army which marched north from Carlisle in 1300. The colour and pageantry impressed him greatly. 'There were many rich caparisons embroidered on silks and satins; many a beautiful pennon fixed to a lance; and many a banner displayed. And afar off was the noise heard of the neighing of horses: mountains and valleys were everywhere covered with sumpter horses and waggons with provisions, and sacks of tents and pavilions. And the days were long and fine.' When the army reached Caerlaverock castle, it encamped ready for the siege. 'Then were the banners arranged, when one might observe many a warrior there exercising his horse; and there appeared three thousand brave men-at-arms; then might be seen gold and silver, and the noblest and best of all rich colours, so as entirely to illuminate the valley.' Tents were put up to accommodate the troops, 'and leaves, herbs, and flowers gathered in the woods, which were strewed within; and then our people took up their quarters'.[2] This vision may not have been all that much of an exaggeration, as far as the élite of the army were concerned. A few years later, early in Edward II's reign, fifteen tents were bought for the king and his army, at a cost of £500. Two were substantial halls, one with seven posts and two porches. There was a four-posted chapel, and even ten stables for the horses.[3]

Comfort could hardly be guaranteed in war. A strikingly realistic account of campaigning is that provided by the Hainaulter, Jean le Bel, who accompanied a troop of his compatriots to England in 1327. The campaign took place in Weardale, directed against a Scottish force raiding south. Things began badly, with a riot in York between the English archers and the Hainaulters. The latter had to confine themselves to their quarters, arms at the ready, constantly alert for further trouble. Four weeks were spent waiting in York; eventually the army moved north, to Durham and then up into Weardale. They could see where the Scots had been, from the fires of

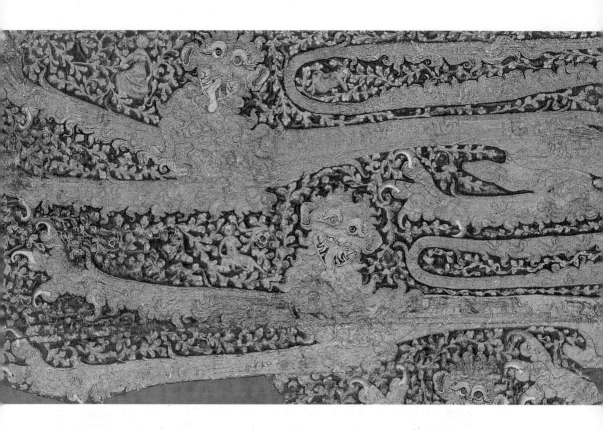

the burning homesteads they destroyed, but two days were spent in
trying vainly to locate them. The infantry was worn out, and could
go no further. The next day saw the cavalry make an early start, and
again there was a fruitless search for the Scots in the wild moorland.
By evening they reached the Tyne, which they forded with considerable difficulty. There were not enough axes to cut down trees to
make shelter; the men had to lie in the open in full armour, holding
the bridles of their horses to prevent them from moving off. The only
food was loaves of bread, which had been carried behind their
saddles, and was soaked through with the sweat of the horses. A few
magnates had some wine, brought on pack-horses, but most of the
men had to drink the river-water. Next morning it began to rain, and
it poured all day long. The following day some provisions were
brought to the army by traders; poor quality bread and thin wine, at
exorbitant prices. The men stayed encamped for four days, their
clothing soaked, their equipment starting to rot. There was no fuel to
make fires. Not surprisingly, the men began to quarrel, particularly
over food. Eventually the army moved off, once again crossing the
Tyne. After three days, news was brought of the whereabouts of the
Scots. Preparations were made for battle, but the Scots were in too
strong a position, high on a hillside. Another intolerably uncomfort-

An early fourteenth-century embroidered horse trapper, showing
the leopards of England. The style and quality of the work, with
coloured silks, silver and silver-gilt thread on a velvet ground,
as well as the royal leopards, suggest that this was made for
Edward III.

The Weardale campaign, 1327, as depicted in a fifteenth-century manuscript of Froissart's *Chronicles*. The Scots occupy the high ground.

able night was spent in the open, in full armour, with no camp fires and nowhere to tie up the horses. Three days passed, with nothing more than futile skirmishing between the two armies. The Scots then decamped at night, and moved off to an even stronger position. Eighteen days were spent with the two sides facing each other. Heralds were sent to try to persuade the Scots to join battle on level ground: they would not agree. Finally, the Scots slipped away by night. Frustrated, angry and exhausted, their horses starving, the English force returned to Durham.[4] The vision of the cold, wet host, huddled by the banks of the Tyne with no proper shelter, in smelly and insanitary conditions, and with no proper food to eat, is surely far closer to reality than depiction of the flower-strewn tents of the idyllic summer of 1300 in Galloway.

It is hardest of all to recapture the experience of the common soldier in a medieval army. Henry V's chaplain brought out some sense of the horrors of dysentery, hunger, dejection at rumours of enemy movements, and occasional cheerfulness. 'And the rest of us in the army (for I will say nothing of those in command), fearing battle to be imminent, raised our hearts and eyes to heaven, crying out, with voices expressing our innermost thoughts, that God would have pity on us and, of his ineffable goodness, turn away from us the

violence of the French.' The men faced heavy rain the night before
Agincourt, and threats that their ears would be cut off if they made
a noise.[5] The images are hardly those of Shakespeare's *Henry V*.

  War took many forms in the medieval period. There were
campaigns aimed at conquest within the British Isles. The subjuga-
tion of Wales began in the eleventh century, and was not completed
until the major expeditions of Edward I's reign, above all that of
1282–3. Henry II's armies in Wales were thwarted by a combination
of terrain, weather and tricky opponents. John was unable to mount
a campaign on the scale that he intended, and sporadic campaigning
under Henry III never seemed likely to bring an increasingly aggressive principality under control. Edward, however, was able to deploy
forces on a quite different scale, sealing his conquest with a spectacular castle-building programme. As for Scotland, William the
Conqueror led an extremely successful campaign there in 1072, but
the period of the Scottish wars of independence proper began with an
apparently triumphal progress by Edward I in 1296. Success beck-
oned in 1298, with the English triumph at Falkirk, and again in 1304
when Stirling fell to Edward's forces. The disaster at Bannockburn in
1314, however, proved what by then needed no demonstration: that
Scotland was not ripe for picking. Indeed, in the early fourteenth
century the Scots were able to bring the war to the north of England
with devastating effect in their raids. War continued under Edward
III, with the English support of Edward Balliol, an unconvincing rival
to the line of kings descended from Robert Bruce. English involvement in Ireland began in 1169, and three kings, Henry II, John and
Richard II, led campaigns there, though Ireland never consumed
English military resources on the Scottish scale. Fortunately for the
English, the attempt of Robert Bruce and his brother in the second
decade of the fourteenth century to extend their rule into Ireland
came to nothing.

  Anglo-French warfare provides a more constant theme. The
defence of the duchy of Normandy was a major preoccupation for
the twelfth-century rulers of England, and although it was lost by
John in 1204, the continued English presence in Gascony ensured
that conflict would not cease. The thirteenth century was a peaceful
epoch, but while the conventional date for the start of the Hundred
Years War is 1337, there is a good case for arguing that the outbreak
of war in 1294 was more important as a turning point. The Hundred
Years War was not, of course, a continuous conflict. It was punctuated by frequent truces, and in many ways is best thought of as a
succession of different, if connected, wars, which finally concluded in
1453. The great period of English success came under Edward III in
the years up to 1360, with a further phase of glory under Henry V;
victory at Agincourt in 1415 was followed by the conquest of

Normandy. The years following the reopening of the war in 1369, and those of the attempt to maintain Henry V's gains during the reign of his son Henry VI were periods of great difficulty for the English. The war as a whole was perhaps as much characterised by the English attempts to defend territory won previously, as by the great offensive raids such as that of 1346–7. The excitement of the *chevauchée*, the destructive raid, was matched for many soldiers by the tedium of garrison duty.

The methods of warfare needed for war in Wales, Scotland and Ireland were very different from those appropriate in France. The Welsh were able soldiers, but their style was that of the guerrilla. They had few, if any, of the heavily armed knights who formed the élite of English armies. They avoided pitched battle, though an English army was constantly at risk of being ambushed. Their forces were hard to engage, being capable of melting away into the woods and mountains where they could not be pursued by troops less knowledgeable about the terrain. They were very capable of capturing castles by surprise attack, though they did not have the capability of mounting large-scale sieges, lacking as they did substantial armouries of stone-throwing engines and other machinery. The Scots could present similar problems, although they had the capability of fighting battles. They developed effective tactics designed to counter the power of English cavalry, employing massed formations of spearmen whose ranks were hard to penetrate. The Irish shared many of the characteristics of their Celtic brethren, with warfare dominated by raids in which captives and cattle were carried off by warring chieftains. Exposure to English forces brought some adaptation, and by about 1300 they had adopted some at least of the techniques used by their opponents. In France it was the élite knightly cavalry which dominated battle, fighting in traditional chivalric fashion with sword and lance on horseback, until challenged in the fourteenth century by the very different style developed by the English, in which men-at-arms fought on foot, supported by the deadly fire provided by longbowmen. France was where the castle had its origins, and siege warfare was an important element in some campaigns, though the English in their swift mounted raids were often able to bypass fortifications.

Another form of warfare in which Englishmen were involved was crusading. Of all forms of war, this was regarded as the most meritorious, conferring on its participants not merely fame and distinction, but also spiritual benefits. The Third Crusade was the only one in which a reigning monarch, Richard I, led a considerable English contingent, but there was a major English contribution to the Second Crusade, when English troops were largely responsible for the capture of Lisbon. The future Edward I led a small and unsuccessful expedition to the Holy Land shortly before his accession to the throne. Many other crusading ventures had substantial English involvement.[6]

Nor, of course, was war simply a matter of fighting external foes. For men in the twelfth century at least, the phrase *tempus werrae*, 'time of war', meant civil war, not war against external foes. Civil war characterised the reign of Stephen, while the rebellion of 1173–4 was a major threat to the ordered government of Henry II. The end of John's reign and the start of the minority of his son, Henry III, saw the country wracked by civil war and invaded by French forces. The baronial reform movement, which began in 1258 in a spirit of high idealism, collapsed into civil war by 1264. The political system was likewise unable to cope with the failures of government under Edward II, and a brief war in 1322 resulted. When the royal and baronial armies confronted each other at Burton on Trent, Hugh Despenser begged the king not to order his banner to be unfurled, for that would amount to a formal declaration of war. By that time war and peace had acquired a meaning closer to that of the present day; it was possible in ordinances reforming the exchequer to distinguish between the financial methods needed in wartime, and those of the *temps de pees*.[7]

The length of time that the country was technically at war was perhaps less important than the length of the campaigns. The Caerlaverock campaign of 1300 in south-western Scotland saw the army muster early in July; by the end of August those of the army who had not already deserted were back in England. It could be seen as not much more than a pleasant summer outing, particularly since the Scots chose not to offer any serious resistance in the field. One of the institutions of medieval warfare was geared around campaigns of this scale, for the length of formal feudal service was a mere forty days. Yet many expeditions took place at much less pleasant times of the year than July and August, and many lasted far longer than forty days. The rebellion of 1173 against Henry II began in May, and though there some brief truces early in the next year, due to winter weather, campaigning did not end until September 1174. Winter did not always mean an end to fighting. King John led a highly effective force to the north of England in January 1216. He was at Doncaster on the first day of the year, and reached Berwick two weeks later. The campaign was concluded by late February. In 1282 the war against the Welsh began with rebellion at Easter, 22 March. The first English troops were on the payroll by 7 April. The feudal muster was ordered for 2 August. The first significant engagement took place on 6 November, when an English force was defeated after it crossed from Anglesey to the mainland. The Welsh prince Llywelyn was killed on 11 December, but it was not until the following June that

Hugh Despenser the Younger
(d.1326), from a stained glass
window in Tewkesbury Abbey.

his brother Dafydd was finally taken prisoner, and the war was
eventually at an end.

The Hundred Years War saw troops on the royal payroll for
extended periods. William Bohun, earl of Northampton, was in royal
service continuously for 579 days, starting on 22 July 1338, and this
was matched by others who were with the king in Flanders.[8] Much
of that period was spent in pleasant lodgings, but hard campaigning
could last a long time. In 1346 the Crécy campaign began when the
fleet first sailed from Portsmouth on 28 June, only to be driven back
by contrary winds. The landing in Normandy was made on 12 July.
The battle of Crécy was fought on 26 August; the army then marched

north to lay siege to Calais early in September. Surrender did not come until 3 August 1347. Preceded by a raid led by the duke of Lancaster in October, what was planned as the greatest of Edward III's campaigns set out from Calais early in November 1359. It was intended to culminate in his coronation as king of France, but the gates of Rheims were not opened to Edward, and no ceremony took place. The king did not return to England until mid-May of the following year. In addition to the campaigns themselves, of course, there were the long years in which many men were engaged in garrison duty. Just as in more recent periods, soldiering in the middle ages was rarely a matter of swift and decisive campaigns conducted in good weather. Men often served for long periods, through hard winters, in constant discomfort.

One of the most potent historical theories about the nature and impact of war is that of the 'military revolution', originally propounded by Michael Roberts for the period 1560–1660. His starting point was tactical changes and drill, and he then moved on to argue that improvements in this area made possible a revolution in strategy which entailed a major growth in the size of armies. War could be fought on a wholly new scale. This inevitably entailed a radical change to the administrative and other burdens that war placed upon society. For Roberts, the high point of the military revolution was the achievement of Sweden's Gustavus Adolphus. There has been much argument and debate over this thesis, though revision has consisted of suggesting modifications, rather than challenging the basic concepts. The chronology of the 'revolution' has been challenged, with some historians seeing major advances earlier, in the sixteenth century, and some later. The pre-eminence of Sweden has also been questioned.[9]

There are many ways in which elements of the early modern military revolution were anticipated in the middle ages, as will become apparent in later chapters. Medieval soldiers knew little of formal drill, but the importance of being able to order troops to advance in good order was well recognised. As Simon de Montfort remarked of his opponents in 1265, 'By the arm of St James, they are advancing well. They have not learned that for themselves, but were taught it by me.'[10] Numbers might be very considerable, and there was a rapid increase in the size of English armies in the late thirteenth century which parallels that of the so-called military revolution. There was no lack of grand strategy in the medieval period, with wars against France being planned in terms not only of the mobilisation of substantial English armies, but also of the organisation of complex alliances, timed to swing into action in effective co-ordination. In terms of the impact that war might have on the countryside and towns, and those who inhabited them, the

military commanders of the Thirty Years War had little to learn that
was not known to those of the Hundred Years War and before. The
Scottish wars brought devastation to the north of England;
the English wars in France wrought havoc in the French countryside.
The techniques employed by troops were simple: fire is as potent a
weapon distributed by lighted torches as it is by modern incendiary
bombs. Wooden buildings, with thatched roofs, offered tempting
targets. One single house set alight in Carlisle in 1296 led to the
destruction of most of the city. Cattle could easily be driven away,
and other animals slaughtered. In France, much damage could be
done by destroying vineyards. Defence against swift moving raids or
chevauchées was not easy. Castles could be bypassed, and as the
experience of 1327 showed, forces who did not wish to fight were
very hard to engage. It was, according to the chronicler Walter of
Guisborough, only God and St Cuthbert who opposed the Scots in
Durham in 1296, by bringing down severe weather with snow and
frost, which forced the Scots to retreat.[11] An army could destroy
territory in a wide swathe. The English boasted in 1346 that as they
marched through Normandy to Caen, they destroyed and robbed for
five or six miles around, burning many places.[12] One entry on the
Close Rolls for 1346 lists the manors and places in Cumberland
'burned and totally destroyed, with the corn, animals and other
goods therein, by hostile incursions of the king's Scottish enemies,
after Michaelmas last'. Some seventy places were named, and
pardoned all payment of tax, such was the level of devastation.[13] It
would be tedious to multiply examples. There is some academic
debate about the speed that regions could recover from the devastation of medieval warfare; but there can be little doubt that, in the
short term, the effects of a visitation by an army bent on doing its
worst with fire and sword were appalling.

The logistics of medieval warfare were complex. Again, the later
military revolution has its precursor. In the early modern period, it
was from the 1640s that the French began to calculate the precise
needs of their forces. Contracts with merchants were drawn up, and
a system of magazines, or victualling bases, was established.[14] All this
can be paralleled from the English experience in the fourteenth
century; victualling bases for Scottish operations were set up at
Berwick and Carlisle, elaborate calculations were made of what
quantities of foodstuffs were needed, instructions were issued to
sheriffs to collect them, and the expertise of merchants was drawn
upon. Success in campaigns in the medieval period was not achieved
solely by knights in shining armour, with pennons waving in the
breeze, or by courageous longbowmen, but in part by pen-pushing
clerks in military headquarters, by officials requisitioning victuals,
and by the men who ensured that the supplies reached the men who
did the fighting.

The history of war used to be the history of battles, written by old soldiers. Military experience no doubt provided an insight not available to those who have not experienced war, but it could also lead to misinterpretation of the past. Times have changed, and the new orthodoxy is that medieval commanders sought to avoid battle wherever possible, seeking instead to wear down their opponents by waging wars of devastation. 'What is certain is that he did not adopt a battle-seeking strategy' is a recent verdict on one of the most apparently glamorous and chivalrous of medieval soldiers, Richard I.[15] The ravaging of enemy territory was central to Richard's conception of warfare. Yet the case should not be overstated. Certainly, battle was often avoided, and the civil wars of Stephen's reign may have seen no more than one major battle, at Lincoln early in 1141. In contrast, however, the brief civil war of 1264–5 saw two major conflicts, at Lewes and Evesham. The early stages of the Scottish wars of independence witnessed major battles at Stirling Bridge, Falkirk, Bannockburn and Halidon Hill. The great battles of the Hundred Years War may not have resulted in eventual victory, but their importance cannot be easily denied. There is no doubt that battle was sought on many occasions, and its part in the structure of medieval warfare should not be dismissed, as some recent commentators have tended to do. Battles were without doubt the high-points of many campaigns.

Battles were swift in the medieval period; it was highly exceptional that fighting at Bannockburn in 1314 should take place on two days. Sieges were a very different matter, for while towns and castles might be taken by a rapid escalade, it more commonly took a matter of weeks and months for a substantial fortification to be reduced. The great siege of Kenilworth, the last major military operation of the civil war of the 1260s, lasted from the spring until mid December 1266. There were laws and conventions which governed the conduct of medieval warfare; the slow progress of many sieges provided opportunity for these to be put into operation in a way which might not apply so readily in the turbulence of battle.

War had its glory. Men could win honour and fame to the sound of the trumpets and the clash of steel. There was glamour in the gaudy coats-of-arms, excitement in the snorts and thundering hooves of the great warhorses. Another side should not be forgotten, and one example from the multitude that could be cited makes the point. In the late 1320s Beatrice de Ryhill petitioned the queen. She had been ruined by the Scots and their use of fire. Her husband and twenty-eight of her tenants had been killed, she had nothing left, and did not dare to live on her lands.[16] War was savage, and codes of chivalry did little to soften its impact.

2

The Military Elite

The knight sits mounted on his caparisoned charger, fully armoured with richly decorated surcoat bearing his coat of arms, and is presented with his helmet by his wife, while his daughter-in-law waits to hand him his shield. Sir Geoffrey Luttrell, as depicted in the Luttrell Psalter, is an archetype of the élite soldier of the middle ages. The glowing power of the artist's vision is remarkable; here, it seems, is the true knight, the man at the heart of a medieval army. What was the reality behind this? Jean le Bel's description of the 1327 Weardale campaign, with men tired, their armour rusting in the rain, their inadequate victuals soaked by horses' sweat, and no shelter available, provides a very different and more convincing image of knights at war.[1]

It is conventional to think of medieval armies as divided into cavalry and infantry. This may be convenient, but it presents some difficulties, as the 'cavalry' might well dismount to fight, and the 'infantry' be mounted on the march. Until the fourteenth century, there was a clear division and distinction between two main elements of the army, which reflected the social differences between those who rode, and those who went on foot. These two elements of the army were organised quite separately. Geoffrey de Mandeville, formidable soldier of Stephen's reign, provides early evidence of this. He had two lieutenants, one of whom commanded his cavalry, the other his infantry. These were his marshal and constable.[2] The cavalry and infantry forces were still quite separate under Edward I, to judge by the pay records. The situation changed, however, with the Hundred Years War, when magnates recruited archers, particularly mounted archers, as part of their retinue. The social distinction between those of high status, who fought as knights and men-at-arms, and the bowmen, was no doubt as apparent as ever, and it is with the élite that this chapter is concerned.

Ranks

There were surprisingly few distinctions of rank in a medieval army. In the eleventh and early twelfth centuries all those who fought with shield, lance and sword on horseback were termed knights (*milites*), but by 1300 there were bannerets and knights, followed by men apparently of equal status: sergeants, squires and valets. At this level the different terminology seems to have been as much the result of clerical whims as of genuine differences.

The bannerets clearly had responsibility for organising the cavalry forces, with authority to give orders to the knights and others, but how this worked in practice is not revealed by the sources. In terms of pay, a banneret received twice as much as a knight, who in turn received twice as much as a squire or sergeant. Rank did not reflect military ability or experience alone: it was also an indication of social status. Bannerets were distinguished from ordinary knights because they bore rectangular banners, rather than simple pennants. This distinction began to be apparent in the late twelfth century.[3] The

Sir Geoffrey Luttrell (1276–1345), being handed his helmet, lance and shield by his wife and daughter-in-law, from the Luttrell Psalter, *c.* 1320–40.

Histoire of William Marshal suggests, when describing the household of the Young King, that since he had fifteen bannerets, he must
have had at least 200 knights at his disposal. Each banneret would
therefore have had, on average, some thirteen knights in his following.[4] The rank of banneret was almost exclusively military. It was not
an hereditary status, but depended on personal standing and reputation. It did not carry with it the kind of ideological baggage that
was attached to knighthood, but had practical implications for the
command of men. When a poet (and herald) described the army that
invaded Scotland in 1300, what concerned him was to list all the
eighty-seven bannerets present. These were the men of real significance. Some wealth was necessary to be a banneret. Under Edward I,
Brian FitzAlan, a soldier of distinction, had explained to the king
when refusing appointment as warden of Scotland that he did not
have the money to lead a troop appropriate to a banneret.[5] John de
Coupland was granted £500 a year in 1347, to maintain himself as
a banneret, a rank he received because he had captured King David
of Scotland at Neville's Cross. In a more conventional case in the
same year William FitzWarin was granted two manors by Edward III
to support his newly acquired status of banneret. Peers of parliament
were not automatically bannerets; John de Cobham was one of those
who received a summons as a lord of parliament some years before
his promotion in 1354.[6] By the late fourteenth century the rank of
banneret was losing its original military significance; to obtain the

Edward III of England shown with David
II of Scots, who was held captive from
1346 until 1357, when he was released for
a promised ransom of 100,000 marks.

status a man needed sufficient lands to maintain his position. In 1361 John Chandos had entered into an indenture with the king, agreeing to serve as his lieutenant in France and Normandy with a force of forty men-at-arms. One of his subordinates was to be a banneret, and it is very remarkable that he did not at this stage have this rank himself.[7] His promotion to the rank of banneret is described in a famous passage in Froissart, when Chandos presented his long-tailed banner to the Black Prince, asking that he should display it 'in whatever manner shall be most agreeable to you'. The prince then cut off its tail, and returned it to Chandos, so formally acknowledging an elevation in rank.[8] By the time of the Agincourt campaign, although the contracts specified numbers of bannerets, knights and esquires to be taken, there was no longer mention in the retinue roll of whether men were bannerets or not; the distinction was decreasing in significance. More important in social terms was whether or not men had the right to be summoned as barons to parliament, and as David Crouch has pointed out, the bannerets who had this right thought of themselves as barons, while those who did not were indistinguishable from the knights, who by this time were a far more exclusive group than in the past.[9] The title of banneret did not, however, finally disappear until the 1640s.

Below the bannerets were the knights. In England, in contrast to the continent, knighthood was not purely hereditary. The eleventh-century knight might be a man of low social standing; the very fact that the English applied the word *cniht* to the armed and mounted Norman soldiers suggests that they were seen as followers of no great status, not as leaders. The term knight, or *miles*, was one which could safely be applied to a wide range of men, from substantial landholder to landless retainer.[10] In many contexts the word meant little more than mounted soldier. In the great majority of cases men in this period probably became knights simply because they were provided with the appropriate equipment, though this would soon change. The business of making men knights in a formal ceremony was almost certainly initially confined to the highest ranks of society. There is a story told of William Rufus's reign, but written in about 1140, of a magnate bringing his followers to be knighted by the king. In 1147 King Stephen 'ceremonially girded with the belt of knighthood his son Eustace'.[11] Although there was obviously an assumption that the son of a knight would receive his father's rank, this was not necessarily the case. By the early thirteenth century there were cases where men did not seek knighthood. An ability to fight or to command men does not normally appear to have been a significant element in the elevation of a man to knightly status. The criterion used in the thirteenth century to decide whether or not a man should become a knight was primarily financial, though this did not mean that a knight was not expected to play his part in war.

In 1224 an order required everyone who possessed a knight's fee to become a knight by Easter of the following year. The criterion was not a satisfactory one, and when a similar order was issued in 1241, it was laid down that anyone in possession of land worth £20 a year should be knighted. A holder of a knight's fee was liable only if he had demesne land worth £20. Further distraints of knighthood, as this method of compelling men to become knights has become known, were issued in the 1250s. One in 1254 was linked with the knighting of the king's own son. From 1246 the articles of the general eyre, the great judicial inquiries that were held by justices on circuit through the land, included a question as to whether there were men of full age who possessed £20 of lands and were not knighted. These various orders were undoubtedly linked with military plans; there was a desire to increase the number of knights who could fight in the king's wars in France and in Wales. At the same time, the Crown became keenly aware in the 1250s that it was possible to obtain fines from men who did not want to accept the burden of knighthood. It may have been the costs of campaigning that deterred men from becoming knights, though it seems much more likely that the major deterrent was the burden of local administration, above all jury service, placed on the knights, that made men reluctant to accept the status.[12] There has been much discussion of the question of whether or not there was a 'crisis of the gentry' in the thirteenth century. This is a matter which will doubtless continue to provide much employment for medieval historians; what is clear is that whether or not there was a general crisis, there were certainly many individual knights and potential knights who found times hard.[13] In the military context it is important to realise that it was not solely the knights who were expected to fight, fully armed, on horseback. Although the practice of distraint of knighthood was therefore not necessary as a method of obtaining cavalry forces, it was not abandoned, but continued to be employed in the fourteenth and fifteenth centuries. It was, indeed, to be revived by a Stuart monarchy anxious to make use of ancient precedents as money-making expedients.

Below the level of the knights, the terminology used to describe men's status, both social and military, was shifting and often imprecise. The term sergeant could, particularly in the twelfth century, mean a multiplicity of things, from an ordinary infantryman to a man holding land by some special form of service. The mounted sergeant, armed and horsed in much the same way as the knight, began to appear in the records in the later twelfth century. This was not a development unique to England. Early evidence for sergeants comes from southern Italy, France and the Low Countries. The *Catalogus Baronum*, drawn up in the Norman kingdom of Sicily and

Southern Italy in 1167–8, gives details of feudal military service by over 8,500 knights and more than 11,000 sergeants. The latters' service was not part of the original obligation on the fiefs, but was owed as part of the *augmentum*, the additional service owed for major expeditions. Precisely how these sergeants were armed, and indeed whether or not they were mounted, is not apparent from the record.[14] In 1187 the count of Hainault provided Philip II with 110 knights and eighty sergeants, equipped in the same way as the knights, and the French royal accounts for 1202–3 reveal payments to 174 mounted sergeants.[15] Peter Picot, probably a Fleming, had twenty-seven sergeants, mounted and equipped with hauberks, in England in 1173. The garrison of Newcastle under Lyme in the same year contained five knights, six mounted sergeants, and seven infantry sergeants.[16] Under Richard I knights were paid 1s a day, and mounted sergeants with hauberks 6d. A sergeant who had no hauberk and only one horse received 4d, and a foot sergeant 2d. In 1200 payment was authorised to a force of 160 sergeants, 105 of whom had three horses each, and the remainder two.[17] There were sergeants employed in Henry III's household in 1220, whose inferior status to the knights was demonstrated by the rabbit-fur trimmings on their green robes; the latter had squirrel fur.[18]

By 1300 the position was more complex. Within the royal household the ranks of those below knight were those of sergeant (*serviens*), and squire (*scutifer*). Elsewhere in the accounts men in receipt of similar wages are called valets (*valletti*); that this was synonymous with squire is apparent from a list of valets who are termed squires in the margin.[19] *Armiger* was another word that could be used, but of all these terms that of squire would become the most important. Definition was not easy; when in 1324 the sheriffs were asked to send in lists of knights and men-at-arms in their counties, they did not all use the same criteria to define the latter. In Lancashire men with £15 of land qualified as men-at-arms, but in Cornwall the level set was £40.[20] By the start of the Hundred Years War the normal cavalry retinue was formed of knights and squires, but the phraseology used was not always consistent; for example, Dietrich de Mauny, a knight, served with nineteen followers described as men-at-arms (*homines ad arma*), a catch-all term also applied to men who would earlier have been called sergeants. In most cases the term squire was interchangeable with man-at-arms, but William de Norwell had in his retinue two squires paid 18d a day each, and eighteen men-at-arms who received the normal 2s daily.[21]

A squire was a man who aspired to knighthood, but who increasingly might not take it up. The records of payment to soldiers of the late twelfth and early thirteenth centuries do not distinguish esquires from knights, or indeed from sergeants; by Edward I's reign the esquires were a clearly identifiable group in the army pay-rolls. They received the same rate as the mounted sergeants-at-arms. The distinction between knight and squire was a significant one. When in 1319 Philip de Chetwynd agreed to serve Ralph Basset of Drayton with two horses in time of peace, and three in war, he was an esquire, and the agreement specified that if he became a knight during the year that it was due to run, then the terms would be renegotiated.[22] The rank of esquire became increasingly significant, and in the fourteenth century the esquires began to use coats of arms of their own; a significant landmark came in 1389 when Richard II made the first grant of arms to an esquire, John Kingston. The squire emerged to take up the place that the knight had occupied in society a century or so earlier.[23]

Equipment

Much of the discussion of the knights and men-at-arms by historians has concentrated upon the question of formal obligations to serve, and on the development of contractual paid service. While this is important, and will be discussed in the next chapter, it has led to a lack of attention to the question of how these forces actually fought and were organised in the field. While there was considerable change between the eleventh and fourteenth centuries with regard to formal obligation, there was much greater continuity with respect to the reality of troops in the field.

Knightly equipment was transformed in the course of the medieval period.[24] The Norman knight as depicted in the Bayeux Tapestry wore a conical helmet, open in the front, with the only guard for the face being a nasal. A mail coif, worn under the helmet, protected the neck. He had a long mail hauberk, which must have been worn over heavily padded clothing. The Tapestry shows the hauberks as trousered; this must have been an error, as other evidence shows clearly that they were in fact designed with a split skirt, far more practical for riding.[25] The wooden shield was long and kite-shaped, curved to fit the user, so as to provide full protection for the left side of the body.

Change came slowly. In the mid twelfth century round-topped helmets appeared. Then face-guards were introduced, and by the early thirteenth century flat-topped helmets, pot-helms, which enclosed the head fully, were coming into use. These provided much better protection for their wearers, but at the same time limited vision. Body protection was still provided by the mail hauberk; this offered superb flexibility, and good security against the cutting edge of a sword. After about 1150 mail chausses, or leggings, came into

Fully armed eleventh-century Norman knights, from the Bayeux Tapestry.

David and Goliath, depicted in mid-twelfth-century military equipment, from a leaf intended for the Winchester Bible, *c.* 1150–80. In contrast to the Bayeux Tapestry, the hauberk is shown forming a split skirt.

A colour-washed drawing of a praying knight crusader, in mid-thirteenth-century equipment, from a Matthew Paris manuscript.

use, and from the late twelfth century the sleeves of the hauberk were sometimes extended to form mittens.[26] Mail left the wearer vulnerable to crushing blows, and could be pierced by arrows or crossbow bolts. The Norwegians knew the use of iron plates by the late twelfth century, but these were apparently not copied by the English.[27] A splendid colour-washed drawing by Matthew Paris, or one of his assistants, of a mid-thirteenth-century crusader shows him wearing a mail coif on his head, a hauberk with split skirt and, apparently, integral mail gauntlets. Whereas the knights of the Conquest seem to have worn textile leggings, this knight has shin-bands of metal plate or hardened leather, and shoes of plate. He is not wearing a helmet, but this is held by a squire in the background; it is a great helm, an elaborate version of the pot-helm, finely decorated with slits both for vision, and to enable the wearer to breathe. No shield is shown, but other sources reveal that the long Norman shield had by now become much smaller, still retaining a roughly triangular shape. The round top of Conquest days had become less pronounced by the mid twelfth century, and by the thirteenth century shields were flat-topped.[28]

Documentary evidence on armour supports the visual, and shows the way in which mail was supplemented by pieces of plate armour from the thirteenth century. There is a reference in 1224 to a hauberk and a pair of iron greaves being placed in pledge for *6s 8d*. An inventory of goods stolen from a chest in 1289 included not only two hauberks, but also iron greaves, two 'pairs of plates', probably breast-plate and backplate perhaps made of overlapping pieces of

A splendidly decorated piece of *cuir bouilli*, hardened leather armour. This is designed to protect the right upper arm, and dates from the first half of the fourteenth century.

Memorial brasses provide a good record of the development of armour. (*From left*) Sir Roger de Trumpington (Trumpington, Cambs, 1326); Sir John de Creke (Westley Waterless, Cambs, *c.* 1340–45); Sir R. Staunton (Castle Donington, Leics, 1458).

metal, cuisses, or thigh pieces, iron gauntlets and a plate gorget, or neck piece.[29] As an alternative to steel plate, hardened leather, or *cuir bouilli*, might be used to make pieces of armour. The great helm was cumbersome, and lighter, more rounded helmets were developed, known as bacinets. By the fourteenth century these might feature movable visors. Fashion, rather than military need, may explain the adoption in the late thirteenth and early fourteenth centuries of aillettes, miniature shields worn on the shoulder rather like elaborate epaulettes. Inventories of goods forfeited after Boroughbridge in 1322 suggest that by that date a knight would be expected to have as his helmet a bacinet, with some form of protection for the neck, a mail hauberk, plate armour for thighs and shins, with iron gauntlets and shoes. A will of 1325 mentions 'a pair of plates'.[30] Yet as late as 1327, according to Jean le Bel, English armour was very old-fashioned. The English, apparently, had no plate armour, but were still wearing antiquated hauberks, topped not with modern bacinets, but with great helms of iron or hardened leather.[31] The fine memorial brass of John de Creke, dating from about 1340–45, shows him wearing mail armour substantially reinforced with plate. Rather than an elaborate helmet, he has a skull-cap, or bacinet, on his head. Brassarts protect his upper arms, and gauntlets his hands and wrists.

A late thirteenth-century aquamanile, or water vessel, in the form of a mounted knight. He wears a surcoat over mail armour; the shield and lance are missing. This fine object was found in the River Tyne, and is probably English.

On his legs he has poleyns, while greaves protect his shins, and jointed sabatons cover his feet. The flowing surcoat makes it hard to distinguish the body armour clearly, but he may even have worn a 'coat of plates', formed of iron plates riveted to leather or cloth, between the surcoat and the hauberk. The triangular shield is small and manoeuvrable.

There followed during the Hundred Years War a rapid move towards the full-scale adoption of plate-armour. The great helm, often featuring an elaborate crest, had become a piece of specialised tournament armour. For battle, the lighter bacinet was far more practical. One characteristic form was fitted with a projecting snout-like visor, which could be easily raised. Breastplates may have developed first for tournaments, but were soon incorporated into battle-armour. Unfortunately, the habit of wearing flowing surcoats, or tighter jupons, over body armour makes it impossible to determine many details with precision. In 1368 Thomas Erskine, a Scot, was given permission to buy armour in London and take it to Scotland where he needed it to fight a judicial duel. He needed a bacinet, breastplate and backplate, a pair of 'bracers' for his arms, with cuisses and greaves for his legs. He also required a chanfron, or head-piece, for his horse.[32] These were individual pieces, but by the

A late fourteenth-century misericorde from Lincoln Cathedral. Back-plates are rarely depicted, but are clearly shown in this carving.

fifteenth century it is clear that the fully articulated suit of plate-armour had emerged, the wearer's pride in it such that the cloth coverings of earlier periods were abandoned and the armour worn 'white', polished and shining. By then the shield, which had been steadily becoming ever smaller, had been abandoned as unnecessary. The mail aventail which had protected the neck was replaced by the plate gorget, and elaborate fan-shaped guards protected vulnerable joints at the elbow. A popular type of helmet was the sallet, rounded in shape and reaching down to the shoulders, with a visor covering the face-opening. The manufacture of this full plate-armour was very skilled; the market was dominated by Milanese and German armourers.

Royal accounts provide the best evidence of the costs of armour, but the equipment provided for kings is likely to have been of the highest quality, and proportionately costly. Early in John's reign a hauberk cost £1, and a habergeon (rather smaller than a hauberk) one mark. Two hauberks, four habergeons and six helmets cost, a little later in the same reign, £7 8s.[33] Two surcoats, two corslets, presumably of mail, and two pairs of iron boots were bought in London for Henry III for sixteen marks.[34] Seven haketons (reinforced

A rare surviving example of a habergeon, or mail shirt, probably dating from the fourteenth century. It is made of alternate rows of riveted and one-piece rings.

leather jackets) bought for Edward II early in 1312 cost 10s each; repair of the royal sword came to 9s 4d.[35] In 1316–17 the king's armourer, Hugo Cole, was employed making armour in York from September until April, with three assistants. Including materials, the cost came to just over £20.[36] In 1321 the king bought a new habergeon, two new swords, and had a range of equipment repaired, for a total cost of £10 5s 8d. The king could afford the best: an account presented by one of Edward III's armourers, Hugh de Bungay, gives an impression of the costs of the best-quality equipment. A pair of plate gauntlets cost 6s 8d. A pair of greaves with poleyns (covering shins and knees), with burnished fittings, came to 26s 8d. A war helmet cost £2, and a further 5s was spent on a painted crest for it. Two bacinets, much simpler helmets, were bought for 13s 6d. Surprisingly, the most expensive single piece of equipment was the cotton and fustian trapper worn by the royal charger, to protect him from being rubbed by his iron armour. This cost 52s 8d.[37] Edward could be extravagant in buying armour; in the preparations for the 1359 expedition, £113 was spent with one of his armourers, and over £30 with another. Unfortunately, the accounts do not reveal the details of what he acquired.[38] Even these levels are not startlingly high, and the costs borne by normal knights must have been much lower than those of the king. An inventory of goods stolen in 1324 from John de Swynnerton shows that a habergeon with mail fittings (aventail, pisan and collaret), was worth ten marks. Bacinets were valued at 10s each, and, surprisingly, war swords at a mere 3s 4d – half the price of longbows. A set of leg armour (jainbers, cuisses and poleyns) came to 15s. Two tents, necessary for campaigning, were valued at six marks.[39] An account of arms purchased by Thomas de Melchebourne for equipping a royal galley at the outset of the Hundred Years War shows that adequate armour need not cost a fortune. Haketons, padded jerkins, cost 5s each. Bacinets, fitted with aventails to protect the neck, were a mere 3s each. Iron gauntlets cost 1s a pair, and lances 6d each. This equipment, however, was perhaps more appropriate for well-armed footsoldiers than for cavalrymen.[40] A well-off knight might possess a substantial quantity of armour. Fulk de Pembridge, in his will of 1325, left his eldest son a haketon, a hauberk, a 'pair of plates' (breastplate and backplate), a tournament bacinet, a helmet for war and another for tournaments, an aventail, gauntlets, poleyns, cuisses, two swords, two horse coverings, some horse armour, spurs and other equipment. Two other sons also received a full set of armour each, with the fourth receiving two hauberks.[41] Fulk's investment in armour was considerable, but the equipment lasted a long time, provided it was properly maintained. It is unlikely that many considered that the cost of providing it was an intolerable financial burden.

Armour provided valuable protection, but must also have created problems; no matter how well fitted it was, movement must have been hampered, while a helmet with visor lowered would limit vision and communication.[42] It would have been extremely difficult to organise an advance, followed by a charge, with troops prepared in full battle array. It was perhaps for reasons of communication as well as of comfort that the helmet was the last item of equipment to be put on. This is demonstrated by the celebrated case of the Earl Marshal at the battle of Lincoln in 1217, when a squire reminded the veteran warrior at the last minute that he had not yet donned it.[43]

The knight's main weapons were sword and lance, though others such as the mace might be used. Lances were made of ash. The light weapons of the Conquest era, apparently capable of being wielded overarm and even thrown, developed later into more substantial implements. The length was probably about fourteen feet; the weapon was carried vertically until lowered for the charge. The lance depended for its effect on the combined momentum of horse and rider; it was therefore of little use after the initial shock of impact. Lances were easily broken, and were of little value in a mêlée.[44] The fight before the walls of Le Mans in 1189 was marked by much breaking of lances, and William the Marshal even lost his horse when

Part of the will of Sir Fulk de Pembridge, 1325, listing the armour he is leaving to his sons.

it trod on one of the broken pieces which littered the ground. The lance was certainly effective in skilled hands; the Marshal killed the future Richard I's horse with a single thrust in one celebrated encounter.[45] It was possible to convert the lance for use in fighting on foot: at Nogent in 1359 Eustace d'Aubrichecourt ordered the English cavalry to dismount and to cut down their lances to five feet in length.[46] An important innovation of the late fourteenth century was the lance-rest, a device attached to the breastplate which enabled a rider to couch his lance far more effectively, resting it securely rather than carrying its considerable weight.[47]

Medieval swords were the product of a technology which, with comparatively simple methods, succeeded in producing highly sophisticated weapons. They might vary considerably in size, from massive two-handed implements that could be wielded only on foot, to superb cavalry weapons. One is described in a legal record of Edward I's day. It was a Cologne sword, the blade an ell in length (45 inches), the hilt, made of iron, five inches long. The pommel was of steel, round in shape. The handle was fitted with two plates of maple wood, decorated with a yellow and green filigree pattern.[48] Such a weapon was clearly a prized possession. The most usual types of sword had a flat blade, and were clearly designed for cutting rather than thrusting. In the thirteenth century, however, some were produced with a strong central rib and a sharp point, clearly intended to be thrust, much like a lance. By the mid fourteenth century this type was much the most common. Clearly there was little point in using a cutting weapon against plate-armour; a powerful thrust might, in contrast, find a weak joint and penetrate. Very large swords, used one-handed, were fashionable in the late thirteenth and early fourteenth centuries, while from the mid fourteenth century great two-

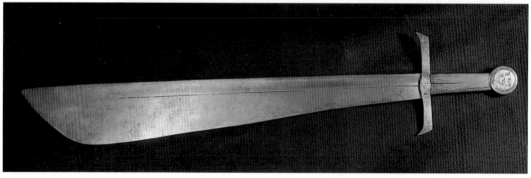

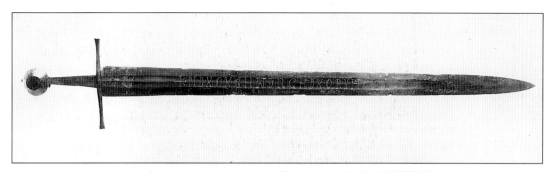

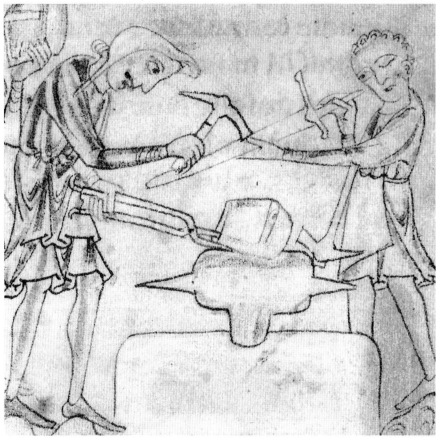

(*Above left*) Ferocious figures in the thirteenth-century Douce Apocalypse wielding falchions and a war-hammer, with (*below*) a surviving falchion from Durham Cathedral. This was used for ceremonial purposes as a symbol of the Conyers family's tenure of Sockburn. (*Above, top*) A sword with broad double-edged blade, probably dating from 1250–1330. The illustration below it, from a thirteenth-century manuscript, shows armourers at work, making a sword and a helmet.

handed weapons were sometimes used for fighting on foot.[49] Froissart describes how on one occasion the Scot Archibald Douglas dismounted when he approached the English, and then set about them to great effect with an immense sword, so heavy that hardly anyone else could have lifted it.[50] A weapon similar to the sword and popular in the thirteenth century was the falchion, a short broad-bladed implement which could be used to deliver a powerful cutting blow. Swords were highly effective, and it is interesting that at the battle of Lincoln in 1141 the earl of Gloucester's men did not use lances in the initial encounters but charged from the first with drawn swords. In this way they succeeded in breaking through the lines of King Stephen's men. Later in the twelfth century, Gerald of Wales noted how John de Courcy, fighting in Ireland, 'lopped off now a head from someone's shoulders, or again arms or hands from their body', so effective were the blows from his sword. Roger Wendover's account of the rebellion of Richard Marshal in the early thirteenth century reveals how devastating a sword could be in the hands of a skilled, fit man.[51] Other weapons were also used, such as battle-axes, maces and war-hammers, though the sword normally predominated.

Horses

A vital element in the knight's equipment was the horse, 'which is so necessary to him that it could rightly be described as his faithful companion. For with his horse he both charges and puts to flight the enemy, or, if need arise, escapes from his own pursuers.'[52] The warhorse was the most expensive possession of a knight or man-at-arms. A destrier, the most specialised of warhorses, was not an ordinary animal. It was a highly trained, expertly bred beast, capable of carrying an impressive load of man and armour in the terrifying conditions of battle. Mares were not used for this task; the spirit and aggression of a stallion were considered essential. Destriers were not common; of twenty-seven horses lost by members of the earl of Derby's retinue in Flanders in the late 1330s, only two were of this type. By the later middle ages, the destrier was known as a great horse; the type appears to have vanished from England in the seventeenth century, and is most unlikely, as is sometimes suggested, to have been the ancestor of the modern carthorse. Coursers were another highly prized type of horse. More ordinary animals were described as rounceys, or simply as *equi*, or horses. All of these were suitable for use in war; in general, warhorses were clearly quite distinct from palfreys, or riding horses, and from the various types of farm horses. The finest horses had proud names. Among the Black Prince's destriers were Grisel de Cologne, Morel de Burghersh,

Bayard de Brucell and Bayard Dieu; a small hackney had the more appropriately homely name of Wellfed.[53]

Men needed more than just one horse; important men needed a considerable number. Horses might become sick or lame, and remounts were needed. Warhorses were not suitable for riding long distances; a knight would possess at least two other horses in addition to his charger. The treaty between Henry I and the count of Flanders in 1101 provided that each man should have three mounts.[54] An actual, rather than a theoretical, figure for the mid thirteenth century is that of a force of thirty-eight men with sixty-four horses, which went to take over Nottingham castle in 1266. Under Edward II, the household sergeants-at-arms were allowed one warhorse, one riding horse, and one pack-horse each.[55] Early in the Hundred Years War the warlike bishop of Lincoln, Henry Burghersh, had six horses for himself, five each for his bannerets, four each for his knights, and three each for his squires. Other magnates were paid for taking similar numbers across the Channel.[56] The levels were higher by Henry V's reign, when it was assumed that a duke would have fifty horses, an earl twenty-four, a baron sixteen, a man-at-arms four and a mounted archer one. Even higher figures are given for the earl of Suffolk's retinue in the army of 1417. He claimed to have twenty-four horses for each of his five knights, six horses each for his twenty-four other men-at-arms, and four horses for each mounted archer, which adds up to 624 horses for a total of 120 men. The change in battle tactics that took place in the second quarter of the fourteenth century, with the decision that men-at-arms should fight on foot, did not apparently diminish the importance of the horse to the medieval soldier.[57]

There is no way in which the breed of the medieval warhorse can be properly reconstructed. To argue from the evidence of seals that the horses of William I's day were altogether more slender and lighter than those of Edward I's is to place an unwarranted reliance on the artistic skills of the engravers of seal matrices. Descriptions of destriers as having upright necks and large buttocks make it plain that these were not potential Derby winners, but are of little more assistance.[58] Reliable documentary evidence reveals the colours of warhorses, along with estimates of their value, but not their size or breed. They could be black, white, bay, white-spotted, grey, iron-grey, chestnut, or tawny, and were often marked with white on heads and feet.

England was not a premier country for the production of horses, and very considerable numbers were imported. Robert de Bellême brought Spanish horses to his Shropshire estates as early as the late eleventh century.[59] In 1214 King John bought considerable numbers from merchants in France. A little later others were acquired from

Lombardy and Spain.[60] Under Edward I, horses were bought in France to provide for the needs of the army at the time of the first Welsh war in 1277; the king and his advisers made a major effort to improve the quality of horses available to the English cavalry. Southern Europe, particularly Spain, was a favoured region from which to import horses; the element of Arab blood had no doubt improved the quality of the breeds there. Near the end of Edward's reign the citizens of London decided to present him with a Spanish charger.[61] Early in Edward III's reign horses were bought in Sicily and Spain for the king, though after 1334 importation from Spain ceased. The Castilian monarchy was hostile to the export trade, and the English found other sources of high quality bloodstock.[62] In 1358–9 Edmund Rose, keeper of the royal great horses, bought horses abroad, on one occasion acquiring thirty-eight at Malines from a single Italian merchant for almost £3,000. Others were bought in England, some from a German trader. Some of these were described as being from Hungary, and others from Rothenburg, Regensburg and Nuremburg.[63] Other horses were acquired on campaign. The earl of Stafford was unable to take all his horses with him on campaign to Gascony in 1352, since there was insufficient shipping, and he had to buy mounts locally.[64]

As well as importing horses, much care was taken over breeding animals in England. The records of John's reign provide the earliest full evidence for the activities of the royal stud-farms: the king took a great interest and pride in his stables. Records show the movement of royal horses from one part of the country to another. In 1210 at one time there were forty royal horses at Northampton; Thomas de la Lande took twenty-one to Cirencester, and Geoffrey of Wales thirty-five to Oxford. Accounts from 1212 detail the costs of thirty-three horses, each with its own groom, at Newport Pagnell and elsewhere.[65] By Edward I's reign, when detailed accounts first survive, there was an elaborate organisation of royal studs, spread over the country. In the north, Macclesfield and the Peak were much used; Odiham, Chertsey, Woodstock, Hertford, St Albans and Breaumore were among the more important in the south. Richard Foun was for many years keeper of Edward's horses; this was a highly skilled, professional task, and it made no sense to make frequent changes. Under Edward III, Richard de Framesworth held positions dealing with the royal horses for at least thirty years. There are many accounts for the studs, which reveal the stock figures, the movement of horses between studs, and the varied items of expenditure. The numbers of horses are not easy to calculate, as the surviving accounts may provide no more than a partial picture. The records suggest that in 1284 there were seventy-three, and in the mid 1290s over a hundred royal horses.[66] The accounts of Richard de Stanes, marshal of the king's horses at the start of Edward II's reign, show great fluctuations in numbers, but the maximum number in his care was no more than forty-eight. The record reveals the king's fondness for his favourite Piers Gaveston, who was given several horses as presents, and who was provided with royal mounts for tournaments.[67] In the late 1350s Framesworth, as keeper of the horses south of the Trent, had custody of between fifty and sixty animals. Perhaps not surprisingly, given the king's unwarlike character, the accounts of John Staward (master of Henry VI's horse) drawn up in 1439, reveal a relatively small establishment of forty-two horses.[68]

These records of the keepers of the royal horses reveal something of the care that was taken with these animals. Orderic Vitalis had commented in the twelfth century on the fact that oats were needed to keep up the strength of horses in a northern climate, and the royal horses were allocated impressive quantities.[69] Framesworth's account for 1352–4 shows that in the winter months each horse was allowed half a bushel of oats every twenty-four hours, along with three loaves of horsebread, baked from beans and peas mixed with oatmeal. In winter, the stables were lit with oil lamps. Shoeing was a regular expense, and substantial quantities of cloth were bought to make halters and head-stalls. If the horses fell ill, there was a considerable range of medicaments available. Wine, vinegar and olive oil might be used, and there was also white ointment, pitch, mastic, fenugreek, frankincense, ginger and dragon's blood. The cost of maintaining a single horse in December was 2*d*, the same daily rate as was received by an infantry solider, though the figure was halved by the spring. That was because fodder became cheap; it does not seem that the horses were ever put out to graze. Each horse had its own groom; these were pampered animals.[70]

The scale of activity of the royal studs naturally correlated with the needs of war. The period of Edward III's greatest successes in the Hundred Years War was also the time when the crown's horse-breeding activities were at their highest. The years of peace which followed the truce of Brétigny saw a rapid decline in the studs. When the war reopened in 1369, the king was no longer so active, and the royal household had been substantially reduced in scale.[71]

These surviving stud accounts simply deal with the king's horses. The crown did not as a rule supply horses to those fighting in its armies; even household knights appear to have been expected to provide their own mounts. In 1210 John provided four knights with money to buy horses, rather than giving them royal ones.[72] The royal horses were for the king's own use, and for the needs of his immediate household. Great magnates would have had stud farms themselves, while many knights must have been dependent on horse-traders to find mounts of a high standard.

Good quality horses were extremely valuable. The evidence points to a rapid price rise in the late twelfth and early thirteenth centuries. Under Henry II a standard price appears to have been £2, though one horse was bought for £6 13s 4d. From Richard I's reign there is evidence of destriers costing a mere 10 marks for two; towards the end of John's reign figures for purchase of horses show that the price could vary from 50 *li. Ang.* to as little as 14 *li. Ang.* (there were roughly four Angevin pounds to each pound sterling). Two Lombard horses cost £38 13s 4d, but five Spanish horses were bought for £40 from a crossbowman called Gilot.[73] The ample early thirteenth-century Pipe Roll evidence of warhorses and palfreys owed to the crown in part payment of fines demonstrates that they were highly prized. Where the price is given, the normal level is 30 marks, though how far what is clearly a notional value related to market price cannot be determined. Higher prices of £50 were not unknown for good warhorses.[74] The high value John put on horses is demonstrated by many entries in the records. In one year the earl of Chester offered two of the best and most beautiful warhorses, and three of the best palfreys, to obtain rights to an heiress. Brian de Lisle offered two good valuable horses to be quit of £100 he owed. The earl of Winchester owed the king a good chaser, like the silver-grey he already had. Fulk FitzWarin promised to pay £100, along with a beautiful warhorse, the finest to be found in Wales. In one of those curious entries in John's records that tantalise more than explain, it was stated that Robert de Vaux owed five of the best palfreys to buy the king's silence in the matter of the wife of Henry Pinel.[75]

By the end of the thirteenth century, the best warhorses were very expensive. In 1297 Edward I sold a horse for £33 6s 8d, and bought a replacement for £66 13s 4d. Prices for the best horses continued to rise; in 1337 Edward III bought one charger in the Low Countries for £168 15s, and another for £162 9s. It would be wrong, however, to judge horse prices in terms of the highest prices that could be obtained; a horse given by Edward III to the count of Nassau cost only £10, and presumably was regarded as a worthwhile gift. The fullest evidence for horse prices is provided by the lists of the valuations of horses made at the start of campaigns, and of the compensation paid when animals were lost. The problem is that these were not true market prices, but were values put on the animals by royal clerks, no doubt after some haggling with their owners. Men would, of course, have only their best horse valued: ordinary riding horses and baggage animals were much cheaper than those listed in the valuations. In 1300 the highest compensation for loss of horses was that awarded to Ralph Manton, an influential clerk in the royal administration, one of whose animals had been valued at 80 marks. This perhaps reflected the position of the horse's owner at least as much as its quality.

The evidence of horse valuations has been carefully considered by Andrew Ayton. The mean price was at roughly the same level, at £8 10s, for Edward I's second Welsh war in 1282, as it was for Edward III's 1359 expedition, when it stood at £9. Between those dates, however, it fell as low as £7 12s in 1337, and rose as high as £16 8s in 1338–9. There were considerable variations within these figures. The earl of Salisbury's retinue in the Low Countries lost sixty-five animals in 1338–9, at an average price of under £20 each, yet John Moleyns's thirteen horses lost cost the crown over £30 on average.[76] The figures are complex to interpret; the contrast between the low horse prices for Scottish campaigns in the 1330s and the high ones for those serving in Flanders at the end of the decade may well reflect a perception that better horses would be needed for fighting against the French. They may also reflect a generosity on the part of the crown's valuers in Flanders, paralleling the unprecedented offer of double wages for the campaign. What is abundantly clear is that good horses were a very major investment for their owners.

The horses had to be properly equipped for war. At the time of the Norman Conquest, the horse bore no more than a saddle, high at front and rear with pommel and cantle to provide support for the rider, and the normal reins, bit and bridle. Horse armour began to make its appearance in the later twelfth century in France and the Low Countries. In 1187 the count of Hainault provided knights with armoured horses for the French king Philip Augustus, and in 1198 Richard I captured 200 French destriers, of which 140 were armoured.[77] By the thirteenth century a full covering for the charger was the rule, and pictorial evidence therefore rarely reveals whether the horse was equipped with armour under the gaudy caparison. Most of the horses shown in the pictures in the Painted Chamber at Westminster – known only from later copies – were fully caparisoned, with a cloth covering that displayed their owner's arms. One appears to be wearing a full coat of mail, both costly and extraordinarily heavy.[78] Under Edward I, warhorses were frequently described as 'covered horses' (*equi cooperti*). Again, how far this covering was purely heraldic, and how far it was padded so as to provide some genuine protection for the horse, is not clear. By the early 1340s metal plate armour was in use; Edward III's charger had an elaborate cloth, or *frette*, of cotton and fustian made to fit under his armour, with a thick padding intended to absorb sweat. A trapper with royal arms would then have covered the whole, looking magnificent.[79] The picture of Sir Geoffrey Luttrell shows his horse with an elaborate trapper, and even a splendid crest on the horse's head to match that on his own helmet. The fashion for the fully covered warhorse did not last long. The splendid memorial to Sir John Hawkwood painted by Ucello in 1436 shows his horse with an

AD PRELIVM: CON TRA HAROL DVM REGE

(*Above*) Knights riding to battle, from the Bayeux Tapestry. Note the straight legs, with forward-mounted stirrups, and saddles which support the rider front and rear. (*Right*) A knight from the late thirteenth-century Painted Chamber at Westminster, showing his fully-caparisoned, or barded, horse. The trapper bears his personal symbol. (*Far right*) A drawing of a mid-twelfth-century knight, probably Robert earl of Gloucester (d. 1147), showing the straight-legged riding style.

elaborate harness but no trapper.[80] Most fifteenth-century illustrations of warfare show the horses uncovered, but with a certain
amount of armour, above all chanfrons to protect their heads.

The riding style of the medieval knight looks to have been
thoroughly awkward, with the body held near vertical, and legs
almost straight, not bent. The long stirrups appear in many contemporary illustrations, placed inconveniently far forward. Sir Geoffrey
Luttrell, as depicted in the Luttrell Psalter, has his legs straight, and
his pelvis almost fully enclosed in an elaborate saddle, a clear ancestor of the seventeenth-century 'great saddle' which supported the
rider 'like the body of a well-padded library chair'.[81] This aided
balance when wearing armour, but there was no way that a knight
thus equipped could have risen in his stirrups to engage in swordplay.
Even when a lower saddle was used, it is clear from a multitude of
illustrations that medieval knights did not rise up in their stirrups.
The weight of armour helps to explain the style of riding, with the
knight firmly balanced in the saddle, thrusting down on his stirrups,
and not using his thighs to grip his mount. The way that the saddle
was raised from the horse's back meant that it was hard to sense the
movements of the animal.[82]

The royal household

The cavalry in medieval English armies was made up of a multiplicity of households and retinues, of which the royal household was by far the largest. The knights, squires and sergeants of the household formed the core of royal armies from the eleventh century until at least the mid-fourteenth century. Indeed, much earlier, Anglo-Saxon rulers went to war accompanied by their household retainers. King Alfred was said to have reserved one-sixth of his revenues from taxation to pay his warriors, surely men retained in his household. In the tenth century it is interesting that Aelfric translated the Latin word *miles*, or soldier, as *cniht*, a word which implied that the man was retained by a lord, normally in his household, and that he rode with him. Under Cnut the thegns and *cnihtas* of the tenth-century Anglo-Saxon kings were replaced by the housecarls, household warriors of Danish origins and descent, who were provided with food, lodging and equipment by the king. Under Edward the Confessor, the military retinue probably contained a mixture of elements, thegns, *cnihtas*, some housecarls and a few Normans.[83]

After the Conquest, a formidable military household was one of the keys to Norman success in England. Under Henry I this body, the *familia regis*, had a military pre-eminence that was rarely to be matched later. The evidence comes not from financial accounts, as in later periods, but from chronicles. It is striking that the chronicles of, say, Edward I's reign make little of the military role of the household, clear though it is from record evidence. That so much about the Norman household can be gleaned from the pages of Orderic Vitalis is a powerful demonstration of its importance. It was the household knights who were the key element in the campaigns of William Rufus and Henry I. They were much more than a personal force following the king: at times the household virtually formed an army in its own right, capable of fighting battles with no other support, as at Bourgthéroulde in 1124. They also provided an occupation force when divided up into castle garrisons. The household enabled the crown to put forces into the field at short notice, and its members could be relied upon to remain on campaign for lengthy periods.[84]

The household under Henry II is surprisingly obscure; the documents that would have revealed its importance have not survived, and the chroniclers rarely emphasise its role in the way that Orderic Vitalis did for the early Norman period. There are some hints of its importance, in addition to the well-known fact that it was four household knights who were responsible for Becket's death. In 1173–4 the Pipe Roll refers to the payment of £9 16s 8d to seventeen household knights at Nottingham, to cover their losses. During the rebellion of that period William de Mandeville crossed to Normandy with the military forces of the royal household in thirty-seven ships. In 1176 the king sent William FitzAldelin with ten knights of the household to Ireland. John de Courcy, Miles de Cogan and Robert Stephen who went too were probably also household members. Disaster struck the household in 1187, when many of its members drowned in a storm at sea, when crossing to Normandy.[85]

John's household knights have been carefully studied by Stephen Church. The reign is important, for it is the first from which house-hold records survive, though unfortunately they do not contain the kinds of lists of fees paid to household knights which feature under Edward I and later. Records of John's expedition to Scotland in 1209 show that he was accompanied by at least thirty-six household knights, while it is probable that he had some forty-five with him in Ireland in the following year. A muster roll for 1215 lists forty-seven household knights. In some cases a knight would bring others with him on campaign, so increasing the overall total. It can be argued that there should be added to these figures the numbers of mercen-aries whom John hired in the Low Countries, who received money fees from the household. The 1215 muster roll lists no less than 375 knights, nearly all of whom fit into this category. Although there was substantial recruitment in the final, disastrous, years of the reign, the evidence suggests that there was considerable continuity of service in John's household. Fifty-three knights served for six years or more, twenty-eight of them for over ten years. At the very end of the reign a list of those in receipt of fees and robes suggests that there were thirty-five household knights on the strength, but this may not be a complete record.[86] These numbers may not appear large, but they do not reveal the full military strength of the household. Each knight would have brought his own followers with him, and mounted sergeants would also have been retained.

Unexpectedly high figures for the size of the military household are revealed by muster lists from the 1220s. One, from 1225–6, shows a total force of ninety-seven knights. In 1228 there were seventy, and in 1229 sixty-seven. Given that Henry III himself was barely of age, and that the country was recovering from the civil war with all its financial implications, it is surprising that such large numbers were retained. Nor were these all, for two of the lists show that some of the knights were expected to bring others with them, bringing the total force for 1225–6 to about 200. There are surprisingly few names shared by all three lists – a mere eleven. Thirty-nine, however, appear on two out of the three lists.[87] Curiously, the numbers of men the knights were expected to bring with them varied from list to list. The fact that it proved necessary to summon these men suggests that few were actually resident in the household at this period; they should perhaps be regarded as forming a wide royal affinity rather than a coherent body of knights such as existed in other periods. There are no similar household muster lists available from other periods, and some caution is therefore needed in comparing the figures with those drawn from different types of source. There is no doubt, however, that Henry III could muster surprisingly substantial household forces. He had a core of thirty or more knights in receipt of fees from the exchequer, and could normally put at least a hundred into the field in a military emergency.[88]

There is a wealth of evidence from the reign of Edward I detailing the personnel and activities of the knights and squires of the royal household, and the pattern continued until Edward III's French war temporarily ceased with the treaty of Brétigny in 1360. Numbers fluctuated in accordance with the king's need and the state of the royal finances. Early in Edward I's reign there were about fifty household knights and bannerets, while in 1285 the strength totalled seventy-seven. In 1290 the figure stood at fifty-eight, the same number as in the year of political and military crisis: 1297. In 1300 there were thirty bannerets and fifty knights, but numbers were not maintained at such a level, and by the end of the reign there were forty-five in all. These figures, of course, provide little indication of the total military strength of the household, for they do not include the retinues that these knights would bring with them on campaign, nor do they include the squires and sergeants of the household, who totalled about 170 in the mid 1280s. The overall numbers that could be put into the field by Edward I's household were impressive. The pay accounts separate the household men neatly from others who accepted royal pay. They show that 527 out of a total of 895 were provided by full members of the household for the campaign in Flanders in 1297. For the Falkirk campaign of the next year the figure rose to almost 800 out of some 1,360.[89]

The household knights continued to provide a significant military force under the unwarlike Edward II. Numbers fluctuated considerably, but in 1314–15 there were no fewer than thirty-two bannerets and eighty-nine knights on the books. In the following year economies, and perhaps policy reassessment in the aftermath of the defeat at Bannockburn, saw the equivalent figures as seven and forty-five.[90] When Edward III was in Flanders in the late 1330s, he had in his household seventeen bannerets, some newly promoted. Knights numbered forty-four. There were almost ninety squires, who included such names of future renown as Nigel Loring and Guy Brian.[91] In 1347 there were fourteen bannerets and sixty-six knights, but by the time of the major campaign of 1359 numbers had fallen to ten and thirty-seven, of whom eleven were recent appointments to the household. It is perhaps significant that the account for the royal expedition to France does not distinguish in the wages section between the household knights and the other knights on the payroll in the way that had been done early in the century. With the resumption of war in 1369, Edward III himself did not play the leading part he had done previously, and there was no longer the same need for a large royal military household.

In the middle years of the fourteenth century nomenclature began to change, from household knights to 'knights of the chamber'. The distinction was not clear before 1360, but thereafter there was a defined inner circle of chamber knights. The term 'household knight' vanished quite abruptly. The change was not simply one of nomenclature. Given-Wilson has argued persuasively that the chamber knights provided service to the king that was both more domestic and more varied than that of the earlier household knights. Though the chamber knights campaigned when necessary, that was not their prime function. A further change took place under Richard II, with the appearance of men simply termed 'king's knight'. These men received annuities from the exchequer, rather than fees from the household. They were not as closely linked to the king as the former household knights had been, but made up a wider affinity. These men provided the heart of royal armies at the end of the fourteenth century, much as household knights had done earlier. Richard II's Irish expedition of 1394 contained eighty-nine bannerets and knights who headed retinues. Forty-eight of these were king's knights. When the king returned to Ireland in 1399, out of forty-nine bannerets and knights, thirty were king's knights.[92] The reasons for these changes to the institution of the household knight in the third quarter of the fourteenth century were, no doubt, complex. The fact that Edward III himself took no further active part in warfare after 1360 was one important element; another was that the Crown was copying the way in which great lay households were organised, and abandoning its own somewhat dated traditions.

Retinues

Just as the king had his household, so too did his more illustrious subjects. The great magnates had very substantial followings, their size increasing considerably in the course of time. There are no comprehensive retinue lists earlier than those of the late thirteenth century. In 1297 Roger Bigod, earl of Norfolk, retained five bannerets, nine knights and seventeen men-at-arms. According to the *Song of Caerlaverock*, the earl of Lincoln had twelve bannerets in his company. Less than a hundred years later, in 1282, John of Gaunt retained seven bannerets, seventy knights and ninety-six squires. These huge retinues were, of course, made up of many smaller ones.

John de Segrave had agreed to provide Bigod with twenty cavalry in time of war. John Neville was contracted for life to Gaunt, to serve with twenty men-at-arms and the same number of archers.[93] The average size of a banneret's retinue in the English armies in Scotland under Edward I was, to judge by the horse valuation lists, between thirteen and fifteen. Such averages, however, conceal considerable variations. In 1300 Robert Clifford had a retinue of four knights and eighteen squires, John de la Mare one of two knights and eight squires, while Arnald de Gaveston had a mere four squires. Some of the bannerets were themselves members of much larger retinues. By 1322 the average size of a banneret's retinue had risen to twenty-one, the largest, that led by John Darcy, consisting of forty men. In Scotland in 1341–2 the average had risen to thirty. The trend continued, and by 1359 the figure for a banneret's following was sixty. In that year the Black Prince commanded a retinue of seven bannerets, 136 knights and 444 squires. The average size of the banneret's following rose much higher still after the renewal of the French war in 1369, to almost 200. In 1415 the duke of Clarence agreed to serve with 240 men-at-arms and 720 mounted archers, while Gloucester contracted for 200 men-at-arms and 600 mounted archers. These large retinues were made up of many smaller retinues, provided by sub-contractors; there is no indication of any organisation into tens or twenties.[94]

The ways in which men recruited others to serve in their followings have been intensively studied.[95] The most obvious source of men was the lord's own immediate family. Secondly, there was his tenantry, particularly those who held land by knight service. Thirdly, there were those specially retained to perform military or other services. The broad assumption of most historians has been that there was a shift from a reliance on tenurial obligation to a dependence on the recruitment of paid retainers, which took place between the twelfth and fourteenth centuries. It may be that this shift is more apparent than real, a result of changing forms of evidence rather than of changing patterns of behaviour. Personal ties in the medieval period, as in any other, were complex. Different elements could overlap each other in a confusing medley of family, tenurial and financial relationships.

Kinsmen must have provided a central core to many retinues and followings throughout the medieval period. Pay records do not normally provide full lists of names, but other sources such as the lists of horse valuations and requests for writs of protection are more informative. The Berkeley contingent on the Flanders campaign of 1297 was headed by three members of the family. In 1298, for example, William de Montgomery, Robert de Mohaut, and William Echingham, to name just three, all had brothers serving with them. In

December 1303 John Botetourt's retinue in Scotland contained two men who shared his name, William and Paul, clearly relatives.[96] Analysis of the retinue that Sir Ralph Mobberly took to serve under the Black Prince in 1355, consisting of himself, a squire, and some thirty-two mounted archers, reveals the presence of three of Ralph's relations. The attendance of men with the same surname in the retinue, such as John and William Warburton, and Hugh and William Vernon, further shows that family members might well fight together. David Hulgreve's retinue in 1380 contained three members of his immediate family.[97] The retinue of the earl of Devon in the 1380s included five members of the Courtenay family. Many retinues, however, contained no duplication of surnames.

A lord would expect to be served in war by members of his permanent household staff. In the Norman period there is some evidence both for officials and knights as members of noble households. In the early twelfth century William Peverel of Dover gave land assessed at half a knight's fee to his steward, Thurstin. A knight called William is described as being of the house and *familia* (household) of Hugh de Lacy. Orderic Vitalis described the lavish following of the obese earl of Chester, who 'went about surrounded by an army instead of a household', and clearly possessed a very substantial force of household knights.[99] Early in Henry II's reign Robert de Valoignes entered into an agreement with William de Bacton, promising that he would provide for him, and his man, in his household, and that he would give him furred robes.[100] The story told of the deathbed of the great Marshal in 1219, when he refused to allow the furs and robes he had in store to be given away in alms, because they should be distributed to his knights, helps to demonstrate how important these men were.[101] By the early fourteenth century, such retaining of household knights might be on a massive scale. Thomas earl of Lancaster probably had over fifty knights and twice as many squires in his household at one time. At the end of the century John of Gaunt's household was of similar size.[102]

If land was held in fee, then tenants were under a formal feudal obligation to provide their lords with military service. Yet relations of tenants with their lords may often have been more antagonistic than mutually supportive, marked by litigation not co-operation. Men frequently held land from several lords, but could serve with only one. Sub-enfeoffment weakened the lord's hold, as did the strengthening of the hereditary right of the tenants. From at least the late twelfth century, men of the knightly class, though holding their lands as tenants, possessed considerable independence of action. Evidence from the eleventh and twelfth centuries for the detailed composition of the contingents men took to war is inevitably largely lacking. From a very early stage some tenants paid scutage instead of performing physical service, and it is not even clear to what extent lords were able to rely on their tenants to provide their formal quotas of feudal military service.[103] At the time of the civil war at the end of John's reign, tenurial ties were certainly an important part of the complex mosaic of loyalties. In 1216 the garrison manning Peter de Brus's castle of Skelton consisted largely of his tenants, men who owed castle-guard service.[104] Yet analysis of the following of William Marshal early in the thirteenth century, based on the lists of those witnessing his charters, shows that only one-third of the knights who served him were his tenants.[105] In the mid-thirteenth-century civil war, the Montfortian Henry de Hastings was able to obtain the service of one of his tenants, David de Esseby, only by distraining his lands and goods. In contrast, many of those knights who supported Simon de Montfort did so quite independently of their lords.[106] Often it is not possible to be certain of men's status, but the fact that two lists of Roger Bigod's household, one from 1294–5, and the other from 1297, contain no more than five names in common, suggests that he was not relying heavily on his tenantry. In the first two decades of the fourteenth century only two men featured with any regularity in the Berkeley military retinues. Though both lived in areas where Berkeley influence was strong, it is not clear that either were tenants. A little later, in 1355, and at a lower level of society, Ralph Mobberley's tenantry did not make a significant contribution to his retinue. On the other hand, John of Gaunt was a landholder on such a large scale, particularly in Lancashire from where he drew most of his retainers, that thirty-two out of a sample of eighty-nine held some land from him.[107]

Study of the composition of retinues, above all in the late thirteenth and early fourteenth centuries, demonstrates that there was a strikingly rapid turnover of membership. Men would serve with a different lord on each campaign, and lords such as Robert Clifford who attracted a genuine personal loyalty were rare. Clifford's following was strongly regional in character, featuring such north-western names as Vipont, Wigton, Leybourne and Lowther.[108] More typically, of twenty-four men in John de Warenne's retinue for the 1303–4 campaign in Scotland, only three appear to have served with him on other occasions. The only regulars campaigning with Aymer de Valence were his steward, Roger of Inkpen, and his son.[109] More research is needed to establish later patterns, but few of those who were with Ralph Mobberley in 1355 served with him on the 1359 campaign. Even so great a late-fourteenth-century magnate as John of Gaunt found that a substantial proportion, perhaps half, of his men-at-arms had to be recruited year by year, with no effective continuity of service.[110] In the fifteenth century, to judge by a careful study of the retinues that served John Talbot, earl of Shrewsbury, the pattern of a rapid turnover continued. Taking the muster rolls of the years 1439–41, A.J. Pollard demonstrated that only half of the men-at-arms served for a whole year. Over the two-year period, no more than a third remained in Talbot's service throughout. There was a small nucleus of men who formed a personal following. Very few of Talbot's men had links with him in England; their connections with him were forged in Normandy. Talbot's retinue had a simple but effective organisation. An experienced soldier headed it, ready to take command should Talbot himself be otherwise engaged; this post was held by different men every year. There was a paymaster, and a clerk who was responsible for recruitment and supply of foodstuffs and equipment.[111]

The analysis so far has concentrated on the vertical links within retinues, the connections between men and their lords or commanders. There were in addition significant horizontal links, which might be permanent or temporary. In the late 1170s William Marshal entered into what appears to have been a formal partnership with another noted knight, Roger de Gaugi. The two engaged in a highly successful tour of the European tournament circuit, capturing no less than 103 knights in a couple of years.[112] It seems very likely that this was an early example of the practice of entering into the type of agreement known as brotherhood in arms. These agreements formalised partnerships between soldiers, agreements to share profits and losses, to be of mutual support and aid to each other. Those knights in Edward I's household who are listed in the records as *commilites* were almost certainly men who served with their companion-in-arms. A very rare surviving brotherhood agreement dates from 1298; the document is scarce, but the practice was common.[113] A most notorious brotherhood agreement was that which was almost certainly made between Piers Gaveston and the future King Edward II; this was highly abnormal, as the two men were not of equal status.[114] Many of these brotherhood agreements were made during the Hundred Years War. The arms of Hugh Calveley and Robert Knollys feature on alternate panels on the tomb of the former. The two men were not related by blood, but surely this tomb bears witness to more than the respect and affection of each for the other, and proclaims their adoptive brotherhood. In 1421 two squires, John Winter and Nicholas Molyneux, made a typical agreement to be brothers-in-arms, combining their gains in war and sending them back to England to be wisely invested in land.[115] These were business agreements, but there was more to them than that. The comradeship born of campaigning together was a link that has left only a weak trace in the records, but it must have been a powerful bond in the field.

In addition to the substantial retinues led by bannerets, the pay records of the years of Edwardian rule show that many knights came

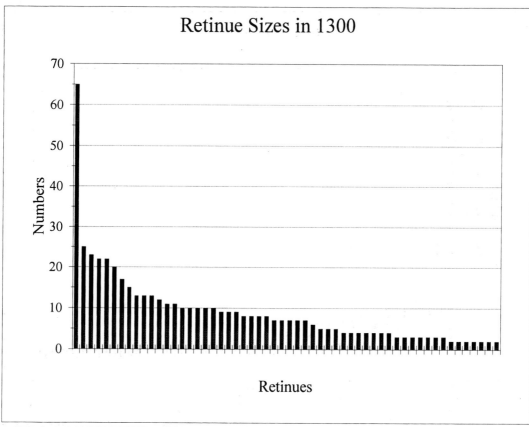

Retinue Sizes in 1300

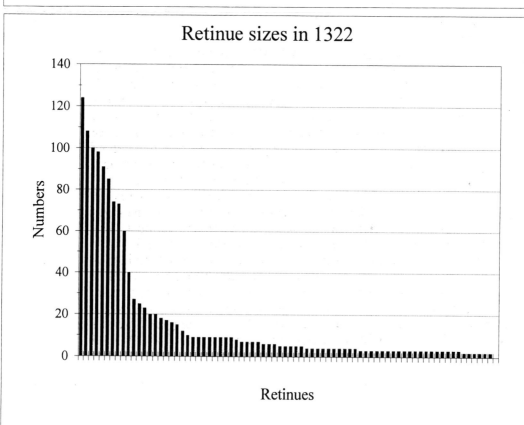

Retinue sizes in 1322

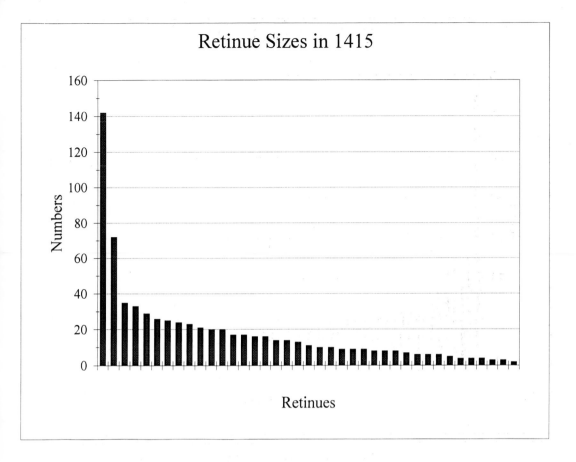

Retinue Sizes in 1415

Numbers

Retinues

on campaign with a following of no more than one or two men, and were paid independently. How these men were integrated into the command structure is not apparent from the sources, but it is unlikely that they were formally brought into larger retinues; if they had been, this would surely have been reflected in the way they were paid. They may have been organised into informal groupings for tactical purposes, but it seems most likely that they did indeed operate with a measure of independence within the larger 'battles'. The figures opposite show the spread of retinue sizes for the campaigns of 1300 and 1322 in Scotland, while that above is for the Agincourt campaign. The latter diagram does not include the numbers of mounted archers who formed part of the retinues. The normal pattern was for there to be a remarkable range between the largest retinues and the smallest. In 1300 John de St John had by far the largest retinue listed in the year's account book, but it reached sixty-five only because other retinues were incorporated in it. More striking than the large retinues were the many small ones which feature in the record for every army. In 1300, for example, there was John de Bicknor, knight, who served with one squire. The figure of

Chaucer's knight, accompanied as he was by no more than a squire and a yeoman, may seem at first sight surprising, but Thomas of Bradwell, knight, went on the 1359–60 expedition to France accompanied by no more than one squire and one archer, and eight horses between them. He was far from unique.[116]

Organisation in the field

Important as the individual skills of knights undoubtedly were, for effective use in battle the men had to be organised into groups. The largest groups were the 'battles'; it was normal for armies to be divided into three or four such main divisions. The army which marched north to Scotland in 1300, for example, was divided into four units, termed *eschieles* by the author of the *Song of Caerlaverock*, while at Crécy Edward III divided his army into three.[117] The sources are usually fairly clear on these main divisions of the army. It is more difficult to identify the next layer down in the organisation of the cavalry forces. In the Norman period, some evidence suggests that units of ten men, or multiples thereof, known as *conrois*, were usual. Wace, in his accounts of warfare, treated the *conroi* as one of the basic military units, and the Templars rode in groups of ten knights. The French prince Louis, during the civil war at the end of John's reign, is described as organising his army into battle, and ordering it to ride *en conroi*.[118] J.H. Round argued long ago that the feudal organisation of Anglo-Norman England was based on *constabularia* of ten knights. His very reasonable assumption was that tenurial arrangements reflected the reality of military practice.[119] The constabulary, however, did not become established as a significant tenurial unit; knights' fees were not grouped in fives, tens and twenties as a permanent feature of feudal geography. Yet some twelfth-century evidence from pipe rolls and other sources suggests that tens and twenties were the common currency of cavalry organisation. In 1173–4 there were at one time ten knights, and at another twenty, in Portchester castle. There were contingents of twenty knights in Salisbury and Nottingham, and one of the same number of Flemish knights in Canterbury. Particularly telling is Gerald of Wales's account of operations in Ireland. In 1176, for example, William FitzAdelin was sent to Ireland with ten knights of the royal household; with him went John de Courcy with another ten, and Robert FitzStephen and Miles de Cogan with twenty.[120] Larger units, of roughly twenty-five, are suggested by a muster-list probably dating from 1215, but a document dating from late in Edward I's reign shows the cavalry forces of the royal household still organised into *constabularia* in a decimal pattern. Thus John of

Brittany, Arnald de Caupenne and John Russell together provided thirty knights, who are noted as forming three *constabularia*.[121] This evidence is the last to show this type of decimal division; the bulk of the accounts for Edward I's reign show the cavalry divided differently, into the various retinues of the bannerets and knights. It is not likely that there was a rapid transition from a style of military organisation based on decimal units to one formed more haphazardly from retinues of varied size; what is more probable is that decimal units were common in twelfth-century forces, but that this system gradually fell into disuse in the thirteenth century. A French source dating from the late 1330s suggests a logical ordering of the cavalry into hundreds, each hundred being composed of four bannerets, sixteen knights and eighty squires, but there is no such systematic pattern proposed by any English document.[122] It may be significant that the constabulary of ten knights had largely disappeared by the time that the effectiveness of knights on the battlefield was challenged by footsoldiers, as at Stirling Bridge in 1297 and Bannockburn in 1314; without systematic organisation, the cavalry charge was far less likely to prove a decisive weapon in battle.

The retinue, which could vary so greatly in size, must have provided a basic building block for the organisation of the cavalry forces, but at least as important was the support that each individual knight received from his immediate followers. In the twelfth century knights presumably operated in much the same way as was envisaged in the Templar Rule. When they were formed up for battle, each knight would have two squires: one in front carrying his lance, one behind, leading the spare horses. Before battle began, the latter were led to the rear. The lance-bearer handed the weapon to his knight and made ready to charge after him on the spare war-horse.[123] A touching early fourteenth-century visual representation of the knight with his immediate following is provided by a tomb in Exeter cathedral, probably of Richard de Stapledon, in which a knight is shown accompanied by his squire, page and horse.[124] Later in the century, the organisation favoured by the great English condottiere John Hawkwood was the three-man lance, in which two men-at-arms were accompanied and served by a single page. This method was designed for fighting on foot; the men-at-arms would stand back to back in a mêlée, while the page would bring up the horses at the end of the encounter. Froissart's account of the battle of Crécy shows how James Audley fought, with the support of a small body of no more than four squires.[125] What the English did not do was to develop the 'lance' as a unit in the way that the French were to do in the mid fifteenth century. In 1445 a royal ordinance set out the six-man lance as a basic military unit, consisting of a man-at-arms, a well-armed *coutillier*, two archers and two pages.[126]

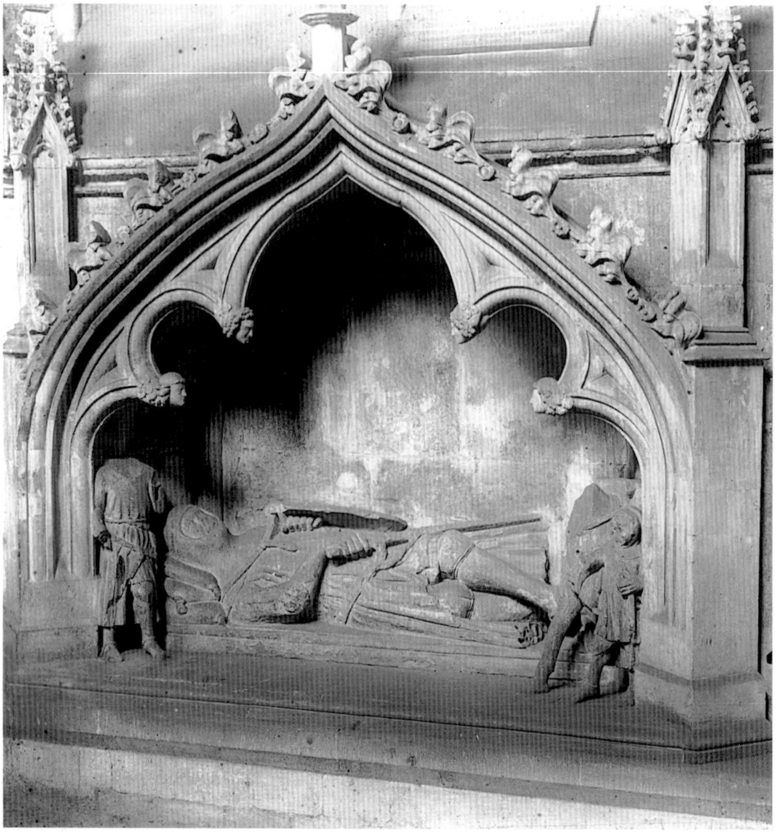

A knight's tomb, probably of Richard Stapledon, in Exeter Cathedral. He is accompanied by his squire on the left, and his horse and page on the right.

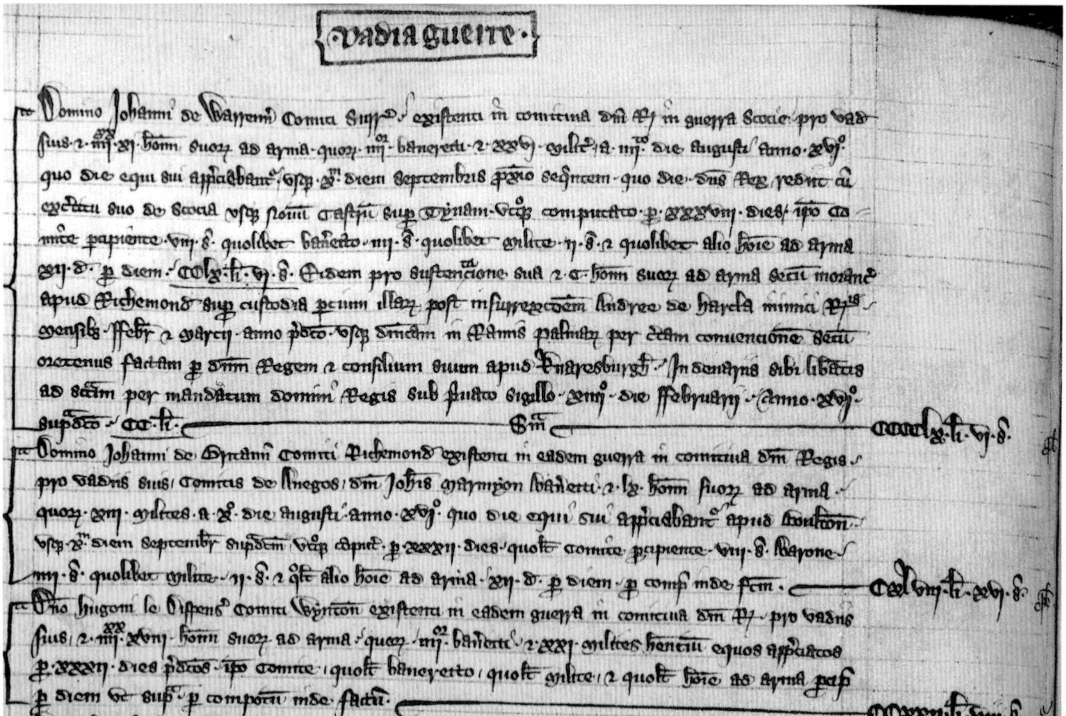

Vadia guerre

Knights and sergeants

The evidence of military pay records from the late thirteenth century makes it possible to examine the way in which the proportion of knights as against sergeants, squires and other men-at-arms changed. Under Edward I between a quarter and a third of the cavalry forces were knights, and this level did not change substantially until the third quarter of the fourteenth century. In the second Welsh war, of 1282–3, of those mustered at Chester 28 per cent were knights or bannerets, as were 24 per cent of those who mustered at Gloucester.[127] On the Caerlaverock campaign in 1300 about 22 per cent of the cavalry in royal pay were knighted, and on the ill-fated 1322 expedition to Scotland the level was 24 per cent. Salisbury's troop in Scotland in 1337 contained 18 per cent knights.[128] In Brittany in 1343 22 per cent of Henry of Lancaster's retinue were knights, though Walter Mauny's contained only 16 per cent. Perhaps, as a foreigner, he found it harder to recruit men of status in his service.[129] In the Black Prince's massive contingent in the 1359 campaign, the proportion stood at 24 per cent.[130] The transformation in these proportions began after the reopening of the Hundred Years War in 1369. John of Gaunt's retinue in 1369 showed no change from earlier patterns, for 27 per cent of his cavalry troops were of knightly rank. But this level fell rapidly, and for Gaunt's great *chevauchée* of 1373 it was no more than 13 per cent, and for the 1375 Brittany expedition it fell to under 5 per cent. In 1380 it stood at 6.5 per cent.[131] This sudden change in proportions can hardly be explained by an equally rapid shift in English social structure. Rather, it must be the result of changing attitudes towards the war. Sherborne's researches showed that between 1369 and 1380 only eight knights of county gentry origins served as captains of retinues in France, and of those, six were king's knights at the time. He was disinclined to see this as evidence of a fall in the overall contribution of the knightly class to the war, but taken in conjunction with the indications of the sudden fall in the proportion of knights in the armies of this time, it points firmly in that direction.[132] In the Agincourt army, the proportion of knights stood at about 8 per cent.[133] The figure fell as enthusiasm for the French war declined. There was concern in Henry V's later years at the situation, and a growing recognition of the fact that squires now had attained the status that knights had possessed in past periods. The king was anxious to be served by men, be they knights or squires, who had the right to coats of arms, and in military records it was noted when men were 'de nom et d'armes'.[134] In 1437 those of knightly and higher status formed 3.5 per cent of the army. In the Duke of York's force of 1441 the level was 2.4 per cent. In 1439 it was decided that

Part of a page from a royal wardrobe account book, detailing some of the cavalry wages on the 1322 expedition to Scotland. The first entry is for John de Warenne, earl of Surrey.

Huntingdon should take a force of two bannerets, sixteen knights and 280 men-at-arms, with 2,000 archers, to Gascony. His actual force slightly exceeded this in men-at-arms and archers, but he could raise no more than six knights. When in 1443 Somerset took some 600 cavalry to France, approximately 1.3 per cent of the force were of knightly rank or above. He noted, not surprisingly, a 'lakke of barons, bannerets and knights' prepared to accompany him.[135] Where heads of knightly families were prepared to serve Henry V in 1415, it was the younger brothers and sons who served in the wars in the reign of Henry VI. In Derbyshire, only two significant gentry families, the Gresleys and the Blounts, provided men who had important military careers.[136] The evidence strongly suggests that knightly numbers remained reasonably static for a hundred years from the 1270s, and that after that there was a rapid and startling decline in numbers.

A further element in the mounted forces put into the field was lightly armed horsemen, often termed hobelars. Troops of this type are to be found in records of military service on the Welsh march from 1166: fifty-one such tenures are known. In this region they were based in castle garrisons, and it is not clear to what extent such troops formed part of major field armies.[137] The hobelars proper were troops of Irish origin, first used in Scotland in 1296. They were lightly armed cavalrymen, 'light lancers, moss-troopers or border prickers' as J.E. Morris explained in terms perhaps more comprehensible when he wrote in 1914 than today. In 1301, 390 hobelars came over with the Irish contingent of troops, and soon troops of this type were recruited in England, particularly the north, as well as in Ireland. In 1319, 845 hobelars were present at the unsuccessful siege of Berwick.[138] Such men had obvious value in campaigns against Scottish or Irish forces; they were highly mobile, had hardy mounts that could put up with the rigours of mountainous terrain, and had the advantage of being relatively cheap, with wages of 6*d* a day. It was noted in 1325, however, that they were unlikely to prove useful in densely populated Gascony; their value lay more in war fought in a wide and open countryside.[139]

Numbers

There is a great deal of information on the numbers of cavalry employed in English armies, but despite the bulk of pay records and horse-valuation lists, it is not easy to provide definitive figures. The Norman period provides the figure of a little over 5,000 knights' fees in England, and it might be tempting to assume that that represents a reasonable assessment of the total available cavalry. There is, however, no evidence to suggest that the full 5,000 were ever mustered, and it is unlikely that the quotas of service were set after careful consideration of the probable total manpower available. Large numbers were not inconceivable; the treaty with the Count of Flanders of 1101 allowed for the count to serve with 1,000 knights. Orderic Vitalis credited William Rufus with mobilising a force of 1,700 knights in Maine in 1098.[140] Gerald of Wales, whose evidence on numbers appears more trustworthy than that of most chroniclers, thought that Henry II took a force of about 500 knights, with many archers both mounted and on foot, to Ireland in 1171.[141] A feudal muster for a Welsh expedition in 1223 yielded a force of 387 knights and 145 sergeants, and in 1228 an estimated 545 knights took part in a further campaign in Wales.[142]

By Edward I's reign much evidence from pay-rolls is available, and while these are not necessarily precisely accurate, there is no reason to doubt the overall picture they provide. The greater financial resources available to the state, above all from direct taxation and customs duties, with credit mechanisms provided by Italian merchants, enabled Edward to recruit much larger armies than those of the past. However, many magnates did not accept royal pay, and so any figures calculated from the pay records tell only part of the story. The paid forces of the royal household seem to have provided about a quarter or a third of the troops in such major expeditions as those of 1298 or 1300. The horse valuation lists show that some 1,300 men accepted pay in 1298, so the total force of knights, squires and sergeants may have been in the region of 4,000.[143] It was not until Edward III's reign that all the magnates were ready to accept royal pay, making it possible to produce more reliable calculations. Payrolls, however, are not always to be trusted, particularly when they show contingents remaining at precisely the same strength through months of campaigning. In 1335 there were some 3,200 men-at-arms in the army that went to Scotland – a huge force. In the autumn of 1339 the king had some 1,600 men-at-arms with him in the Low Countries. No similar figures can be precisely calculated for the Crécy–Calais campaign as the accounts do not survive, but the estimate is that there were between 2,700 and 2,900 men-at-arms present. The detailed accounts for the 1359 expedition show that the force was yet larger, with some 4,750 heavily armed cavalry. Those were exceptionally large expeditions, but cavalry were recruited in substantial numbers for less significant campaigns. John of Gaunt had over 2,000 heavily armed cavalry for his march in 1373 from Calais to Bordeaux. There were almost as many present in the Brittany campaign of 1375. A final example is that of the Agincourt army, of which about 2,600 were men-at-arms.[144]

Such global figures derived from pay accounts are probably fairly realistic estimates of the numbers of actual fighting men. Yet the true size of cavalry contingents is not properly revealed by the accounts. The Crown was, understandably, concerned to pay only those who were of fighting value, and valets, grooms and camp-followers would not have appeared. As already noted, Maltravers's indenture with the earl of Salisbury revealed that he had three servants with him in addition to the two archers for whom he received war wages.[145] An account of a nobleman from Ponthieu, the lord of Varannes, who served on the Courtrai campaign under Philip IV, is very informative. The total force consisted of five knights, twenty squires, a chaplain, two clerks, six chamberlains, sixty-one servants (*garçons*) and one washerwoman, with a total of eighty-four horses. Varannes' personal contingent consisted of himself, eight squires, and twenty chamberlains and servants, with thirty horse.[146] An English pay-roll would probably have recorded him as campaigning with five knights and twenty squires. There is no reason to suppose that practices not far across the Channel were radically different from those in England, and these figures suggest that for every combatant cavalryman, there would have been at least two people in a supporting role.

The knightly career

How long a military career would a member of the social élite have? The legal convention for the populace at large was that all men between the ages of fifteen and sixty were supposed to bear arms. It is clear that many of the knightly class continued to take an active part in war long after they would have been encouraged to retire in more recent times. There is a mass of evidence provided by the elaborate hearings in the chivalric dispute between Richard Scrope and Robert Grosvenor in 1386, but unfortunately some of it is rendered less than reliable because many of the witnesses had no accurate idea of their own age. John de Sully claimed to be 105, and had memories of battles from Halidon Hill in 1333 until Nájera in 1367. He would, if his age is accepted, have been eighty-seven at the latter battle; it is more realistic to accept that he had a long military career lasting over thirty years. Perhaps the most implausible example is that of John de Thirlwell and his father. John was fifty-four; his father, 'the oldest squire in the north', had died at the age of 145, having borne arms for sixty-nine years. A more typical entry is Walter Urswick's. He was, he said, sixty years old, and had borne his coat of arms forty years and more. Despite his age, he went on the Scottish expedition in 1385. Some men claimed to have first borne arms in their teenage years: John de Loudham, aged thirty-four, had done so at fourteen, and Simon Moigne at sixteen.[147] Other evidence backs up the picture provided by the Scrope–Grosvenor hearings. Hugh Calveley can be shown to have campaigned as early as 1344, and as late as 1385, a career of over forty years. His companion Robert Knollys, who died in his nineties, was in arms for almost as long. John Talbot, earl of Shrewsbury, was killed in battle at Castillon in 1453 at the age of about sixty-six. Nor was it solely during the Hundred Years War that men had long military careers. William Marshal was knighted in 1167, aged twenty, and rode into battle for the last time at Lincoln in 1217, at seventy. John Botetourt first campaigned in Wales as a squire of the household in 1282, and fought last as a banneret in 1322. Evidence from tournament rolls in the early fourteenth century shows that the average age of the participants was just over thirty, with the oldest being in their fifties. War was not an occupation solely for the young.

It is not easy to determine what proportion of those qualified in terms of wealth and ability to fight actually did so. There must have been men who, despite all the propaganda and pressure, did not care for campaigning, with all the risks and discomforts it entailed. Unpopular campaigns, such as that which Edward I led in Flanders in 1297, might attract few men. The king tried to attract men by offering pay after his attempt to impose a form of compulsory service failed. Replies from the sheriffs of three counties asking them to send to Winchelsea those who had agreed to serve show that only one man, and he a household knight, was prepared to do as he was asked. Records suggest that from the whole of England Edward was able to recruit only sixty-three cavalrymen by these means.[148] That was exceptional. The evidence of attempts to compel men to take up knighthood suggests that the great majority did not try to evade their responsibilities, and they were prepared to fight. In 1333, 150 men were returned as not being knights when they had sufficient wealth, and in 1366 the figure was 170. In 1360 the sheriff of Northumberland reported that there was only one knight available in his county, and he was unfit; the others were all engaged in war.[149] An inquiry of about 1420 gives a slightly different impression. Seventy Yorkshire gentlemen (the term is the contemporary one) offered excuses, in some cases promising that they would serve if their circumstances changed. Many claimed poverty; others ill-health. In many cases they pleaded that they were paying for brothers and sons to fight. The excuses were not all considered valid: thirty-seven men were considered by the commissioners to be capable of service in the French war.[150] Nevertheless, there can be no doubt that for most of the medieval period the upper echelons of English society were thoroughly militarised. The knights and gentry expected to fight, and the great majority of them must have done so at some time in their careers.

The cavalry forces underwent major changes between the Conquest and the fifteenth century. The essential offensive arms, sword and lance, perhaps changed least, and the essential style of fighting on horseback, relying above all on the combined weight of horse and man to provide a massive impetus, a shock attack, altered little. The knights and men-at-arms did not, however, invariably fight from the saddle; they could be highly effective in a defensive line on foot, as was demonstrated in battles both in the early twelfth century and in the Hundred Years War. Armour changed radically in the first half of the fourteenth century; breeding and the importation of animals from Spain and elsewhere doubtless improved the quality of the mounts. The way in which the élite forces were organised in the field is not easily discerned from the sources. There is a logical pattern of constabularies or ten knights, or on occasions more, evident from some records, but from about 1300 there is no clear indication that troops were organised along such lines. Men came on campaign in retinues, which might vary in size from a small group to what virtually amounted to a small army. The élite warrior at the same time remained an individual, often reliant on personal skills and abilities at least as much as on the collective power of an organised group. If the existence of a 'military revolution' depends, at least in part, on systematic organisation and drill, insofar as the cavalry was concerned it would be hard to argue for such a revolution in the middle ages. In other terms, however, there were times when change could well be described as revolutionary. The initial impact of the Norman mounted knight in eleventh-century England was undoubtedly one such moment. Another came in the early fourteenth century, with the transformation of fighting methods in the tactical revolution which brought the English victory at Halidon Hill, Crécy, Poitiers and elsewhere.

3

Military Obligation

Men fought for a wide range of reasons. There were exalted motives, particularly if crusading was involved. In a warlike society, the desire to gain personal glory in combat should not be underestimated. Successful service in war was a good way to a monarch's heart; the unwarlike Edward II rewarded John de Bermingham with the earldom of Louth, and Andrew Harclay with that of Carlisle in grateful recognition of their services at the battles of Faughart and Boroughbridge respectively. There were profits to be made from war, ranging from grants of conquered territory to booty and ransoms, and even pay. The overbearing strength of cultural expectation was that men, particularly those of knightly standing, should fight, unless they were clerics. There was little intellectual doubt about this. Canon and Roman lawyers displayed great skill in developing notions of the just war, and by the thirteenth century any war fought by a monarch could be said to be just. There was no condemnation of warriors by use of the argument that those who live by the sword should die by the sword. The common good provided a full justification for the waging of war.[1]

Feudal service

The concepts of the just war provided by Roman and canon law could not be translated easily into specific formal duties. There were other roots to the forms of military obligation to which the English Crown appealed. The first type that needs to be examined is feudal service. The term 'feudal' is one which many historians frequently try, with considerable justification, to avoid. It carries too many different meanings, from the general to the very specific. It can mean little more than 'medieval', which is hardly helpful, and can be applied to any system in which men perform services in return for their land. It may be used more specifically to refer to the legal relationship between lords and their vassals, and can be used with some precision in relation to military service. In this last sense feudal service was the military duty owed by the holder of a fief to his lord, as part of the obligation incurred following the act of homage. This service was unpaid, and normally lasted for a period of forty days. A summons would demand that service be provided in accordance with the fealty and homage owed to the king. Such service was not, of course, termed 'feudal' by those who performed it; magnates were normally asked to provide their *servitium debitum*, or obligatory service.[2]

Was such feudal service an innovation following the Norman Conquest? There undoubtedly was a tradition of military service in Anglo-Saxon England which could be built on, but identifying and defining that tradition is not easy. The study of military obligation in the Anglo-Saxon period is a topic more prickly than the spears of a fourteenth-century Scottish schiltrom. The dominant orthodoxy is that there were two related but separate structures, a general duty on all free men to defend their locality, and a more specific obligation which made a select force, or fyrd, available to the king.[3] There is in fact remarkably little evidence for such distinctions, and references such as one from 1016 to the summons of all men capable of service are difficult to take literally. There are certainly no Anglo-Saxon texts which clearly demonstrate that there were indeed two separate systems of military service, distinguishing between the 'great fyrd' and the 'select fyrd'. Both are historical constructs resting on remarkably flimsy foundations, although it is clear that an obligation to provide military service of some sort had existed since at least the eighth century.[4]

One distinction that can be demonstrated from the texts is that between those who were summoned personally to fight, and others who simply owed service. A key Domesday passage, describing the military customs which applied in Berkshire, explained that if anyone who had been summoned did not go to fight, then he would lose his lands. If, however, a personal summons was not involved, then a fine of fifty shillings was the penalty. The entry for Worcestershire drew a distinction between a free man, himself a lord in possession of some rights of jurisdiction, and a free man over whom a lord had rights. The former was in the king's mercy for all his lands if he disobeyed a military summons; the latter was merely liable to pay a forty-shilling fine. The implication is that the king summoned his major lords to go on campaign, and that they brought their men with them.[5] The obligation lay on those who held land from the king, either by a formal charter or book (book-land), or by loan (loan-land), and was not a universal duty of all citizens. There was certainly no question of the performance of homage.

How many men was an Anglo-Saxon lord expected to provide? The Berkshire Domesday entry suggests that one soldier was to be

An initial letter D, showing a knight kneeling before a king, holding a sword. He is perhaps acknowledging fealty or homage. This is from a late thirteenth-century English bible, and marks the start of the Book of Wisdom.

provided from every five hides. How far this was a national system is not clear, but the hide was a unit of land used for fiscal purposes, and there was thus a direct relationship between the military and financial burdens imposed on estates. The same system may have applied elsewhere in England. The key to the Anglo-Saxon military system is more likely to have lain in the personal summonses, than in the hideage assessment, as is usually supposed. A lord in receipt of an individual summons would most probably have attended the king with an armed following appropriate to his rank, rather than one carefully calculated at one-fifth of the number of hides he held.[6]

If Anglo-Saxon armies are thought of in this way, then there was not perhaps so much of a contrast with the methods introduced by the Normans after the Conquest. There has been much intense argument between those who hold that feudal knight service was a wholesale innovation under William I, and those who seek continuity with the Anglo-Saxon past. This is one of the most intensively mined of all historical quarries, with each scarce nugget of information given microscopic examination. Only one eleventh-century writ of summons survives. It is addressed not to a Norman lord, but to one of the few Anglo-Saxons who retained power, Æthelwig, abbot of Evesham. This writ asked him to summon all those under his authority who owed knights to send them to Clarendon, where he was also to appear himself, together with the five knights he owed in respect of his abbey.[7] As in Anglo-Saxon practice, there appear to have been two classes, those who received individual summonses, as Æthelwig himself did, and those who were summoned indirectly. The term used in the writ, knight (*miles*), was the same as that used by the Domesday commissioners to describe the pre-Conquest Berkshire soldiers. Yet this writ was used by the redoubtable J.H. Round in his classic paper on the introduction of knight service as a linchpin for his argument that such service was introduced by the Conqueror. The obligation to provide five knights was the same as that owed much later by the abbey of Evesham, but it cannot be demonstrated that it derived from any Anglo-Saxon precedent. This level of service, however, was far lower than that of the great lay magnates; Evesham was highly favoured by having such a low assessment.[8]

The most substantial evidence for the new system is the great survey that was made by Henry II in 1166 into knight service. No example of the request Henry issued has survived, but from the responses it is apparent that he wanted to know the number of knights enfeoffed under Henry I, at the date of his death (the old enfeoffment), and how many had been granted lands since then (the new enfeoffment). The returns were also to specify how many knights there were on the demesne, with their names.[9] Round used the results of this inquiry to show that in very many cases knight service was plainly assessed in units, or constabularies, made up of multiples of five. This, he argued, 'is absolutely destructive of the view that it always represented the number of five-hide (or £20) units contained in the fief'. Military obligation was not decided by the extent of a man's estates, 'but was fixed in relation to, and expressed in terms of, the *constabularia* of ten knights, the unit of the feudal host'.[10] These decimal units could not have been based on Anglo-Saxon military practices, but must have been arbitrarily allocated by the Conqueror in the course of his reign.

Round's arguments were very powerful, but the case for a continuity between the Anglo-Saxon five-hide units and the post-Conquest knight's fee has not been without its supporters. Round's case was primarily based on the quotas owed by the tenants-in-chief to the king; examination of the way in which those great men obtained service from their own sub-tenants reveals that in some cases an Anglo-Saxon five-hide unit became an Anglo-Norman knight's fee, demonstrating a measure of continuity. That is not surprising; it is nonetheless clear that the quotas of the tenants-in-chief were not calculated by adding the number of hides under their control, and dividing by five.[11]

More recently, John Gillingham has argued ingeniously in support of continuity across the thin red line of the Conquest. He pointed out the extraordinary lack of contemporary evidence for the kind of fundamental change in social organisation that would have been involved in the introduction of a brand new form of military service. In addition to the writ to Æthelwig of Evesham, Round used the evidence of Roger of Wendover, writing in the thirteenth century, the *Liber Eliensis* of the later twelfth century, and the Abingdon chronicle. This latter was written in the early twelfth century, but though it states that the burden of knight service was recorded under William I, it does not state that it was introduced by him. The range of sources used by Round was small, and Gillingham cogently argues that fifteen contemporary authors writing in some twelve different churches or monasteries did not mention new burdens arising as a result of the introduction of knight service. Nor did Archbishops Lanfranc or Anselm complain about what would appear to have been a heavy additional burden imposed on the English church. Ingenious, if not wholly convincing, argument suggests that when Orderic Vitalis wrote that William I distributed lands so as to ensure that he would have 60,000 knights available to him, he did not mean that knight service was newly imposed. A particularly striking part of the case is that in a charter dated 821, but in reality forged in the post-Conquest period, clear reference was made to military service with twelve vassals. Surely no forger would have been so stupid as to refer in this way to a military system known to have been recently introduced? Gillingham's suggestion is that in Anglo-Saxon times there must have been a system of quotas very like that of the Norman period.[12]

It may be that Gillingham overestimated the historical awareness of the Anglo-Norman forger, and it is perhaps asking too much of contemporary chroniclers to concentrate on the social changes which interest twentieth-century historians, but his points have consider-able force. At the very least, it seems likely that contemporaries were not as aware as historians today of the implications of the changes that took place in the way that military service was demanded by the Normans. Yet one at least did clearly indicate that there was a fundamental difference between the Norman and the Anglo-Saxon periods. The vision of Boso, a Norman follower of the bishop of Durham, in the 1090s vividly contrasted the Northumbrian spearmen of the past, mounted on fat horses, with knights of his own day, clad in armour riding chargers.[13] This was not a matter of the technicalities of systems of obligation, but of the realities of warfare.

The fact that the many of the quotas revealed by the returns to the 1166 inquiry were assessed in multiples of five and ten strongly suggests that they were indeed arbitrarily imposed in the Norman period, and not inherited from the Anglo-Saxon period. There were, however, many quotas which did not fit into this convenient mathematical pattern. These were examined by Holt, who argued convincingly that the decimal quotas were clearly older than those of an apparently random character. The random quotas were the pro-duct of a process whereby estates were broken up, sometimes by accidents of descent, sometimes by confiscation following rebellion. He also showed that it was possible under Rufus and in the early years of Henry I's reign for newly formed baronies to be allocated decimal quotas, as was done in the case of Plympton in Devon, established by 1107.[14]

Another set of arguments over the possible continuity between Anglo-Saxon and Norman military institutions relate to the length of the period of military service. The Berkshire Domesday passage specified this as sixty days; the conventional feudal service of later periods was forty days. Hollister argued that in the century after the conquest the length of service remained at the Anglo-Saxon level. The case depended on calculations based on the assumption that rates of scutage, the money payment that could be made instead of service, were calculated in terms of the cost of hiring substitute knights. A 30*s* scutage would pay for a knight to serve for sixty days at a daily wage of 6*d*.[15] The problem with this argument is that the evidence for a 6*d* wage in the reign of Henry I is unconvincing, while the varied rates at which scutages were levied makes it impossible to argue that there was a standard equation linking scutage, wage rates and the length of service. Nor is there any evidence for the Crown agreeing to reduce the length of service from sixty to forty days. The arguments of those who see the Normans introducing to England the forty-day term of service are far more convincing, though it has to be admitted that there is no evidence that this was the customary period of service in pre-Conquest Normandy.[16]

The evidence for the actual enforcement of the feudal obligation on holders of knights' fees to serve for forty days is surprisingly limited. There is no full record of the performance of service until the thirteenth century, and one of the implications of Henry II's 1166 inquiry is that the crown did not itself even possess a central record of what service was owed. Stenton argued that 'it is easy to under-estimate the frequency with which the feudal army was summoned by the Norman kings', and it may be that such summonses were so normal an event that chroniclers did not think them worth record-ing.[17] It is only because William II complained about the quality and suitability of the knights provided by Archbishop Anselm for one of his expeditions to Wales that it is clear that a feudal summons had been issued.[18] Henry I certainly appears to have considered service important at the outset of his reign, for in his coronation charter he promised not to levy geld or other services on the demesne lands of knights who held their estates *per loricas,* by their hauberks, so that they would be properly provided with horses and arms, ready to serve the king in the defence of the realm.[19] Yet the promise was not one that he kept; mercenaries proved to be of more use than knights provided in response to requests for service. The full scale of feudal service amounted in theory to some 5,000 knights, an impressive number. It is hard to imagine that a force so large could ever have been mustered, and it is not surprising to find that Henry II demanded a third of the total in 1157. Two years later he preferred to take scutage from the bulk of his tenants-in-chief, rather than require *agrarios milites,* rustic knights, to go on the Toulouse expe-dition. In 1165 he obtained promises from many tenants-in-chief that they would provide specific numbers of sergeants for a period of six months service.[20] Yet Henry did not abandon knight service. Feudal service was requested for the expedition to Ireland in 1171, and for that to Galloway in 1186. At the very end of the reign, in a striking contrast to the policy adopted in the 1150s, it was reported that all the knights in England, even if feeble and poor, were summoned to serve in France.[21]

Henry II's far-reaching inquiry into feudal obligation, made in 1166, provides the bulk of the evidence for military service in the twelfth century. The king's motives for ordering the inquiry were probably fiscal rather than military, and were related to the aid for the marriage of his eldest daughter to Henry the Lion of Saxony. The unit of assessment for such an aid was the knight's fee, and so it is not surprising that the returns should provide detailed information about knight service, though there is little on how it was actually performed.[22] This information should have provided the evidence for a reassessment of military and fiscal burdens. In practice, the returns were insufficiently standardised to be of much use.

The patterns that emerged from the inquiry were predictably varied. Some responses were very straightforward. Herbert de Castello, a Shropshire lord, reported that he had five knights of the old enfeoffment, each of whom he named as holding a knight's fee, and all of whom had performed homage to the king. There were no knights on the new enfeoffment. On the barony of Skipton in Yorkshire, on the other hand, there was a complex pattern. There were twelve fees on the old enfeoffment, but from one it was impossible to obtain service. Two tenants held half fees. The new enfeoffment consisted, for the most part, of land whose value was assessed in carucates, or ploughlands, rather than knight's fees. Thus, 'Walter FitzWilliam, ten carucates of land, of which fourteen carucates make a knight's fee'. It was reported that in Northamptonshire Richard Basset had held 184 carucates for the service of fifteen knights, 'but no knight on the old enfeoffment was specifically enfeoffed for a knight's fee. Each carucate was assessed to perform a fifteenth part of all knight's services, both in armies, castle-guard and elsewhere.' At Ramsey abbey, under Henry I, a hideage assessment was used to divide the burden of knightly service between the tenants. In the case of the honour of Wallingford, the return distinguished between the knights who had been enfeoffed, and whose obligations were set out in the form of knight's fees, and the free tenants, who were assessed in terms of hides and virgates. William de Beauchamp stressed that he owed seven knights on the old enfeoffment, but listed seventeen knights, with a total service of sixteen. In contrast, Hugh de Scalers owed service of fifteen knights, but had only eight and a fraction enfeoffed on his lands.[23]

It would be unwise to draw too many conclusions from such exceptional examples in the 1166 returns. It is striking, however, that the neat decimal pattern of distribution which Round observed in the obligations of the tenants-in-chief to the crown is rarely to be found in the details of the way that service was imposed by these men on their own tenants, save in the case of those with very substantial obligations. For the most part, it was a matter of men owing a single knight, or a fractional service. The earl of Gloucester, however, had one tenant owing fifteen knights, and six, including the quaintly named Elias Goldenballs (*aureis testiculis*) owing ten. The smaller holdings on his lands were not, however, so logically assessed for service. The distribution pattern of the old enfeoffment on his estates was as follows:[24]

No. of knights owed	No. owing this service
15	1
10	6
9	4
8	1
7	4
6	1
5	5
4	6
3	3
2	7
1½	2
1¼	2
½	9

In contrast, Patrick earl of Salisbury's response showed that there was no pattern of consolidation of fees into fives or tens within the forty that he owed to the Crown:[25]

No. of knights owed	No. owing this service
7	1
3	3
2½	2
2	4
1½	2
1	8

Details of how service was actually performed are rare in the 1166 returns, for they were not requested by the king. The Evesham return noted that the abbot paid the expenses of the knights on the old enfeoffment when they served in the king's army.[26] It was noted, 'as old men testify', that the substantial FitzAlan estates in Shropshire owed service of only ten knights in expeditions and *chevauchées* within the county, and only five outside it. The FitzAlan return is interesting, since it, exceptionally, gives details of non-knightly service, that of *muntatores*. These were lightly armed cavalrymen, whose service was based in the castle at Oswestry, and who were obviously valuable in dealing with the hit-and-run border warfare practised by the Welsh. Later, two of these men would be counted as equivalent to one knight, but the 1166 returns give no hint of any such equivalence.[27] Another interesting entry reveals that there had been considerable argument about the obligation of the knights of the honour of Arundel over service in Wales. The king had chosen four of the oldest and wisest to testify to the obligations, and it was the results of their deliberations that were reported in response to the king's inquiries. The fact that in some cases tenants-in-chief in 1166 clearly had some difficulty in establishing what their military obligation actually was, and that they had to consult with their own tenants to discover the answers, strongly suggests that by this period knight service did not bear a close relationship with military reality.[28]

Where the evidence for military service becomes startlingly thin is precisely where it might be expected to yield a rich seam of knowledge. There is astonishingly little evidence as to how men actually fulfilled their obligations before the thirteenth century. The surviving charters granting land in return for, among other things, military service are thoroughly uninformative. There is much more evidence for the performance of castle-guard service than there is for service in royal armies. The implication of the silence of the evidence is that obligatory service in royal armies was not regarded as particularly important. It may be that there was no possible doubt about what was entailed in the service of a knight, so making any closer definition unnecessary, but this would be surprising given the care that was taken much later, in the fourteenth century, to define the precise terms of service in military indentures. It is also striking that the financial records of the exchequer reveal very few cases where men were accused of failing to provide their service. Stenton gave the example of William Lovel who was disseised in 1197 because he had not attended the royal army in Normandy.[29] It is not, however, even clear that Lovel's obligation was a feudal one.

The size of the holdings from which knight service was expected could vary very considerably. Sally Harvey argued from Domesday Book for the existence of knights of very lowly status, and equivalently small landholdings, in the late eleventh century. She worked out the average size of a knightly holding to have been a mere one and a half hides. The case is hardly a convincing one since her analysis was based on those knights whose names are not given in Domesday; had she included those great men who were named, and who were undoubtedly knights even though not specified as such, the results would have been strikingly different. The very term *miles*, while it could apply to men of standing, does not in the eleventh century bear the full connotations of knighthood that accompanied it later.[30] Some knightly holdings were certainly small. Stenton, looking at twelfth-century evidence, showed that while there is good evidence for the existence of knights' fees valued at a substantial £20 a year, there are also examples of fees being created that were worth £10. In the early 1140s the earl of Lincoln gave £10 of land in two widely separated parcels to Peter of Goxhill in return for the service of one knight.[31] The Crown, of course, had no need to take an interest in the way that its tenants-in-chief allocated the burdens of service on their own tenants. The very considerable local variations that existed suggest that military needs were not the predominant element in determining the tenurial structure. Indeed, many knights held little if any land. They were household knights, professionals who were retained by lords and paid for their services, but not rewarded with estates.

Mention should be made of the obligations that existed to perform non-knightly service. Land could be held by sergeanty service. This service might take many forms, but most of them were non-military in nature. Such duties as looking after the royal hawks, rearing royal puppies, even counting the king's chess-men and putting them back in their box after use, were among the sergeanties. Perhaps the most celebrated among historians is that attached to the manor of Hemingstone in Suffolk, whose tenant was to leap, whistle and fart for the king's amusement every Christmas Day. Some sergeanties were more straightforward, with their holders being obliged to provide men armed with relatively simple equipment for campaigns.[32] The contribution of sergeanties to English armies was a very minor one, and it is significant that when an attempt was made in the mid thirteenth century to review the system many were converted into rents or knight service. Adam Gurdon held an estate in Hampshire by sergeanty, but in 1254 it was converted into half a knight's fee.[33]

Arguments from silence are always dangerous, but given the surviving evidence it is difficult to argue that feudal service provided the major element in the cavalry forces of eleventh- and twelfth-century armies. The limitation of the period of service to forty days would certainly have presented considerable problems, unless the troops were simply taken into royal pay at the end of the obligatory forty days. The difficulties involved in assuring the quality of the troops provided were no doubt great; it is hard to believe that Anselm's were the only unsatisfactory knights. It was surely the case that the real value of the system of knight's fees was not military, but fiscal. The mechanisms of scutage and of feudal aids were surely what were of real significance to the Norman and early Angevin monarchies. Yet service obviously was performed, as well as scutage paid. When magnates served in twelfth-century armies, they may well have considered that in so doing they were fulfilling a clear military obligation. It seems likely, however, that what was in practice expected of them was that they should campaign with a respectable contingent, rather than a specific and carefully assessed number of knights.

The reduction of quotas

The end of the twelfth century, and the beginning of the thirteenth, saw a major, swift and dramatic transformation of feudal military service, no doubt because it was increasingly apparent that the existing structure did not meet contemporary requirements. What Richard I needed was 300 knights to fight for a year in France, as he demanded in 1197, rather than a huge host which disappeared within six weeks of mustering.[34] Had the burden of the traditional knight service been equitably distributed, then it might have been appropriate for the Crown to have demanded a proportion of it, much as Henry II had done in 1157 when a third was demanded. However, by John's reign, and probably earlier, the Crown had to be content with tenants-in-chief appearing on campaign with a fitting contingent, one appropriate to their status but not related by any formula to the traditional obligation. For example, on the Irish expedition of 1210 Geoffrey FitzPeter provided ten knights, not the ninety-eight and a third that he owed. Gilbert de Gaunt provided six knights as against a quota of sixty-eight and a third. In the Poitou campaign of 1214 the earl of Devon served with twenty knights, not the eighty-nine of his formal obligation. In the Unknown Charter, drawn up in the negotiations that preceded the issue of Magna Carta, a scheme was suggested whereby anyone who owed more than ten knights would have their service appropriately reduced, on baronial advice.[35] Summons lists from this period do not confine themselves to the major tenants-in-chief, with the expectation that they would provide substantial contingents. Rather, as a list from 1213 shows, John was summoning the individual knights from great honours such as those of Peverel, Leicester and Tickhill, most of whom are noted as either coming alone, or with one knight.[36] There were clearly problems in getting lists of summonses right. This is surely the explanation for the curious Pipe Roll entry, noting that Hugh de Neville offered (or bet) five tuns of good wine that Geoffrey Sauvage of Staffordshire would be summoned to serve in Poitou, and that Geoffrey Sauvage undersheriff of Hampshire would not be summoned.[37] There is no doubt that feudal military service was a reality in this period; the reductions in the numbers of troops expected meant that the Crown could expect men to turn up with appropriate quotas. One lady, Albreda of Lincoln, paid twenty marks to recover her land of Norton, which had been confiscated because she did not have a knight doing service for John in Ireland. Duncan de Lasceles owed sixty marks and one palfrey to regain three and a half knights' fees, taken from him on the king's orders because he had not attended with horses and arms on the Scottish expedition.[38] Near the end of the reign the tenants of one half of the honour of Leicester offered to pay £254 5s 3d to be quit of whatever quota of military service was demanded from them. Had service been a largely nominal burden, no such offer would have been made.

Feudal service was not normally rewarded with pay.[39] Under John, however, prests, or cash advances, were issued to men who were performing feudal service in his armies. Holt has argued that the demands of war at this period were such that monetary payments were needed in order to ensure that service was provided. In time, these would have to be repaid, but the suggestion is that the use of these prests was an acceptable means of rewarding men who considered that their status would be adversely affected if they accepted wages in the full sense. The modern analogy might be with sportsmen who receive lavish 'expenses' in order to maintain their amateur status. In the case of the army which mustered at Dover in 1213, the summons did not take the full feudal form, but in two instances, the Irish expedition of 1210 and the Poitou expedition of 1214, prests were certainly paid to an army which mustered in response to a feudal summons demanding the performance of knight service. The prests were probably intended in many cases as advances against the scutage that magnates and knights could expect to collect in due course from their own tenants, though the implications of the entry stating that Geoffrey de Neville received a prest of fifteen marks 'on the hairs of his head' remain unclear. King John had a strange sense of humour.[40] These prests were not a stage in a transformation of feudal service into paid service, but represent an evolutionary dead-end, a product of the particular circumstances of the early thirteenth century. It is also possible that rather than representing a form of payment for feudal service, they were a form of recognition of the fact that the period of service would stretch beyond the traditional forty days; the Irish campaign lasted some eighty days, and that in Poitou eight months. They were not an advance on wages, since it was expected that they would be repaid; the Pipe Rolls of Henry III's reign show that men were indeed charged with these prests, and receipt rolls show that some at least were repaid.[41]

The Crown conceded no formal reduction in feudal service in Magna Carta. All that was included was an anodyne clause promising that knights' fees would not be burdened with more service than was due from them.[42] Yet the process of establishing new levels continued, by individual bargaining rather than national agreement. The pattern was one in which the great tenants-in-chief saw their quotas reduced very substantially; smaller men benefited to a much lesser extent. Lists were drawn up of all those from whom service was individually demanded. These were based on a register of 157 names. The reasons for selection are far from apparent. There was no attempt to include all tenants-in-chief, and the omission of the Earl

Marshal from the register on which the lists were based is curious.
The inclusion of four countesses shows that the basis of the lists was
not service in person. A demand for service in 1229 yielded a force of
some five or six hundred knights in all. Walter de Lacy, who owed
fifty-one and a quarter knights, was asked to provide a mere four.[43]
By the time of the Welsh campaign of 1245, most of the new reduced
quotas were firmly established. These quotas were in many cases well
short of the actual numbers of men provided by the magnates on
campaign. The earl of Winchester was obliged to attend in 1245 with
three knights and one sergeant, but he mustered with ten men. Peter
of Savoy, on the same campaign, acknowledged the service of five
knights, but provided a further seven *de gratia*.[44] The following table
gives some examples.

	Old quota	Knights supplied	Service acknowledged
Peter of Savoy	140	13	5
John de Courtenay	92	3	3
Earl of Winchester	60	10	3½
Robert St John	55	5	3
Saher de Wahull	30	2	2
Abbot of Abingdon	30	4	30
Ralph Basset of Great Weldon	15	2	15
Robert de Newborough	15	2	12
Philip de Columbars	10	3	2
Henry Hose	2	1	1
Ralph de Kaines	3	4 sergeants	2
Robert Belet	1	2 sergeants	1
Roger St John	1	1	1
William de Hampton	1	1 sergeant	½

These new, massively reduced quotas, represent a major success
for the magnates in their relationship with the Crown. This success
was not the product of a single crisis or even, it seems, of a major
debate, but the scale of the reduction was very remarkable. The old
quotas were unrealistically large in early thirteenth-century terms, as
John had been ready to recognise, but the new quotas reduced the
obligation of the greater tenants-in-chief to equally unrealistic levels.
But the change was not a total victory for those who owed service,
for the old quotas, while abandoned as far as service was concerned,
were not forgotten by the exchequer for fiscal purposes. Scutage, for

example, continued to be demanded on the basis of the old quotas. Nor were the new quotas accompanied by the creation of new, massively enlarged, knight's fees; the tenants-in-chief did not reorganise their own estates to mirror the change in the obligation they owed to the Crown.

Feudal service was one of the means used by the Crown to recruit men during the Barons' Wars of the 1260s. Early in 1263 an interesting summons was issued to William Mauduit and twenty-six other men, using full feudal terminology with an appeal to the fealty and homage that they owed to the Crown, but asking them to come well supplied with men and arms to serve at the king's wages. This, however, did not presage any general move to combine feudal obligation with paid service. In May of the same year there was a reversion to more traditional methods, for 133 tenants-in-chief were sent individual summonses asking them to muster at Worcester, while the sheriffs were asked to summon all those who held at least a knight's fee. The clergy were asked to send their service as well. There is unfortunately no record of the result of this summons; the political circumstances of the day must have meant that response was limited. Presumably the greater tenants-in-chief were expected to appear with the new-style reduced quotas, but the demand that all with at least a knight's fee should attend amounted to a considerable extension of military service. In the next year a summons to serve against Llywelyn of Wales made no use of the feudal terminology of homage, but appealed in more general terms to the fealty and affection that was owed to the king, and demanded that the service owed should be provided. Unfortunately the writs summoning John Balliol and other northerners were lost by the royal messenger as he traversed Sherwood Forest; their replacements included an appeal to homage, so this muster as a whole should probably be regarded as a traditional appeal for feudal service.[45] Nor were these the only feudal summonses in the period of civil war; obligatory service was requested for the siege of Kenilworth in 1266.

The last stages of feudal service

From 1277 to 1327, regular use was made of feudal military summonses by Edward I and Edward II. Records survive giving details of the numbers of troops who mustered. For the Welsh war of 1277, 228 knights and 294 sergeants served for forty days without pay. Two sergeants were counted as the equivalent of one knight in fulfilling the obligation. The level of service in 1282 was lower, with 123 knights and 190 sergeants, but it may be that records for the year are not complete. In 1300 forty knights and 366 sergeants appeared

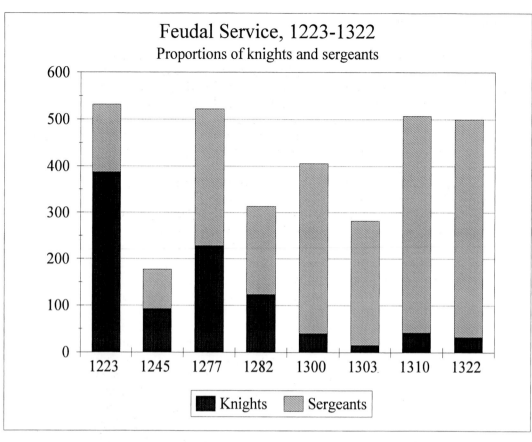

Feudal Service, 1223-1322
Proportions of knights and sergeants

Legend: ■ Knights ▨ Sergeants

on the Caerlaverock campaign, and in 1303 fifteen knights and 267 sergeants. The figure above shows the changing proportions of knights and sergeants. By 1310 the emphasis was placed on how many barded horses were provided, rather than on whether the men were knights or sergeants. Thus the earl of Pembroke provided one knight and eight sergeants with ten barded horses to fulfil a five-knight obligation. In all, forty-two knights were enrolled as doing service, and 465 sergeants. The total number of cavalry performing service in 1322 was again about 500.[46] These are significant numbers, but clearly feudal service could not provide an army. It could produce perhaps a quarter of the cavalry forces for a limited duration. The obligation to perform service was not one which lay heavily on men in an individual sense. There was no personal duty involved, and the obligation was fully satisfied by sending substitutes. It is striking that during the reigns of Edward I and II, when there are reasonably full details of how service was actually performed, even when tenants-in-chief were present in the army, it was very rare for them to register as doing service themselves. Out of about 200 tenants-in-chief providing service in 1300, only a dozen were recorded as serving in person. Curiously, incomplete records for service in 1306 show that while in July only two out of twenty-seven tenants-in-chief served in person, in October eighteen out of twenty-nine did answer individually for their feudal obligation. When men did serve in person, the size of their feudal quota bore no relationship to the actual number with them on campaign. In 1306 John Botetourt enrolled himself as performing the service of one knight, but in fact he had a contingent of three knights and eleven squires with him in Scotland.[47]

The sources do not normally reveal whether those performing feudal service were formed up together as a single body in the army, or whether, once they had registered their service with the Marshal or officials responsible for keeping the record, they were dispersed among the army. In the case of the small feudal muster of July 1306 the men were instructed to proceed with all speed to Perth, and not to join up with any other retinues.[48] The circumstances of that campaign may, however, have been exceptional, with several small corps operating in Scotland rather than one single large army.

In many cases, men would simply detach part of their retinue to be enrolled to perform feudal service. Ecclesiastics, if they did not pay fines in lieu of service, normally contracted with some military professional to do their service for them. In 1300 the bishop of Hereford arranged for William de Grandson to represent him, for 120 marks. Robert Constable of York specialised in this, providing service for the bishop of Ely in 1322, and the archbishop of York in 1327. In 1314 William de Fauconberg entered into an elaborate contract with John de Beauchamp, for the service due from three knights' fees and to pay him sixty marks if he failed to perform.[49] There is nothing to suggest that those who performed service under Edward I or his son were incompetent or ill-equipped, apart from a small lunatic fringe. There were a few cases where some antiquated sergeanty service was owed, when the holder insisted, perhaps out of a misguided sense of humour, in performing his duty. Thus in 1282 one man came to the muster carrying a side of bacon, which he ate, and promptly departed. John de Langford was obliged to attend on a horse worth five shillings, bearing a stick with a sack tied to the end, while Hugo FitzHeyr offered his service which consisted of 'following the king in his war with a bow and an arrow. As soon as he saw the king's enemies, he loosed off the arrow, and returned home.'[50]

It was not essential to issue a feudal summons in order to recruit an army. There were no such summonses for the Flanders expedition of 1297, the Falkirk campaign of 1298, the campaign of 1307, or that of 1319. Edward I's initial intention in 1282 had been to summon an army that would be paid royal wages, and it was probably only after protests from the magnates that a traditional feudal summons was issued. It was aristocratic, rather than governmental, conservatism that meant that feudal service continued to be demanded for so long. The burden of service, once the new quotas were firmly established by the middle of the thirteenth century, was not great. In some cases quotas continued to fall. The earl of Warwick's fell from six and a half knights in 1277 to five in 1310; while thanks to royal favour, Piers Gaveston as earl of Cornwall under Edward II owed no more than three knights, as against the fifteen due from his predecessor as earl. Forty days was not long. There were expectations that the Crown would reward those who served with lands, should the campaign be successful. Tenants-in-chief also benefited in financial terms, for they were able to collect scutage from their sub-tenants on the basis of the old twelfth-century quotas. The earl of Lincoln received £125 from his Pontefract tenants as scutage for the 1300 campaign. Above all, the magnates were probably anxious to maintain traditional forms of summons for fear that any alternative might impose far greater demands on them. There were also some limited advantages for the Crown. It could also benefit in financial terms, but receipts were relatively low. It might obtain either scutage paid on the basis of the old assessment, or fines derived from the new quotas. The latter yielded about £2,000 in 1300, but scutage less than £400. It was also important that there could be no argument about a feudal summons; the duty to provide men could not be challenged, unless it was intended to take the army to somewhere that was not hallowed by custom. There were no problems about issuing feudal summonses for Wales or Scotland; Gascony was a different matter. In 1294 Edward I did ask for a feudal muster to send troops to Gascony, but there were considerable problems. Some troops undoubtedly appeared: the abbot of Ramsey sent men. But the muster had to be postponed, no doubt because the response to the summons was inadequate, and it looks as if it was quietly abandoned by a government whose attention was soon distracted by the news of rebellion in Wales.[51]

The system of feudal military obligation, in its second generation as reconstituted in the early thirteenth century, lasted in a more or less unchanged form until 1327. That was the year of Edward III's sole feudal summons. The technique was then summarily abandoned, though the terminology of asking men to come in fealty and homage, the customary vocabulary of a feudal summons, was not given up.[52] Unfortunately, there is no record of any discussions that took place, nor is there any indication that political hostility lay behind the move. It was not surprising, for feudal service bore little relationship to the realities of fourteenth-century armies. The armies mustered by means of the summonses of 1314, 1322 and 1327 had all been conspicuously unsuccessful, and a new generation of royal advisers must have calculated that there was no merit in standing by traditional methods, if they failed to produce adequate results. Yet the case for regarding feudal service as obsolete, an anachronistic survival, was perhaps not quite so clear-cut. In Scotland at the start of the fourteenth century the English introduced a form of feudal tenure. Those who were granted lands in Scotland were, by a decision reached in parliament in 1302, expected to provide men-at-arms to garrison Scottish castles.[53] In Ireland, more significantly, knight service which had been important in the thirteenth century continued to be demanded in the fourteenth and even the fifteenth centuries. The character of warfare in Ireland was very different; military obligation based upon land made good sense when warfare was primarily local and defensive in its nature. Though scutage was paid in Ireland, there clearly was strong feeling, expressed in the Irish parliament in 1342, that service should be done in person. In Normandy, after the conquest by Henry V, the king carefully reserved his rights to feudal service when making grants to his followers, while also imposing new obligations on the most important fiefs. The service of Norman nobles was also insisted upon. In all, some 1,400 men could, at least in theory, have been recruited by feudal means, and summonses were issued with great frequency.[54] Feudal service was not abandoned in England after 1327 because the concept was outdated. Rather, given the reduction in the English quotas, such service was not worthwhile, as relatively few troops could be raised and scutage could no longer be collected.

There is one postscript to the story of feudal service in England. Through all the campaigns of his reign against the Scots and the French, Edward III made no use of the system. It was, however, revived in 1385 for a Scottish campaign. This was almost certainly done for financial, rather than military, reasons, though there may also have been a view that if no feudal summons was issued under Richard II, precedents would lapse, and the Crown would lose its right to demand such service in the future.[55]

Extensions of obligation

As well as the specific obligation to provide knight service, there was a much more general one to which the Crown might appeal. One possibility was to make use of the widely accepted general principle that all free men should be prepared to bear arms in defence of their country. Henry II in the Assize of Arms of 1181 set out the military equipment that all men were expected to possess, and required that they should swear to bear arms in the king's service at his command.[56] It was possible to ask for service in terms of the allegiance and affection (*in fide et dileccione*) which subjects owed to the king.

In 1263 the 'bachelors' of Herefordshire were asked in these terms to muster at Hereford.[57] This type of writ was used to recruit the army that won victory for Edward I at Falkirk in 1298. Such an appeal might also be appended to a feudal summons; tenants-in-chief in 1300 were asked to bring as many men with them as they considered they could provide, as well as the formal quotas.[58] In 1297 Edward argued that he was risking life and limb in venturing with his expedition to Flanders. His subjects should support him, 'as good and loyal people should and are bound to do to their liege lord in so great and high a matter'.[59] This again was not a request for the *servitium debitum*, but a broader statement of the loyalty and duty that subjects owed to the king. It is very hard to be precise about this general obligation, but it is equally hard to deny that it had considerable force, particularly when linked to the intangible but important expectations of the chivalrous classes. There was an ill-defined expectation that a knight should be prepared to fight. The legal treatise known as 'Bracton' stated that the chief distinction of knighthood lay in selection for fighting in defence of the land.[60] The virtues of prowess and honour, the skills in the use of arms, were best demonstrated by fighting in a just cause.

'Bracton' was written in a period when the number of knights in the country was in decline, as families that had been able to afford the honour found it increasingly beyond their means. Distraint of knighthood provided a means to try to increase or at least maintain the numbers of knights. All those initially with at least a knight's fee, and subsequently with at least £20-worth of land, were expected to become knights. Henry III did not, however, extend the principle further and try to impose an obligation to serve on all those qualified for knightly rank.[61] The next reign, with the increased military requirements of Edward I, would see this happen.

Edward I's first Welsh war, in 1277, was accompanied by a distraint of knighthood, but whereas in Henry III's reign distraint preceded the campaigns, now the distraint of all those with at least £30 of land followed the Welsh expedition, in 1278. It was presumably chiefly intended as a method of raising money from those who had not fought in the campaign. Then, soon after the outbreak of the second war at Easter in 1282, the same class were ordered to prepare themselves with war-horses and proper armour. In November all those with £20-worth of land were summoned to appear at York or Northampton early in the next year. County representatives were also summoned, so that a grant of taxation might be made. It does seem that it was intended to persuade the £20 men that they had an obligation to fight, and at York a grant of military service was initially made, but this was then abandoned in favour of the grant of a tax. The Northampton meeting had already made such a grant. In the mood of post-war euphoria the level of wealth required for knighthood was relaxed to £100, though in 1292 it was brought down again to a more realistic £40.[62]

The period of war that began in 1294 provided many incentives for the king to find new methods of enforcing service. There was now no question of limiting requests to serve to those who had formally assumed the rank of knighthood. Wealth alone was the criterion adopted by the Crown. Early in 1295 the sheriffs were asked to inquire into all those who held at least £40 worth of land. Such men were ordered to be ready to set out on campaign at three weeks' notice, properly equipped, at royal wages. It was said that this was to provide troops for Gascony, but how successful it was as a method of recruitment is not clear. The instruction was, however, repeated in 1296, and may well have assisted in gathering troops for the Scottish expedition that year. There were no immediate objections to these measures, but when in 1297 the king extended the principle to all £20 landholders, he thrust a stick into a hornet's nest. These men were formally summoned to muster at London, and resistance was widespread. It is not clear how many turned up at London, but the results persuaded the king to try again, this time with an offer of wages. Replies from three sheriffs, those of Devon, Herefordshire and Lancashire, show that only one man from the three counties was prepared to go. The account book for the campaign in Flanders suggests a total recruitment for the whole country of a mere sixty-three men. In the sheriffs' returns listing the £20 landholders, which survive for thirteen counties, 713 men had been named. The attempt to extend obligation to this class had been conspicuously unsuccessful.[63]

Edward I's problems in 1297 had been acute. There was virtually no support beyond the ranks of his own household for the campaign in Flanders, and it was not surprising that attempts to extend military obligation should have failed dismally. Scotland was perhaps a different matter, and in 1300 Edward tried once again to establish a wealth qualification for service. Lists were drawn up of £40 landholders, and their paid service was requested. Objections were raised, on the grounds that these men were either not tenants-in-chief, and so did not owe service, or were tenants-in-chief, in which case they already had a feudal obligation. The argument was powerful, and the scheme was not repeated. Instead, in 1301, no doubt making use of the lists of £40 landholders, no fewer than 935 men were sent individual summonses, promising pay. There is no way to discover how effective these summonses were, but the experiment was not tried again. Either it failed to produce results, or political hostility was too great. In his final years, Edward I abandoned innovative forms of recruitment and attempts to extend obligation; nevertheless, he was able, by conventional means, to recruit very adequate numbers for his Scottish campaigns.[64] The contribution of those who could not fight was not forgotten; they were expected to pray for the king's success in war. Edward claimed, perhaps sincerely, to put more trust in the prayers of his subjects than in his military strength.[65]

The obvious lesson from Edward I's experience was that it did not pay to try to extend military obligation, and that other methods of recruitment were far more satisfactory. Yet the difficult circumstances of Edward II's reign, with a disastrously unsuccessful Scottish war and a high level of political discontent at home, were hardly propitious for voluntary recruitment. In 1316 a feudal summons was issued. This, as was quite normal, asked the tenants-in-chief to bring as many additional troops as they could. What was not normal was that this additional request was linked to homage, while the writs made wholly new threats that lands would be confiscated if the order was not obeyed. In addition, the service of £50 landholders was requested, again under threat of confiscation of estates. The precise form of obligation was not set out, nor was pay promised. Such measures aroused inevitable hostility, and led to the withdrawal of the earl of Lancaster from government. A fragile political truce was shattered, and no successful recruitment along the new lines followed.

The destruction of Lancastrian opposition at the battle of Boroughbridge in 1322 meant that the government could once again try to extend military obligation. For the Scottish campaign of 1322 the sheriffs were asked to make proclamations asking all cavalrymen who were not retained by any lord to muster at Newcastle. Lists of such men were drawn up with varying success: the sheriff of Essex returned the names of fifty-six bannerets and knights, and of eighty-one men-at-arms, while his Huntingdon colleague listed no more than two knights and seven squires. Further attempts were made in 1324. In a remarkable move all knights were asked to come to Westminster to discuss matters of state, and an order for distraint of knighthood was issued. Sheriffs drew up lists of all the knights and men-at-arms in their counties. These are not complete, and different criteria of wealth for men-at-arms were used in different counties, but the surviving returns provide the names of about 1,150 knights and 950 men-at-arms. These were clearly measures undertaken as preparation for a new system of military obligation. For the war in Gascony, commissioners were appointed to array all knights, squires and men-at-arms, and returns were to be sent in, listing those men who were members of magnate retinues, and those others who were ready to serve. Orders then went out requesting specific numbers of men-at-arms, light cavalry, and infantry, with the total number of

Comment les gentz qe esteient de venz la Citee de Jertm ne voleient ren
tre la Citee a David. e David p force les combati e maÿna la Citee.

Warfare in the early fourteenth century, from the contemporary Queen Mary's Psalter. A city is
attacked by mounted knights and miners with picks in the upper scene. Battle rages in the lower panel.

fully armed cavalrymen totalling about 650. In 1325 the sheriffs announced that all men were to be ready to serve when requested. A new distraint of knighthood was instituted. Taken together, these were radical measures. The use of commissioners of array was normal for recruitment of infantry, but to extend their role to cavalry forces was quite new. There was a clear assumption made that all men of the knightly class, and all those who had the equipment appropriate to a man-at-arms, should be under a compulsion to serve. That such policies should have been introduced during the harsh and unsympathetic rule of the Despensers should not be a surprise, and that they were abandoned in 1327 was equally unsurprising.[66]

There was one final attempt made to establish a new system of military obligation. In 1344 Edward III introduced a graduated scale to assess men for their contribution to the army. Everyone with an income of £5 or over was included, with the scale extending right up to those with £1,000 a year or more. All were to find troops in proportion to their wealth. A £5 landholder was to provide an archer; a £25 one a man-at-arms. In the 1330s the king had revised the Statute of Winchester of 1285, itself ultimately derived from the Assize of Arms of 1181, and had laid down that a £40 landholder should have appropriate arms and horse for himself and a companion, but this extension of the system in 1344 was radically new. Commissioners were duly appointed to assess the wealth, and hence the obligation, county by county. In 1345 orders went out to recruit men on the new basis; those who were not fit to serve could provide substitutes. The move was extremely unpopular, prompting protests in parliament, and winning promises that no precedent was intended. Had the campaign not been triumphantly successful at Crécy and at Calais, there would surely have been a major political crisis, such was the scale of the king's demands. As it was, the Commons petitioned the king in 1352 that no one should be obliged to provide military service, except by common consent and grant in parliament. The concession was duly made, and the system abandoned.[67]

There were some other methods of forcing men to fight, in addition to the use of general systems of obligation. These were on an individual basis. The king might bargain, with magnates, and take fines in place of military service. Under King John, Robert de Berkeley agreed to provide ten knights for a year in return for the writing off of a fine of 500 marks. Robert FitzAdam agreed to find two knights for a year, in payment of a fine of £72 10s. Robert de Vaux exchanged a debt of 1,000 marks for the service of a force of three knights and forty sergeants for a two year period. In 1213 John obtained a force of over 150 knights and twenty sergeants by pardoning all or part of debts owed to him.[68] Edward I used similar techniques, if not on such a scale. In 1306 the king pardoned Thomas and Maurice de Berkeley a fine of 1,000 marks imposed for various felonies committed in Gloucestershire, provided that they provided ten men-at-arms for as long as the king remained in Scotland.[69] Edward was also prepared to threaten that long-standing debts would be collected unless men co-operated with his military plans. In 1295 a group of nineteen magnates, headed by the earl of Arundel, refused to go to Gascony. The exchequer was duly instructed to do all it could to compel them to do so. These magnates owed impressive long-standing debts to the Crown, Arundel's totalling £5,232. The threat of collection was a potent one, and they duly sailed for Gascony.[70]

Walter de Milemete, a royal clerk anxious to curry favour with his master, commissioned a fine illuminated manuscript at the end of Edward II's reign to present to the heir to the throne. The text is, for the most part, dull and highly derivative. On military service, however, Walter is interesting. He divides service into three types, voluntary, paid, and compulsory. Of these, the first was much the most commendable. Paid troops, either the king's own subjects, or foreigners, were important, but compulsory service was the least significant. In all cases, the prudent ruler should reward and thank those who fought for him, and make a proper distribution of any lands that were captured.[71] This puts obligation into a proper perspective. Despite all the efforts made by the Crown, troops serving under formal systems of obligation were never more than a minority in royal armies. Had it not been for the fact that feudal service was so integral a part of the land-holding structure of the country, and had considerable financial implications, it would surely never have lasted as long as it did. It is not easy to assess the effectiveness of feudal obligation in the eleventh and twelfth centuries, but it is abundantly evident that such obligation alone was not sufficient to enable the Crown to recruit the armies it needed. The importance of the system in fiscal terms is far easier to demonstrate than is its military significance. The radical reduction of the quotas in the early thirteenth century emasculated the system of obligation so that it could never provide more than a fraction of the required forces. The alternative schemes of obligation based on wealth that were tried in the late thirteenth and the first half of the fourteenth centuries incurred such political hostility, and raised so few troops, that it is surprising that the Crown, under different monarchs, was so persistent in attempting to enforce them. There were other means of obtaining service, by using systems of pay and rewards, that were far more effective.

4

Rewards

The men who rode out from Carlisle towards Scotland with Edward I in those fine summer days in 1300 did so for a variety of reasons. For some, there were no doubt elevated motives; a desire to win renown through glorious deeds. Others were there under a clear obligation to serve their king or their lord, perhaps because of the terms on which they held their land, or because they had entered into a formal contract. Many, no doubt, hoped to better themselves, through pay and by obtaining booty, ransoming prisoners, and perhaps obtaining grants of land in return for good service. There is no easy way to separate the lures of material gain from the more intangible factors of a desire for fame and glory, but there is no doubt that the former were important. It is also not easy to separate the rewards of war from the broader issues of royal patronage, but this chapter will concentrate on the immediate gains derived from military activity, and not extend the discussion to include the many grants made in England to those who assisted the Crown in its military enterprises.

Pay was an obvious reward for military service. The fact that many men in the Norman period served for wages is well established, although there is debate as to what the normal rates were. Some were undoubtedly mercenaries hired in the Low Countries, but the twelfth-century evidence suggests that ordinary English troops were also frequently paid for their service. Wace, in his descriptions of warfare, laid due emphasis on the need to pay troops. In his account of the Conqueror's troops waiting to embark at St Valéry he explained that 'some required pay, and allowances and gifts. Often it was necessary to distribute these to those who could not afford to wait.'[1] The story of the future Henry II's unsuccessful venture to England in 1147, when his knights were hired, not for cash in hand, but by promises of future payment, and he had to turn in desperation to King Stephen for help, suggests that pay was the normal method of rewarding soldiers.[2] In 1173 when Earl Richard de Clare went on an expedition to Ireland, his supplies of treasure soon ran out, so that he could no longer pay his troops. Nor were they able to capture any booty, given the slothful character of the constable commanding

The young Edward III shown, fully armed, being presented with shield and lance by St George in Walter de Milemete's treatise written early in 1327.

them. Mutiny was threatened, a new commander appointed, and military success brought with it the booty with which they could be properly rewarded. The way the story is told by Gerald of Wales suggests nothing unusual: the implication is that these were the normal means of rewarding troops. Walter Map made it clear that wages were paid to those who joined the royal household under Henry I, at the rate of 1s a day. Evidence from Henry II's Pipe Rolls demonstrates that the normal knight's wage was 8d a day, with sergeants receiving a mere 1d. Early in John's reign, Geoffrey Luttrell was ordered to take pay 'as the other knights of my household receive it', at a rate of seven Angevin shillings a day, or just under 2s.[3] By 1212 Flemish soldiers in John's service were being paid at 2s a day for a knight, and 1s for a sergeant. Welsh infantry received 2d a day, with the vintenars, men in charge of groups of twenty men, 4d.[4] The period from about 1180 to 1220 was one of rapid inflation, and military wages were no exception to the general rises that were taking place. There were particular difficulties in the closing stages of the civil war that ended in 1217, for money was extremely short. A number of soldiers were accordingly paid in sapphires, diamonds and emeralds. Godescall of Maskeline, a Flemish mercenary, received twenty-four sapphires and fifteen diamonds to pay the knights and sergeants in his force.[5] In this period, to use the jargon of economics, there was a true market for soldiers. Wages were set in accordance with the laws of supply and demand.

Rates of pay

The levels of pay established in the early thirteenth century were soon stabilised. Two shillings a day became the standard wage for a knight, with mounted sergeants normally receiving half this sum. In the latter stages of the civil war of the 1260s Welsh archers were being paid 3d a day.[6] Under Edward I they remained at similar levels. The king was in a monopoly position, able to dictate wage rates with little reference to market forces. Pay was standardised at 4s a day for a banneret, 2s a day for a knight, 1s a day for a sergeant or man-at-arms, 6d a day for a hobelar or lightly armed horseman, and 2d a day for an infantryman. When mounted archers were introduced in the 1330s, they were paid 6d a day. It was not possible for others to keep wages as low as the Crown could: under Edward II the archbishop of York, desperate for troops to deal with the threat of Scottish invasion, envisaged that it would be necessary to pay knights, if any could be found, 3s 4d a day.[7] In the initial phase of the Hundred Years War Edward III, conscious of the problems involved

King Edward II, an unwarlike king, as depicted in a later medieval manuscript.

in recruiting for overseas service, offered double wages in July 1338. He was able to maintain this generosity until November 1339, and then was compelled to revert to the previous level. Rates were adjusted in relation to the number of horses men had with them; one group of men-at-arms were paid no more than 12*d* daily because they had only two horses each.[8] That remained the level of 'customary wages', but on occasion increased levels were paid. In 1369 John of Gaunt contracted to be paid wages at one and a half times the usual rate, rising to double should his force be besieged. In 1370 double wages were offered to the main military contractors. On occasion lower than normal rates were paid. In 1359 some of the troops waiting for embarkation to Calais were paid a low rate. Thomas de Bradwell received $4^1/_2d$ a day during September, but from then until 11 April 1360 was paid at the 1*s* rate. He was then promoted to knightly rank, even though he had only one companion, an archer, and was paid 2*s* daily.

The purpose of wages was not so much to provide a reward for service, as to meet necessary expenditure. It seems likely that for the most part the costs of campaigning were not in fact fully covered. The true costs to individuals are hard to determine, but arrangements made in 1322 and 1327 by military contractors to fulfil the feudal service owed by major ecclesiastics are perhaps indicative. Five knights were provided for a forty-day period for a sum of £100, which works out at 10s a day for each knight – five times the rate at which the Crown paid wages.[9]

The Crown found ways to increase the level of financial rewards without changing the basic wage rates. The regard was an important introduction in the 1340s. This was a form of bonus, paid quarterly, the normal rate being 100 marks for the service of thirty men-at-arms. This might be increased, and paid at one and half times, or double, the standard level.[10] In many cases it seems likely that these rates were not passed on precisely to all members of the retinue. The earl of March contracted in 1374 to serve for customary wages and a double regard, but one of his retinue, John Strother, received a regard from March at an even higher rate, and paid his own men at a lower rate, so maximising his profits.[11]

It often made sense to offer men sums in advance of their wages, and then to set these sums against the total due when the time came to draw up accounts. Such advances were known as prests. The Pipe Roll for 1173 records that Ralph Brito paid £15 16s 8d to fifteen knights and five sergeants in Colchester castle in wages on one occasion, and £30 on another as a prest. He also paid out £20 in prests to the garrison at Walton.[12] There was an obvious administrative convenience in a system which allowed royal paymasters to pay lump sums out of such funds as were available, avoiding the complex calculation of daily wages. Under John, separate rolls of prests were kept; that for 1210 provides invaluable information on the army that the king took to Ireland. At Dublin on 28 June advances totalling over £300 were made, with most men receiving £1 or £2. John's practice of granting prests to men who were performing feudal service was a short-lived experiment, though the use of prests as one of the means of rewarding those who did accept royal wages continued.[13] It depended, of course, on the Crown being in possession of sufficient quantities of cash; while it was possible for Edward I to pay out substantial sums in prests in Wales in 1294,[14] it became increasingly difficult for him to do so as the Scottish wars took their inevitable toll of his treasury. Most of the prests paid out by Edward III against military wages in the initial stages of the Hundred Years War were to foreigners who had entered his service. They clearly needed more inducements than did his own subjects. Some English knights were nevertheless paid prests. In 1339 William Stury, a household knight, received a huge prest of £200 at Antwerp, paid over to him by William de la Pole. More typical were prests paid to him in the next year of £2 and 16s 6d.[15] At this period the bulk of prests went to princes and others allied to Edward III, and to the bankers and merchants who did so much to finance the king's expedition to Flanders, rather than to the soldiers themselves.

Payment of wages

Not only were wages often inadequate, they were also frequently left unpaid, or paid extremely late. A great many examples could be provided; a few may perhaps suffice. By the later years of Edward I's reign the financial system was severely over-stretched. In 1301 the king wrote to the exchequer to complain that most of the troops with him 'have now left us, and we have no ability to prevent those who are still staying with us from departing day by day, and all this is for want of money'.[16] In that year the garrison at Berwick mutinied because money sent to them was insufficient, particularly when some of it was sent to the troops at Jedburgh and Roxburgh.[17] John Lovel, who served with a troop of five squires in Scotland in 1300 was owed in wages, fees and robes, and the cost of one horse which died on campaign, a total of £57, to which was added in the account £20 still owing from 1298. All he received in cash in 1300 was £20, though liveries of wheat, oats, flour and wine reduced the amount finally owed to him to £49.[18] The record of wages paid to the troops on the 1337 expedition to Scotland noted that the earl of Salisbury was owed £2,845, and that he had received a bill promising payment. The sum was eventually paid by John de Wesenham, one of the wool merchants who did so much to assist the financing of the war, and recorded in the Pipe Roll for 1349.[19] There were very substantial war debts when the campaign in Brittany was concluded in the truce of Malestroit in 1343. The earl of Lancaster alone was owed £2,343, and the total of debt recorded in the royal account book approached £20,000. On Thomas Dagworth's death, his widow filed claims for payment of debts due to him totalling £2,790.[20] John of Gaunt's payment of wages was 'often dilatory and erratic, and the income to be gained from this source was never to be relied upon'.[21] When he went on his major, and eventually unsuccessful, *chevauchée* of 1373, he and his captains were promised that they would receive prior to sailing their regard for six months, wages for three months, and a guarantee of payment for the next three months. Twelve thousand pounds would be sent out to France after the initial six months. In practice, no money was sent to France, and when the captains presented their accounts at the exchequer, between 1374 and 1380, the total due to them was almost £20,000. It was common for men to have to wait at least ten years for payment, and payment was often made only because men acquired the right degree of political influence.[22]

In 1415 Henry V solved the problem of his inability to pay wages promptly by handing over jewels and plate as security for their future payment. The duke of York received a splendid golden alms dish, in the form of a ship mounted on a bear, worth £332, while the earl of Salisbury took a silver-gilt nef, complete with twelve figures of men-at-arms on the deck, which weighed an impressive 65 lbs. These were not redeemed by the crown until 1430. Thomas Haulay was given as security for £12 8s 0½d a pair of gold spurs, a gilt ewer, and a sword decorated with ostrich feathers, which had been the king's before his accession.[23] Late payment of wages, however, continued to be a problem in the final stages of the Hundred Years War. In 1438 John Talbot claimed that he was owed £3,800 in wages since 1435, and by 1443 this figure of arrears had risen to £4,627 10s 6½d. By 1446 the duke of York was owed almost £40,000 for his expenses, largely military, as governor of Normandy.[24]

The calculation of wages on a daily basis could be a considerable administrative burden. On major campaigns, such as those conducted by Edward I, it is clear that the infantry troops were mustered at fairly regular intervals, and their number counted. Payment was based on these figures. The cavalry were not counted in the same way, but when account was made, the leader of each troop had to account precisely for the number of men he had under him. In 1300 William de Grandson accounted for himself, one knight and three squires from 12 July until 10 August. He was then joined by another knight, Thomas de Bermingham, and seven squires. One knight departed on 26 August; a squire left on 11 September, and another on 16 October. Grandson himself and the remaining knight and six squires finally left royal service on 3 November.[25] It was complex to account in such detail, although the staff of the royal household provided the Crown with the clerical resources to operate such a system, and it was also possible to appoint special paymasters. It was simpler, however, to recruit and pay men on a contractual basis.

Contracts

The origins of contracts have been much discussed. It was by means of short-term contracts that a large proportion of the cavalry forces were recruited, from at least the late thirteenth century. The earliest known documents recording such agreements date from 1270, when Prince Edward was forming his crusading expedition. The documents are imprecise in their terms. Adam of Jesmond agreed to go with four knights; Payn de Chaworth and Robert Tiptoft jointly with eight. Service was to be for a year, and payment of expenses was at the rate of a hundred marks for each knight, together with the costs of sea transport for as many horses and men as was appropriate for a knightly company. No mention was made of any recompense for loss of horses, of arrangements for distribution of the spoils of war, or other details that would commonly feature in later contracts.[26] A crusade was an exceptional venture, and these contracts were certainly not following a common form of agreement for military service. But it would be wrong to argue from silence that contracts had not been used previously. Such references as that to £20 paid by Edward to Drogo de Barentin in 1259 in return for service with two other knights show that the prince was not doing anything particularly innovative in 1270.[27] The absence of earlier written agreements is not a particularly strong argument, for there were no good reasons for preserving agreements of a temporary nature. Many contracts may not have been put down in writing.

It would be wrong to see the need for a military retinue as the prime reason for the development of systems of retaining in the thirteenth century. Some early indentures, such as those by which William de Swynburne retained William de Kellawe and John de Lisle, did not mention military service.[28] The shift from a reliance on feudal tenants to one where lordship was exercised by means of contracted retainers is a topic which has been hotly debated, the more so the earlier that it has been placed. One suggestion sees the origin of the late thirteenth-century indenture in the political treaties of the first half of the twelfth century.[29] Another view stresses the need for magnates to acquire the service of highly professional estate managers and other servants, and sees this as an important incentive to find new types of relationship. A range of systems of contracts and annuities was developed in the thirteenth century which enabled lords to obtain service without the concomitant liabilities involved in feudal tenure.[30] To distinguish military service from other needs that lords had is perhaps artificial; what was taking place from at least the late twelfth century was a shift in a range of activities away from a system of rewarding men by means of land held in feudal tenure, and a consequent development of other methods based on contract. As far as military service was concerned, the development of the new reduced quotas of feudal service in the early thirteenth century must have made it far more difficult for lords to rely on their tenants to provide them with assistance in times of war, since service was no longer related to the individual knight's fee. One late thirteenth-century example shows that it might even be necessary, if a lord wanted to obtain military service from one of his tenants, to make a contract with him, for Philip of Hartshill, who contracted to serve

Edmund Stafford in Flanders in 1297, was one of Stafford's tenants.[31]

Contracts for service rapidly became more elaborate after their first appearance in 1270. A highly unusual one for the Welsh war of 1287 was almost exclusively concerned with the question of compensation for loss of horses. The ten horses provided by Peter de Maulay in serving with Edmund Mortimer were described and valued in detail, in a way not done in later contracts. By the last decade of Edward I's reign it was usual for indentures to specify the robes and in some cases the saddles to be granted to retainers. *Bouche à court*, meals in the lord's household, were often offered. Wages were to be paid at the normal rates. Service in tournaments was usually, but not always, demanded. While promises to compensate for horses lost in war were usual, the animals themselves were not listed in the contracts. Thus in 1297 Thomas de Berkeley agreed to serve Aymer de Valence with five knights and six squires as well as servants, for a fee of £50. He was to receive robes, and he and his men would be provided with food. Wage rates were set at the same level as those paid by the Crown. If service was to be overseas, the fee would be increased to 100 marks. Losses of horses would be recompensed. Provisions were also made for Thomas's son Maurice. Unusually, when John de Grey retained Thomas Fillol in 1313, it was conceded that the latter would not have to serve in Wales or Scotland if he did not wish to do so. There was little difference in the terms of time-limited indentures and those that were made for life, save that in the latter case, payment was often promised out of the revenues of some particular manor. Thus John de Segrave was enfeoffed with the manor of Lodden in Norfolk by Roger Bigod, earl of Norfolk, when he entered into a life indenture with him in 1297.[32] It was typical of late-thirteenth- and early-fourteenth-century society to seek to define in writing a form of relationship that can hardly have been new. The intention must have been to make the agreement enforceable in law, yet cases where the terms of the contract were breached are surprisingly rare. There was a dispute over a life indenture made by William de Cressy with William de Doylly in 1294. In 1297 Roger de Mowbray complained that Walter de Burnham had agreed to serve with him in Flanders, but had not done so; in 1320 Nicholas Kingston complained that Alan Plokenet had failed to provide him with robes as he had promised.[33]

It is hardly surprising to find that the Crown also made use of contracts. The *fief-rente*, or money fief, was in effect a form of contract with a long history. William I granted 300 marks a year to the count of Flanders in return for military service prior to the conquest of England. In 1101 Henry I reached agreement with the count for the service of 1,000 knights in exchange for a fee of £500 a year. The count of Hainault also agreed to provide service for Henry in return for an annual £100. Many more examples can be cited; Richard I and John made extensive use of the *fief-rente* in their struggle with the French monarchy. Lengthy lists can be drawn up of knights in the Low Countries who accepted fees from John. It has been calculated that he granted almost 300 *fief-rentes* in the course of his reign.[34] Similar techniques of buying the service of continental allies on a massive scale were employed by Edward I in the 1290s, and by Edward III. Whether such arrangements can be seen as the antecedents of the use of contracts to recruit the Crown's own subjects for war is debatable.[35] If the diplomatic of the documents is studied, then there seems little connection; on the other hand, the content of the agreements had a very great deal in common. Content is surely more significant than form, though it makes little sense to search for a single origin for contractual arrangements.

What is surprising is not that the English Crown entered into contracts for military service with its own subjects, but that apparently it did not do so before the 1290s. As king, Edward I initially used contracts when armies were sent to Gascony. Edmund of Lancaster agreed to serve in 1294 with 140 men-at-arms for 4,000 marks. The earls of Lincoln and Cornwall also entered into contracts to fight in the duchy. It made sense to pay these great men large sums in this way, so avoiding the bureaucratic complexities involved in payment of wages to a large number of men on a regular basis. Although paymasters were sent to Gascony, the full-scale administrative resources of the royal household were not available there. Similarly, in the autumn of 1297 a group of magnates agreed to provide service in return for lump-sum payments in two instalments. The king himself, with his household administration, was at the time campaigning ineffectually in Flanders, so the normal mechanisms for payment were not available. The sum was not calculated on the normal basis of wages, for it averaged at about 3s 5d per man per day. It may be that the figure was set at a high level in lieu of meeting the cost of horses lost on the campaign. The actual contracts themselves, if indeed they were set in writing, do not survive.[36] It was also practical to use contracts where there was a need to provide garrisons for castles outside the campaigning season; it was administratively much simpler to enter into a contract with a castle constable, offering a set sum of money in return for his service with a set number of men. Thus in 1301 John Kingston agreed to keep Edinburgh castle with a force of thirty men-at-arms, fifty-four foot, and ancillary staff for £220 between the end of November and the following Whitsun. Payment was to be made in four instalments, with the dates carefully set out.[37]

In the autumn of 1316 Edward II began to make a number of contracts with leading magnates for service in war and peace. Bartholomew Badlesmere, for example, agreed to provide a hundred men-at-arms, as did the earl of Hereford. A year later the earl of Pembroke contracted to serve with 200 men-at-arms in return for land worth 500 marks, and a wartime fee of 2,000 marks payable quarterly. There had been considerable difficulties in recruiting forces in the summer of 1316, when the earl of Lancaster appears to have taken exception to the type of summons used by Edward. There was also a serious Scottish menace in the north, while the king undoubtedly regarded Lancaster's huge retinue as a threat to his rule. It is likely, therefore, that the contractual arrangements that were entered into represented an attempt to build up the strength of royal forces in a new way, one which imitated the methods by which the magnates themselves recruited their own followers. The terms were much more generous than those used to retain household knights and bannerets.[38]

It was not until 1337 that an entire army was engaged on a contract basis. This was again for an expedition to Scotland at a time when the king was occupied by events in Flanders. The experiment was not wholly successful. The smaller contingents, in particular, failed to achieve their intended numbers, and desertion thinned the ranks. The military operations themselves could not be counted a triumph.[39] Contracts, however, were proving their value as a recruitment method. Indentures continued to be used for garrison service; in April 1340 John Mowbray agreed to take charge of Berwick for a year starting in May, with a total force of 120 men-at-arms, 100 hobelars and 200 archers. He himself was to provide sixty men-at-arms, twenty hobelars and sixty archers. The king would recruit the rest, and the watchmen needed to ensure the Scots did not approach. Edward also promised to provide two warships and a barge, and most importantly assured Mowbray that if a siege began, he would come to relieve it within a quarter of a year.[40] When the king himself commanded an expedition, it was rare for contracts to be used. During Edward's ineffective campaigns in the Low Countries in the late 1330s, it appears that only Henry Burghersh, bishop of Lincoln, and Geoffrey le Scrope served under the terms of contracts, rather than simply being paid wages in the traditional fashion.[41] Contracts were normally used for service away from the king's side, in circumstances where the administrative resources of the royal household would not be available. An exceptional plan was drawn up in 1341 for a contract army to be led by the king, but this was designed to accommodate an unusual method of payment. Rather than receiving normal wages, the magnates were to receive assignments of wool to cover the costs of their wages for forty days. In the end, the expedition did not take place.[42]

The contracts made by the Crown under Edward III rarely promised lump sums in return for service with specified numbers of men. Instead, wages were to be paid at the normal rates, usually paid quarterly with the first instalment handed over in advance. In the case of one agreement made in 1342 with Thomas Berkeley for service on the Scottish March, a bonus of £100 was promised because he had undertaken to serve although 'he is sick in body and has few riches'.[43] This perhaps presaged the important introduction of the regard. This term appeared in the mid 1340s; John Charnels, one of the warlike clerics who served Edward III, received a regard in 1345. Another early example is provided by the indenture made by the earl of Northampton, the earl of Oxford and John Darcy with Thomas Dagworth in the same year, in which Dagworth was promised a regard, as advised by Northampton and others.[44] Fees might still be used in this period as well as regards. In April 1347 Edward contracted with Thomas Ughtred to provide service for a year. Ughtred was to provide twenty men-at-arms, of whom six, himself included, were to be knights. In addition, his contingent would include twenty mounted archers. The fee for the year was £200, half to be paid at Easter. Wages were payable once Ughtred and his men reached the coast, ready to cross to France. Instalments would be quarterly, the first in advance. Ughtred would receive livery of foodstuffs and other items on the same basis as the king's other bannerets. The king promised to provide Ughtred with a horse appropriate to his status, and he was promised compensation for any horses lost on campaign. The king also agreed to provide shipping for both outward and return journeys to France.[45]

Contracts were not normally entered into for Edward III's own major expeditions to France, for they could be easily administered directly by the officials of the royal household, just as had been the case under Edward I. Thus contracts were not needed for the great 1346–7 army, or for that of 1359, though there were no doubt informal understandings between the king and his main captains. For other expeditions, in which the king was not involved, contracts recorded in indentures were used. The formulas used for these indentures became increasingly standardised. The rate of wages would be specified, as was the regard, or bonus paid quarterly. The normal level for this was 100 marks for thirty men-at-arms each quarter. Most commonly by Edward III's later years indentures specified normal wages, and a double regard, though double wages was not unknown. Payment would be quarterly in advance. An exceptional indenture was that made with Robert Knollys in 1370, when he agreed to fight for two years in France, with 4,000 men of whom 2,000 were to be men-at-arms. These would be paid double wages, and a regard and a half for the first quarter. All who went with Knollys were to receive general writs of protection, and the ports

(*Above*) King Edward III in old age, as shown in the initial letter of a charter, with (*right*) a portrait of his son, John of Gaunt, duke of Lancaster (1362–99).

along the south coast from Rye to Mousehole were to be open to any
who wanted to join the expedition. Provisions were included about
land which might be taken from the French.[46] Indentured service had
become the norm, and there is some surprise indicated in a note in
the record of service in Wales under the future Henry V in 1403, to
the effect that the earl of Worcester had no contract, that he was *sine
indentura*.[47]

Just as the Crown made indentures with the captains employed in
war, so the captains made indentures with those who served under
them. A great many contracts have survived, notably those made by
John of Gaunt, duke of Lancaster, whose retinue has been ably
studied by Simon Walker. The duke offered his men the same
financial terms as did the Crown, and in addition substantial fees.
Two-thirds of the profits of war, such as plunder and ransoms, could
be kept by the retainer.[48] A contract made by the earl of Salisbury
with Roger Maltravers in 1371 is typical. Roger agreed to serve the
earl for a year, with two archers in his company. He was to provide
his own horses, and be properly equipped for war. The earl agreed to
pay the cost of shipping for overseas service; interestingly, it is clear
that Maltravers' total company included three servants as well as the
two archers, and that they required seven horses in all. Pay and a
regard were promised, along with a fee of £20 for Maltravers and the
two archers. One-third of any booty was to go to the earl.[49] It begins
to be possible to see a pyramidal structure of sub-contracts underlying agreements. John Strother, a Northumberland knight, made
seven sub-contracts in 1374, and Sir Hugh Hastings, preparing for
war in 1380, made twenty-four sub-contracts. It is clear that there
was a real market in operation, for many of the sub-contractors were
prepared to accept lower rates of pay than those being offered to the
contractor himself by the Crown. There could well have been some
uncomfortable moments around the camp-fire as Hastings' men discovered that they were not all being offered equal rewards, while the
level of Strother's profits may well have aroused jealousy.[50]

In the early days of contract service it is unlikely that very much
was done to ensure that the contractors properly fulfilled the terms of
their agreements. There was obviously much scope for abuse, however, and therefore regular musters were instituted. Initially, musters
were primarily required for garrison troops, as in 1345 when Henry
of Lancaster made an indenture with two Gascon magnates, appointing them captains of Bergerac with a substantial force, which was to
be mustered every eight days.[51] Such frequent musters deprived the
contract system of its original simplicity, but were an obvious measure to prevent abuses. In 1372 the earl of Salisbury's troops were
mustered at the start of the expedition, and when he came to make
his final account deductions of £21 14s 6d from wages, and of £13

6s 8d from the regard were taken because the muster rolls revealed that there had been absentees.[52] The system was certainly not perfect, as was shown when John Neville was charged in the Good Parliament of 1376 with taking fewer troops, of poorer quality, than had been agreed with the Crown. Musters became more common, no doubt to check further corruption. A list of the retinues of two squires, John Sandes and Richard Craddock, serving in Gascony under Neville in 1379–80, shows that great care was taken to avoid a repeat of the charges against the latter; dots were placed against the men's names to record their attendance.[53] In 1387 the victualling officer appointed to Brest was required to take musters as often as needed. He was to send lists to the exchequer both of those present, and of those who had deserted.[54] In the fifteenth century musters were made regularly, as an essential check on recruitment, and on desertion. In 1442, according to the indentures he made with thirty-five captains, John Talbot's army in France should have been 2,500 strong but in practice it numbered 2,228.[55]

Restoration of horses

Restoration of horses, or *restor*, was an important element in the contracts for military service. One indenture, made by Edward III in 1346 with three men from the Low Countries, promised them this right, stating that it was 'according to the English custom'.[56] It is not clear when this custom, which was not in fact exclusively English, began. The treaty made by Henry I with the count of Flanders in 1101 promised that the Flemish knights serving in England would have compensation for losses as was customary in Henry's household. Horses were not specified, but may have been intended.[57] The Pipe Roll for 1193 reveals that three marks was paid to Hugh de Vilers for horses lost at Swansea, and the account for the Tower of London has a payment of £2 3s 4d for loss of a charger and two rounceys.[58] The records of John's reign reveal many instances of the king buying horses for his mercenary soldiers, which may in some instances be cases of *restor* being provided. Two agreements made by Philip Basset, probably in about 1270, provide that he would replace lost horses, and it was normal practice under Edward I for such payments to be made.[59] Conventionally, each man could have only one horse valued, although in 1357 an indenture with the earl of Salisbury allowed him *restor* of his own mount, and of what is described as his horse of arms.[60] Should a horse die, its owner would then present its ears and tail to the royal clerks as evidence for his claim for compensation. This somewhat grisly procedure was an obvious protection against fraud. It was not, however, only for death that compensation was given. Some horses are noted down in the rolls as being 'handed over to the caravan' (*redditus ad karvannum*). These were animals which were no longer capable of active campaigning, but which were handed over to become part of the pool of horses available for other duties. One in 1336 was noted as being returned to the caravan, and then handed over to John Polayn, royal carter, to serve as a carthorse.[61] Yet others were noted in the rolls as being 'handed over to alms' (*redditus ad elemosinam*), a mysterious phrase which eludes explanation, but clearly shows that the horse concerned was no longer fit for active service.[62]

The process of valuing the horses, and repaying their owners, was highly bureaucratic. Impatient men must have had to wait in long lines for their animals to be inspected. Lengthy rolls were compiled, containing details of the colour and distinguishing marks of the horses, and of their value. Payment for losses had to be carefully accounted. It was tempting to simplify the process, and in 1362 John Chandos submitted a claim to the exchequer for compensation for the deaths of a hundred horses at an average value of ten marks each when he commanded a force going to Gascony. This crude estimate appears to have been accepted; perhaps the exchequer considered that the large round number for losses was compensated by the very low valuation put on the animals.[63] It was simpler still to give up the system, and Edward III had indeed negotiated its abandonment in some of the Scottish campaigns in the early years of his reign. Early in 1342 Henry Percy received a grant of £500, in compensation for military costs, and because he had agreed not to make claims for *restor*, when fighting in Scotland.[64] In the wars in France, however, *restor* was provided until the Treaty of Brétigny in 1360. With the renewal of the war in 1369 the *restor* element in indentures was for the most part dropped. It was highly exceptional for John of Gaunt to include it in an indenture with Thomas de Wennesley in 1384. Some indentures were drawn up which expressly excluded it; the financial terms were made more generous instead, with a double regard, or bonus. In 1372 the earl of Salisbury explicitly promised not to demand *restor*. It is unlikely that it was the cost of *restor* that prompted its abandonment; it is more probable that a desire to streamline cumbersome administrative arrangements lay behind the change.[65]

Voluntary service

Pay was not always acceptable, particularly to great men who resented subordination to a paymaster. The evidence from Edward I's reign shows that the majority of the cavalry forces were not paid by the Crown. Various lists were drawn up in the later years of the reign of the great men present on campaign. In 1298 this was done for the production of a heraldic roll; in 1300 the author of the *Song of Caerlaverock*, itself a heraldic poem, names all the bannerets he could remember being present in the army. There are also lists of those present in the army in 1304. These lists of names can be compared with the very full pay records that survive, and demonstrate that many men did not accept the king's penny. In 1298 sixty-two out of 110 bannerets were not paid; in 1300 sixty-four out of eighty-seven. As for 1304, out of 140 men named, at least a hundred do not appear on the pay records. This evidence is quite clear. Under Edward I the earls were plainly very reluctant to accept pay for normal summer campaigns in the British Isles; winter expeditions and war in Gascony were a different matter. In 1282 the king's initial plans for a fully paid expedition to Wales were revised at a very late stage, almost certainly because the earls objected to the subordination and loss of status that would be involved in their accepting wages. If a traditional feudal summons were issued, then they would have better expectations of receiving a proper distribution of lands should the campaign prove successful. It is not, however, the case that those who served, but not for pay, were all performing feudal service. As already shown, this service yielded relatively few troops. The bulk of the cavalry came in response to an additional request to provide as many troops as was appropriate. In the cases of the Falkirk campaign of 1298 and the 1301 campaign, there was no feudal summons issued, yet the majority of the cavalry served without accepting royal pay.[66]

Voluntary service continued to be performed under Edward II. There is no record of Piers Gaveston, earl of Cornwall, receiving royal wages, though he obtained much else from the king. If the royal favourite was not paid, neither was the king's chief political opponent, Thomas of Lancaster. The earl of Gloucester, who died at Bannockburn, was another magnate whose position did not require him to take pay from the king. Most of the earls, however, had fewer scruples. Arundel, Norfolk, Hereford, Kent, Pembroke, Richmond, Warenne and Winchester all accepted pay at some time during the reign. No magnates of significance attended the 1322 campaign in Scotland at their own expense.[67] Doubtless economic realities had their part to play in this change of attitude by the earls, while the fact that few had their hearts in the Scottish war since there was little chance of profiting from conquests must also have influenced attitudes. Under Edward III there was no longer any question of unpaid service on a large scale; wages were offered and willingly accepted. Jean le Bel exaggerated when he noted that in 1339 there were many lords, barons and knights who 'so loved the king that they wanted to

William Marshal, earl of Pembroke (1199–1219), from the effigy on his tomb in the Temple Church, London.

serve him at their own expense, and would not take wages or liveries at court'.[68]

Evidence for what is best termed voluntary service is difficult to find for periods prior to the reign of Edward I. It has been suggested that in the difficult days of the minority of Henry III, many important men 'carried out essential administrative and military duties on their own initiative, and presumably at their own expense', but they were able to set many of their expenses against receipts such as those from sheriffdoms. William Marshal's accounts for this period show that the costs of knights, sergeants and footsoldiers were met by the Crown, rather than paid out of his own pocket. There is no evidence, however, that he took wages for himself. The Marshal also took pay in 1193 for a considerable number of troops under his command, though again there is no evidence that he received daily wages himself. One earl, Salisbury, took an annual fee from King John, though whether he also accepted wages must be doubtful.[69] It seems likely that voluntary service emerged on a substantial scale as traditional feudal service was cut back radically in the early thirteenth century. Prior to that time there were no doubt occasions when magnates agreed to remain on campaign after the end of the forty-day period for which they were formally bound to serve. Conditions of civil war, too, might prompt men to serve at their own expense. Once feudal quotas were established at the new low levels of the thirteenth century, it was inevitable that great men would bring more substantial contingents with them than the formal *servitia debita*, if only for reasons of prestige.

Rewards and ransoms

Men could expect notable service, whether paid or unpaid, to attract additional rewards. When advising the young Edward III as to how he should conduct himself as king, Walter de Milemete stressed in his treatise the need to reward with conquered possessions those who served him in war.[70] Such grants of lands were important, conveying not merely wealth but also, in some cases, status. The acquisition of lands in Brittany enabled Robert Knollys, a man of lowly origins, to call himself '*Seignour de Derval et de Rouge*'.[71] The chronicler Pierre Langtoft was very clear about this; Edward I would have had no difficulty in conquering Wales had he been prepared to grant out the land to his followers, to hold by knight service.[72] In 1298 it was a dispute over the grants of land made by Edward I in Scotland that led to the departure of the earls of Norfolk and Hereford from the campaign. Subsequently, Edward attempted to ensure the loyalty of his troops by making grants of lands prior to their conquest.[73] Even under so relatively an ungenerous master as Edward I, there were major territorial gains made by English lords in Wales in the aftermath of conquest. The great lordship of Denbigh went to the king's close associate, the earl of Lincoln. The lordship of Bromfield and Yale was Earl Warenne's prize. Chirk went to the younger Roger Mortimer, and Dyffryn Clwyd to Reginald de Grey. Knightly families dependent on these great lords, such as those of Crevequer and Breous, moved into these lordships as the Welsh landholders were moved out; there were also English settlers of lower status, peasants and artisans.[74] In Scotland war did not yield so substantial a territorial dividend. Edward I made significant grants of Scottish estates to men such as the earl of Lincoln and Aymer de Valence, but the unsuccessful course of the war meant that there was little profit in them. The prospect of the original Scottish owners changing sides created further difficulties.[75]

Military indentures did not normally include promises about grants of conquered lands until the 1370s. Then John of Gaunt was promised all captured lands which were not held in royal demesne, or by the Church. Robert Knollys was to hold lands in Normandy which had been part of the demesne in Angevin days, until the war was concluded, in which case they would revert to the Crown. In 1372 a series of documents included promises that castles, towns, lordships and lands taken from the French might be held in accordance with statute.[76] Indentures were, of course, the product of bargaining between the Crown and the military contractor; it is interesting that in a period when the war was going badly for the English, hopes were still high of acquiring territory.

In the Hundred Years War, it was only Henry V's conquest of Normandy that gave an English king estates to distribute to his followers on a substantial scale. Henry's policy was carefully considered, taking into account strategic military considerations and social status. The military commanders were the first to be rewarded, with strategically important estates; in 1418 the earl of Huntingdon received the lordship of Bricqueville-sur-Mer, the earl of Exeter the county of Harcourt, and John Cheyne the barony of La-Haye-du-Puits. After the capture of Rouen in 1419 the process of distributing land proceeded apace. It was not just the great men who received grants; relatively humble men-at-arms profited from the conquest and obtained lands in Normandy. In all, 358 grants are known to have been made, most in response to petitions. Henry was not simply operating a policy of rewarding those who had fought well; he was considering the best way of securing the future for the duchy in English hands.[77]

If a man performed some particularly notable deed in war, he could expect an appropriate reward. After the battle of Poitiers the Black Prince made a number of grants to men who had distinguished themselves. James Audley headed the list, with a promise of £400 a year for life. Among the others, a yeoman, Nicholas Bonde, was to have fifty marks a year; interestingly, the scale of reward did not reflect social status, for two knights received lesser promises of forty marks and £20 a year respectively.[78] John de Coupland, who captured David of Scotland at Neville's Cross in 1346, was made a banneret and was granted £500 a year, initially out of customs revenue. He was promised that he would receive land when it became available, as it did within a couple of years, when Coupland received estates in Lancashire which had belonged to William de Coucy.[79]

The hope of acquiring booty and ransoms must have been a strong incentive to go to war. The author of the *Gesta Stephani* was in no doubt that the activities of warlike magnates in the 1140s could yield rich dividends. Miles of Gloucester achieved many triumphs, 'to say nothing of the immense plunder, beyond computation, that he collected from every quarter, nothing of the terrible burnings of villages and towns, which he reduced to deserts, nothing of the great numbers of men, of different positions and callings, whom he put to the sword or bound with thongs for ransom'.[80] It was very important to John's mercenary captains in Normandy that they should be able to take their plunder where they wished, and they duly obtained appropriate royal writs safeguarding their gains. The record of the legal cases heard during the 1296 campaign in Scotland shows how men banded together to share the profits of plunder, and how they might use such profits, for example to buy cattle. So determined was one group of men to find plunder that they quenched a fire in a malt-kiln, and dug under it looking for treasure.[81] The importance of plunder in motivating men to fight was demonstrated when, prior to the

1333–4 campaign in Scotland, Edward III and his ally Edward Balliol in a blatant recruiting ploy announced that all who wished to set out against the Scots could keep everything that they seized by way of goods and chattels.[82]

A grant by King John to Ralph Archer, permitting him to profit as he wished from the king's enemies, saving the rights of the king himself and his knights, shows that there were recognised principles, established by long convention, as to how plunder should be divided out.[83] The curious rights of the marshal and constable to parti-coloured and hornless cattle, to pigs and unshod horses, though known only from fourteenth-century sources, clearly go back to a distant past.[84] In the businesslike world of the later fourteenth century it was important to set out the rights that men had to booty with some precision in the contracts they made. The normal principle then was that one-third of the profits of war should be paid to the lord. This can be traced back to the practices of the Welsh march in the thirteenth century and earlier.[85] However, in Edward III's French war up to 1360, it seems that half the profits were commonly claimed by the lord. Most indentures did not specify what proportion was to be handed over in this way, but in 1347 the earl of Salisbury made an elaborate life indenture with Geoffrey Walsh, which specified that ransoms and other gains in war were to be equally divided, and in the same year Ralph Stafford retained Hugh FitzSymond on similar conditions. The Black Prince's normal practice was to demand half of all booty.[86] Andrew Ayton has suggested that the differing pro-portion may be explained in terms of *restor*: where payment was made to compensate for lost horses, the high proportion of a half was demanded; when *restor* was abandoned, as it was by the 1370s, the less stringent request was made for one-third. This principle was clearly set out in an indenture between John of Gaunt and Nicholas de Atherton in 1370.[87] The argument is persuasive; it is unfortunate that there are not more indentures specifying the proportion dating from the 1340s and 1350s which might finally prove the point. It must, however, be doubted whether in practice such conditions could be enforced; it would have been a remarkably honest soldier who declared all his gains. Details of booty taken in war are rare, but a note of goods taken from Robert Knollys in 1354 reflects the profit-ability of campaigning in France. A silver basin and a ewer, with a combined weight of over seven pounds, four silver chargers, eighteen silver saucers, and other pieces of plate headed the list, which con-cluded with less costly items, such as two goatskins and two new pairs of boots.[88]

In 1373 royal indentures specified that after the first six months of service, profits from ransoms would be set against wages. In the following year it was hoped that ransoms would be forthcoming in

An imaginative reconstruction from a fifteenth-century manuscript of Froissart's *Chronicles* of the battle of Neville's Cross, 1346, in which David II of Scotland was captured.

sufficient quantity to pay for the military operations after the first half year.[89] Ransoms were certainly highly profitable in the right sort of war. There was nothing to be gained in ransoms from the Welsh, while as far as the Scots were concerned, it was only the capture of King David in 1346 that led to payment of truly substantial sums to the English. When Thomas de Lucy sold two important captives, Dougal MacDowell and his son, to Edward III, he was promised 700 marks a year as payment – a very low price in comparison to the great ransoms of the French war. When Thomas Holland captured the Count of Eu in 1346, he handed his prisoner over to the king, receiving in exchange a grant of 80,000 florins, or about £12,000, payable out of the customs duties on wool.[90] Although high ransoms were not wholly new with the Hundred Years War, there certainly was an inflation in the fourteenth century. Under John the capture of Conan, son of the vicomte of Léon, had brought Gerard de Furnival a profit of 4,000 *li. angevin*, or about £1,000 sterling.[91] John de St John, captured by the French in Gascony in 1297, had his ransom set at 20,000 *li. tournois*. Fluctuating exchange rates make it hard to give a sterling equivalent, but £5,000 was the contemporary estimate.[92] One of the first men to be captured in the Hundred Years War was Guy of Flanders, illegitimate brother of the count of Flanders. He was taken by Walter Mauny when he raided the island of Cadzand in 1337, and was handed over to Edward III in return for £8,000.[93] The ransom of Charles of Blois, captured in 1347, stood at 700,000 écus. Of this, however, only 100,000 écus, almost £17,000, was paid. Charles's sons remained in England as hostages; one of them was eventually ransomed in 1387 for 120,000 gold francs, about £16,500.[94] The capture of kings, of course, brought massive ransoms. Richard I, captured by the duke of Austria on his return from crusade, and then handed over to the emperor Henry VI, was charged a ransom of 150,000 marks, though not all of it was paid. King David of Scotland, taken at Neville's Cross, was worth 100,000 marks, payable over ten years, to the English. As for King John of France, his ransom was a staggering 3,000,000 écus, or £500,000, although again not all of it was handed over.[95] The man who was actually responsible for John's capture, a renegade Frenchman, Denis de Morbeke, gained little reward. There was dispute between himself and a Gascon, Bernard de Troie, but when a legal committee went to see Morbeke in London in 1360 they found him in a pitiful state, very ill in bed, his limbs withered, dried up and so weak that recovery seemed quite of the question.[96]

The business of obtaining and trading in ransoms was far from straightforward. There might be confusion over who actually captured a prisoner. At Poitiers the count of Dammartin initially surrendered to a squire, John Trailly, who removed his bacinet and

Scenes depicting the capture of Richard I (*above*),
and asking for forgiveness from the Emperor Henry VI
(*below*), drawn by the South Italian scholar Peter of Eboli.

Illustris rex anglie a ierosolimis rediens capt psentat augusto.

Rex anglie d morte machiois accensat quod abnegas se ensina manu excusaturu pmittit.

tande ueniam petes ut absoluat

gauntlet, and took his sword. Then a Gascon approached threaten-ingly; the count gave him a escutcheon bearing his coat of arms as a symbol of capture. A third would-be captor in turn obtained the count's fealty. Wisely, this man stayed with the count, and handed him over to the earl of Salisbury. It was no easy task to decide whose prisoner in reality he was, and so who should receive the ransom. Substantial legal costs were involved. Not surprisingly, given his rank, it was the earl whose claim was upheld, and who paid the Black Prince £1,000 as his share.[97]

Payment of the large sums involved was not easy to organise. John Chandos complained to the French king in 1366 that he had received only 12,500 francs of the 20,000 that he was owed for the ransom of Bertrand du Guesclin.[98] Cases might be very complex. In 1359 Jean de Melun, a French knight, had been captured by an English squire, Henry Poinfroit. A ransom of 1,500 *moutons d'or* was agreed, and partly paid. Poinfroit resorted to the French courts during the years of truce that followed the treaty of Brétigny. The decision went in favour of Melun; his English captor was ordered to repay the ransom money, with damages, and to make amends in all the places where Melun's arms had been displayed reversed. The unfortunate Poinfroit was imprisoned in the Chatelet, where he became in course of time the most senior prisoner; in 1380 the court ordered Melun to pay him six *deniers* a day maintenance.[99] The most celebrated case is that of the count of Denia, taken at Nájera in 1367. Arguments about the huge ransom led to the imprisonment of the two squires who had taken the count, Robert Hawley and John Shakell, in the Tower. They escaped in 1378, but were pursued by the Constable of the Tower. Hawley was murdered in Westminster Abbey, which was a major scandal. Complex litigation between Hawley and Shakell, and others, over the ransom continued for over a century.[100]

While the hope of obtaining ransoms must have been a powerful incentive to many, there must also have been the fears of financial catastrophe resulting from capture. In 1204 one of King John's knights was granted ten marks to assist in the payment of his ransom, a small figure compared with later levels.[101] In about 1320 Ralph Neville petitioned Edward II. His brother Robert had been killed by the Scots, and he with another two brothers had been captured. He had a ransom of 2,000 marks to pay to gain his freedom.[102] Thomas Felton was taken prisoner in Gascony, and wrote to Richard II in 1379, explaining that he had undertaken to pay 30,000 francs on strict terms. If he did not pay in time, he would lose money he had already raised in loans and sale of land. He promised to make over all his lands in Norfolk to the king in return for £6,000 which he desperately needed.[103] Robert, Lord Hungerford and Moleyns, was taken at Castillon in 1453. The ransom totalled almost £8,000, and the family had to sell and mortgage property on a massive scale to meet the bill. On the other hand, such financial demands were preferable to Robert's end; he was taken prisoner at Hexham by Yorkist forces in 1464, and promptly executed.[104] It was only in exceptional cases that the Crown itself came to the rescue, assisting with ransom payments. Edward I made every effort in 1298 to secure the release of John de St John, while Edward II was also prepared to help those taken prisoner during the Scottish wars. Humphrey de Bohun, earl of Hereford, was granted 1,000 marks to assist him after he was captured at Bannockburn, and John de Segrave £1,000. Henry de Sully, taken by the Scots at Byland in Yorkshire in 1322, was given 1,000 marks.[105] Later in the fourteenth century the Crown contributed £3,000 towards the ransom of Henry Percy, taken in the night battle at Otterburn. John Talbot, captured at Patay in 1429, could not afford his 'unreasonable and importable raunceon'.

The battle of Nájera in 1367, showing the Black Prince with Pedro of Castile.

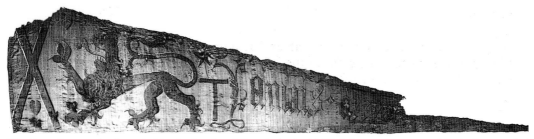

The Douglas standard carried in the battle of Otterburn in 1387. It bears the cross of St Andrew and the lion of Scotland. The motto 'Jamais areyre' refers to the Douglas's claim to lead the Scots into battle.

The Crown granted him £9,000 out of taxation to be levied in Normandy, and contributions from the public provided further help.[106] Lesser men could not hope for such assistance, and even quite small ransoms could prove disastrous. Luke de Wharton, captured some time between 1317 and 1327, was charged no more than forty-four marks as a ransom, but to pay it he had to mortgage his lands to the keeper of Berwick castle, and he never recovered them.[107]

In addition to ransoms paid for the release of individual noble prisoners-of-war, it was possible to impose ransoms or *appatis*, virtually protection money, on whole districts. At Bécherel, Vannes and Ploërmel in Brittany in 1359–60 over £10,000 was collected in this way, in return for the English forces agreeing not to plunder or burn. Three-quarters of the income at Vannes came from ransoms. There was some system to the practice, with attempts to match demands to capacity to pay, reductions for areas where troops had been billeted, and reduced rates for friendly areas. A decade later William Latimer was said to have collected 145,000 francs in the Bécherel region.[108] How much of these sums provided for the personal profit of the English soldiery is not apparent. The records of those that were properly accounted for suggest that the receipts were largely used to maintain castles held by the English in France. There must have been much illicit ransoming as well, which never went through the official books.

The French were often prepared to buy their way into English-held castles. In 1358 the castle of Poix, close to the Norman border, was captured by some English soldiers serving the king of Navarre. In the next year the French agreed to purchase it back for 15,000 *moutons d'or*. The local inhabitants agreed to contribute, on condition that the castle was destroyed; the lord of Poix, to avoid this, agreed to pay 6,000 *moutons* himself, of which 1,000 were promptly handed over.[109] There might thus, disgracefully, be profits in defeat. The trials at the Good Parliament in 1376 produced serious accusations about the way in which Bécherel and St Sauveur had been lost.

Thomas Catterton, commanding at St Sauveur, agreed to accept 40,000 francs for the surrender of the fortress, with 12,000 francs in addition for himself, and 3,000 francs for two of his companions.[110]

Protections

It was important that those who fought should not suffer losses at home as a result of their absence on campaign. In 1299 a royal memorandum noted that

> To preserve from harm the earls, barons, knights and all others who come in person to our army with us . . . by the counsel and assent of the bishops, prelates, earls and barons, and the other nobles of the land who were with us at Carlisle at the octave of St John the Baptist in the twenty-seventh year of our reign [29 August 1299] . . . we have ordained and provided that all the assizes of novel disseisin which are brought against those who have gone or are going to our present war in their own person in our army, should be respited until Easter next.[111]

It was normal practice to provide those going on military expeditions with letters of protection, so that they would not suffer harm through their absence from home. The 1220s provide the earliest evidence of writs of protection being issued in substantial numbers. These were simple protections, and excluded pleas of the Crown. For the Poitou campaign of 1230, writs issued in addition to the normal writs of protection provided safeguard against legal action. From 1242 it was possible to add an additional clause, *Volumus*, to the writ of protection to deal with lawsuits. Actions of novel disseisin, dower, *darrein presentment* and *quare impedit* were not normally covered, hence the special decision that was taken by the king in 1299. In 1346 Edward III explained that it was not his policy to provide protection for men who had recently made disseisins (seized lands), although older cases were to be stayed.[112] A special clause protecting the earl of Warwick's position was added to an indenture made in 1373; the king promised that no lands inherited or acquired by the earl in England while the latter was abroad would be escheated to the crown on the grounds that the earl had not performed homage or fealty.[113]

The policy of giving protection to those going on expeditions was a feature of crusading; the 1215 Fourth Lateran Council established a clear set of privileges to be accorded to those who took the cross. How far there was cross-fertilisation between these crusade privileges and those offered by the Crown for its own military campaigns is not clear, but it was clearly common currency from the early thirteenth century that some measure of protection should be made available. Interestingly, there is a link in the early thirteenth century between the provisions guarding men from legal actions brought against them while they were on campaign, and expeditions for which no formal feudal summons had been issued. This was probably in order to aid recruitment in years when there was no compulsion to serve. Whether men had to pay for these writs is not apparent, but by Edward I's reign at least it was normal practice for anyone leading a retinue to war to submit a list of names to the Chancery, so that the writs of protection could be duly made out.[114] Of course, in many cases royal letters of protection were of little use. John de Beauchamp complained in 1347 that a gang largely composed of parsons, chaplains and clerks had attacked his manors at Sibford in Oxfordshire and Tredington in Worcestershire, carried away his goods, and assaulted his servants while he was under the king's special protection. Richard Elton, not surprisingly, ignored the protection granted to Robert Henbury who raped his wife in 1379.[115] On the other hand, in the mid 1340s Robert Neville thought it necessary to write to ask for the protection granted to John Lowe of Canterbury to be released, so that Neville could take legal action against him for acting contrary to the agreement between them.[116]

Profits and losses

It is often hard to tell whether or not men really did benefit from war. The earl of Arundel, writing to the king in 1297, was sure that he did not. He argued that he had been impoverished by military service, and that he could not even find anyone to take on the manors which he had been compelled to try to lease out. Further campaigning was beyond his means. Brian FitzAlan's refusal to accept command in Scotland is telling evidence of one man's view of the likelihood of profiting from Edward I's war in the north.[117] Whether the rewards that the earl of Lincoln received from Edward in the form of lands in Wales and Scotland and other favours outweighed his expenditure on war is impossible to tell. In the case of the Scottish wars it is clear that some men were seriously impoverished. Robert de Reymes made the serious mistake of acquiring estates in Northumberland in the very year, 1296, that the Scottish wars began. Invasion threats meant that he had to extend and fortify his manor house at Aydon. Capture at Bannockburn and consequent payment of a ransom combined with rapidly falling rents to put Reymes in an increasingly difficult position. Even so, the family survived, and did not abandon their Northumberland lands.[118]

The fullest evidence is that for the fifteenth century. The most detailed case to have been studied is that of John Fastolf. K.B. McFarlane showed that Fastolf had a sophisticated financial machinery available to him so that he could send back to England the profits he made in Normandy in the 1420s and 1430s, to be invested with merchants. He was able to build up a very substantial estate; his inheritance had been worth no more than £46 a year, but he purchased manors worth £775 a year from the profits of war. He built a fine castle, out of the most up-to-date material, brick, at Caister, and spent lavishly on jewellery, plate and even books. Fastolf's success is the more striking in view of the fact that he was active in a period when the war was not going well for the English.[119] Fastolf's greater contemporary, John Talbot, earl of Shrewsbury, was probably less fortunate, above all in being captured at Patay and having to meet a part of his ransom costs. He also had to pay the ransoms for two of his sons, captured in other engagements. Talbot, however, made the best of the opportunities that an increasingly unsuccessful war offered, acquiring much booty in Le Mans and Laval in 1428, and gaining 'great riches and fatte prisoners' in a campaign in 1434. Lands in Normandy provided a useful income, and his position as marshal of France brought profits. Talbot built no great castles, but his family were left comfortably off after his death in 1453. A detailed balance sheet cannot be calculated, but his biographer estimates that Talbot probably made a small profit out of the war.[120] Even moderate financial success was far from guaranteed. William Peyto's military career in France began in the early 1420s. He was an important commander of the second rank, on one occasion leading a force of fifty men-at-arms and 508 archers. He suffered capture and ransom at the hands of the French in 1443. Although the ransom was only £500, Peyto had to mortgage his estates. He suffered, as did so many, from non-payment of wages by the Crown. He was given exchequer tallies to a value of £266 13s 4d, but was unable to exchange them for cash. He was eventually able to recover two of his mortgaged manors, but the third was still in the hands of creditors when he died in 1464. Clearly, this was a man whose hopes of profiting from the war had been dashed.[121]

The way in which men were rewarded for military service has been seen by historians as one of the most important keys to understanding the changing nature of society. The concept of a transformation from a feudal structure, in which men provided service in respect of the land they held from the king or from a lord, to a more commercial society in which service was essentially paid, has dominated a wide range of historical writing. It is here that many have implied that the true military revolution of the middle ages may lie. Yet it is

difficult to see *when* the transformation occurrred. Historians, not surprisingly, all identify it in their own specific period. For J.C. Holt, the early thirteenth century saw John compelled to make use of cash rewards, to obtain the service of his liege-men. J.E. Morris saw the significant change taking place under Edward I, with the use of pay as the key; while H.J. Hewitt considered that it was at the time of the Hundred Years War that 'obligatory service was superseded by voluntary contract'.[122]

The reality was not a simple one of a replacement of service based on land tenure by pay, and there was no one transformation, no single revolution in the way in which men were rewarded for their military duties. In 1120 Henry I decided to pay generous wages to his knights who had fought well for him in Normandy, and to grant some of them extensive honours in England.[123] These methods of reward would not alter throughout the medieval period. In other ways, however, there was change. There was a first phase of knight service, which came to an end in the late twelfth and early thirteenth centuries when the quotas were radically reduced, and a second phase which lasted in England until the early fourteenth century. The development of contract service in the fourteenth century was a highly significant change, accompanied as it was by the virtual abandonment of formal systems of obligation. But beside all the evidence of the use of pay, and of systems of obligation, it is necessary to set the other reasons why men fought. There was the hope of gaining wealth through war, from booty and hostage-taking. Men undoubtedly had good reason to expect that they might do well out of war. The range of rewards available to the successful soldier was wide. Anyone in the later fourteenth century contemplating the great new front built at Warwick castle, or the new castles of the period, such as those built by Edward Dalyngrigge at Bodiam, John de la Mare at Nunney and John Lovel at Wardour, must have been impressed by the profits to be made from war. Yet the calculations men made would not have been dominated by thoughts of profitable balance sheets. The status indicated by those castles was more important than the material wealth of their owners. Someone listening to the often tedious depositions in the famous late-fourteenth-century chivalry case between the Scrope and Grosvenor families as to which had the right to bear *azure, a bend or*, could not but have been impressed by the prestige attached to military fame. Important as wages and the various potential profits of fighting were, war was not simply a matter of profit and loss accounts; the intangible factors that made up what is thought of as chivalry form another set of motives which need analysis.

The interior of the late fourteenth-century barbican at Warwick Castle.

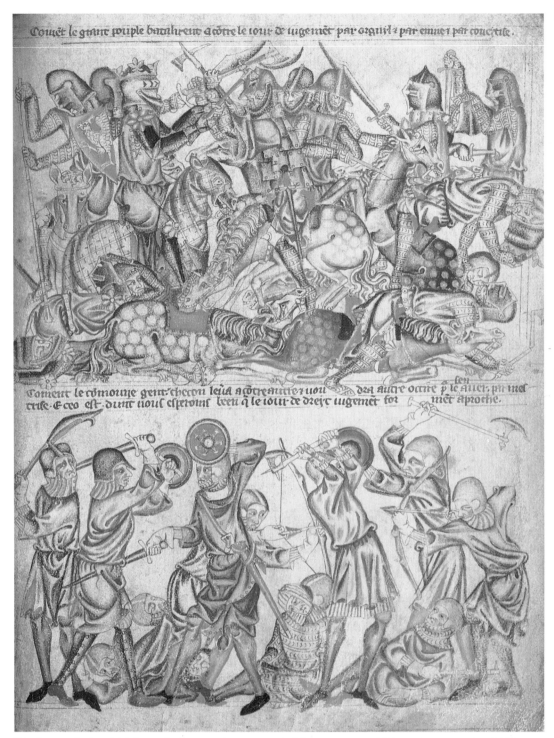

Warfare as depicted in the early fourteenth-century Holkham Picture Bible Book. The upper classes fight on horseback in the top panel; below them, the less well-equipped common people struggle on foot.

5

Infantry

The splendid early fourteenth-century Holkham Picture Bible Book contains two pictures of warfare. The upper drawing shows armoured knights (*le grand peuple*) fighting from horseback with sword, lance and war-hammer. The lower depicts the common people (*le commoune gent*), at most protected by helmets and leg-armour, and small round bucklers, fighting with bow and arrow, sword, falchion and axe.[1] Honour and glory in war may have gone to the knights; but the role of the common soldier was frequently vital. The English learned to their cost how effective footsoldiers might be at Stirling Bridge in 1297 and at Bannockburn in 1314. In the same period the French learned a similar lesson at Courtrai in 1302, and the Austrians at Morgarten in 1315. It was, however, the English longbowmen in the great battles of the Hundred Years War who provided the most stunning demonstrations of the potential of the ordinary soldier, when equipped with an extraordinary weapon: the longbow.

Numbers

Infantry were important in the warfare of the Norman period, but there is no reliable evidence to indicate the scale of recruitment. Chroniclers cannot be relied upon, for they would not themselves have had good information about numbers. It is nonetheless interesting that in his description of the battle of Bourgthéroulde, Orderic Vitalis noted that it was forty bowmen in the front rank of the English army who succeeded in bringing down many of the enemy horses as they charged. He later referred to 3,000 archers in Normandy.[2] Gerald of Wales in his accounts of warfare in Ireland in Henry II's reign provides some plausible figures detailing the numbers of archers involved. Some are specified as being *arcarii*. These men were almost certainly mounted archers, for they are distinguished from others clearly designated as foot archers, *sagitarii pedestrii*. A typical example is that of reinforcements brought from

Wales by Raymond le Gros. A fleet of fifteen ships brought thirty knights, a hundred mounted archers and 300 foot archers.[3] Record evidence from the reign of Richard I gives a good impression of the scale on which infantry forces were recruited. In 1193 Geoffrey FitzPeter retained 500 footsoldiers from the Welsh marches, and took them to the siege of Windsor. In addition, his infantry forces included sixty-seven slingers. William Marshal also had 500 foot in pay at Windsor, as well as 450 at Gloucester. Two years later the sheriff of Hampshire paid the cost of transporting 1,300 footsoldiers, along with fifty-five mounted sergeants, across the Channel to Normandy.[4] The Pipe Roll for 1196 records larger numbers: some 2,100 Welshmen were recruited and sent to Normandy. One knight was in charge of every 500 infantry; he was assisted by a number of mounted sergeants. The counties did not have to bear the cost of paying these troops for long. The sheriff of Herefordshire paid those for whom he was responsible for a mere four days, just long enough to get them to a muster point. The cost of transport across the sea to Normandy was borne by the sheriff of Hampshire, but the bulk of the men's wages was probably paid by the chamber, whose accounts do not survive.[5] It would be dangerous to see these figures as accurate totals of the infantry forces that could be deployed in this period; there are no accounts which clearly reveal the full scale of the numbers of men employed. They do, however, give an impression that the levels of recruitment were relatively modest in comparison with those of a century later. It is not until the later thirteenth century that pay rolls provide evidence which makes it possible to give a more accurate assessment of the overall numbers of infantry in English armies. Though footsoldiers undoubtedly had their part to play in the civil wars of the 1260s, the sources provide remarkably little information on their numbers and even their role in warfare.

Edward I's reign saw the recruitment of infantry on a scale not seen before, and which was not equalled for the rest of the medieval period. The accounts for the first Welsh war are hard to disentangle, but the king probably had some 15,500 footsoldiers in pay when the army was at its largest. About 9,000 of these were drawn from South Wales. For the war of 1282–3, calculations are again difficult, as levies were moved up week by week, and troops sent off to join different armies. In mid June there were 7,000 in pay. Early in August the number of footsoldiers on the headquarters payroll was only 3,360, but by the end of the month the figure was 8,180. These were Englishmen, drawn from the border counties, Derbyshire and Lancashire. In January 1283 a fresh recruitment drive brought 5,000 men to the royal army. Substantial numbers of Welshmen were employed, numbering perhaps 6,000. There was also a force of about

1,300 Gascon crossbowmen.[6] To deal with the rebellion of 1287, the regent (Edward I was in Gascony) assembled almost 11,000 infantry, of whom a third were Welsh. The largest number recruited for service in Wales was that of the 1294–5 rebellion, when in November there were probably over 31,000 serving in the various English armies, though that number was not maintained for long.[7]

Numbers of infantry for Edward I's later campaigns did not remain at this peak. In Flanders in 1297 the king had some 7,800 foot, of whom about a third were Welsh. Transporting troops overseas presented obvious problems; there was less difficulty in obtaining almost 26,000 men for the Falkirk campaign of 1298. That was the largest single concentration of troops seen in the reign. The maximum strength in 1300 was about 9,000; in 1303 it was about 7,500. The final campaigns against Robert Bruce probably saw fewer than 3,000 foot in royal pay.[8] The decline at the end of the reign was a reflection in part of the financial collapse that had taken place, and probably also of a realisation that to take a very large infantry army to Scotland created more problems than it resolved. Yet that was not the end of the notion of the large host. Figures are not so easy to compile for Edward II's reign, but the concept of recruiting very large infantry forces was not abandoned. The army which was defeated at Bannockburn was described by one contemporary as the most considerable which had ever left England. Over 20,000 men were requested, but actual numbers must have been lower. The best guess is that 15,000 were recruited.[9] The futile campaign of 1322 probably saw at least 12,000 in the normal county levies, and an additional 6,800 provided by a unique demand made on the towns. To these should be added 2,000 men in a separate force raised in Cumberland and Westmorland, making an overall total of some 20,000.[10]

These very large numbers were not maintained in the armies of the Hundred Years War. The change from very large, ill-equipped forces to much smaller, more skilled and better armed forces was very important. In 1339 the army contained about 1,500 mounted archers (who fought on foot) and about 1,650 footmen. In Brittany in 1342 there were 1,890 mounted archers and 1,150 foot. Unfortunately such records as there are for the army which landed in Normandy in 1346 and which achieved victory at Crécy do not enable an accurate calculation of numbers to be made. There were probably some 8,000 footsoldiers, and 3,000 or more mounted archers and hobelars (lightly armed cavalrymen). Many more troops joined the army for the siege of Calais in 1347, and one much later summary of accounts, now lost, suggests a total force of 32,000 men, though other versions put the figure at about 26,000. The figure represents not the total achieved at one single date, but the overall figure of those present at some time during the siege.[11] The infantry forces (including mounted archers) could perhaps be estimated at between 23,000 and 29,000. That was a wholly exceptional army. The great army which Edward III recruited in 1359, for what he hoped would be the final campaign which would win him the French crown, probably contained only about 6,600 mounted archers and infantry.

The English field armies at the end of Edward III's reign, after the reopening of the war in 1369, were small. It was common for the number of mounted archers to be the same as that of the men-at-arms; by this date foot archers and spearmen had vanished from the English inventory, though there were still some provided from Wales. In 1369 mounted archers and Welsh probably totalled some 3,000 men. In the next year Robert Knollys agreed to serve with a force of 2,000 men-at-arms and 2,000 mounted archers, though in practice he went with 1,500 of each. On his major, and ill-fated, *chevauchée* of 1373, John of Gaunt probably had approaching 3,000 mounted archers with him, of whom just over 2,000 were drawn from England. For this period, pay-rolls no longer provide reliable evidence of numbers, but analysis of the indentures made by the commanders with the Crown give a reasonable impression of the overall scale of military resources that were available.[12]

In the fifteenth century there was no further transformation of the scale of English armies. The indentures made with military captains show that there was a standard proportion of archers to men-at-arms expected; three-quarters of any force would normally have been bowmen. Henry V's invasion of 1415 was with a substantial force, numbering probably about 10,000, of whom 2,500 were men-at-arms and the remainder mounted and foot archers. Not all could fight at Agincourt, as sickness at Harfleur took a considerable toll. His force of 1417 again numbered some 10,000. These were as large as any English armies to go to France, with the exception of Edward III's huge host assembled for the siege of Calais, but they came nowhere near to matching the size of the expeditions to Scotland of the late thirteenth and early fourteenth centuries. Later fifteenth-century expeditions under magnate command were naturally smaller. In 1428 the earl of Salisbury contracted to provide 600 men-at-arms and 1,800 archers, all mounted; he had discretion to change the balance of the force, and substitute a further 600 archers for 200 men-at-arms. In 1439 the duke of Somerset agreed to serve for six months with a hundred men-at-arms and 2,000 archers; accounts show that he in fact raised 1,980 of the latter. In 1443 he provided a much larger force, of about 600 men-at-arms and almost 4,000 archers.[13]

The scale of infantry involvement in warfare, therefore, underwent dramatic changes. From what were probably relatively small numbers from the Norman period through to the mid thirteenth century, there was an astonishing explosion in quantitative terms under Edward I, with up to 30,000 men being recruited. Such a level of numbers, which presaged the armies of the seventeenth century, was not maintained even for a century; the Hundred Years War was for the most part characterised by the recruitment of much smaller, more specialised forces, with the obvious exceptions of the armies of 1346–7 and 1359.

The explanations for these changes are complex. Changing patterns of recruitment need to be considered. The question of how infantry were equipped was also significant: to what extent were the smaller forces of the early and later periods composed of much better armed men than the large hosts of the late thirteenth and early fourteenth centuries? Shifts in the scale of military forces were a reflection of changes in the type of war being fought, but also reflected the capacity of the state to recruit men.

Obligation

Obligation was less important in recruiting the lower ranks of an army than it was for the cavalry. Common soldiers lacked the political power of their betters, so there was less argument about the nature of their obligation to serve. In their case, their relative poverty meant that it was normally essential that the Crown provide them with adequate payment for what they did.

The Norman Conquest did not bring with it any new system of obligation for common soldiers which paralleled the introduction of knight service. Nor were there clear Anglo-Saxon precedents for the recruitment of ordinary infantry troops. The question of whether there were two different types of fyrd service, 'select' and 'general', has already been discussed.[14] The main proponent of the hypothesis that there were, wrote that 'it is by no means easy to distinguish between the great fyrd and the select fyrd in the numerous military campaigns' mentioned in the narrative sources'.[15] It would have been remarkable indeed if contemporaries had been able to draw distinctions which were first made by historians in the twentieth century. It is hardly surprising that when marauding Vikings were knocking at the gates, all able-bodied inhabitants turned out to try to drive them away. That does not mean, however, that they were acting under some formal obligation. When men fear that their throats may be cut, they are not much concerned with legal niceties. The principle of a general obligation to serve was certainly not clearly set out in the laws of the Anglo-Saxon kings, though the apocryphal 'Laws of William I' did declare that all free men had a duty of fealty to the king, and to defend his lands and honours against enemies and foreigners. References from the *Anglo-Saxon Chronicle* to 'the entire English nation' being summoned to fight in 1015 and 1016 should not be taken literally, and surely mean no more than a nation-wide summons of a limited number.[16] The existence of evidence from the late twelfth and thirteenth centuries for militia service does not mean that the system, such as it was, was based on Anglo-Saxon precedent. Much later Edward III could confidently declare that 'each and every one of the realm is bound as strongly and powerfully as can be to defend it against enemy attacks', but it would be unwise to read such an obligation back into pre-Conquest days.[17]

English infantry were used extensively during the Norman period, but the sources largely fail to reveal whether they were forcibly compelled to serve, served in respect of a formal obligation, or were paid to fight. It is, however, recorded that in 1088 William Rufus appealed to his English subjects to assist him in the siege of Rochester; those who did not would be regarded as *nithing*. The appeal was perhaps to a sense of honour; the threat one of effective outlawry. Promises of good government also played their part. How important formal obligation was in this is not clear, though it may have been an element. Six years later the king demanded English troops for service in Normandy. They assembled at Hastings, but instead of arranging their transport across the Channel, Ranulf Flambard took 10*s*, which had been given to each man for his expenses, from each of them, and sent the money to the king. This was probably a cynical misuse of the Anglo-Saxon five-hide system of obligation.[18]

Infantry forces undoubtedly played their part in the warfare of the twelfth century. King Stephen used considerable numbers of infantry, some archers and some armed with slings, at the siege of Exeter in 1136, but the sources give no indication of how they were recruited, save that the slingers were brought from distant parts. The remark suggests that recruitment was normally local.[19] Henry II, recruiting for his Welsh campaign in 1165, experimented with a system of recruitment which paralleled knight service. A promise was made at Northampton in 1164 that infantry would be provided by the magnates. Rather than ask for men, Henry II chose to ask for money to pay for soldiers, and assessments were made based on units of 15*s* 3*d* Assuming that the men, termed at this period sergeants, were paid a penny a day, the sum implies that they were to serve for a six-month period. In many cases, a knight's fee was charged with providing five such footsoldiers. In the north, the assessment was based on service for a quarter of the year rather then six months. This was a unique experiment; no precedent was made of it, and no future attempt made to establish a system along such lines for the provision of infantry soldiers.[20] A very different system of obligation was set out in 1181 when Henry II promulgated the Assize of Arms. This laid down the duties of free men to possess military equipment. There was a sliding scale, extending from those who held a knight's fee, who should have a coat of mail, helmet, shield and lance, from those with lands and chattels worth ten or fifteen pounds, down to ordinary free men who were to have a gambeson (a quilted jerkin), simple helmet and spear. Judicial inquiries were to make sure that the system operated effectively. The assessment to arms was based directly on wealth, not on how land was held. The overriding concern was to ensure that men had appropriate weapons, rather than with the obligation to serve, although there was a general requirement that everyone was to swear 'to bear his arms in the king's service according to his command'. In the nineteenth century Stubbs could safely argue that the Assize 'was intended to create a force for national defence, safer and more trustworthy than the feudal levies'.[21] National defence, however, was not a major issue in 1181; the purpose was probably more to improve local peacekeeping, by trying to ensure that law-abiding men were well armed, than to provide a means of raising armies.

This general obligation to bear arms was used to raise men for local defence and was appealed to in times of clear necessity: it had less relevance for normal military recruitment. Men were called up under the terms of the assize in 1193, when John rebelled, and in 1205 when he was king, John made very full use of it when invasion from France threatened. 'It is provided that if aliens come to our land, all should unanimously go to oppose them with force and arms without any interference or delay.' Again in 1213 a general summons was sent out to provide for the defence of the country.[22] Interestingly, these demands did not arouse complaints from the magnates, and nothing in Magna Carta related to them. This may have been because in practice the demands had not been particularly onerous, nor those on whom they fell politically influential; it may also have been because even John had limited the use he made of this type of obligation to cases of obvious national necessity.

The Assize of Arms was reissued and updated on several occasions under Henry III, notably in 1242 and 1253. Remarkably, it was only in 1242 that the wealthier men, those with land worth at least £15, were required to possess horses. The context of the 1253 order was very clear; it was not one of military recruitment, but of the maintenance of law and order through such mechanisms as the hue and cry. The idea that order should be kept by making sure that as many men as possible possessed weapons may seem curious, but it finds a modern parallel in the United States, where the right of all to possess deadly weapons is jealously guarded by some.[23] What the measures did not do was to explain what obligation lay on the ordinary freemen to fight in the king's wars. In Henry III's reign those sworn to arms were certainly expected to turn out when requested. In 1224 the sheriff of Shropshire and Staffordshire was told to levy a force using horn and hue, to go to the siege of Bedford castle. In 1231 the sheriff of Gloucestershire was asked to provide the wealthier of those sworn to arms, those with armour of iron, for a Welsh campaign. The lesser men were to provide victuals for 200 axemen. Other counties were asked for one-third of those sworn to arms. The role of these militia forces, however, remained primarily local, and it is not surprising that the principle was used in 1264, when Simon de Montfort needed to have the coasts guarded for fear of invasion. By now, the troops were to be selected, with the best men from each vill chosen; they were to be provided with their expenses by their community, and would serve for forty days.[24]

There were stronger traditions of service in the border regions towards Wales and Scotland than in the rest of England. The conditions of a frontier society naturally led it to be more militarised than the rest of England, with provision for infantry as well as cavalry. According to Domesday Book, the burgesses of Shrewsbury and the tenants of Hereford had to accompany the sheriff on Welsh expeditions. The men of Archenfield in Herefordshire by custom provided the vanguard for armies going into Wales, and the rearguard on their return. Later evidence shows that they were to provide forty-nine sergeants for fifteen days' service in Wales at their own cost. The vanguard and rearguard duties were paralleled in the north, where they were borne by the men of Cumberland. A form of tenure, cornage (common in the north), involved a duty to serve against the Scots. Service was not always unpaid, however. One Shropshire estate was burdened with the duty of providing a constable to be in charge of footsoldiers in armies going to Wales, but this was to be at the king's cost.[25]

Recruitment of infantry soldiers was carried out on an extensive scale in Wales, particularly in the south and in the Marches. Here it was possible to make use of traditional Welsh systems of military obligation. A Welsh prince was entitled to the service of freemen, for an unlimited period within his own lands, and for six weeks beyond them. One text suggests that in the former case the men were to provide their own provisions, and in the latter the lord would do so. Another form of service was much more limited. There were some tenures in Wales which obliged their holder to serve for three days at their own expense, this sometimes being followed by longer service at the lord's cost. This was evidently a system intended to provide military resources when there was some immediate danger. The evidence for these systems of military obligation in Wales is relatively slender, but they formed some basis for recruitment of Welsh troops by Edward I; an inquiry in Chirk in the late fourteenth century described the way in which troops went 'with their lord at his will, using his provisions just as they used to receive in the former times of the Scottish war in the days of Edward, King Henry's son'.[26] No doubt in many cases threats, and perhaps the offer of pay, were enough to recruit Welshmen, without recourse to appeals to traditional obligations.

What Edward I had, therefore, available to him in recruiting footsoldiers was a principle that free men should possess proper military equipment, and a tradition whereby those sworn to arms could be mustered on a county basis by the sheriff for local defence purposes, and paid their expenses by the local community. The terms of the Assize of Arms were updated in the Statute of Winchester of 1285, but its prime intention was not the provision of troops; there was no need to make arrangements for that a couple of years after the conquest of Wales. It was intended as a means of maintaining public order, not as a method of providing 30,000 men to fight in Wales.[27] There was no clear general duty to serve in royal expeditions to Wales, Scotland or France, although there were local customs that applied to those living in the Welsh and Scottish marches. The king could also use traditional Welsh systems of obligation in recruiting Welshmen to his armies. Edward built on the tradition of local obligation as a means of recruitment, but used royal pay to reward the men, or at least provide them with adequate subsistence, on his expeditions.

Commissions of array

The major development in recruiting methods under Edward was the use of special commissions of array. In 1277, for the first Welsh war, responsibility to collect together footsoldiers was laid upon the sheriffs, but in 1282 the king employed some of his household knights on the task, men such as Hugh Turberville, Grimbald Pauncefoot and Roger Lestrange. The importance of recruitment is shown by the way in which leading justices and councillors were given this responsibility in 1294. For a time it was usual to appoint important knights to act together with a royal clerk, but by Edward's later Scottish campaigns reliance was placed wholly on magnates and knights with military experience. The earlier commissions were appointed for large areas: in 1294 Hugh Cressingham, Roger Brabazon and Peter Malore had to select troops in six northern counties. In the next year two commissioners had responsibility for selecting 4,000 troops. By the end of the reign the commissions were much more limited, being confined to single counties, ridings of Yorkshire, or even baronial liberties.[28]

The commissioners were too few to undertake the detailed work of recruiting at a local level. Local officials must have taken the lead in the villages and hundreds. In some cases it seems to have been the entire local community who selected those who were to go to fight. In other instances villagers decided to raise money instead, to hire men to go on their behalf. Abuses were rife. Bribes were offered, and accepted, so that service might be avoided. Those selected to go might fail to do so. From the Crown's point of view, the system was scarcely ideal as a method of obtaining effective troops. It was most likely to serve as a means of collecting together the weak, the imbecile and the outsiders of village society. The commissioners of array would muster the men when they were brought to the county collection points, and no doubt the most unsuitable were weeded out, but this was no way to recruit promising soldiers.[29] What the commissions of array produced was quantity, not quality.

Commissions of array continued in use for the rest of the medieval period and beyond. Those appointed to them did not always find their task easy. In 1315 John Botetourt reported that those recruited for his company were 'feeble chaps, not properly dressed, and lacking bows and arrows'. In the next year William de Montague complained that the bailiff of Gloucester had provided forty-eight men, not the hundred he had been asked for. Those he did bring to muster at Monmouth were of no value, and he admitted taking bribes to leave the competent men behind.[30] In December 1341 arrests of commissioners were ordered, because they had failed to provide the troops Edward III wanted for Brittany and Scotland.[31] In Rutland in the 1350s, commissioners found that they could recruit no more than two men, who did not have sufficient wherewithal to arm themselves properly. The earl of Warwick, Lord Zouche, Lord de la Warre and other magnates had apparently already recruited all the able-bodied men in the tiny county for their own retinues.[32] Abuses continued. There was much potential for corruption in the procedures for recruiting footsoldiers and light cavalry forces. In the early 1330s three men were selected in Clacklose hundred, Norfolk, to serve as hobelars, lightly armed horsemen, in Scotland. They received £3 each for their horses, equipment and expenses from the local community. Then, however, the king cancelled the levy. The three men were asked to repay the money, but refused to do so. One of them, it turned out, had gone to Scotland, 'and he there spent the said money in the king's service, and he came back in great distress and worn out'. On the other hand, the other two had quite improperly pocketed the money.[33] Inquiries in 1341 in Lincolnshire revealed that six years before Walter de Trekyngham, acting on behalf of John de Ros, had taken 13s 4d unjustly from one village to provide archers with food supplies. His clerk took a helmet worth 5s from another place to exempt it from providing one archer; it cost another 26s 8d for an exemption from a demand for two archers. The constable of Bassingham was accused, with another man, of trying to extort 13s 4d from the men of his locality by threatening to recruit them for the war in Scotland. Another arrayer allegedly extorted 26s 8d from Grantham to exempt it from a demand for two archers. The system of array was, hardly surprisingly, not popular. In 1346 an arrayer was assaulted in Birmingham, and forcibly prevented from doing his duty.[34]

The methods that had been developed under Edward I were effective in bringing together very substantial numbers of troops, but numbers were not everything. More effective armies were levied when men-at-arms and archers were recruited as an integrated force. This major change in recruitment patterns took place under Edward III, when the Crown began to include in the indentures negotiated with commanders a demand for specified numbers not merely of men-at-arms, but also of archers. Recruitment of archers became increasingly the task of the leaders of cavalry retinues and not of the commissioners of array, though use of the latter was not abandoned. Some of the leaders in Scotland in 1337 brought archers with them as part of their contingents. The accounts for the royal forces in Flanders in 1338 show the cavalry quite separately from the common soldiers, but the section dealing with the archers shows that over 1,000 archers, nearly all mounted, served with magnates as part of the retinues. The county levies, with the Welsh, nearly all on foot, numbered roughly 3,000.[35] In the 1359 campaign, some 4,500 of the archers were shown as part of the magnate retinues. The account book lists 1,130 horse archers, mostly in contingents a hundred strong, who were not included in retinues. In addition there were 1,000 Welsh footsoldiers, paid 2d a day.[36] By the time of Agincourt, virtually all the archers were members of retinues. How the recruitment took place for a retinue is far from clear. Archers were not retained in the way that knights and squires were. Presumably magnates looked in the first instance to their own estates, but it is also likely that there was a pool of experienced soldiers ready to be hired.

The integration of archers into the retinues of the bannerets and knights was a change of great importance, even though the archers did not usually fight shoulder-to-shoulder with their superiors. The change was probably the product of a move towards administrative simplicity, rather than being dictated by military logic. It does not appear to have been result of a single policy decision, but the new practice evolved rapidly. The efficacy of English armies was greatly increased when cavalry and archers were better integrated as parts of the same military machine.[37]

Pay and recruitment

Pay was an important element in the recruitment of archers and others who fought on foot. It was not provided at rates calculated to bring men pouring voluntarily into the muster points, but was sufficient to ensure that those who fought were not seriously out of pocket. The obligation in cases of national, or local, defence did not mean that men were expected to serve without receiving sufficient funds to cover their costs. Local communities were expected to pay for expenses incurred within the county boundaries, or to a specified muster point. Thereafter, the Crown took over. Pay was not intended as a reward, but was meant to provide the men with their subsistence. At 2*d* a day in the thirteenth and early fourteenth centuries, the footsoldier was certainly better treated than his successors in more modern periods. The rate was higher than he could expect to receive from work as a common agricultural labourer, although less than a skilled craftsman might expect. The mounted archer naturally received more when he came on the scene, for his costs were higher. In the Hundred Years War the normal rates were 6*d* a day for a mounted archer, and 3*d* a day for a footsoldier.

There was a range of inducements that the Crown could offer. A share in the proceeds of war was always tempting. In 1319 Edward II promised that everyone could take up to £100 worth of goods from his Scottish enemies for himself – an offer which thousands found attractive.[38] Pardons could be obtained in return for good service. In 1294 Edward I scoured the country's prisons to find men for his armies. Pretending to be inspired by feelings of mercy, he appointed two justices to grant pardons in return for service. Over 300 men were recruited in this way to go to Gascony, and the expedient was one which was to be extensively used in the future. Men knew that by serving in the wars they could win pardons. A typical entry in the patent roll for 1347 reads 'Pardon, at the request of Henry earl of Lancaster, and for good service done in his company in Gascony, to Thomas son of Randolf Barfote of Pynchebek of the king's suit for the death of John son of Alan Houtered of Pynchebek, killed before Whitsunday in the nineteenth year, and of any subsequent outlawry.' Robert White, who served at the siege of Calais, had an extensive criminal record, for he was pardoned for 'homicides, felonies, robberies, rapes of women, and trespasses'.[39]

The burden of providing troops was not spread equitably. It made obvious sense to collect men from areas near to the campaigning area, or close to the port of embarkation. Under Edward I it was the shires close to the Welsh border, and of course South Wales, which bore the bulk of the burden during the Welsh wars. When the campaigns were in Scotland, the troops were largely drawn from the north and the north midlands. Yorkshire was much called upon. In 1322 Edward II's administrators cast their net more widely. It may have been equitable to draw not merely on counties such as Yorkshire, Derbyshire and Nottinghamshire, but also on counties in the south and west such as Kent, Sussex, Wiltshire and Gloucestershire, but it displayed a lack of practical sense.[40] Some counties established a military tradition. The men of Cheshire were frequently called upon for campaigns in Wales, and the county continued to be a major recruiting area throughout the medieval period. A late-fourteenth-century chronicler commented on the Cheshire men, and claimed that 'because of former wars and disputes among themselves they are better trained in arms, and more difficult to control than other people in the kingdom'. Cheshire probably saw a higher proportion of men recruited into later medieval English armies than any other county.[41]

Wales itself was a prime recruiting ground. The English had good reason to know how effective were Welsh bowmen from the south, and spearmen from the north. Their arms were light, so that their agility was not impeded. All their traditions were to fight on foot, though they might use horses for pursuit or flight. In the late twelfth century Gerald of Wales commented on the men of Gwent, who were particularly noted for their warlike skills, and above all their archery. In a famous passage he described how William de Braose was pinned to his saddle by an arrow shot right through his thigh; it even penetrated through the saddle, killing the horse. Another knight was similarly struck from both sides, pegging him firmly in his saddle.[42] Tough and hardy, with a long military tradition, the Welsh showed little reluctance to be recruited into English armies. Their country was, for the most part, poor; it may be that fighting in France or Scotland seemed to offer a way of escape from a hard way of life. Good soldiers though they were, Welsh troops might present some problems. They were too often as ready to take up arms against their English companions as against the enemy. In Scotland in 1296 there were several incidents of trouble between English and Welsh troops; one Englishman was even hanged for murdering a Welsh soldier. The deputy marshal, John Lovel, had to intervene in a major Anglo-Welsh dispute which took place when the army reached Edinburgh.[43]

Organisation in the field; desertion

Once recruited, the men were formed into units of twenties and hundreds. Each twenty had its officer, or vintenar, every hundred its mounted constable. Early evidence of this is provided by the recruitment in 1193 of 500 Welsh infantry, out of whom twenty-five were officers.[44] A multitude of pay records of Edward I's day reveal this structure of hundreds and twenties. By the time of the Hundred Years War, organisation might be yet more complex. This grouping into hundreds and twenties was the usual way in which the arrayed men were organised; the records do not reveal how the archers recruited by magnates as part of their retinues were arranged in the field. Curiously, it was the Welsh contingents in Edward's reign which appear to have been the best officered. In 1339, 374 foot from North Wales were accompanied by six mounted constables, ten other men-at-arms, a chaplain, a clerk, four doctors, a crier or proclaimer, seven standard-bearers and nineteen vintenars. Similarly, the hundred men who came from Anglesey in 1342 to fight in Brittany were led by a staff consisting of chaplain, interpreter, standard-bearer, crier, doctor and four vintenars, and the records for 1359 show the same pattern.[45] It may be that there were equivalent positions in the English troops, but the records provide no evidence of it. It was presumably tradition combined with decisions of the local communities, rather than of the Crown, which led to the Welsh troops being apparently so well organised.

There was probably little continuity in the infantry forces from year to year. Nothing suggests that the system of recruitment at a county level gave rise to any sense that anticipated later regimental loyalties. No doubt there were many veterans who served in a great many campaigns, but it rare to find any corps of infantry maintained in being for longer than a single expedition. Castle garrisons provide an exception to this, as do mercenary bands. An unusual small corps, effectively a bodyguard, was formed by Edward I in his Scottish wars, from the members of the garrison of Stirling castle after it had fallen to the Scots in 1299.[46]

Desertion was a significant problem, particularly in wars within Britain; abandoning the army was not so easy when it was operating across the Channel. Under Edward I, armies in Scotland suffered a constant haemorrhage; indeed, desertion began the moment levies left their county muster points. Of one contingent of 643 men in August 1300, only 407 arrived. In 1300 the king complained that the Yorkshire footsoldiers 'have wickedly deceived us and have traitorously failed us in our affairs'. Because local officials were thought to have abetted the men, special commissioners were to be appointed to punish the deserters. In 1303 a harsh ordinance was drawn up. Anyone suspected of desertion was to be imprisoned, and wages paid to them were to be forcibly recovered.[47] In 1322, 186 archers from Sussex mustered at Northallerton on 27 July. By the end of the campaign, early in September, their number had fallen to 147. The figures for other English counties were similar; the 401 men from Wiltshire were reduced in number to 310. The Welsh, on the other hand, had a better record in what was a thoroughly unsuccessful campaign. A large contingent of 978 men left Builth on 11 July; 958 returned on 22 September. Troops from Anglesey and elsewhere in the north numbered 1,931 when they left the Menai Straits on 15 July; 1,794 was the number still on the payroll at the end of the campaign.[48] It must have been much harder for a Welsh deserter, so easily identifiable from his language, to return home than it was for an Englishman. Later accounts are not drawn up in a way which makes it easy to identify deserters: they record periods of absenteeism, but without making it clear whether the men were merely temporarily absent. Thus in 1338–9 John Ward led a troop of 202 archers in Flanders. Over a period of 483 days, forty men were absent for thirty-two days, and eight for two days. In 1359 one contingent of a hundred men, led by Thomas Stafford, had its wages reduced because, as the account had it, eight men had been absent for a total of 154 days. It is not clear, however, whether these were true desertions, or absenteeism due to sickness.[49] It cannot have been easy to desert from an army in France, although some were no doubt tempted to join the Free Companies and continue to fight on a private basis.

Equipment and training

The evidence for the Norman period strongly suggests that the normal infantry weapon was the bow. The role of the archers at Hastings is well known, but according to William of Poitiers, the Conqueror also had better-armed mailed infantry, placed next in line behind the bowmen. Chronicle accounts are often not specific about the equipment or role of the infantry, but at Bourgthéroulde in 1124 archers played an important part, shooting at the vulnerable right-hand side of the enemy knights – the side unprotected by a shield. It is not clear how large were the bows used in this period. They may have approached the size of the later longbows, but the illustrations in the Bayeux Tapestry show the archers drawing not to the ear, as with the later longbow, but simply to the chest.[50]

The infantry weapon which was regarded with awe and fear in the twelfth century was the crossbow. Its use, except against infidels, was forbidden by the Fourth Lateran Council of 1139, and it does not appear to have come into widespread use until the late twelfth century.[51] Richard I used crossbows extensively, and John retained small troops of crossbowmen in his service. Some were specially recruited in 1205 for his planned but abortive expedition to France. Peter the Saracen was employed to make crossbows. Expenditure in this one year on these troops came to over £800.[52] The crossbows

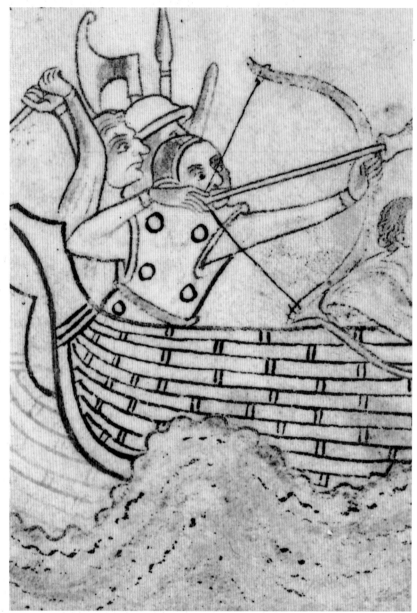

The archers shown in the lower margin of the Bayeux Tapestry drew their bows back to the chest. In contrast, the thirteenth-century archer in the drawing of naval warfare by Matthew Paris drew his bow back almost to his ear.

were not all of the same design; some were described as with one
foot, and others with two. This referred to the stirrup, or stirrups,
used by the crossbowman to hold down the weapon while the
bowstring was hauled into place. Another kind was *à tour*, in which
the bow-string was stretched with the aid of a cord, hooked to the
man's belt, and a pulley. The bow itself was of composite construction, using horn and wood.[53] The crossbow was something of an élite
weapon, which because of its relatively slow rate of shooting was
better suited to siege warfare than to the battlefield. It was certainly
not appropriate for arming very large infantry forces. By the time of
his Welsh wars, Edward I could call upon the services of no more
than about 250 crossbowmen from England, though he also
recruited 585 Gascon crossbowmen in 1282, the majority of them
mounted.[54]

Far more important than the crossbow in English armies was, of
course, the longbow, which proved to be a most potent weapon,
above all during the Hundred Years War. When it came into widespread use is not clear, but it is often argued that the reign of Edward
I was a decisive period. There is scant evidence for the length of
bows; normally the only distinction drawn was that between the bow
and the crossbow. Records, unlike some historians, do not distinguish between longbows and shortbows. A murder case of 1298
provided a description of the weapon employed: a bow with a
circumference of 6 inches and a length of an ell and a half, or $67\frac{1}{2}$
inches – roughly the height of a man. This certainly should qualify as
a longbow, though in another legal record, a generation later, a bow
of this length was described as 'Turkish'. This latter record also
describes a yet more massive weapon, a longbow by any standard.
This was made of Spanish yew, and was two ells in length, or $7\frac{1}{2}$
feet. It was four thumbs thick, and shot a long 'clotharrow'.[55] Such
longbows, however, are unlikely to have been a new development.
The evidence of contemporary illustrations does not suggest any
significant change in the late thirteenth century. Drawings by Matthew Paris in Henry III's reign show bows being pulled back to the
ear, one of the marks of the longbow. There is a change visible in the
bows themselves in the first half of the fourteenth century. Whereas
those of around 1300 are shown rough-hewn and knobbly, in drawing and paintings of around 1340 the bows are depicted as smooth.
Whether this would have made any real difference to the power of
the weapon must be doubted, though if it represents the use of
different types of wood, elm or yew, it does indicate quality. The best
bows were of yew, often imported from Spain and elsewhere.[56]

The skill of the bowyer in making use of both heartwood and
sapwood was vitally important. He had to give the weapon power
derived from the compression of the former, and the expansion of the

latter, as it was bent. The draw weight of a full-sized medieval longbow was very considerable: probably from 100 lbs to as much as 175 lbs. An experienced archer might have been able to shoot as many as twenty arrows in a minute, although a more conservative rate is half that level. The maximum range is not particularly relevant; what is important is that at 200 yards the bow was highly effective.[57] The value of the longbow was still appreciated as late as 1776, when Benjamin Franklin argued for its introduction into the rebel American army. The case was a good one. A bow could be shot four times as fast as a musket. The smoke of discharge did not obscure the soldier's view. A flight of arrows would terrify an enemy, and a man once hit in any part of his body was *hors de combat*.[58] It was, however, no easy task to shoot with a massive longbow; considerable strength was needed, and also extensive practice to acquire the steadiness of arm. Experience alone could teach an archer the degree of elevation to achieve particular distances, and the allowance he should make for the wind. The modern rifle is a far simpler weapon with which to shoot.[59]

Under Edward I, to judge by the pay records, the infantry were dominated by archers. In the first Welsh war, of 1277, some of the foot were described as *lanceati*, or spearmen, but by 1282 the great majority were listed as archers. Edward recruited extensively from south Wales where the bow was the traditional weapon. J.E. Morris argued that it was as a result of knowledge, acquired as a young man, of the excellence of the bowmen from that region that Edward developed the use of archers in his campaigns.[60] The argument is attractive, but does not convince. In 1277 one specialised corps of archers did indeed come from south Wales; the other, however, was drawn from Macclesfield. There were other regions as well as south Wales that were noted for their archers: the Weald was one.[61] At the one battle where Edward commanded as king, Falkirk, the Welsh infantry took no part in the fighting until it was clear that the English had won the day. The contribution of archery to that success was made by the bowmen of Derbyshire, Lancashire and Cheshire.[62] Curiously, Sherwood Forest, with its mythical links with archery, in 1303 provided not bowmen, but slingers.[63]

A further argument against the case that the longbow transformed the infantry under Edward I is that fact the footsoldiers of his day were startlingly ill-equipped. Pay records usually referred to the men as *pedites sagitarii*, 'foot archers', but this was probably little more than common form used by the clerks, which disguised the fact that many were not in fact bowmen. The most detailed evidence for recruitment, in Norfolk in 1295, shows that the men were provided with knives and swords, not bows and arrows.[64] The Crown made virtually no attempt to provide the weapons that were needed; this

Figures from the Luttrell Psalter. Those on the left show longbowmen, the lower stringing his bow. On the right is a crossbowman bending his bow.

was left to the men themselves and their local communities. The results cannot have been satisfactory, and the Crown's determination to recruit such large numbers of men of such questionable value is mystifying. There was certainly a revolution in the quantity of troops marched to the wars by Edward I, but there was no revolution in quality.

In Edward II's reign the government took measures to deal with the inadequate nature of the infantry forces, with the emphasis placed on defensive equipment rather than on the longbow. In 1316 there was a plan to recruit men equipped with padded jerkins, or aketons, and helmets, as well as offensive weapons. Although the plan was abandoned, it was revived in 1322. Not only was there a request for one man to be sent from each township or vill, but a proportion of the ordinary county levies were to be equipped with aketons, helmets and iron gauntlets. Cheshire, for example, provided 186 infantry armoured in this way, and 355 who were, as the pay record somewhat quaintly put it, 'naked'. The number of men specified to be archers was few. None of the Welsh were so named; 186 Sussex men were termed archers. Pay varied with equipment: the best-armed infantry received 4*d* a day, those half-armed 3*d*, and the rest 2*d*.[65] In 1324 a third of the infantry recruited for Gascony were to have padded jerkins, hauberks or plate armour, helmets and gauntlets.[66] One plan from Edward II's final years asked for as many as 5,100 fully armed infantry to be recruited.[67] Morris argued that this experiment in using armoured infantry was a complete failure. Of the 1322 expedition, he wrote 'The men cannot but have been an untrained mob, and their fighting power contemptible', and he pointed to the fact that the experiment was not repeated by Edward III.[68] The problem in practice was one of mobility. The English army of 1322 marched as far as Edinburgh, but totally failed to engage an unwilling Scots enemy. The armoured infantry were not put to the test of battle.

The idea of heavily armed infantry was not, however, wholly abandoned. Although only thirty-nine such men served in Flanders in 1339, a plan for recruiting an army in 1341 included just over 1,000 well-armed footsoldiers, and a memorandum for the following year requested 2,000 men with steel helmets and long spears. There were in addition to be 4,000 English archers, and 4,000 Welsh troops, of whom two-thirds should be archers and one-third spearmen.[69]

The real revolution in the infantry forces came not with the armoured footsoldier, but with the introduction of the mounted archer in the 1330s. There can be no doubts about this innovation, in contrast to the alleged introduction of the longbow under Edward I. The demand that archers should have horses transformed the mobility of armies. The long columns of weary men plodding their way northwards into Scotland, so easily avoided by the Scots, were no more. Swift, smaller forces, capable of rapid manoeuvre, made far more sense. Mounted archers, however, were not a complete innovation. Some were used in the Norman conquest of Ireland in the late twelfth century. The *arcarii* referred to by Gerald of Wales were horse archers: he suggested that they should be intermingled with the cavalry squadrons.[70] William Marshal in 1193 had paid wages to a small force of forty archers, each with two horses, and four mounted archers were included in the little force, largely composed of Welshmen, that John sent to Norway in 1201.[71] Earlier twelfth-century chronicle evidence also makes it clear that mounted archers were, if not common, certainly not unknown at that period. It is conceivable that these men, unlike the later mounted archers, shot from horseback; there is no evidence to reveal the way they fought.[72]

The fourteenth-century horse archer first appeared, to judge by the surviving records, in 1334. No formal request is recorded among the writs of summons for such troops to be recruited, but the numbers that came to take part in the campaign that began in November were such as to show that a deliberate policy had been adopted. The royal household was at the forefront. John Ward was captain of the king's archers, who were drawn from Cheshire, and numbered over 200, all horsed. Adding to their number other mounted archers, some volunteers, some members of knightly retinues, the royal household provided almost 500 mounted archers. Many magnates provided not only men-at-arms but also mounted archers; it has been calculated that from this source the king obtained 818 heavily armed cavalry, and 771 horse archers.[73] These numbers suggest that the concept of the mounted archer cannot have been absolutely brand new in 1334. Similar pay records do not survive for the previous campaign, when the English won the battle of Halidon Hill, and it seems likely that mounted archers had been recruited then. Although none seem to have been employed in 1327, towns had been ordered that year to provide the infantry they sent to the host with a horse, worth thirty or forty shillings, for each man, so that he could ride to the muster – a measure which could be seen as a precedent for the mounted archer proper.[74] J.E. Morris argued that the origins of the mounted archer lay in the hobelars. There is, however, no evidence to suggest that hobelars dismounted to fight. While it is possible that the value of these lightly armed cavalry in the Scottish wars gave someone the idea of mounting the infantry, the mounted archer was more probably an archer put upon a horse, rather a hobelar given a bow and a quiver of arrows.[75] It is surprising that the initial decision to employ mounted archers is not echoed in the writs ordering recruitment in 1334, though the answer may be that these men were organised to march, and presumably to fight, alongside the traditional cavalry. They were not part of the normal county levies, who were recruited according to more traditional formulas.

The foot archer still featured in the mid fourteenth century. At the siege of Calais in 1347 they probably outnumbered horse archers by three to one. In the Black Prince's own retinue at Poitiers there should have been, according to his contract, 400 mounted archers and 300 on foot. The swift-moving *chevauchées* had to rely on mounted archers, but larger expeditions contained their measure of ordinary foot. In the indentures of Edward III's final years, after the renewal of the French war in 1369, mounted archers were normally specified rather than footmen. In the Agincourt army mounted archers outnumbered those on foot. However, in the Wars of the Roses, when many armies contained hastily assembled local levies, the great majority of the troops were almost certainly footsoldiers, rather than mounted archers.[76]

A significant addition to the archer's equipment was made, if the author of the *Gesta Henrici Quinti* is to be believed, on the express orders of the king himself, shortly before Agincourt. Every bowman was ordered to prepare a stake about six feet long, sharpened at both ends. These, driven into the ground in front of the archers, and with some further back, would provide a valuable defence against cavalry attack. Later instructions by the earl of Shrewsbury were that the stakes should be eleven feet long. The use of such stakes was not a complete novelty in 1415; they had been used for defensive purposes by Turkish troops opposing French and Burgundian forces at the battle of Nicopolis in 1396. It had long been customary for archers to dig pits in front of their positions, and it would not have required much imagination to see that stakes might be an effective alternative, far quicker to set up. What was perhaps new at the time of Agincourt was the systematic use of stakes, which made it possible for the archers to establish a new defensive position with great speed. These men had, in addition to their bows and stakes, the equipment to fight in the mêlée; they had axes, mallets or swords at their belts, and for all that some were barefoot and bareheaded, their trousers rolled to the knees, they were a formidable force.[77]

No further major changes to the equipment of the common soldier followed the introduction of the mounted archer, until the appearance of the musket in the sixteenth century. Handguns were certainly known in the fifteenth century, but not until Elizabeth's reign was it clear that they were superseding the bow. There was little need, indeed, to try to improve on the longbow. In the hands of the archers of the fourteenth century it was a devastating weapon. When archers shot in unison, the sight and sound of the arrows approaching must have been terrifying. Fitted with a sharp bodkin-shaped steel arrowhead, they could pierce even plate armour. Horses would have been panicked and stampeded by the stinging impact of arrows. The rapidity with which arrows could be shot from the longbow, and the

A late medieval handgun.

range at which it was effective, enabled the English to carry out a revolution in battlefield tactics. That could be achieved, however, only when there was a sufficient number of trained and experienced men available, who were provided with the proper equipment.

How far men were trained in archery, and indeed practised it, is difficult to determine from the surviving evidence. To have been as effective as they were, however, the English archers of the fourteenth century must have had ample practice. Scattered references show that there were shooting butts: in 1276 Richard son of Avelin was using his crossbow to shoot at targets in London, when he accidentally killed Walter Sanztere. A well-known illustration from the Luttrell Psalter of about 1340 shows archers practising at very modern-looking targets. However, in 1363 a royal order claimed that the art of archery was almost defunct, since people amused themselves by playing football or other unsuitable games instead of training with crossbow or longbow – a complaint which was still being made as late as 1596.[78] Training was not necessarily highly regarded. In the fifteenth century the Burgundian Philippe de Commynes argued, perhaps with his tongue in his cheek, that while archers were a vital element in an army, 'those who have never had a day's experience of their job are more valuable than those who are well trained; this is the opinion of the English, who are the world's best archers'.[79]

To fight effectively, archers should shoot in unison. A single arrow might kill a single man, but successive showers, visible and audible, could terrify a whole army. To shoot simultaneously demanded a degree of drill; but there is nothing in the written records to suggest that any attention was paid to the drilling of troops in the medieval

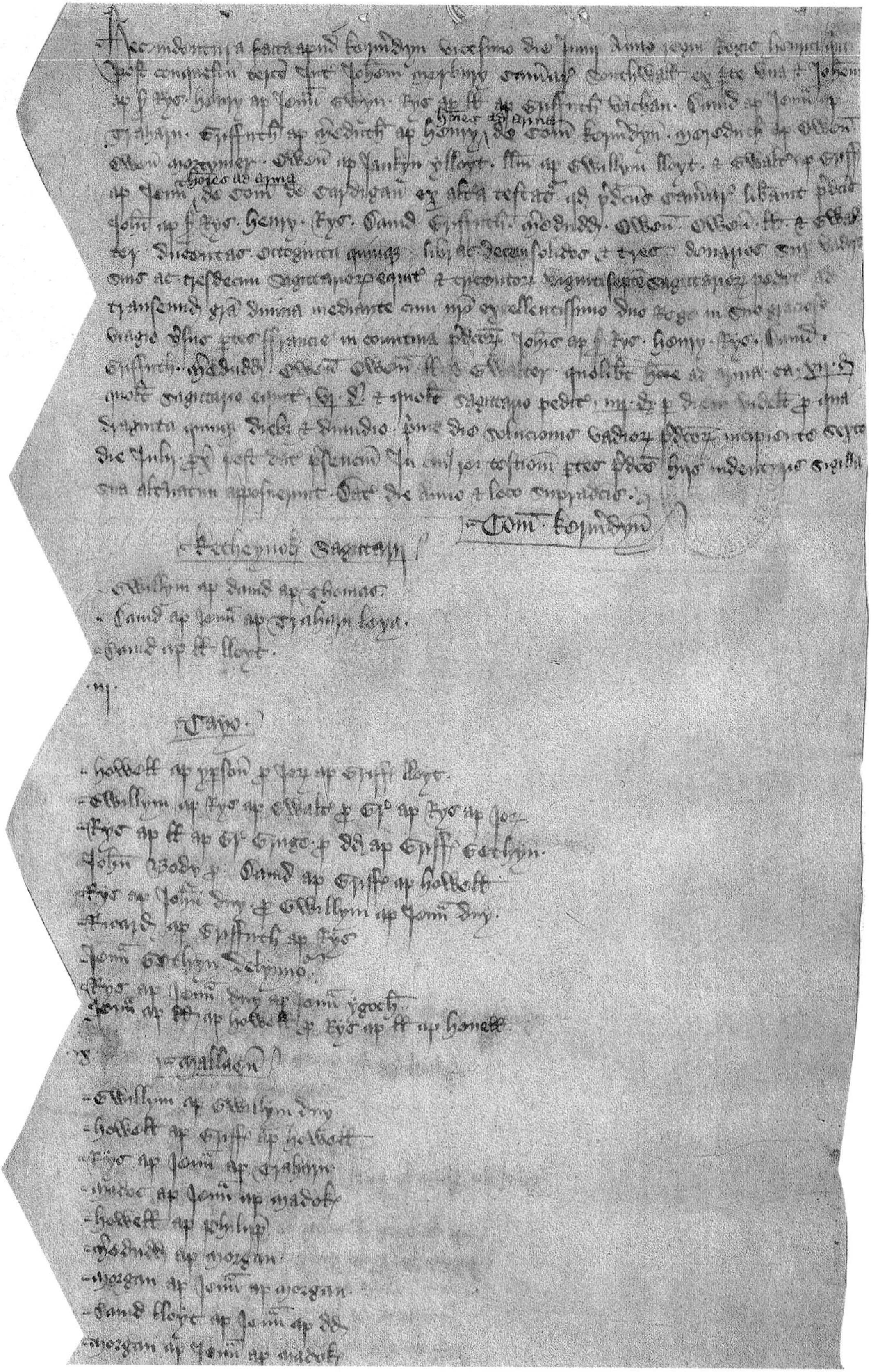

Recordatur a sarra... Keynddyn vicesimo die Juny Anno regni Regis henrici...

Com Keynddyn

Rethegnok Sagrayn

- William ap Dauid ap ... hemav
- Dauid ap Jeun ap Trahayn loya
- Dauid ap ll lloyt

.iij.

Taw

- holbech ap yr son p Jeu ap Gruff lloy
- William ap Kyr ap Walter ... Gr ap Kyr ap Jou
- Kyr ap ll ap Gr Grug ... DD ap Gruff Kethyn
- John Body ... Dauid ap Gruff ap holbech
- Kyr ap John Dry ... William ap Jeun Dry
- Lleud ap Gruffuch ap Kyr
- Jeun Kethyn Delymo
- Kyr ap Jeun Dry ap Jeun hooth
- Jeun ap DD ap holbech ... Kyr ap ll ap llauett

.x.

Mallaen

- William ap William Dry
- holbech ap Gruff ap holbech
- Kyr ap Jeun ap Trahayn
- Madoc ap Jeun ap madok
- holbech ap yehlug
- hodruch ap morgan
- morgan ap Jeun ap morgan
- Dauid lloyt ap Jeun ap DD
- morgan ap Jeun ap madok

period. Yet pictorial representation of armies in battle during the Hundred Years War show archers carefully lined up, bows all drawn, and it would not be wise to dismiss this as mere artistic licence.

The army pay-rolls, which provide details of the numbers of men employed as archers, do not indicate the very great difficulties there must have been in transforming peasants into effective fighting men. Surviving records of infantry musters, on the other hand, do hint at these. Several survive from Suffolk for 1346. The men are listed in their groups of twenty, each with its *vintenar*. Their arms are noted. Most had no more than a sword and a knife, some a *gisarme* and a knife. In Blything hundred, two men appeared with axes and knives; only two out of about fifty men were equipped with bows. The musters of Colneis hundred give exactly the same impression; here some men had no more than a staff and a knife.[80] Inspections of arms and arrays in Norwich a decade or so later also suggest that archers were hard to come by. One roll listing fifty-four men specifies only two as archers, while eight others possessed bows and arrows. Interestingly, those specified in these records as archers look to have been of relatively good social standing. Their numbers included a painter, a mercer, a tailor and, surprisingly, a goldsmith. Very unusually, these Norwich records reveal that two men, both leading citizens, had guns and gunpowder.[81]

Local communities had to pay out considerable sums in order to ensure that the men setting out to the wars were adequately equipped. In the Norfolk hundred of Launditch 187 men were arrayed in 1295, at a cost of over £50 in equipment and expenses. In some Yorkshire villages in 1300 the cost at about 5s per man was very similar. Under Edward II, with the demands for properly armoured infantry, costs rose to over £1 per man, and once mounted men were being provided, to about £2 early in Edward III's reign.

(*Left*) An indenture of 20 June 1415, detailing the recruitment of troops from South Wales for the Agincourt campaign. (*Above*) Archery practice in the fourteenth century, from the Luttrell Psalter of 1320–40.

The burden on local communities was heavy.[82] Under Edward III the Crown itself began to make far greater efforts than in the past to see that the men were properly supplied with the weapons they needed. In 1338, 1,000 bows and 4,000 sheaves of arrows were ordered, and as the Hundred Years War proceeded, so the supply and manufacture of bows and arrows became better organised. Sheriffs were given orders; in 1345 a hundred bows and 600 arrows were to be sent with all speed to Ralph Stafford in Gascony. Much was done centrally: in 1359 William de Rothwell, the clerk in charge of the armoury at the Tower of London, was commissioned to take armourers, bowyers and fletchers and to put them to work for the Crown. Any who were not co-operative were threatened with imprisonment. Between 1353 and 1360 Rothwell had added to the stock of arms in the Tower over 4,000 painted bows, 11,300 unpainted bows, 4,000 bowstaves and almost 24,000 sheaves of arrows. The cost of bows naturally varied, but to give one example, the sheriff of Somerset bought 120 at 1s 3d each in 1347, along with 456 sheaves of arrows, mostly at 1s 4d each, all for delivery at the Tower. In 1371 orders went out for the

collection of 16,500 sheaves of arrows, all to be of good dry wood.[83] The scale on which Henry V aimed to provide arrows for his forces was most impressive. The use of ash for clogs and shoes was forbidden in 1416, so that the wood could be reserved for making arrows, and in the next year the sheriffs were ordered to take six feathers from every single goose in their counties, to flight the arrows. Numbers of arrows bought by the crown rose from some 150,000 in 1418 to over 425,000 in 1421.[84]

It made sense for men to wear uniforms. This resolved the problem of recognition in battle, and, probably more importantly, made it easier to impose discipline by making men identifiable. It was not so easy to desert in uniform. In Edward I's Welsh wars the infantry wore armbands bearing the cross of St George. Quite exceptionally, winter camouflage clothing was used in 1283, when the garrison of Dolwyddelan were equipped all in white. The men recruited in Norfolk in 1295 were all equipped with standard *blaunchecotes*, white jerkins, worth 3s each. Early in Edward III's reign some contingents were ordered to wear uniforms, paid for by the local communities. The Welsh were all dressed in the same way. In 1347 a contingent of sixty miners, recruited for the siege of Calais, were equipped with uniform linen tunics and woollen hoods. In some cases, uniforms became quite elaborate. On the Black Prince's 1355 expedition, the men of Cheshire and North Wales wore green and white parti-coloured hats and tunics. The development of such garb was associated with the tendency for lords to provide their men with standardised livery robes. The problem of identification in battle was not fully resolved if each lord dressed his men in a distinctive way, and Henry V ordered that 'every man of what estate or condition that he be, of our party, bear a band of St George', much as Edward I's troops had done. The move towards elaborate liveries was not to be halted: in the Wars of the Roses even towns demonstrated pride in the men sent to fight through the clothes they wore. In 1463–4 the red coats of troops from Nottingham even bore a slogan of some kind, picked out in white letters. The basic white coat, however, remained the standard wear until the late Tudor period.[85]

There was a small number of specialised troops employed in major armies: the forerunners of modern engineer corps. In 1300 Edward I took eleven carpenters, fourteen masons, a dozen smiths, and a similar number of miners on his Scottish campaign. Similarly, in 1359, for example, Edward III had his pavilioner, with sixteen men under him, in charge of the royal tents. There was also a troop of twenty-five smiths, and thirty masons. Carpenters numbered fifty-two, and there was a similar number of miners, men whose services and expertise might prove vital in siege warfare. The account also details payments to the three minstrels who must have had a difficult

English archers (*right*), shown wearing the cross of St George, oppose Genoese crossbowmen at the battle of Crécy in 1346.

time in keeping the king's spirits up during what proved to be a very disappointing campaign.[86]

Coastal defence

In addition to recruiting footsoldiers and mounted archers to take part in campaigning proper, it was necessary to organise a system of coastal defence service at periods when French invasion threatened. The schemes that were developed not surprisingly bore a close relationship to the methods that were used to recruit infantry for campaigns. There was an obligation to turn out in defence of the locality to which appeal could be made. In 1212 John summoned men to Dover to defend England against a threat of attack; all who could bear arms were required to turn out. There is evidence from 1214 for the muster of a hundred men from Dunwich, in Suffolk, to defend the coast. In 1264, when there was an invasion scare, elaborate arrangements were made for the guarding of the coast; even the men of Cambridgeshire and Huntingdonshire, both inland counties, were brought into the system. Under Edward I public proclamations stressed the need for all to be armed and ready to deal with attacks, and in 1295 magnates and knights were commissioned to see to the guarding of the coasts. Peter of Dunwich, a royal clerk, co-ordinated the arrangements.[87] The Crown depended on the obligation, set out initially in the Assize of Arms under Henry II, on all free men to bear arms in defence of the country; this continued to be the case much later. Under Edward III special keepers were appointed to command an area six – or on occasion twelve – leagues from the coast, the *terra maritima*; they operated in conjunction with commissioners of array, though in the 1370s the Crown initiated the amalgamation of the two into a single organisation of commissions. The arrangements were elaborate, though how effective they were is not clear. Beacons were set up to warn of French attacks, and arrangements were also made to ring church bells. There was widespread alarm when Winchelsea was attacked in 1360 by a French force: it was reported that thirty-five men of the town were killed and nine women raped. The 1370s witnessed a series of French raids on English coastal ports, causing considerable damage and panic: 1377 saw particularly serious attacks and even a brief French occupation of the Isle of Wight.[88] It has to be doubted whether the defence system, relying as it did on local levies of inexperienced peasants and townsmen, could have done much to deal with a major invasion force, had the French ever been able to organise one.[89]

The common soldier

The individual common soldier is not easy to identify. Many names can be recovered: for example, records from the middle years of Edward III's reign provide lengthy lists of the names of those selected to go to fight, notably at the siege of Calais in 1346–7. These lists are long, narrow documents, originally made in two copies, and then separated as an indenture. The names of the men, Richard Moris, John Merswode, Roger Grey, Henry Clerk, John le Baker, Walter Goldfinch, William Bollard and many, many others, are evocative. These particular individuals, from little villages in Somerset and Dorset, are not commemorated in any other way. Local records that might reveal something of their family background do not survive. Their experiences in France can only be imagined, not truly recaptured, yet it was such men who formed the bulk of the English army in that most successful period.[90] It is not even possible to do more than surmise at the way in which changes in recruitment must have altered the social composition of armies. The shift from common footsoldiers to mounted archers meant that the very poorest were no longer suitable for military service; the mounted archers are likely to have been drawn from the élite of village society. The infantryman up to the early fourteenth century was likely to have been of villein status; the archer of the Hundred Years War of yeoman standing.

A very few men succeeded in rising from the ranks, but far too few for there to be any suggestion that service as an archer was a normal route to social advancement. Robert Lewer was an infantry constable towards the end of Edward I's reign, and may well have begun his career as a common soldier. He certainly never lost the rough manner of the soldier, but he found some favour in Edward II's court. His expulsion from court was demanded by the political opposition in 1311, but did not take place. He became constable of Odiham castle. When it was taken from him, he turned against the king, and was arrested, only to escape. He came back into favour briefly in 1321–2, when the king needed experienced soldiers to deal with baronial rebellion, but in 1323 he rebelled himself, and died a painful death through *peine forte et dure*, squashed by heavy weights.[91] Of the great captains of the Hundred Years War, Sir Robert Salle was said to have been of unfree origins. If the story is correct, his early military career must have been as an archer. Sir Robert Knollys may have been a Cheshire archer when he first fought in France in the company of Sir Hugh Calveley.[92] More typical was William Jodrell, who held thirteen acres in Macclesfield forest, and who served with the Black Prince in Gascony in 1355. He was given a pass allowing him to return home, the only one of such documents to survive to the present day. He prospered when he returned to Cheshire, and at the time of his death in the mid 1370s was in receipt of rents totalling £3 a year. His son became a squire, and founded a gentry family. To what extent the fortunes of the Jodrell family was founded on the profits William made on campaign is, however, no more than a matter for guesswork. William's kinsman John Jodrell had a more colourful, if less profitable, career. He also served with the Black Prince in 1355, deserted, and rejoined the army in 1356. He profited at Poitiers, taking as booty a silver salt-cellar, which he sold to the prince for £8. He pursued his career in France, rather than his native Cheshire, and the English John Jodrell was metamorphosed into Jean Jaudrell de Peytowe [Poitou].'[93]

A view of the mêlée at the battle of Poitiers in 1356. The French King John, who was captured, is shown prominently.

The common soldier underwent the most extensive transition of any who served in the medieval English army. Numbers were transformed, from relatively few in the twelfth and early thirteenth centuries to substantial hosts as large as 30,000 by Edward I's reign. The longbow was developed as a remarkably powerful and effective weapon, and in the fourteenth century many of the archers were provided with horses. There was a very real military revolution in the use of infantry, which became a key element in the English battle tactics of the fourteenth and fifteenth centuries. As will be shown in Chapter 13, the longbow proved to be a decisive weapon in the Hundred Years War on many occasions. In contrast to the cavalry, the ordinary infantry soldiers were organised into their hundreds and twenties in a highly systematic manner, which can be compared with the practice of the early modern period. They did not, however, march in step. In many cases they were provided with uniform clothing. Their wages were normally better than those they could have received as unskilled agricultural labourers, though for all that, soldiering did not become a profession for many such men in the way that it did for some of their betters.

For Wellington, the infantry were 'the scum of the earth', yet it was 'that article', the common infantryman, that was primarily responsible for his victories. The medieval common soldier, above all the archer, was of equivalent importance. Decisive as his contribution was, however, he is bound to remain a somewhat shadowy figure. The names of common soldiers are sometimes known, as is the nature of their equipment. The acute physical hardships of life in a medieval army can be imagined, even if the personalities of the men themselves are hard to recapture. There are glimpses of heroism, and of tragedy. Thomas Hostelle was badly wounded by a bolt from a springald at Harfleur in 1415, losing one eye. He nevertheless went on to fight at Agincourt, where his hand was smashed, and his body partially crushed. Despite his wounds, he lived, to petition Henry VI in 1429 to assist him, 'he being sore febled and debrused, now falle to greet age and poverte, gretly endetted'.[94]

6

Mercenaries

The mercenary has always been an unpopular figure. To fight merely for money, rather than for patriotism or some other apparently lofty purpose, has been to invite comments such as Bishop Stubbs's remark on the mercenaries of the twelfth century: 'Sprung, no doubt, in the first instance from the lands whose names they bore, they had practised for generations, it would seem, a trade of war, recruiting their numbers by the incorporation of criminals, and by the children borne to them in almost promiscuous concubinage.'[1] All too often historians write of 'mercenaries', when they mean no more than 'paid soldiers', and some definition is needed.[2] The term is better applied to professionals who fought for pay, and who were not much concerned by whose money they were taking. Hardened foreign soldiers, not subjects of the English Crown but effectively stateless, often recruited in the Low Countries, serving for gain, were mercenaries in a proper sense. Such men had a major role during the Norman period, and King John placed much reliance on them; their prominence did not, however, continue far into the thirteenth century. The Hundred Years War provided ample opportunities for mercenaries to practise their trade, although the English did more to supply than to use such men; the war also saw men of high birth and international standing serve for pay under the banners of different rulers.

The eleventh and twelfth centuries

There is considerable evidence for the use of mercenaries in the eleventh and early twelfth centuries.[3] The Conqueror hired knights for the campaign which witnessed the harrying of the north in 1069–70. The threat of invasion in 1085 was the occasion for the recruitment of large numbers of mercenaries. Rufus employed such troops, as did Robert de Bellême in his rebellion at the start of Henry I's reign. Breton mercenaries played an important part in Henry I's defence of his duchy of Normandy against the French monarchy. What sort of troops these early mercenaries were is not clear from the

One of the most famous of English mercenaries, Sir John Hawkwood, fought extensively in Italy. This memorial to him was painted by Ucello in 1436.

sources, but it seems likely that they were *milites*, mounted soldiers rather than infantry troops.

The importance of mercenaries in Stephen's reign is well known, though there are not perhaps as many specific denunciations of mercenaries in the chronicles as might be expected. The core of the army that defeated the Scots at the Battle of Standard in 1138 consisted of mercenaries under the earl of Aumale and Walter of Ghent. William of Ypres was the best known of the mercenaries of Stephen's reign; he commanded the king's household knights. A man of status, being the illegitimate son of a count of Flanders, he was surprisingly mentioned only once in the *Gesta Stephani*, where his behaviour in fleeing from Lincoln in 1141, before he had joined battle at close quarters, was condemned. The same chronicle noted as the soldiers closest to Stephen not any Flemish mercenaries, but the Oxfordshire knights Roger and William de Chesney. Elsewhere, however, the author wrote about the activities of Henry and Ralph de Caldret, Flemings, 'utterly steeped in craft and treachery', who terrorised Gloucestershire. They captured castles, plundered churches, and imposed intolerable burdens on the populace. The author also condemned 'a savage body of barbarians, who had swarmed to England in a body to serve as mercenaries, were affected neither by bowels of compassion nor by feelings of human pity over sufferings so many and so great, but everywhere in the castles they conspired with one mind to commit crime and outrage'.[4] England in a time of civil war was an attractive target to such men, and their expulsion was an important element in the restoration of order in the 1150s. Foreign troops that Henry brought with him to England in 1153 'were shamelessly guilty of murder and pillage and various abominations, and so savagely and brutally did their reckless and unblushing presumption rage without pity against all, and especially the possessions of the churches, that the barons of England shuddered in utter loathing of their company, and being unable to endure their bestial and brutal presumption any longer suggested to the duke that he should allow them to go home'.[5]

In 1159 Henry II, according to the chronicler Robert of Torigny, chose to take scutage from his tenants in England and Normandy rather than demand service in person. He therefore took on the Toulouse campaign his chief barons, and a large number of mercenary troops. The truth of this statement was questioned by J.H. Round, who pointed out that the exchequer records showed that the king received from scutage in England a total of 2,561 marks, representing the service of 1,280 knights, roughly a quarter of the full total of service due. The remaining majority of tenants, argued Round, served abroad with their quotas, and so this was not a largely mercenary army. The soundness of Round's argument was queried by Richardson and Sayles, who suggested that the tenants-in-chief may well have preferred to serve with mercenaries rather than tenants. This cannot be proved, and the evidence of the documents strongly suggests that only a minority of the army was composed of mercenaries hired by the king out of the proceeds of scutage.[6]

The rebellion of 1173–4 lured a fresh influx of mercenaries to England by the hope of rich rewards during civil war. Many men may have considered that in a difficult situation of divided and shifting loyalties mercenaries were likely to prove more reliable than Englishmen. The earl of Leicester, for example, brought a large Flemish contingent with him when he invaded in 1173, though they were soon defeated at Fornham. Whereas the earlier evidence suggests that the mercenaries were for the most part knights, many of those involved in the 1173–4 war were infantrymen, recruited in the populous cloth-making towns of the Low Countries. Jordan Fantosme in his chronicle stated that most of those brought over by the earl of Leicester 'were weavers, they do not know how to bear arms like knights, and why they had come was to pick up plunder and the spoils of war'.[7] Henry II's mercenaries were far more skilful than these levies recruited in the Low Countries by his opponents. The king's forces were extremely effective against the Breton rebels, and in particular demonstrated their abilities with an astonishingly rapid march from Rouen to Dol. This led to the surrender of Hugh, earl of Chester and of Ralph de Fougères.

A French historian, Jacques Boussard, argued that English armies were transformed under Henry II. There was, he claimed, a change from traditional hosts composed of magnates and knights serving under terms of feudal obligation to a corps of mercenaries, fighting in well-organised units on foot, capable of astonishing speed of march, well equipped both for battle and for siege warfare.[8] Some events in the war of 1173–4, such as the capture of Dol, certainly bear out Boussard's view. But his argument also depended on demonstrating that there were very large numbers of mercenaries – Flemings, Brabançons and Welsh – recruited, and this is questionable. He suggested that the maximum reached perhaps 6,000, and based this on a statement in a Pipe Roll, that William de Mandeville with the royal military household crossed the Channel in thirty-seven ships. It is most unlikely that all of this force consisted of mercenaries, and improbable that the ships carried an average of a hundred to a hundred and fifty men. Forty passengers in each vessel is a more plausible guess, with a total mercenary force of perhaps 1,000.[9] A better clue to the probable level of numbers is a Pipe Roll entry recording the issue of cloth to 166 sergeants from overseas.[10] It is hard to argue from such evidence that there was a real revolution in the way in which war was fought under Henry II, particularly given the evidence that the employment of mercenaries was hardly new in this period. Nor was it peculiar to Henry's England. The role of the mercenaries, Brabançons, Cotereaux, Catalans and others, was an international phenomenon. Many of them were younger sons, illegitimates, impoverished figures on the fringes of society, men who had few prospects in an increasingly ordered world. There was an international trade in mercenaries at this period. When the rebellion in England was over, the Flemings and Brabançons moved to the service of the emperor, Frederick Barbarossa, to campaign in Italy.[11] The outbreak of war between Richard I of England and Philip II of France provided such men with new opportunities in the west.

The extent to which Richard I, and above all John, recruited mercenaries demonstrates the success of the government in obtaining financial resources on a quite new scale. It also demonstrates the fact that John was not able to rely sufficiently on his own subjects. Mercadier, Richard I's famous mercenary captain, described his service to the king in these words: 'I fought for him strenuously and loyally. I never opposed his will, but was prompt in obedience to his orders. In consequence of this service I gained his respect and was placed in command of his army.' He first entered Richard's service in 1184, and was indeed consistently loyal until Richard's death at Chaluz. He almost certainly did not, however, accompany Richard on his crusade; perhaps it was felt that he was needed to help guard the Angevin possessions in France, or perhaps the disapproval of the Church for his profession meant that he had little enthusiasm for the journey to the Holy Land.[12]

The precise definition of a mercenary becomes difficult in John's reign. Some of the captains he employed who originated from the Angevin lands on the Continent were not true mercenaries as they were at least in a sense his own subjects. Men such as Philip Mark, Gerard d'Athée and Engelard de Cigogné, though they had military commands, were much more than mercenary soldiers, for they played a significant role in politics and administration. Savary de Mauléon led a corps of Poitevin troops in John's support, but was himself a great noble and distinguished poet, hardly a soldier of fortune. Equally, some of those recruited by money fees and other means in the Low Countries do not fit the mercenary label, if it is considered that it should not be applied to men of high social status.[13]

The exact terms and conditions of service of John's mercenaries are not known, but many knights from the Low Countries were paid retaining fees and offered other rewards. In 1202 promises of money and land were made. A writ to the Provost of Bruges in 1203 summoned all those in receipt of fees to come to the king at Easter.[14] Expectations of other profits from war were no doubt an important element in recruitment. Letters on behalf of one of John's most noted mercenaries, Louvrecaire, reveal the importance of booty. Special instructions were given to safeguard his loot as it was carried through Normandy. Martin Algais, a Spaniard in John's service, was also particularly highly regarded and well rewarded. His booty was protected, his merchants were quit of customs duties, and he was given the high office of seneschal of Gascony and Périgord. John wrote of him 'We esteem the service of Martin Algais more highly than any other person.'[15] John did not abandon his mercenary troops after the loss of Normandy. Small companies of crossbowmen were stationed in particularly strategic castles. Some of them were highly rewarded. In 1205 one called Kempe was granted land from Newcastle escheats to the value of £5 until the king could provide him with an heiress. He was stationed in Newcastle for a year, receiving from the city £22 17s 6d in livery.[16] John used mercenaries in his Irish campaigns. In 1210 the records show that he had at least some sixty-five knights from the Low Countries with him in Ireland.[17] He relied more and more on mercenaries in the political crises of the last years of the reign. This was hardly surprising given the unreliability of his own subjects. The household *Misae* roll of 1212–13 contains the names of about 115 knights from Flanders and elsewhere in the Low Countries, the highest ranked being the duke of Limburg, who were in receipt of annual fees. A group of nine were all paid fees on 18 August 1212. Later in the year Walter le Buk, who had served in Ireland in 1210, brought four knights and thirty-five sergeants from Flanders to join the king's service; he would serve again in 1216. A household record from 1212–13 names about 115 Flemish knights in receipt of money fees. In 1214 foreign soldiers began to pour into England from Poitou as well as from the Low Countries. John's fury at the news of the shipwreck of the fleet in which Hugh de Boves was bringing reinforcements from Flanders is well attested. A muster list dating from 1215 names no less than 375 knights, most of whom appear to have come from the Low Countries.[18]

There were obvious advantages in employing mercenary troops. The *Dialogus de Scaccario* of Henry II's reign suggested that there was a case for employing mercenaries since this would avoid putting the Crown's own subjects at risk.[19] Political complexities might be avoided if troops were simply hired; mercenaries might not expect to receive such extensive grants and favours as the king's own subjects. For an unpopular king such as John, mercenaries might well prove more reliable than native-born Englishmen. It is not easy to identify the special expertise of mercenaries from the sources, but their skills in the art of war must have provided good reasons for recruiting them from abroad. Practice and experience alone must have been important elements in their superiority. Clearly if mercenaries were to continue to find employment, it was important that they should fight well, maintaining their reputation. Robert of Bellême's mercenaries at Bridgnorth in 1102 felt this strongly, and considered that they were let down by the local inhabitants who wanted to surrender. Henry I acknowledged their position, and allowed them to leave the castle with their horses and arms.[20] Their use of the crossbow may well have been an important element. The author of the *Gesta Stephani* noted Robert FitzHubert's ingenious capture of Devizes castle by means of leather scaling-ladders, a 'remarkable feat'.[21] Another way that they displayed their quality was in speed and mobility: the march from Rouen to Dol took seven days, a distance of about 140 miles – no mean feat for an infantry corps.[22]

Yet there were also obvious disadvantages. The late classical author Vegetius, in the main textbook on military matters used in the middle ages, advised against the use of mercenaries, arguing that it was far better for a ruler to train his own subjects, 'than to take and reteyn under him grete foison of strange souldeours that he knoweth not'.[23] Mercenaries could prove unreliable, particularly if their pay was not forthcoming. Henry of Anjou discovered this on his expedition to England in 1147, when his troops, whom he had not paid, failed him and fled.[24] In the last resort, foreign troops were anxious to save their own skins. At the siege of Rochester in 1215 it was Savary de Mauléon, the Poitevin, who argued that the defeated garrison should not be hanged, in case he might suffer the same fate should the fortunes of war be reversed. Men would not be willing to serve John if his policies meant that their lives were put uncecessarily at risk.[25]

There is no doubt, too, that the use of mercenaries was extremely unpopular. Louis VII and the emperor Frederick Barbarossa agreed, in a treaty of the mid 1160s, to expel them, both horse and foot, from their dominions.[26] Widespread revulsion at the savagery of the Brabançons and other *routiers* led to their condemnation in the Third Lateran Council of 1179. Walter Map accused them of many horrors, including heresy.[27] It was not the taking of pay that was reprehensible. Payment of fees and wages was central to the military organisation of the period, and was not a matter for criticism. It would indeed be hard to see much distinction between a man retained by means of a money fee, and another who received his fee in land.[28] What singled out the *routiers* for condemnation was their cruelty, the lack of respect that they showed for churches (an excellent source of booty), and the fact that they seemed all too often to be quite uncontrollable. Under John, there were additional reasons for hatred of the mercenary captains. Grants of lands and offices to them were extremely unpopular. Not only did Robert of Béthune receive military command as constable of John's army; he was also promised the lands of the great earldom of Gloucester. Philip Mark was sheriff of Nottinghamshire and constable of Nottingham castle; at the very end of the reign the joint shrievalty of Lincolnshire was added.[29] In Henry III's minority Falkes de Bréauté held the sheriffdoms of six counties. At various times he had custody of the castles of Bedford, Buckingham, Cambridge, Hertford, Northampton and Oxford. John had arranged his marriage to the wealthy widow of the earl of Devon, through whose right he held Plympton in Devon as part of her dower lands. The rise of such a man could not but be seen as threatening. The low social origins of some of John's favoured mercenaries made it hard for them to become accepted. Peter de Maulay entered John's service as a household usher. Robert de Gaugi was a Flemish sergeant. Falkes de Bréauté was illegitimate, and began his career as a poor sergeant.[30] It was not simply as soldiers that these men were widely hated; they represented a threat to the social order.

The decline of mercenaries in the thirteenth century

Magna Carta in its 1215 version promised that all foreign knights, crossbowmen, sergeants and paid soldiers would be removed from the land. Mercenaries were used very little by the English after the civil war ended in 1217. In part this can be explained by the wider European context, for it was not merely in England that the bands of *routiers* vanished from the scene. The social and political circumstances that had spawned them changed, with the growing authority of the French monarchy, and greater prosperity in the regions from which the mercenaries had been drawn. In England the peace that prevailed from 1217 until Simon de Montfort's political opposition erupted into civil war in 1264 provided little opportunity for them. Memories of John's reign would have made it extremely dangerous for anyone to try to recruit such men.

In 1263 Prince Edward did return to England from France with a small force of foreign knights, mostly French. They were used on a campaign in Wales; the Marcher lords objected to their presence, and refused to assist Edward. Later in the year he garrisoned Windsor castle with these men, and it is possible that it was because of the need to pay their wages that he resorted to the desperate financial expedient of robbing the Temple in London. It was only when the mercenaries had been dismissed that he was able to win the support of an important group of magnates, among whom the Marchers were dominant.[31] Once on the throne, Edward made virtually no use of mercenary troops. The valiant corps of Gascons who fought in Wales in 1282–3 were the king's own subjects, and were hardly professional soldiers like the *routiers* of the twelfth century. A few foreign knights entered Edward's service, but men such as Pascual of Valencia, known as the *Adalid*, were hardly the equivalent of John's mercenary captains. Otto de Grandson, from Savoy, was one of Edward's most faithful companions, and never incurred the sort of opprobrium that had been attached to John's mercenaries. Rather, he was a man of considerable chivalric renown.

The Hundred Years War

The fourteenth century, like the twelfth, proved to be an age of opportunity for the mercenary soldier. The conditions in Italy, and in the France of the Hundred Years War, provided the chance for men to follow careers as soldiers of fortune. The pattern was very different from that of the twelfth century, however, for although some men who could well be classified as mercenaries served in Edward III's armies, England now became more noted as a provider of such men, rather than as a purchaser.

In the early stages of the reign, the familiar pattern of English employment of mercenaries from the Low Countries reasserted itself. Edward's own accession to the throne in 1327 was in considerable measure due to the military support provided to his mother, Isabella, by the count of Hainault, and there was a body of Hainaulters, including the chronicler Jean le Bel, present on the Weardale campaign of the same year. Edward also obtained assistance from the Low Countries in the Scottish campaigns of the 1330s; the count of Namur and his brother, and the count of Jülich were with him in 1335. The strategy of forming alliances with the duchies and counties of the Low Countries, which was adopted on the outbreak of war with France in 1337, inevitably brought men from that region into Edward's service. Walter Mauny, the most notable, was a Hainaulter who had first come to England in the service of Queen Philippa in 1327.[32] The consistent loyalty he showed to Edward III makes it hard, however, to categorise him as a soldier of fortune. The accounts for 1338–40 also reveal such names as Conrad of Esch, from Luxembourg, the Germans Winand von Dunzenkoven, Gerard de Blankenheim and Winand of Gymnich, and the French knight Goblin de Lancy, among many others. Edward's reputation was such that he even attracted into his service Italians such as Jolinetto de Visores.[33] It was, however, those from the Low Countries who were much the most important of the foreigners who served Edward. Walter Mauny and Eustace d'Aubrichecourt were the most prominent among them, and it became hard to distinguish them, and their role, from the great English captains. They served for a similar wide range of motives, rather than merely for the money. Eustace, for example, was a Hainaulter who married Philippa of Hainault's niece Elizabeth, the widow of the earl of Kent. Members of his family had served the English Crown much earlier, under John. Such a man was more a foreign favourite than a mercenary or foreign adventurer. Although he received a wardship from Edward III he obtained little land in England, but gained much wealth in war. In the 1359–60 campaign he extracted rich ransoms from the Burgundian countryside. In the years of truce after 1360 Eustace continued to fight, in France, Gascony and Ireland. In 1366 he entered the service of the king of Navarre in return for an annual fee of 1,000 *livres tournois*. Although in his deed of homage he reserved his allegiance to Edward III and the Black Prince, he did not reappear in English service.[34] Another member of the family, Sanchet, was one of the founder members of the Order of the Garter, and two of the next generation of the family, Sanchet's sons or nephews, John and Nicholas, established themselves as members of the English gentry.[35]

The Hundred Years War brought some men into English service for purely mercenary reasons. In Brittany the English captain Walter Bentley complained about the men who appeared whenever a large army landed. These were soldiers who fought for their own profit, who were of low social status, and would not fight unless they had their shilling a day and forty marks a year in fees.[36] There was not, however, the systematic employment of mercenaries as there had been under Henry II. Edward was certainly not reliant on mercenaries to fight his wars for him. In 1359, when it became known that he was planning a major expedition which was to set out from Calais, a large number of would-be mercenaries from the Low Countries, Germany and elsewhere came to join him. Edward's financial situation was such that all he could offer was a share in the profits of war; he could not afford to pay them wages, or offer to recompense them for horses lost on campaign. A few were prepared to accept such terms; the majority returned home. That is Froissart's account; the record evidence tells a rather different story, for the account book for the campaign shows that at least 450 foreign men-at-arms, nearly all from the Low Countries, to judge by their names, accepted English pay for the campaign. These were not men who regularly served Edward, and were not brought into his service as a result of major diplomatic initiatives, for all that their number included a margrave. The opportunity presented by Edward's campaign was simply too good to miss.[37]

The Hundred Years War saw the reversal of the pattern whereby the English employed mercenaries from the Low Countries and elsewhere. The expertise that men acquired serving as captains to Edward III was highly saleable. The truce made in 1360 was not welcome to many such men, who duly sought employment as mercenaries. It must have been attractive to them to be able to fight without the constraints of discipline imposed in a royal army, and to be free of an obligation to pass a proportion of booty over to the Crown. In 1361 two men were ordered to go to France to find those English subjects who were still oppressing the French, taking prisoners, and seizing castles as if it was still wartime. Those who refused to leave France within a given time were to be arrested. In 1364 the king wrote severely to Eustace d'Aubrichecourt, Robert Scot, Hugh Calveley and others, and condemned the way in which they had joined the king of Navarre in attacking France. He had gathered that 'You have entered the said kingdom with a large following and numbers of men-at-arms, archers and others, and that you are openly making war there by seizing, robbing and ransoming the people, burning and destroying buildings, violating and ravishing widows, virgins and other women, taking, occupying and detaining fortresses.'[38] Spain in the 1360s offered good chances of employment to Englishmen trained in the French wars who wanted to continue to profit from fighting. Italy, too, became a noted hunting ground for English (and other) mercenaries in this period. Sir John Hawkwood, who does not appear to have had a particularly distinguished career in the Anglo-French wars, became a great figure in Florence. With his name metamorphosed to Giovanni Acuto, he was one of the most noted of the condottieri. The growth of the free companies was an international phenomenon, to which the English made a distinctive contribution.

The use of mercenaries has sometimes been seen as a way in which warfare was transformed, though medieval historians have too often confused the use of pay with the employment of professional soldiers. The true mercenary was a product of periods of endemic warfare, and had a central and important part to play in English armies in the twelfth and early thirteenth centuries, when the Angevin monarchy was becoming reliant on a hired army of foreign mercenaries to maintain its political dominance in England. The numbers of those employed, however, should not be exaggerated. The use of mercenaries by Henry II was certainly highly effective, but Boussard's argument that this amounted to a military revolution presumes too much. Such troops were indeed skilled in war, but their superiority was not such as to transform tactics, much less strategy. King John certainly hoped for much from his mercenary captains, but his lack of success in war demonstrates that in the end he did not receive value for money from them. Recruitment from the Low Countries on a very substantial scale at the end of his reign failed to resolve the military stalemate in his favour, but did much to discredit the use of mercenaries. John's reign marked the end of a chapter; mercenaries were never to be so important again in English armies. The campaigns of Edward I were fought with little if any aid from mercenary troops; such hardened soldiers were not a vital ingredient for success. In the fourteenth century, men such as Walter Mauny and Eustace d'Aubrichecourt played a significant part in the Anglo-French conflict, and in the fifteenth century the Spaniard François de Surienne with his attack on Fougères contributed unwittingly to the final collapse of the English cause in France. But the transformation of warfare in the hands of the English in the fourteenth century was not the achievement of mercenary troops. The tactical revolution came with the use made of the longbow, and the dismounting of the men-at-arms to fight in defensive formations, both purely English developments.

Edward III shown granting Aquitaine to his son Edward
the Black Prince, in 1362.

7

Command

Ability in military command was not a quality that was admired as much in the medieval period as in other ages. Success in generalship did not necessarily bring with it fame and fortune; there were no medieval Marlboroughs, Wellingtons, or even Eisenhowers. Though successes such as the victory at Poitiers were celebrated in the streets of London, triumphs after the classical fashion were not accorded to victorious generals. Chroniclers were not even in agreement as to who was in command of the force which defeated and slew the Welsh prince Llywelyn ap Gruffudd in 1282.[1] It was rare for those responsible for victory in battle to be rewarded with earldoms; the example of Andrew Harclay, created earl of Carlisle after his services at Boroughbridge in 1322, and executed for treason in the following year, was not an encouraging one. Rulers might well be praised, as were William the Conqueror and Richard I, for their military skills. William of Poitiers even provided a favourable comparison of the former with Caesar and other Roman heroes.[2] Yet John of London, who wrote a lengthy *commendatio* on Edward I, never attempted to analyse the qualities of command that made him successful in war.[3] Individual valour was considered more worthy of praise than successful generalship.

Yet the fact that contemporary sources did not always give due credit to brilliant commanders does not mean that generalship was unimportant in the medieval period. There can be no doubt that there were great generals in the middle ages. Richard I, Edward III and Henry V all deserve high praise, and the roll of honour of commanders of lesser rank during the Hundred Years War is a long one. Nor were contemporaries completely unaware of the commander's role. Simon de Montfort emphasised one aspect of the role of a good commander, when he saw Prince Edward's forces advancing on him at Evesham and declared 'By the arm of St James, they are advancing well. They have not learned that for themselves, but were taught it by me.'[4] The consequence of the lack of effective command were noted in Edward II's reign, when the defeat of a locally-raised army in 1319 at Myton-on-Swale was explained by one chronicler: 'Not having a leader, or instruction in how to fight, they were dispersed by the enemy, and a considerable slaughter of the English followed.'[5]

Command structure

The command structure of any modern military operation is highly complex. In contrast, there was little formal organisation in a medieval English army. These armies were, for the most part, expeditionary forces which did not stay long in being. A substantial host would be divided into three or four main divisions. At Falkirk in 1298 there were four; on the Caerlaverock campaign two years later there were three. In 1327 once the army came within range of the Scots it was divided into three main battles, each with two wings of cavalry. The great army which marched full of optimism out of Calais in 1359 was similarly divided into three main divisions. Normally, one of these divisions or battles would be led by the king or whoever was in charge of the army as a whole; the others would each have their own commander, though these do not seem to have been very formal appointments. On some occasions the allocation of commanders appears to have been made on the eve of battle itself. The chronicler Jean le Bel described the way in which in the morning of 26 August 1346 Edward III gave the first battle at Crécy to his son, aided by the earls of Warwick and Stafford and other magnates, the second to Northampton, Suffolk and the bishop of Durham, while he retained command of the third. The battle itself began in the late afternoon of 27 August.[6]

Defensive operations needed a rather more permanent structure than might be required in a field army, and commanders might hold office in twelfth-century Normandy, or later in Gascony for extended periods. In the thirteenth-century Welsh marches, wardens might be appointed on an *ad hoc* basis at times when trouble threatened. In 1242 the men of Shropshire, Cheshire and Staffordshire were ordered to obey John Lestrange; John of Monmouth had authority over those from Hereford, Worcester and Gloucester.[7] Such wardenships did not become permanent, but in the north of England the wardenships of the Marches developed into a lasting institution in the later middle ages, one increasingly dominated by the great families of the Percy and Nevilles. In the fifteenth century, after Henry V's conquest of Normandy, a permanent military structure was established, with lieutenant-generals in charge of separate areas, and below them captaincies based on important castles.

Selection of commanders

Selection of a commander was often entirely straightforward, as the choice might be determined by rank and heredity. There may seem little to commend such a system, but though it certainly produced some bad results, it also yielded excellent ones. Kings were expected to lead their armies to war. In the twelfth century John of Salisbury in his *Policraticus* stressed the importance of kings having a military training, and it was highly appropriate that the treatise presented to Edward III in 1327 by one of the chancery clerks, Walter of Milemete, should have concentrated on military matters.[8] Henry III, no soldier, was present, and at least theoretically in command, in all the major campaigns of his reign. There was no question of removing a proven incompetent such as Edward II from this role; the disaster of the Bannockburn campaign was followed by the dismal failure of the siege of Berwick in 1319, and the futile expedition to Scotland of 1322, both undertaken under the king's direction. Even Henry VI was expected to command his armies. Age, of course, might excuse a ruler. Edward III did not lead an army to France after his campaign of 1359–60, though there were plans for him to do so in 1372. If the king was not available, then a close relation, preferably a son, might be expected to take his place. An elaborate indenture set out the details of the appointment of the Black Prince in Gascony in 1355. On one occasion John of Gaunt was appointed chieftain of the king's war, explicitly because the king and the Black Prince were absent.[9] In Edward III's final years, five major expeditions took place, and the king's sons took pride of place in leading them. Two were led by Gaunt, one by Thomas of Woodstock, while Edmund of Langley shared in command of another. The king's son-in-law, the earl of Pembroke, was put in charge of the force intended for Gascony in 1372. These were young men, of little experience.[10]

It was the men of the highest rank who provided the largest contingents of troops for the armies, and it was only to be expected that they would be chosen as commanders. In 1359 the biggest force was the Prince of Wales's, with 587 men-at-arms and 900 archers. Lancaster had 582 men-at-arms and 423 archers; the next largest was Warwick with eighty men-at-arms and a hundred archers. It is hardly surprising that one of the three columns of the army was commanded by the king himself, and the other two by the prince and the duke of Lancaster. In the Agincourt army the dukes and earls alone provided over a third of the total forces. It was in the final decade of the Hundred Years War that the high nobility, with the occasional exception such as John Talbot, ceased to take so active a part in the war.[11]

The effigy of Edward the Black Prince, from his tomb in Canterbury Cathedral.

The appointment of a man of the highest rank to command might, of course, be largely nominal. A person such as Henry III, who had little military expertise, would obviously rely on his subsidiary commanders to a much greater extent than could be imagined with Richard I, Edward I, or Edward III, though a wise general would always take proper counsel. When Edward I gave his son Edward command of one of the two armies operating in Scotland in 1301, effective authority was in practice exercised by the earl of Lincoln. The Black Prince was constantly guided and assisted at Poitiers in 1356 by John Chandos, a man whose worth was widely acknowledged. At Auray in Brittany in 1364 the army led by John de Montfort, duke of Brittany, was in reality commanded by Chandos. At Nájera in 1367 it was Chandos who provided advice and instruc-

The battle of Poitiers in 1356, showing the Black Prince (*right*) with his standard-bearer, and King John of France (*left*), with Geoffrey de Charny carrying the Oriflamme.

tion to the young John of Gaunt, nominally his superior. Even when he had gained much more experience, Gaunt was normally careful to take advice from his advisers and military councillors.[12]

There were no standard terms and conditions that applied to appointments to military command. An indenture made by the king with the earl of Northampton in 1345 was thoroughly comprehensive. The earl was to be chieftain and guardian in Brittany, by land and sea, with all powers of high and low justice, and the right to hear all quarrels and issues. He was to conduct expeditions against the enemy in war by land and sea, to take towns, castles and fortresses, to give and take truces, to have the power of pardoning men even in cases of life and limb. He could remove and replace officials, and the king promised to back him in all he did. The indenture also set out the financial aspects of Northampton's position; this was the part of the agreement which was perhaps of most interest and importance to the earl. In the next year, when Hugh de Hastings was appointed as English captain in Flanders, the terms were simple: he was to make expeditions and *chevauchées* against the French, and to fight and destroy them.[13] When, almost a decade later, the king appointed his son the Black Prince to command in Gascony, as royal lieutenant, the question of wages and 'money sufficient for the conciliation of the people of the country' came before such matters as the power to make truces. The prince was careful to cover himself; the king had responsibility for victualling four towns, and if they were lost, no blame would be attached to the prince. If the prince was in serious difficulties, the king promised to rescue him somehow.[14]

It has been suggested that it was not until the Hundred Years War, and above all the later fourteenth century, that command came to be exercised by real 'professionals'.[15] A hypothesis that professional generals emerged in a period of frequent campaigning is certainly tempting, but it is not convincing. It assumes that great magnates were not professional in their approach to the task of military command, yet they, above all, were the men most likely to have been trained for the task.[16] It also assumes that it was not until the later fourteenth century that the Crown was in a position to acknowledge military ability in those of lesser status, and that earlier than this it was unable to promote them to command.

The foreigners who served the English Crown were among the most professional commanders to be employed. During the Anarchy of Stephen's reign, while the earls and great magnates played a major role as military commanders, so also did the Flemish mercenary leader, William of Ypres. It was he who commanded Stephen's forces at Devizes in 1139. In the war of 1173–4, Henry II was opposed by his own eldest son, Henry, the earls of Leicester, Chester, Derby and Norfolk, Ralph de Fougères and others. Rightly suspicious of his aristocracy, Henry chose to fight the war largely by using Brabançon mercenaries. Their captains no doubt provided the necessary professional expertise, and Richard I and John's use of mercenary captains certainly does not suggest any reluctance on their part to give command to 'professional' soldiers.[17]

Edward I did not invariably appoint men of the very highest rank to head his armies. In Wales in 1282 he nominated Reginald de Grey, Roger Mortimer and Robert de Tibetot to three major commands, rather than calling on any of the earls. In the course of the campaign, he appointed Luke de Tany, not a magnate of the first rank, to take charge of a force largely composed of members of the royal household which was sent to Anglesey. Luke and his men appear to have disobeyed orders, and advanced across the pontoon bridge constructed over the Menai Straits while peace negotiations were taking place. On their return to the bridge, the Welsh attacked, and at least sixteen English knights were drowned. Luke may appear headstrong, but he had been chosen for command on grounds of ability. In the same campaign a force led by the marcher lord Roger Lestrange, an important magnate though again not of the first rank, achieved the striking triumph in the same campaign of defeating the Welsh prince Llywelyn at the battle of Irfon Bridge.[18]

Even as powerful a king as Edward I could not, however, always ignore the greatest men in the land in making military appointments. He appointed his brother, Edmund of Cornwall, to command the English troops in Gascony in 1294, although it was not until 1296 that Edmund finally arrived in the duchy, seriously ill. On his death the earl of Lincoln, Henry de Lacy, took over. It was evidently difficult to avoid appointing nobles who possessed wide acres to positions of command. The English custodian of Scotland in 1297 was Earl Warenne, a major magnate and a man of considerable experience. When Edward I entrusted him with the post, he declared, referring presumably to Scotland, 'When you get rid of a turd, you do a good job.' Warenne did not appreciate the king's coarse humour, and preferred to remain in England. The Scottish climate, he said, was bad for his health. To replace Warenne, Edward turned not to another earl, but to a man of lesser baronial status. Brian FitzAlan of Bedale was reluctant. He claimed, with some justification, that he could not afford to maintain the troop of fifty men-at-arms he would need, and that if an earl could not keep Scotland in peace, he did not see how he could do so for less money. The plan was accordingly dropped, and Warenne went on at Stirling Bridge to add his name to the inglorious roll of English commanders who have lost important battles.[19]

Edward I's impatience with another aristocratic commander was displayed in 1304, when he wrote to the earl of March: 'Know that we understand that you have delayed until now in going against our enemies, until they have gone away, and this is still the case up to last Sunday. We are greatly astonished at the slow way you are proceeding. It can only be to put into effect the words used to tell people off, "When the war was finished, then Audigier drew his sword."' The tale of Audigier to which Edward sarcastically referred was a work of remarkable obscenity, betraying an extremely unpleasant scatological obsession.[20]

Nevertheless, Edward continued to appoint great nobles to command in Scotland. In 1306 Aymer de Valence, who was soon to become earl of Pembroke, and Henry Percy were initially appointed to command the English troops in the fight against Robert Bruce. A larger army was then sent north, commanded by the Prince of Wales, the future Edward II, a man of notable military incompetence.[21] In the last stages of the reign, therefore, although Edward I had in the past often appointed men on grounds of ability, social rank outweighed military skill and experience.

The sense that what was really needed was a commander of the highest rank was again well illustrated in the reign of Edward II, when early in 1315 four local magnates, William Roos, John Mowbray, Peter de Maulay and Ralph FitzWilliam were jointly appointed as commanders to defend the north against the Scots. It was soon felt that this was inadequate, and the earl of Pembroke was sent north with other magnates. In June he was appointed keeper of the region between the Trent and Roxburgh. In August, however, the earl of Lancaster, by far the wealthiest magnate in the realm, was named as king's lieutenant and 'superior captain' of all the English forces in the north.[22] Lancaster, unfortunately, for all his status was a man of no military ability whatsoever.

In choosing commanders, kings had to consider many factors. Questions of honour and pride were inevitably often bound up with the question of command. Before the battle of Auray, Sir Hugh Calveley was upset at being asked by Chandos to take command of the rearguard. He refused to do so, for was he not as good as any other? Chandos argued, and eventually said that either Hugh must do it, or he would undertake the task himself. Calveley then agreed.[23] Social position was closely tied up with the sense of honour, and it was becoming harder, not easier, in the later middle ages to appoint men who were not of the highest social standing to command. A council memorandum of the 1340s emphasised the importance of status in clear terms. 'Item, that the earl of Arundel be made Admiral, because no one could do it unless he is a great man' (*un grant*).[24] It was not easy to override social distinction in making military appointments, and a lack of distinguished ancestry could result in difficulties, even for a man of immense military experience. When Robert Knollys was appointed to command a force of 4,000 men in 1370, he clearly had considerable personal doubts, for he proceeded to associate Alan Buxhull, Thomas Grandison and Thomas Bourchier with him, agreeing to share the responsibilities and profits of command. The captains in the force, in an unusual procedure, sealed letters in which they promised to obey Knollys and his associates, to provide aid and counsel, and to do nothing in prejudice of the expedition. Such precautions did not work. Knollys faced considerable problems on this *chevauchée*, with continual disagreements from John Minsterworth, who commanded the largest knightly retinue in the force. Things went so far that Minsterworth took himself and his men off, deserting Knollys' expedition, which soon disbanded. After Knollys returned to England, accusations regarding his conduct of the expedition were brought against him. He was, however, able to clear himself, while Minsterworth was found guilty of treason.[25] It seems very likely that Knollys' lack of breeding was held against him: he had probably started his military career as a mere bowman. Sir John Fastolf put the ideal requirements for a commander briefly in 1450. He should be 'a chevetaine of noble and grete astate, havyng knouledge and experience of the werres'.[26]

In the Wars of the Roses command continued normally to be given to noblemen. Some men of low birth, but of great military expertise,

Robert Knollys riding out in 1370 at the head of his
chevauchée, carrying a baton as a symbol of command,
accompanied by Thomas Grandison.

did have significant roles, but more as advisers to magnates than as independent commanders. A squire, Lovelace, reputed as 'being the most expert in warfare in England', was made captain of Kent and steward of the earl of Warwick's household. Andrew Trollope, who rose to knighthood from the ranks, was another upon whom Warwick depended for military advice. Commanders of urban levies were often men of no great social standing, and popular rural rebellion could throw up leaders of low rank. Major command, however, was reserved to the great men as was normal. As they dominated politics, so they dominated war.[27]

Household knights

Since the royal household played such a major role in warfare, it is not surprising to find that the more important of the household knights might be entrusted with significant commands. At Tinchebray in 1106 the commanders of the main divisions of Henry I's army were household men such as William de Warenne. Members of the household were given the key commands in Normandy during the rebellion of 1123–4. At Bourgthéroulde in 1124 Odo Borleng, a

household man of obscure origins, played a leading part in the battle. Examples could be multiplied: Ralph Rufus, another man of no great social status, was one of Henry's household knights entrusted with command on at least two occasions.[28]

Household knights continued to play a significant role in the command structure. In 1206 Henry de Pomeroy, almost certainly a household knight, was a constable in command of the knights of Devon and Cornwall, sent by King John to Poitou.[29] In the mopping up operations at the close of the Barons' Wars in the 1260s, a significant part was played by Roger Leyburn, who was prominent in Prince Edward's household.[30] As king, Edward relied extensively on his household knights, notably when it was a question of sending relatively small forces on raids against the Scots. In 1304 John Botetourt, a household banneret, led a raid into Nithsdale with 130 cavalry and 1,770 infantry, while at about the same time Robert Clifford and William Latimer, also household bannerets, joined John de Segrave in a similar expedition into Selkirk Forest. In 1307 Botetourt again commanded a raid against the Scots, as did another experienced commander, Robert Clifford.[31] What the sources do not reveal as clearly is the probability that it was men of this type who served Edward as his headquarters staff officers during the major royal campaigns. The role of the steward of the household in particular must have been very important, as he was in charge of the corps of household knights.

It would perhaps not have been politic to appoint household knights to major commands in the fourteenth century, but Edward III solved this problem at one simple stroke in 1337. He simply appointed the four most important bannerets of the household, William Montague, Robert Ufford, William Clinton and William Bohun, to earldoms. Such a step could hardly be repeated, and at the end of his reign the role of royal household knights in war was clear. Out of ten knights employed as captains in the years after the renewal of the Hundred Years War in 1369, six were royal knights, and a seventh entered the household under Richard II.[32]

Churchmen

The clergy were forbidden to take up arms. Among the articles promulgated at the council of Westminster in 1138 was an explicit statement that it was 'ridiculous and inconvenient' for them to do so, and the authority of Pope Nicholas II and even St Paul was cited. The view of canon lawyers was less extreme; bishops could provide soldiers for the army, exhort men to fight a just war, and travel with the army, though they could not themselves fight. In practice they

Odo, bishop of Bayeux at the battle of Hastings, shown in the Bayeux Tapestry holding a large baton.

were not automatically excluded by their cloth from military command.[33] The Bayeux Tapestry vividly shows the part played by the Conqueror's half-brother Odo of Bayeux at Hastings. Anthony Bek, bishop of Durham, was one of the commanders of the English army at Falkirk in 1298. William Melton, archbishop of York, had little success at Myton in 1319, but in 1346 Archbishop Thoresby was one of those heading the army that defeated the Scots at Neville's Cross. Henry Despenser, bishop of Norwich from 1370 to 1406, provides a notorious example of a bishop who was determined to exercise military command. Success in putting down a few disheartened peasants in the aftermath of the revolt of 1381 went to his head, and in 1383 he insisted on leading a crusading expedition to Flanders. It was dignified with the crusading title, since it was directed against supporters of the schismatic Clement VII. The ill-equipped army soon showed that it was deficient in true leadership. There was no proper discipline exercised, and Despenser failed to win the trust of his lay captains. Both bishop and captains under him suffered impeachment in parliament on their return to England from a thoroughly unsuccessful expedition.[34]

The somewhat worldly clerics who served at the heart of royal administration, in the royal household, found it hard to resist the temptation to take up arms. In Edward I's reign, the more important clerks of the king's wardrobe, such as the keeper, John Droxford,

The warlike seal of Thomas Hatfield, bishop of Durham from 1345–81. Bishops' seals were normally oval, not round.

appeared on campaign with retinues fully the equal of those of the household knights. Thomas Hatfield, promoted to the see of Durham after having been one of Edward III's household clerks, was put in command of the rearguard of the English army which invaded Normandy in 1346.[35] His splendid seal shows him as a warrior, not as a pastoral leader.

There was inevitable criticism of military clerks. At the battle of Falkirk in 1298, Anthony Bek, bishop of Durham, commanded one of the English divisions. As they approached the Scots, they had to swing east, to avoid a loch which was between them and the enemy. Bek had trouble holding his men back. 'It is not for you, bishop, to teach us about knightly matters, when you should be saying mass. Go and celebrate mass and leave us to get on with our military affairs.' That was the view of Ralph Basset of Drayton, who with his colleagues ignored Bek's orders.[36] A little later, Ralph Manton, the cofferer of the wardrobe, was killed when on campaign with John de Segrave in 1303. He was severely rebuked, just before his death, by the Scot Simon Fraser (a former household knight of Edward I), for appearing mailed and armed, rather than wearing clerical dress.[37]

Hereditary positions

The king did not have a completely free hand in deciding who should play a part in the command of his armies. The positions of constable and marshal of England were the subject of hereditary claims. The early history of the office of constable is obscure and controversial, and research has advanced surprisingly little since the days of Madox, writing in 1769, who commented 'But 'tis not my purpose to be curious about the Succession or Descent of this Office. I would much rather (if I could) discover the Powers which belonged to it in the ancient Times. But that is a subject too obscure for me to illustrate.' There were probably four constables in the royal household in the Norman period, who had military responsibilities. Walter of Gloucester was one, who attested charters as constable from at least 1114 until his death in about 1130. His son Miles duly became a constable; he deserted Stephen for Matilda in 1139, and continued to act as constable in her service. It was from one of his co-heirs that the title descended, as constable of England, to the Bohun family.[38] In the hands of a family of comital status, the position could no longer remain as a household office. It developed, in a way which is far from clear, into a national post, with formal responsibilities in the coronation ceremony, and claims to a very significant role in military affairs. Humphrey de Bohun, earl of Hereford from 1336 to 1361, was for some reason (probably physical incapacity) unable to campaign. In 1338 he therefore renounced his office of constable in favour of his younger brother William, who had been made earl of Northampton in the previous year. The office came back to the earldom of Hereford when William's son suceeded his uncle in 1363.[39]

The marshal's post was in origin less important than the constable's. Like the constables, the function of the marshals in the Norman period was within the royal household. The *Constitutio Domus Regis*, or *Establishment of the King's Household*, of about 1135 gave the marshal responsibility for keeping tallies as a record of gifts and allowances, and as a record of other expenditure, but more important from a military point of view was the marshal's duty of looking after the horses. He had to provide them with fodder, and may as a result have had wider responsibilities in war for organising supplies. Much later, in 1236, one of the duties of the marshal of England was stated as being the prevention of tumult in the royal household; later in the thirteenth century the marshals of the household had prime responsibility for maintaining discipline.[40]

One of the first known marshals, Gilbert the Marshal, died in about 1130. His son, John FitzGilbert, played a significant role in the warfare of Stephen's reign. His decision to support Matilda no doubt increased the prestige of his office when the Angevin cause was eventually successful. When the office came to William Marshal, earl of Pembroke, in 1194, after the death of his elder brother, it was in the hands of a man of considerable military experience and steadily growing prestige. From being a household post, the marshalship had become the possession of a great earl, the same pattern as applied to the constableship. From a household position it developed into that of marshal of England. After the collapse of the Marshal dynasty in 1245, the office came into the hands of the Bigod earls of Norfolk. When Roger Bigod died in 1306 leaving no direct heirs, the office remained with the earldom of Norfolk. From 1338, the earldom was in the hands of a woman, Margaret, daughter of Thomas of Brotherton and granddaughter of Edward I. This enabled Edward III to make appointments to the post of marshal as he wished, rather than being constrained by the hereditary principle. The king made the earl of Salisbury marshal in 1338, and on his death in 1344 the position went to the earl of Warwick. In 1346 it was he who acted as marshal of the army which was victorious at Crécy.[41]

What was the reality of the claims put forward by the holders of these offices? The earliest evidence for the military role of a constable is that of Henry de Pomeroy, who commanded one detachment of household troops in the Bourgthéroulde campaign of 1124.[42] John FitzGilbert, 'scion of hell and root of all evil' as one chronicler saw him,[43] played a major part in the warfare of Stephen's reign, but nothing he did can be specifically identified as being connected to his office of marshal. As for his son, the great William Marshal, the conclusion of one biographer is that 'the office had become largely an honorary and ceremonial one', while another suggests that 'the one aspect of the Marshal's office in which he may have kept some active concern was the keeping of the records of service done in the royal army'.[44] In Richard I's crusading army, men with judicial responsibility were appointed to assist in keeping order, but there is no evidence of hereditary posts being of significance.[45] There is evidence that William Marshal's nephew John played an active role as marshal, for in 1202 in Normandy King John issued letters ordering all his knights and sergeants to be obedient to John, his marshal, and to perform their service as he instructed. John was the son of William Marshal's elder brother John, and in strict hereditary terms the office should have been his, but it had been granted by royal charter to William in 1200.[46] Later in John's reign, in 1214, a draft ordinance stated that the king should have two marshals from each of his lands, England, Normandy, and his other French possessions. The English marshals were named as Ralph de Bray and Ralph de Normanville: not even lip-service was paid to the claims of the Marshal family.[47]

Arguments from silence are dangerous, but it seems unlikely that the marshals and constables of the twelfth and early thirteenth centuries did much more in war than assist in the organisation of the household troops, and probably also maintain records of the performance of feudal service. Towards the end of the thirteenth century, however, the role of these offices was reinterpreted by their holders, and there was much argument about them.

In 1277 the earls of Norfolk and Hereford performed their function of registering feudal service at the outset of the campaign. The two men remained with the main royal army during the campaign. In 1282, however, Edward's initial plan was to use a paid army. At the council at Devizes in April where the first decisions about the war were taken, the earl of Hereford formally requested that he should be given the proper perquisites due to his office of constable. This suggests that there was some argument over his role. The form of summons was changed in May to a traditional feudal one; it seems very possible that further protests from Hereford may have prompted this.[48] Hereford was not in fact with the main royal army in 1282, as he was in the south, defending his lordship of Brecon. He therefore appointed his uncle, John de Bohun, to act on his behalf; later in the campaign Hugh de Turberville became deputy constable. Norfolk on the other hand was present, and with Geoffrey de Geneville to help him, drew up records of all those performing military service.[49]

It is perhaps indicative of Edward's attitude to the great military offices held by Norfolk and Hereford that the two men did not receive massive grants of land in Wales once the campaign was over, in contrast to Earl Warenne, the earl of Lincoln, Reginald de Grey and others. In 1294 Edward had no truck with hereditary claims, and appointed a household knight, Roger de Molis, to act as marshal in Wales. Norfolk was sent to south Wales to fight there, while the royal army advanced from the north. He clearly protested at the way that his rights were being ignored, with fees due to him being paid into the royal wardrobe. Edward was compelled to issue a formal letter promising that Molis's appointment as marshal would not form a precedent for the future.[50] In Gascony at this time, the post of marshal was given to Ralph Gorges, almost certainly by royal appointment rather than through nomination by the earl of Norfolk. This may have been acceptable, as it most unlikely that the earl would have wanted to serve in Gascony.[51] On the Scottish campaign of 1296 the office was in the hands of John Lovel, acting in place of the earl, and very probably appointed by him as his deputy. It was in 1297 that matters came to a head, with the demand by the king that the marshal and constable should register the troops which had mustered in London in response to a summons of questionable constitutional validity. Refusal by the two led to their temporary replacement by household men, Geoffrey de Geneville and Thomas de Berkeley. Norfolk and Hereford led opposition to the king and his plans in 1297, and remained in England rather than accompany Edward to Flanders. In 1298, the political crisis at home over, the two men accompanied Edward on the Falkirk campaign. At the battle, they were in the forefront of the advance, along with the earl of Lincoln: no doubt they claimed that their hereditary posts entitled them to this honour.[52] After the battle there were arguments over the distribution of lands in Scotland, and when the army reached Carlisle and further campaigning was discussed, the earls refused to participate further. In October 1298 Edward asked the officials of the exchequer to look up the rights and duties of the marshal and constable: he was obviously anxious to counter the arguments put forward by the two men. In reply, all he received was an unhelpful statement of the fees as set out in the *Constitutio Domus Regis*.[53] The earl of Hereford, Humphrey de Bohun, died in 1298; his successor became the king's son-in-law, and the question of the office of constable caused no further controversy. Indeed, for the 1301 campaign Bohun made over to the king his claims to booty. Roger Bigod, earl of Norfolk, took no further part in the Scottish wars after 1298. The question of the marshalship was settled by his appointment of John de Segrave as his deputy; after discussions in 1301 Segrave was paid £100 in place of the perquisites to which the office entitled him.[54] Edward had been unable to counter the claims that the marshal and constable had made, but by the final campaigns of his reign they were of relatively little significance.

Treatises setting out the functions, and more particularly the rights, of the constable and marshal were written in the late fourteenth century; it is hard to determine the extent to which they depict contemporary or past practice, or the unrealisable aims of their holders.[55] The marshal was entitled to payments from all who did homage to the king, and in wartime received all the fines levied in his court, save in the case of the king's household knights and squires. He also had a right to all particoloured beasts taken as booty. The constable had an equivalent right to all beasts without horns, pigs, and unshod horses, and was to receive 4*d* weekly from all merchants and whores following the army. The two men had to organise billeting, the setting up of camp and sentry duty. The marshal had the task of registering the performance of feudal service, and a right to attend councils of war. He had an obligation to maintain order in the army.[56] It is possible that there was evidence which is now lost about the role of the constables and marshals in the Norman period. It is also possible that they were drawing on continental parallels: a tract on the duties and rights of the marshal in the kingdom of southern Italy and Sicily has similarities to the English tract on the marshal, which extend much further than a common right to take fines every Saturday from prostitutes following the court and army. The Sicilian document, of course, may itself look back to Norman origins.[57]

The dispute at the battle of Bannockburn between the earl of Gloucester and the earl of Hereford over who had the right to lead the vanguard reveals another claim that was made. The marshal and constable had a responsibility to prevent desertion; in 1333 Simon Lovel was imprisoned for departing from Simon Warde's retinue in Scotland without permission of the king, the steward and marshal, and Warde himself.[58] In France, after Henry V's conquest of Normandy, it was possible to appoint marshals of France as well as of England. John Talbot was given such a position in 1436. His duties were to undertake military operations that would ensure the defeat of the French, to organise muster and review of the English troops, and to exercise the judicial role of the marshal.[59] There was certainly no question of the traditional posts being regarded as obsolete in the dying days of the Hundred Years War. John Fastolf, in 1450, advising on an expedition to France, argued that the commander should 'have two lordes for to be his constable and marshal of his hooste, welle ensured knightis, that afore this tyme have had grete knoulage and experience in the werris, to gouverne his hooste in executing of the lawes of armes and shoche ordenaunces as shal be thoughte most necessarie'.[60]

Another office which had a hereditary character was that of royal standard-bearer. Edward of Salisbury performed this function at the battle of Brémule, but under Henry II the post was held by Henry of Essex. He, however, was charged with treason by a rival in 1163; he had mistakenly thought that the king himself had been killed when his army was caught in a Welsh ambush in 1157, and had cast away his standard. The case went to trial by battle, and Henry lost: he ended his days as a monk at Reading Abbey. It seems likely that with his disgrace, his office fell into abeyance.[61]

Clerks and paymasters

A commander cannot act in isolation. Not only was support and advice needed from his immediate subordinates, but administrative backing was required if the wishes of the commander were to be carried out. The clerks who were in charge of paying the troops and organising the collection and distribution of supplies were a vital element in the command structure of a medieval army. Although some men were highly experienced in this role, the Crown did not have specialists to call upon. It was, in most cases, the clerks of the royal household who were employed in times of campaign to become, in effect, staff officers. It was less easy to use clerks employed in the exchequer or the chancery, for those departments still had to be run and staffed in times of war as much as in peacetime; the royal household, in contrast, was largely turned over to the concerns of war. The chamber, and above all the wardrobe, were the departments of the household whose clerks were most employed in the business of paying troops and drawing up records of the process, checking horse valuations, ordering supplies, and all the multifarious administrative tasks that were an integral part of campaigning. If the king himself did not take part in an expedition, then it might be necessary to set up a separate administrative structure outside the royal household, as was the case with the army that defeated David Bruce at Neville's Cross in 1346, while the king was on campaign in France.

Until John's reign, the records reveal little of the operations of the royal household, and so little of the administrative arrangements for royal campaigns. The great series of pipe rolls demonstrate the way in which local administrative officers, above all the sheriffs, assisted in the organisation of war, but the central role played by the royal chamber and its staff remains largely in darkness. Household records from John's reign show, for example, that on the Irish campaign of 1210 Richard Marsh was the most important clerk involved; he was the leading official in the king's chamber, and would in 1214 be promoted to become chancellor. He helped to supervise the payment of prests, or advances, to the troops on many occasions, and no doubt performed many other administrative duties.[62]

It is not until the reign of Edward I that the full scale of the administrative effort involved in war becomes clear from the records. An extraordinary quantity of evidence survives, testifying to the detailed work that was done by the clerks of the wardrobe. Accounts were kept in great detail, receipts written and issued, and letters sent back to the exchequer and chancery at York. Accounting was done on a special counting table, using small tokens, pushed up and down columns after the fashion of an abacus. The leading household officials, the keepers of the wardrobe, the cofferers and controllers, all became highly experienced in the arts of war. John Droxford, keeper from 1295, and his senior campaigned with substantial retinues just as if they were bannerets or knights. The work of these officials was impressive; the vast quantity of parchment books, rolls, bills and dockets that survive bear vivid testimony to the scale of the task that faced them.

Very similar administrative methods underpinned the main campaigns led by Edward III in person. The wardrobe account book of William Norwell, keeper of the wardrobe, which covers the period from 1338 to 1340, is very similar to those of John Droxford's keepership under Edward I. In addition to the wardrobe men, two chamber clerks, Thomas Hatfield and William Kilsby, were important in the administration of the early stages of the French war, when Edward spent so many frustrating months in the Low Countries with little action taking place. Kilsby had a retinue of one banneret, two knights and twenty-eight men-at-arms – a most warlike cleric.[63] In 1359 the keeper of the wardrobe, William Farley, headed the administration of the king's army on the great expedition which marched to Rheims in the vain expectation that Edward III would be crowned king of France. He was, as Tout pointed out, 'no mere supervisor of household accounts, but the paymaster of an army and of a diplomatic service'. William Clee, his controller, and Thomas Brantingham, cofferer, assisted in a task which seems to have been too complex even for these experienced men. Farley's account book is much less clear, and much less satisfactory, than the earlier ones of Norwell or Droxford. Entries run confusingly on one from another, and although the exchequer accepted the accounts when they were audited, they have obvious deficiencies.[64]

When the king himself headed a campaign, the administrative machinery of his household was readily available to him. Other expeditions needed to have individual arrangements made. In the French war of 1294–7 special paymasters were appointed for the English troops in Gascony. Peter of Aylesford with his controller, Thomas of Cambridge, clerks without extensive experience in royal administration, performed the task; on Aylesford's death John Sandale, a man who knew how war in Wales had been organised, took his place. English forces in Scotland in 1297 had Walter of Amersham as paymaster, with Robert Heron as his controller.[65] Later, during the Hundred Years War, it did not prove necessary for the Crown to appoint clerks in this way. The system of contract service meant that magnates and captains had to provide their own administrative support, just as the Black Prince employed John Henxteworth, controller of his household, to be his paymaster for the expedition of 1355–6, or Henry, Prince of Wales, his controller, John Spencer, when he fought in Wales in 1404.[66] The Crown's records from the mid fourteenth century do not give the same impression of a high level of bureaucratic management of war as those of Edward I's day. Royal clerks were no longer appointed to see to the day-to-day financial administration of expeditionary forces, and records do not therefore provide the same level of detailed information. It was only with the need to organise forces for the defence of Normandy after Henry V's conquest of the duchy that an elaborate administrative machinery was once again required.

Orders and discipline

The sources are largely silent on the question of how command was actually exercised: how were orders actually transmitted? Jean le Bel in his account of the Weardale campaign of 1327 provides some information. Trumpets were used to give basic orders, as bugles were later. Instructions were issued that at the first blast, everyone should saddle their horses and prepare them. At the second blast, everyone should arm himself, and at the third, everyone was to mount without delay. When the young king himself was paraded in front of his troops, he ordered them not to advance until the order to do so was given. When that order did come, it was to move ahead at a slow pace, *le petit pas*. The formation into three divisions was maintained as the men moved forward.[67] Trumpets were clearly the best means of giving general commands. Richard I's plan at Arsuf in 1191 was for the attack on the Saracens to be signalled by six trumpets. It was by means of trumpets that the Black Prince called his men to arms before the battle of Nájera in 1367. Nor were trumpets limited to giving the simplest of orders; it was by their means that at Agincourt the order to kill the French prisoners was disseminated.[68] In addition to the orders given by trumpet there must have been an efficient system of using couriers to pass instructions to the various commanders so that they could make them known to the troops.

It might be difficult to ensure that orders were obeyed. In 1300 Edward I was advancing into Galloway. Scottish forces were on one side of an estuary, English on the other. An archery duel took place, and then at low tide some of the English foot crossed, to engage the Scots more closely. The king's column, and that led by Earl Warenne, crossed by a ford, but when the force led (at least nominally) by Prince Edward moved up, it halted, watching the archery exchange. The Scots formed up in line of battle, and Edward, nervous of the reception they were preparing for him, decided to recross the ford. He ordered the earl of Hereford to recall his infantry who had made the crossing. Orders were issued forbidding anyone else to cross the estuary. When the infantry saw the earl approaching, however, they thought that he was bringing them reinforcements, and attacked the Scots all the more vigorously. The English knights on the bank, seeing the earl go across, followed his example, as did all the prince's force. Edward promptly ordered his trumpets and horns to be blown, mounted his horse, and hurried to the water's edge, as did Warenne. The Scots promptly fled, 'like hares before greyhounds'.[69] The account shows the way in which commands were given by the king to his leading commanders, the use of horns and trumpets to announce an advance, and the extreme difficulty in a battlefield situation for a commander to make his real intentions understood.

At the taking of Caen in 1346, Edward III drew up his forces in good order, and sent men forward to reconnoitre. The army, however, attacked the bridge leading into the main part of the town 'without command and without order', though, fortunately for them, with success. The earl of Warwick, the marshal, had been ordered to sound the retreat, but the command was not obeyed by the uncontrollable infantry.[70] In 1428 when the earl of Salisbury besieged Jenville-en-Beauce, the English troops, infuriated by the lack of progress of discussions between their leaders and the French, attacked the town on their own initiative, without orders. The atrocities they committed when they forced an entry were too horrific for the chronicler's demure pen.[71]

The maintenance of discipline was an important element in the command of an army. The dangers if this was not done were obvious. In 1137 Stephen invaded Anjou, his army reinforced by Flemish mercenaries. A major dispute took place between the Normans and the Flemings, over a stolen cask of wine. Such was the dissension in the army that the king was forced to abandon the expedition.[72] National differences were a common reason for a breakdown of discipline. A distribution of wine to the Welsh infantry before the battle of Falkirk proved to be a major mistake, resulting in fighting among the troops, and the withdrawal of the Welsh from the English camp. They did not join in the battle until the final stages, when it was clear that the Scots had lost.[73] Similar problems threatened when the English army gathered at York prior to the Weardale campaign of 1327. A game of dice resulted in a major riot between the English archers and the Hainaulters who had come to take part in the expedition, following their count's support for the invasion of Isabella and Mortimer in 1326. The Hainaulters feared for their lives, but in the event, it was 416 Lincolnshire archers who were killed.[74] Ill-disciplined troops might attack their allies with as much ferocity as the enemy; infantry sent to reinforce the English troops in Gascony in 1325 promptly attacked the citizens of Bordeaux, killing and plundering goods of an estimated value of £10,000.[75]

Full ordinances setting out rules and regulations governing the behaviour of soldiers are surprisingly rare. William I and Henry I took measures which limited the excesses of their household troops.[76] Richard I issued decrees at Chinon for the sailors who were to take him on crusade: these dealt severely with those who murdered, stole and swore. The death penalty was imposed for murder; an attack which drew blood was to be punished with loss of a hand; a simple assault by a triple dipping in the sea. Fines were to be paid by those who swore, and thieves would be tarred and feathered. Later regulations for the army dealt with some of the problems of victualling by measures controlling the sale of bread. Richard was clearly a fierce disciplinarian. When he arrived, en route for his crusade, at Messina in Sicily, one of his first actions was to erect a gallows outside his camp. When battle seemed likely, he announced that anyone who ran away on foot should lose a foot, and that any knight who deserted would be stripped of the belt which signified his status. The line of battle was to be drawn up following military discipline.[77] A set of draft military decrees under John emphasised that nothing was to be taken from the Church without prompt payment: this surely reflected the problems John was having with the Church, and was an attempt to deal with criticism.[78]

It might be expected that Edward I, in whose reign so much was done to reorganise the workings of the law in a great series of statutes, would have produced military regulations, but none survive. He did, however, attempt to regulate tournaments. Edward III, when he landed in France in 1346, forbade attacks on the elderly, women and children, robbery of churches, and burning of buildings. A reward of forty shillings was promised to anyone who brought those guilty of such offences before the army authorities.[79] It is doubtful whether this had much effect. Henry V was a far stronger disciplinarian than Edward III. He issued various disciplinary ordinances, at Harfleur in 1415, at Mantes in 1419 and at Rouen in 1421. These were based on ordinances issued by Richard II at Durham for his Scottish expedition of 1385. Attacks on churches, women and priests were condemned. Common soldiers were not to attack castles or fortifications without being ordered to do so by someone of status. There were instructions for the taking of prisoners, and the payment of a third of captured booty to commanders. Men on the march were not to break ranks, under penalty of losing horse and harness.[80] Henry's chaplain told a story about the Englishman who stole a pyx, which he thought was made of gold (though in reality it was copper gilt), who was promptly tried by the king and hanged. On the eve of the battle of Agincourt, Henry ordered anyone who made a noise to be punished: gentleman were to lose horse and harness, and anyone of the rank of yeoman or below, their right ear.[81] A strongly puritanical note was struck by Henry; anyone who found a whore in the camp could take all her money, drive her off, and even break her arm. Regulations preventing the discussion of old feuds and prohibitions against arguments based on nationality – Welsh, Irish or French – suggest some of the problems which existed in the army. Foraging was regulated, especially in conquered territory: there was a major difference between Henry's war of conquest in Normandy, and the *chevauchées* of Edward III's day, for it was important that the local population should not regard the English with hatred.[82]

Unfortunately, only one roll survives recording actual cases from a military court. This is from Edward I's Scottish expedition of 1296, and the record gives unique glimpses of daily life in a medieval army. The cases do not reveal more than occasional incidents of insubordination, such as that when John de Averinthe refused to perform watch and ward, or go on a foray when ordered to do so. Another dispute took place over a sum of fifty shillings, intended as wages to pay footsoldiers, which was misappropriated. The impression is, however, that military discipline was reasonably well maintained. A man who dared to go in advance of the banner of the constable and marshal, contrary to a proclamation, was duly arrested. Two men who left their column to go plundering were imprisoned. One vintenar was arrested for refusing to come to a muster; he, remarkably, was put to *peine forte et dure* (this consisted of being pressed by heavy weights, with a diet of bread and water on alternate days), and survived.

The soldiers on the 1296 expedition were, not surprisingly, responsible for a number of criminal acts. One group of seven men was found guilty of arson attacks on churches and houses in England, and of numerous robberies. Property of various kinds might be mislaid or stolen: there were the cases of Matthew de Forneys, whose grey horse ran away from its groom at Berwick, and of Roger de Beauchamp's vanished (and no doubt favourite) cap. An interesting case came up because a group of four men agreed to pool their profits from plunder. They sold goods worth £110 to the royal treasurer, but one of their number was then accused of keeping the lion's share for himself. It was not always easy to send back booty to England: Hugh Despenser acquired 966 cattle and two warhorses in the course of the campaign, but they were detained in the Borders as Despenser's men were taking them south. One warhorse died, and 166 of the cattle were not restored to Despenser. Billeting was an issue which caused occasional trouble, as men competed for comfortable lodgings. There might also be problems over food supplies: a few men were fined for unlawful profiteering. The roll shows that there was considerable tension between the English and Welsh in Edward I's army, with a particularly serious dispute taking place when the army was in Edinburgh. One English soldier was hanged for murdering a Welshman, although others were acquitted on similar charges.[83]

There is no single model for the successful commander. There are those who lead from the front, displaying charismatic qualities; there are those who direct operations from the rear, making up in organisational skill what they lack in obvious, if foolhardy, example. The medieval period can provide its examples of commanders exposing themselves to danger in the front line or in the midst of the mêlée. At Hastings, Duke William of Normandy was evidently in the thick of things when rumours spread of his death; by raising his helmet he was able to identify himself to his men. Henry I was hit twice on the head at Brémule, and although his helmet and hauberk held firm, he nevertheless suffered a wound, cut by his own armour. At Lincoln in 1141 King Stephen fought to the end with great bravery. When his sword broke, he continued fighting when a Danish battle-axe was put into his hands, and surrendered to the earl of Gloucester only when it was clear that all was lost.[84] Richard I deliberately risked his own life on many occasions, for troops will respect and follow a man prepared to die on their behalf. When the Hospitallers charged at Arsuf contrary to his orders, he had the sense to abandon carefully worked-out plans, and charged directly into the enemy lines. His death came when he exposed himself too readily to danger at Chaluz, and was mortally wounded by a crossbow bolt. At the siege of Stirling in 1304 even the more prudent Edward I narrowly escaped death when he rode too close to the walls of the castle, within easy crossbow range. Impetuosity, however, was not always praised. Gerald of Wales, describing John de Courcy, pointed out that in his headstrong eagerness for battle he abandoned the self-control required for real leadership, acting more as knight than as commander, throwing away the opportunity for victory in his eagerness to win.[85] The wise commander might hold himself back in a position where he could hope to control events. At Crécy Edward III set up his headquarters in a windmill, from where he could see the course of the action. For all that the Black Prince declared at Poitiers 'You shall not see me turn my back this day, but I will always be among the foremost',[86] he did not enter the thick of the fray until a fairly late stage.

There were many ways to win the respect and affection of troops. Edward I, besieged by the Welsh in his brand-new castle of Conwy early in 1295, showed some understanding when the wine ran out. All that was left was one small keg, reserved for the king himself. He, however, declared that in an emergency everything should be shared equally. The gesture was a small one, but it was well calculated.[87] The story told by Froissart of how Edward III ordered his minstrels to play a German dance, and persuaded John Chandos to sing along with them, as his fleet approached the Spanish vessels before the battle of Les Espagnols sur Mer in 1351, shows his grasp of how to keep up morale. So, perhaps, did the king's ordering of wine as he and his men armed for the fight.[88] Speeches before battles, and more effectively, a tour of the lines of men, nervous and eager, drawn up ready for an enemy attack, were obvious ways of boosting morale.

The best medieval commanders certainly were ready to display personal courage, but did not risk all in an attempt to win glory. Successful generalship, in the middle ages as in other periods, demanded a range of qualities: strategic and tactical awareness, boldness in decision-making, persuasiveness, bravery and a measure of good fortune. The tools available to men such as Edward I or the Black Prince were limited. Communications were difficult, command structures were simple almost to the point of non-existence. Given the problems that they faced, the achievements of medieval commanders were remarkable.

8

Strategy and Intelligence

In 1435 Sir John Fastolf wrote a report on how the war in France should be conducted. Sieges were to be avoided, as they were not an effective means of achieving conquest. Instead, two captains should be appointed, to campaign from June through to November, burning and destroying the land as they moved through it, in a 'sharp and cruel war'. Places were not to be occupied and held unless they controlled a major river, or had similar strategic importance. By living off the land, the English troops would force the French into starvation, and would themselves need less wages. Fortification was required in Normandy, in those cases where towns did not already have an adequate castle. Control of the sea was important, and so as to ensure a ready market for English exports of wool, alliances should be made with Genoa and Venice.[1] It may be doubted whether this policy, which was primarily designed to punish those who had treasonably abandoned the English cause in France, would in fact have worked, even if the English had been in a proper position to put it into effect. What Fastolf's advice does show is that careful thought was given to the overall strategy of war.

Historians have often been reluctant to accept that medieval commanders had any strategic grasp.[2] William I's success in establishing control of Normandy and conquering England might appear to suggest that he, and the forces under his command, were capable of putting a highly effective strategy into effect, yet it was with a certain grudging surprise that Stenton wrote that 'Even in the eleventh century a Norman army was capable of something more than an unco-ordinated series of single combats.'[3] In the early thirteenth century, according to Richardson and Sayles, 'warfare called for little strategy, for little military science'. War consisted of 'small bodies of knights and serjeants engaged in cavalry charges where tactics and personal prowess were the only things that mattered'.[4] As for Edward I, according to Richardson, 'However good a tactician he may have been, he was a pitiable strategist.'[5] Nor had matters apparently improved by the time of the Hundred Years War, when according to one distinguished historian, 'Older knights had no

The future Edward I, accompanied by some nobles, shown receiving the wisdom of Vegetius, author of the *De Re Militari*.

doubt acquired some knowledge of tactics, but many campaigns were marked by an absence of strategy. They consisted in devastation – combining insult with injury – along a line of march which might lead to the enemy capital or to no clearly defined objective.' Another historian commented on Edward III, that he was 'a very competent tactician, but a very unskilful strategist'.[6] It is interesting that modern military men have had a higher opinion of medieval strategy than historians. An intelligence report produced on a Normandy raid in 1942 included on a map the track of Edward III's 1346 expedition, 'in the hope of providing historical encouragement'. Detailed study of the Conqueror's operations in Brittany and Normandy formed part of General George S. Patton's preparations for his campaign following the D Day landings.[7]

There was only one treatise read in the medieval period that discussed military strategy. The *De Re Militari* by Vegetius was written in the late fourth century by a man of no practical military experience. It brought together in one volume a wealth of earlier classical opinion, and reflected not the military practice of Vegetius's own day, but that of earlier and more successful periods of the Roman past. The discussion of strategy and tactics was eminently sensible and practical. Above all, Vegetius stressed the avoidance of pitched battles, advocating war by all other possible means. The popularity of the book is attested to by the very large number of surviving manuscripts. It does not appear to have been known in England until after the Conquest, and became increasingly popular in the fourteenth and fifteenth centuries. Edward I's queen, Eleanor, commissioned a translation into French of the work for her husband during the crusade of 1270–2; a translation into English was done for Lord Berkeley in 1408.[8] There is only one known example of a commander specifically referring to Vegetius. In the mid twelfth century Geoffrey, count of Anjou, was found by a monk deeply immersed in the book at the siege of Montreuil-Bellay. When he put it down, the monk picked the book up, and began to read. 'Stay with me tomorrow, dear brother', said the count, 'and what you find in your reading, you shall see put into practice.' Interpretation of the story is not straightforward, for the device that the count used the following day was an incendiary bomb, something not referred to by Vegetius at all.[9] Beyond that one incident, it is impossible to tell how influential in practical terms Vegetius's work was. Did commanders take sensible decisions, avoiding risks and relying on diplomacy and on careful manoeuvring of troops rather than battle, because they had read this late classical author, or because they followed the dictates of common sense? The question is perhaps ultimately unanswerable. It would be hard to argue that so popular a work had no practical implications, but at the same time it is hard to imagine that many experienced campaigners kept a copy in the medieval equivalent of their back pocket for easy consultation. Practical experience must have counted for much more than the dictates of Vegetius.[10]

The formulation of strategy

Evidence for the discussion of strategy is rare, partly for the very good reason that it was often kept secret. It is necessary to rely largely upon examination of the course of events to deduce what plans had been made – a procedure which obviously has its dangers. It would not be right, on the other hand, to assume that the paucity of evidence proves that there was little planning. Grand strategy there certainly was. The devising of crusades provides an example. There may have been little thought beyond journeying to Jerusalem in the minds of those who commanded the forces on the First Crusade, but thereafter much attention was given to the political and strategic problems. Should alliance be made with Egypt or Damascus? Was co-operation with the Mongols a possibility? How could naval forces be used? The attack on the Nile Delta in the Fifth Crusade turned out to have been a disastrous mistake, yet it was a carefully calculated strategic move.

In Richard I, the Angevin monarchy provided the crusading movement with one of its most effective strategists. Richard's crusade was not undertaken in a spirit of disinterested piety; he had strong family interests, for he was a direct descendant of Fulk, King of Jerusalem. His choice of a sea route to the east, in contrast to the German emperor's decision to go overland, enabled him to seize Cyprus, and so gain essential food supplies to support his operations. After the capture of Acre, the evidence strongly suggests that Richard had a clear plan to move against Egypt, proceeding to Ascalon rather than directing his aims to the emotionally satisfying, but strategically sterile, goal of Jerusalem. His decisions were not those of an opportunist, ready to adopt a popular tack; rather, they show every indication of following a carefully thought-out plan.[11]

In the late thirteenth century much thought was given to crusade strategy. A memorandum, possibly written by Edward I's confidant Otto de Grandson, advocated the use of Armenia as a base, and suggested that the crusading troops should arrive in the autumn, to give them sufficient time to prepare for a march on Jerusalem in the following spring.[12] In the early 1290s, following the fall of Acre, there was considerable discussion about the best strategy to adopt, much of it centring on the need for a unified command, and for the establishment of peace in the west before an expedition to the east was mounted. Edward I had hopes of a grand alliance between the

West and the Mongols in the east, and an English embassy was duly sent to the Il-Khan of Persia to try to take these plans further. The strategy may have been hopelessly over-ambitious, but at least it demonstrates that men were capable of planning war on a global scale.[13]

On a lesser, but more realistically drawn canvas, it is impossible to read Gerald of Wales's discussion of how Ireland should be conquered without realising that a great deal of thought went into military operations. His views must reflect many a discussion and debate with his relatives involved in the conquest. He argued for the use of lightly armed men, capable of fighting on both horse and foot, in place of heavily equipped knights. Archers were essential, to ward off the Irish as they rushed forward hurling stones. A strategy of developing a connected system of castles was needed, instead of building fortifications in haphazardly chosen sites, the garrisons of which could not assist each other in times of crisis.[14] Gerald also provided advice on the conquest of Wales. Internal divisions among the Welsh should be fostered, and an economic blockade mounted. Lightly armed troops were appropriate, with fresh contingents regularly brought up. Troops from the Welsh marches and Ireland would be ideal, and Flemish, Norman or Brabançon mercenaries were also suitable. French knights, however, fought in so radically different a way from the Welsh as to be of little value. Gerald was very well aware of the different needs of warfare against the lightly armed Irish and Welsh, as compared to war across the Channel, where the mounted knight and the powerful stone castle were dominant.[15]

Government records do not reveal ideas about strategy with the clarity of Gerald of Wales's writings or Fastolf's memorandum. There were dangers in setting down too much in writing; the discovery by the English in 1346 of invasion plans drawn up by the French in 1338 made for excellent propaganda.[16] There is nevertheless good evidence to show that there was detailed planning of campaigns. Decisions had to be made about the command structure of armies, while the summoning of troops, the collection of food supplies and the impressment of ships had to be worked out in considerable detail. Much expertise was built up. Drafts, orders and instructions survive in some number from Edward III's reign to reveal the process. One dealing with plans for a Scottish campaign began by noting that the earl of Warwick was to be the commander. Commissions of array needed to be set up, as agreed by the council, to recruit men-at-arms, hobelars and archers. Thomas de Ousefleet was to be in charge of payment of wages. Anthony de Lucy was to have custody of Berwick, and a clerk should be appointed to act as chamberlain and chancellor in the town. Negotiations were needed with the various English garrisons in Scotland, and Lucy was given charge of this. The building works in Berwick were to be overseen by John de Swanland, who was also given responsibility for the garrisons in Edinburgh, Roxburgh, Stirling and Bothwell. Two 'peels', simple wooden fortifications, were needed on the coasts of northern England: one in the west, and one in the east. Attempts should be made to provide sufficient Englishmen to inhabit Berwick. Bows, arrows, crossbows and bolts were to be taken to Berwick and the other English-held fortresses, and large (unspecified) quantities of food supplies were to be sent with all haste to Berwick.[17]

Another memorandum, drawn up in the early 1340s, noted that it had been agreed that men-at-arms, their numbers detailed elsewhere, were to assemble at Portsmouth at Whitsun. Two thousand spearmen, equipped with helmets, were to be arrayed, along with 4,000 archers from south of the Trent. Four thousand Welsh, two-thirds of them archers and the rest spearmen, were also to be recruited. Ships, capable of carrying at least 30 tuns, from ports between Hull in the east and Chester in the west, were to be pressed into service. The large vessels were to have double crews. All were to be ready to take the troops, their horses and their victuals to France.[18] A more elaborate plan was worked out for an expedition in 1341, which never actually took place. This set out the various retinues in detail, calculated the number of ships needed at 300, and worked out a detailed budget. The cost of the expedition, assuming it lasted only forty days, would have been just over £25,000, which it was hoped would be met out of the proceeds of a purveyance of 5,100 sacks of wool.[19] One document, dealing with naval preparations, noted 'Item, remember to speak with the king, to see if he wants all the ships assembled at Portsmouth, or part of the ships elsewhere, and in which places.' A marginal note recorded the king's agreement to the suggestion of Portsmouth.[20] It is surely inconceivable that this detailed planning should have taken place without full discussion of the strategy to be employed by the expeditions which were so carefully put together. The strategic decisions, however, did not need to be recorded in the same way as the administrative plans.

There were obviously problems in formulating strategy. In modern times, commanders are faced with a plethora of evidence from maps; but it was not until the sixteenth century that maps began to be used for military planning, and cartography rapidly became an important military science. (It has been suggested that one reason for Spain's military decline in the seventeenth century was the lack of up-to-date maps.[21]) The development of high-quality maps was closely connected to the military requirements of gunners. Such maps as existed in the medieval period were of no use for military planning, though itineraries might provide information of some value about distances. A record was kept of Edward I's Scottish campaign of 1296, giving

details of places and distances, perhaps in part because this information might be of use in future expeditions.[22] No doubt it was
possible for commanders to construct some kind of mental map, but
detailed planning must have been hard. The problems of operating
without maps should not, however, be exaggerated. Medieval armies
did not blunder about the countryside in total ignorance of where
they were going. By following roads and rivers, and in many cases by
taking local advice, it was possible to work out appropriate routes. It
was of particular importance to have accurate information about
rivers and river-crossings; it is clear from campaign after campaign
that these were a prime determinant of events. The most striking
example, of course, is that of the 1346 campaign in France, when
Edward was forced to march virtually to the gates of Paris in order
to force a crossing of the Seine. In 1356 the ambitious plan to link the
forces of the Black Prince with those of the duke of Lancaster failed,
because the Loire could not be crossed due to an unexpectedly high
water level.

The pace at which armies could proceed was an obvious influence
on strategy. When William Rufus invaded Maine in 1098, his army
marched ten to fifteen miles a day. A mounted force could operate
surprisingly quickly, as was shown in 1336 when Edward III took a
small expedition of some 800 men from Perth to rescue the countess
of Atholl at Lochindorb, thence to Elgin, and back via Aberdeen to
Stirling. The entire operation was conducted between 12 and 26 July;
the rate of travel varied from about eight miles on the first day, to
forty on 15 July. Not surprisingly, a good many horses were lost that
day.[23] A large army, however, was a very different matter; its pace
was determined by the slowest and most heavily laden wagons in the
baggage train. In 1300 Edward I left Carlisle on 4 July; he did not
reach Dumfries until 10 July, admittedly by a somewhat circuitous
route. The army had travelled at an average of some four or five miles
a day. It would take them four days to march from Dumfries to
Kirkcudbright, a distance of about thirty miles.[24] In 1346 it was rare
for Edward III's army, encumbered as it was by footsoldiers, to
march more than ten or twelve miles in a day. Even in the advance
towards the Somme, when hastening to avoid the pursuing French, it
did not prove possible to manage more than fifteen miles a day. The
Black Prince on his ravaging raid in October and November of 1355
to Narbonne averaged some ten miles a day, with a maximum of
twenty-five miles in a single day.[25] Edward III's great army of 1359
left Calais on 4 November, and took a month to reach Rheims; the
average daily journey was therefore less than six miles. Henry V's
march from Harfleur to Agincourt was undertaken at breakneck
speed. His men, many of them suffering from dysentery, managed
260 miles in seventeen days, an average of slightly over fifteen miles

a day. To give a more recent comparison, General Sherman in his march from Atlanta to the sea, during the American Civil War, took his army – which was much larger than Henry V's – 285 miles at about twelve miles a day.[26]

Grand strategy

There were very different levels of strategy in the medieval as in any other period, ranging from the grand scale of alliances between dynasties to the planning of individual campaigns. The central problem of grand strategy facing the medieval English monarchy was how to deal with its French rival. By Henry II's reign the English held a swathe of territory from Normandy right down to the Pyrenees, which needed to be defended from an increasingly ambitious and aggressive French crown. The duchy of Normandy was placed under immense pressure by Philip II in the late twelfth century; Richard I's strategy for its defence was complex and ambitious. He set up an elaborate system of alliances among Imperial princes in 1194, offering them fees in return for assistance against the French. His diplomatic links were widespread, extending to Navarre and Toulouse.[27] At a more local level, defences were improved with the building of the magnificent castle of Chateau Gaillard. Richard's construction of this, one of the greatest of all medieval castles, was obviously dictated by the needs of strategy, though whether that strategy was one of defending Normandy against a French attack down the Seine valley, or of providing a base for an Anglo-Norman conquest of the county of the Vexin, is open to question.[28] In 1204, however, Chateau Gaillard, the 'Saucy Castle', fell to the French, and the whole duchy of Normandy soon followed. John's strategy for its recovery was ambitious. The major campaign took place in 1214. English troops under the king himself operated in Poitou; in the north a massive coalition of allies, headed by Otto IV, the German emperor, and including many princes from the Low Countries, was called into action. The idea was to squeeze Philip II in a gigantic pincer movement. The strategy failed on the battlefield of Bouvines, where Otto and the allies, assisted by some English troops under the earl of Salisbury, were defeated. The Bouvines campaign demonstrated the extreme difficulty involved in co-ordinating the efforts of a widespread alliance, but the obvious lesson was not learned from it.

In 1294, when war was forced on Edward I by the French, he took advice from his councillors. The bishop of Durham advised him to mount his charger, take his lance in his hand and (which was much more practical) to seek allies in Germany, Aragon, Savoy and Burgundy.[29] The plan, which was little more than a revival of John's

strategy at the beginning of the century, met with general approval.
An alliance was concluded with the German king, the archbishop of
Cologne, and various minor German magnates. The count of Bar
also promised Edward support. The duke of Brabant, Edward's
son-in-law, was with the king in Wales in the spring of 1295, and
promised his assistance. Guelders and Holland were also brought
into the alliance. The French, however, strove to counter the efforts
of the English agents, and constructed their own alliances. Flanders,
vital for Edward I, was brought into the French network, by a
mixture of bullying and financial promises. Holland was detached
from the English cause early in 1296. Count Florence of Holland was
murdered, however, and his son John lured back into the English
alliance in January 1297. In addition to subsidies, he received the
hand of one of Edward's daughters, Elizabeth, in marriage. The
cornerstone of the English scheme remained Flanders, and Count
Guy turned from Philip IV of France to Edward. A further threat to
the French came in the form of an agreement with some influential
Burgundian nobles with Edward in May 1297. The grand alliance
was, at least on parchment, very impressive, but it had been brought
together at a very high cost. In all, some £250,000 was promised.
The outcome of all this effort was not quite as disastrous as the 1214
campaign, but the strategy scarcely lived up to expectations. Edward
was distracted by rebellion in Wales and what he regarded as
rebellion in Scotland, so the continental campaign was delayed until
1297. He crossed to Flanders with an inadequate force, only to find
that many of his allies had already been defeated. All that could be
done was to negotiate a truce with the French, and to desert in an
ignoble way his Flemish allies.[30]

It might be expected that a strategy which had failed twice would
have been abandoned, but with the outbreak of war with France in
1337, Edward III adopted it once more. It is clear that this was not
a case of reinventing the wheel; much research was done by his clerks
into the precedents of the past, and his grand alliance was built in
very full awareness of such past parallels as those set by Edward I in
the 1290s.[31] Once again, the strategy proved too elaborate and
costly. A great alliance was built up at enormous cost, with much
reliance placed on the princes of the Low Countries and the German
ruler Ludwig IV. William, count and then margrave of Jülich, played
a very important role in the alliance, receiving the title of earl of
Cambridge as a reward in 1340. The allies included the duke of
Brabant, the count of Hainault and the count of Guelders. The costs
were immense: in October 1339 parliament was informed that the
king's debts stood at £300,000. Even the great crown of England had
been handed over as security for subsidies promised to the archbishop of Trier.[32] Despite all the work done by Edward's agents, the

one real English success in the early stages of the war, the naval battle of Sluys in 1340, owed nothing to the allies. An Anglo-Flemish army was defeated at St Omer; and as splits between the allies widened into crevasses, the siege of Tournai failed. The next phase of the Hundred Years War saw a more limited strategy adopted, with intervention in Brittany in support of John de Montfort's claim to the duchy. Of course, as the war continued, alliances were important, as was exploitation of divisions within France. There were to be echoes of the strategy of the grand alliance, as when Henry V sought the support of German princes at the end of his reign, or when Henry VI's government did the same after the duke of Burgundy abandoned the English cause in 1435. International relations were important, but they were not the bedrock of English military strategy in the later fourteenth and fifteenth centuries.[33]

Strategy on the grand scale, based on alliances with empires, kingdoms, duchies and counties was, therefore, attempted. Yet the problems of co-ordinating military action with allies were immense, and the costs of buying support against the French were too high. The grand strategies of the 1290s and the late 1330s were not attempted again. That does not mean, however, that strategy as such was beyond the capability of medieval states. Indeed, at the relatively straightforward levels of using armies in campaigns to achieve specific goals, and embarking on programmes of castle-building, there is much evidence to show that highly effective strategies were adopted.

Wales and Scotland

By the time that Edward I conquered Wales, the English had long experience of the strategic problems posed by a country with major geographical obstacles of mountains and forests, and a people reluctant to come to battle though eager to fight a guerrilla-style war. In 1165 Henry II attempted a march from Oswestry, across the mountains, into north Wales, and was disastrously thwarted both by the terrain and the weather. The strategy was ambitious, involving the use of hired Irish ships from Dublin, but when the king eventually reached the coast near Chester, he realised that this fleet was too small, and it was accordingly dismissed and the campaign finally abandoned.[34] It was far more effective to march a substantial army along the coast of north Wales, as Henry had done in 1157, and indeed, as the Roman general Suetonius Paulinus had done in the first century AD. Edward I demonstrated the effectiveness of such a strategy in 1277, when his army marched from Chester to Flint, and on to Deganwy. Following Henry II's 1157 example, Edward sent a force by sea to Anglesey, where the harvest was collected – a move

Wales: the English conquest.

which simultaneously provided food for the English army and threatened to starve out the Welsh. Initial plans in 1282 were rather different. The muster was first requested for Worcester, but when Edward arrived there in May he issued new summonses for the army to gather at Rhuddlan at the start of August. He moved rapidly to Chester, and began assembling his forces there.[35] It is conceivable that the initial summons to Worcester was a device intended to confuse the Welsh, but it is more likely that the strategy of directing the main thrust in the north was adopted only at a late stage.

Whether Edward should be castigated for indecision, or praised for flexibility, is a moot point. The strategy that was finally adopted was clear. Forces in central and southern Wales under baronial command ensured that the Welsh were in no position to concentrate their forces. The royal army advanced from Chester into the north, with essential naval support. As in 1277, an expedition was sent to Anglesey, and this time a pontoon bridge was constructed to enable it to take the war to the mainland. Roads were cut through the Welsh forests to facilitate the English movements. Inevitably, events did not

Scotland: the Wars of Independence.

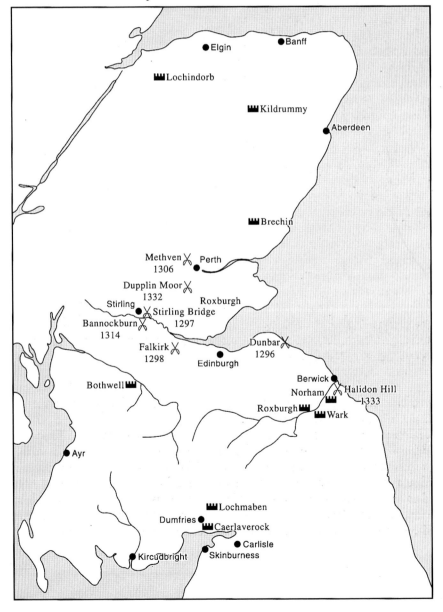

go precisely as planned, but there can be little doubt that Edward was putting a clearly worked-out plan into action in a most effective way.[36]

Scotland presented greater problems in strategic terms than Wales; the country was never, indeed, effectively conquered by the English, although Edward I came near to achieving success in 1304. It was not easy to mobilise armies so far north; there were difficulties in bringing supplies to forces operating in Scotland; and above all the nature of the terrain and its scale ensured that final success for English military operations remained illusory.

Perhaps the most effective strategy employed against the Scots was that of William the Conqueror. In 1072 he launched an astonishing campaign, in which a largely mounted force was backed with great effectiveness by naval forces in a synchronised attack. The army advanced northwards from Durham, and crossed the Forth near Stirling. It then marched to Perth, and in the Tay estuary linked up with the naval forces. No military action took place: Malcolm III, King of Scots, was so overwhelmed by William's arrival that he at once entered into negotiations with him. At Abernethy hostages were handed over, and homage was performed. William had obtained security from the potential menace that Scotland represented, with remarkable speed.[37] Yet the settlement did not prove lasting; later, another army had to be sent north under William's son Robert, and it was to be many years before the frontier between England and Scotland was clearly demarcated. The Conqueror had, however, shown that much might be achieved by speed and an effective co-ordination between army and fleet – points which were not so clearly grasped by the English in the wars which followed the breakdown of Anglo-Scottish relations in 1296.

No major English force invaded Scotland between the reigns of William I and Edward I. By the late thirteenth century there was a well-established border, with recognised procedures for settling disputes. A number of great families held important estates in both England and Scotland, which contributed to the lack of serious tension between the two countries. The outbreak of war in 1296 presented Edward I with problems that had not been faced for generations.

Unfortunately the highly successful 1296 campaign is ill-documented. The English began with the capture of Berwick. The only significant military challenge came at Dunbar, where the Scottish forces were routed with little difficulty. Thereafter, the campaign was hardly more than a triumphant procession, reaching its climax with the surrender of the abject John Balliol, king since Edward had adjudicated in his favour when the succession dispute was resolved in 1292. Edward went much further than the Conqueror had done in

1072. The Forth was again crossed at Stirling, but the army marched as far north as Banff and Elgin before returning south. The success was misleading. Scotland was Edward I's Vietnam: he tried to win the war by sending in large armies at great cost, and failed to develop a strategy to deal with an enemy who after 1298 refused open battle. There is little direct evidence of Edward's plans. In 1296 it is clear that he intended to recruit an army of unprecedented size, demanding that his administrators provide him with 60,000 men – an impossibly large number. In 1298 Edward succeeded in bringing the Scots to battle at Falkirk, but he was unable to follow up that success with conquest. The campaign of 1300 saw him invade on the western route, rather than the normal eastern one; in 1301 the strategy was a highly ambitious double attack, with one army advancing from

The North of England.

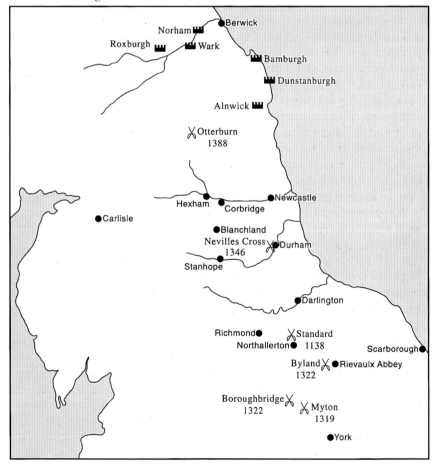

Berwick, and another from Carlisle. It is likely that the two were intended to join forces, but the western army, under the nominal command of the king's ineffective son, never reached central Scotland. Letters sent to the exchequer suggest that Edward thought that if he could only cross the Firth of Forth, he would be able to achieve the final victory that he sought.[38] Naval forces were of course employed, to bring supplies from the eastern counties of England, and across from Ireland, but there was nothing to compare with the remarkable co-ordination of army and navy that had been achieved by William I in 1072. By 1304 Edward appeared to achieve success; with the fall of Stirling castle resistance ended. His problems then were political; and the settlement that was worked out did not last. In 1306 Robert Bruce seized the Scottish throne, and the war reopened. Despite some initial successes, the English had no answer to the problems that Bruce set them.

The Scottish wars of Edward I's reign did not demonstrate that the English had no strategy. Rather, they showed the problems that resulted from sticking rigidly to a formula which steadily proved less and less effective. The lesson was not understood; Edward II's campaigns saw defeat and dishonour, and a barren failure to adopt a new approach to the strategic problems presented by war against the Scots. The campaign of 1322 above all demonstrated the futility of the traditional strategy. A substantial army marched north as far as Edinburgh. The countryside was emptied by the Scots in advance of the English; there was no enemy to engage, and no territory to plunder and destroy. The effect of the expedition was to lay the north of England open to Scottish reprisal, and indeed to expose the king and his army on the march south through Yorkshire to the Scots, who attacked them to considerable effect at Old Byland. It was not until after his initial success at Halidon Hill in 1333 that Edward III came to realise the futility of marching large armies north against an elusive enemy. The English had much to learn from the Scottish wars. Among the lessons was the effectiveness of the swift mounted raid into enemy territory. The middle years of Edward II's reign had seen the north of England suffer raid after raid. The Scots were able to finance their war effort out of the proceeds of their expeditions across the border. There were profits to be made out of plunder, and profits from levying protection money on a massive scale, selling local truces at a high price.[39] These were techniques that the English could adopt to good purpose when fighting in France.

Fire and sword

A strategy based on destruction of enemy territory was of course nothing new; it was a fundamental technique of medieval warfare. It was both punitive and a way of depriving opponents of essential resources. William I, according to William of Poitiers, was familiar with such methods before his invasion of England. His technique for dealing with the county of Maine was to sow terror by means of frequent and lengthy raids, to destroy the vines, fields and manors, to take the fortified places, and to afflict the land with every possible calamity. This strategy the chronicler attributed to his moderation, and his reluctance to shed blood.[40] William used similar brutal methods in the north of England in 1069–70, breaking English resistance with, according to chronicle evidence, no village left inhabited between York and Durham. The warfare of the Anarchy of Stephen's reign was characterised by widespread destruction. A typical passage in the contemporary *Gesta Stephani* recorded the way in which Philip of Gloucester 'raged in all directions with fire and sword, violence and plunder; and far and wide reduced to bare fields and a dreadful desert the lands and possessions not only of those barons who opposed the king, but even of his own father'.[41] There has been some difficulty in equating record evidence with that of the chronicles. Both Domesday Book and the early Pipe Rolls of Henry II's reign contain many references to 'waste', but these are difficult to map precisely against what is known of the pattern of campaigning. The Yorkshire Domesday entries suggest massive depopulation high in the Pennines, rather than in the fertile Vale of York. The counties which, according to chronicle accounts, saw heavy fighting in Stephen's reign, such as Wiltshire, did not show in their returns as much 'waste' as other counties, such as Warwickshire. One possibility is that 'waste' may not necessarily refer to the physical destruction of agriculture, but could have been an administratively convenient way of referring to land from which it was impossible, for whatever reason, to collect revenue. It is impossible, however, to ignore the broad coincidence between 'waste' and warfare, and the anomalies in the evidence are best explained in terms of the time-lag between the physical destruction and the making of the records. The fact that in some midland counties tax receipts from geld fell by over 50 per cent cannot be disassociated from the savage effects of warfare on the land.[42] Nor did the Anarchy see the end of the practice of harrying. William the Lion of Scotland was advised in 1173 by the count of Flanders as to how he should conduct war in England. He should lay waste English territory, firing all in sight. Only then should he start to besiege castles.[43]

The evidence of the effects of destructive raids is clear in records from the north of England in the late thirteenth and early fourteenth centuries. Famine aggravated the miseries of war. Men were terrified of the Scots: in 1315, hearing of their coming, a local parishioner, John Sayer, fled to the church at Houghton-le-Spring and in his fear climbed right to the top of the bell-tower only to fall to an untimely death when he tried to come down again. A range of figures tell an equally gloomy story. In 1313–14 Durham Cathedral Priory drew £412 in tithes from Northumberland. By 1319 tithes could be collected from only one church, yielding £10. The archbishop of York's manor at Hexham was derelict by 1316, and barely any people remained there. In one raid, the Scottish army camped at Fountains Abbey, doing so much damage that it was claimed that there was no longer sufficient means to sustain the community. The church at Pannal in Yorkshire could no longer pay any dues 'because the Scots stayed there and burned it on their retreat'. A tallage taken in 1333 by the bishop of Durham yielded less than half that of 1311. Some lands were spared, because the Scots collected large sums in protection money, but the truces that were bought lasted far too short a time. Cumberland alone was required to pay 2,000 marks in nine months in 1313–14. Ripon was charged with £1,000 in 1318. In Northumberland, the income received from Norham and Holy Island fell by 1329 to 23.7 per cent of its level in 1307. Although some recovery took place later in the fourteenth century, a whole region was transformed by the experience of war.[44]

The Hundred Years War

The English, so recently the victims of savage raids in the north, adopted a similar strategy of destruction in the early stages of the Hundred Years War to that which the Scots had employed. Fire was the chief weapon, as it has been in so many wars. It was one of Sherman's men who, during the American Civil War, wrote 'I do not beleave [*sic*] there is a man in the army but has set fire to one or more buildings.'[45] The march from Atlanta to the sea had much in common with the *chevauchées* of the fourteenth century, and Edward III's soldiers could well have said the same thing. Henry V's view was that war without fire was like sausages without mustard.[46] The *chevauchée*, with its speed and destructiveness, could also be compared to the *blitzkrieg* of the twentieth century. In 1339 the English and their allies burned and destroyed the countryside around Cambrai. Edward III wrote to his son in England: 'The Monday, on the eve of St Matthew, we passed out of Valenciennes, and on the same day they did begin to burn in Cambrésis, and they burnt there all the week following, so that the country is clean laid waste, as of corn and cattle and other goods.' So severe was the damage that the pope made a special grant of 6,000 florins to relieve the suffering of the inhabitants. The report by the official responsible for distributing the funds shows that devastation was spread over 174 parishes, with appalling damage done by fire. In a celebrated incident Geoffrey le Scrope led a French cardinal to the top of a high tower, showing him the land in the direction of France burning over a distance of some fifteen miles. 'Lord', he said, 'do you not see that the silk thread which surrounds France is broken?' One English estimate was that 2,118 villages and castles had been burned and destroyed.[47] Similar methods continued to be used. The *Anonimalle Chronicle* reported proudly that on the Black Prince's raid of 1355, eleven fine cities and 3,700 villages had been destroyed. Baker's account noted the burning of towns and villages, and also of a dozen windmills at Montgiscard, and of twenty at Avignonet. Crops (though not vines and orchards) might recover relatively quickly; windmills were a major investment, costly to rebuild. In 1359 it was not so much the burning of towns and villages that was remarkable, rather the fact that Edward III gave orders that Pontigny was not to be put to the flames, in honour of the shrine there of St Edmund, archbishop of Canterbury.[48] By the late fourteenth century the scale of destruction in France was horrific, with widespread depopulation of rural areas. Not all of it was the work of the English; the *jacquerie* of the late 1350s and the activities of the Free Companies in the years after the treaty of Brétigny laid waste wide tracts of territory, while the economic effects of plague were a further element in the disaster which affected so many villages.[49]

There is no doubt that the strategy of widespread destruction was deliberately adopted as a means of reducing French military capability and of forcing the enemy to come either to battle, or to the conference table. Destruction of French territory was noted by the royal clerk Michael Northburgh in 1346: 'the people in the army rode pillaging and destroying five or six leagues around every day, burning many places.' And 'they fired everything along the coast from Roche Massé to Oistreham, in the harbour for Caen, a distance of 120 English leagues.'[50] The fact that so much destruction took place does not demonstrate the unplanned nature of the expedition; it was an integral part of the strategy. John Wingfield, the Black Prince's steward, writing a newsletter in 1355, stressed the damage that his master's raid to Narbonne had done to French royal finances. 'The land and good towns which are destroyed in this *chevauchée* found for the king of France each year more for the maintenance of his war than did half of his kingdom, excluding receipts from coinage and the customs in Poitou. I can prove this to you from good records which were found in the houses of receivers in various towns.[51] Such a policy of destruction brought material advantages to the English, who acquired food and plunder in plenty as they savaged the French countryside.

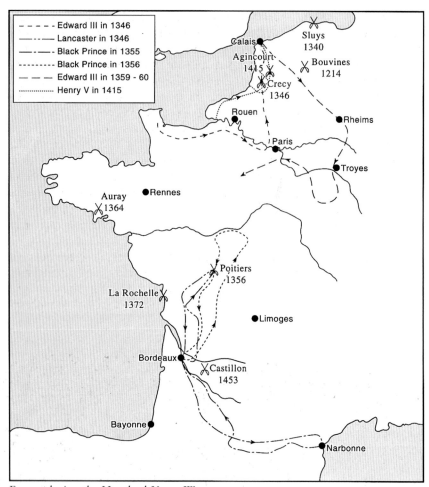

France during the Hundred Years War.

The adoption of these methods of waging a particularly brutal form of economic warfare did not mean that there was no need to plan campaigns carefully. It can be argued that during the really successful years of the Hundred Years War, the period of Crécy and Poitiers, Edward III's strategy was perhaps more opportunistic than carefully planned. His overall war aims probably changed as circumstances altered. It is not clear whether he seriously hoped to become king of France, or whether he aimed to detach the western provinces from the rest of the kingdom, and hold them in full sovereignty.[52] Even so, the evidence of the Crécy campaign itself suggests that a clear plan of action had been worked out. At first the expedition was almost certainly intended to go to Gascony, to relieve the siege of Aiguillon. At a late stage the decision was taken to launch an attack

The battle of Poitiers, from a fifteenth-century manuscript of
Froissart's *Chronicles*.

on Normandy; a renegade Norman, Godfrey de Harcourt, was held by chroniclers to be behind the change, although it may have been simply that the king decided on a shorter crossing, in a direction favoured by the winds, which had held up the final departure from English waters for a fortnight. Clearly the strategy of the campaign developed as the English forces gained in confidence. Most interestingly, after the capture of Caen, the king wrote to the council in England, giving news of the campaign and asking for money, arms, and men-at-arms to be sent to Le Crotoy, at the mouth of the Somme. It is plain that a move north-eastwards was planned. It is doubtful that Edward and his councillors realised that they would have to march as far as Poissy before the army could make a crossing of the Seine, but the march from there to the mouth of Somme plainly fitted in to a predetermined plan to revictual and refinance the force at Le Crotoy.[53]

In 1356 plans were elaborate. Two major armies were sent to France; the Black Prince to Gascony, and the duke of Lancaster to Normandy. The indenture with the Prince, drawn up in the previous year, made it plain that he could expect assistance from Lancaster

and the earls with him. To co-ordinate armies operating in different parts of France was a highly ambitious strategy, but following successes in Normandy, Lancaster moved south into Brittany in August. At the same time the Black Prince began his march northwards. In September the two armies approached the Loire; at night it was possible to see the fires of both, so close were they. The Loire is an unpredictable river, and that year it ran high. It could not be forded, and the French had broken the bridges, notably that at Les-Ponts-de-Cé. The strategy failed, but only just. Then, of course, during the retreat back to Gascony the prince and his forces won the glittering victory of Poitiers. It can be argued that the movements of the armies in 1356 was not predetermined by a calculated strategy, but although there is no documented plan of campaign, it is impossible to believe that the attempted junction of forces at the Loire was not part of an ambitious, deliberate and calculated series of moves.[54] To win a victory in battle must have been one of the hopes of the English, but the battle of Poitiers was the product of the manoeuvrings of the two armies, not of deliberate planning from the outset on the part of the Black Prince and his advisers.

English strategy looked bankrupt by 1359, when Edward attempted to take the French throne by simply marching on Rheims. The campaign was extremely ambitious, but Rheims did not surrender, and the *chevauchée* into Burgundy which followed achieved little. The French initiated negotiations as the English army withdrew in the spring of 1360, and the truce of Brétigny was concluded. Edward achieved limited objectives; he would hold an immense swathe of territory in France in full sovereignty, and abandon his claim to the French throne. The treaty, for complex reasons, was never implemented in full; neither side was content with it.

When the war was renewed in 1369 the English began to face rather different problems. The capture of Calais in 1347 had provided a point of entry to France for English armies, but also a place to be defended. Although the strategy of raiding and pillaging was not abandoned, there was a growing need to provide for the defence of English-controlled lands in Brittany and elsewhere. Campaigns proved increasingly costly, and brought few returns. The offensive strategies which had served so well in the 1340s and 1350s were no longer appropriate, though they were not immediately abandoned. In 1373 it was initially intended that John of Gaunt should take a substantial expedition to Brittany, but when the duke of Brittany fled to England, the plan was changed, and Gaunt embarked on a massive raid from Calais, setting out in August. He marched towards Paris, and then on into Burgundy. After crossing the Massif Central, with much suffering by men and horses alike, he eventually reached Bordeaux by Christmas. To have marched an army so far was a remarkable achievement, but it proved to be of little value. The

Henry V and his army before
the walls of Rouen in 1418.

French refused battle; little plunder was gained, and no cities or
castles were taken.[55] The glories of the 1340s and 1350s could not
easily be repeated. The days of the grand. *chevauchée* were over.
Strategy needed to be changed.

In 1378 the chancellor, Richard Scrope, explained the developing
English strategy in a speech in parliament. 'Barbicans' were to be
established in France, English-held fortresses on the coasts which
would provide effectively for the defence of England. Brest was
leased, and plans made to take over Cherbourg on a similar basis, to
serve as 'barbicans'.[56] A defensive strategy was much more difficult
to operate than an offensive one, but the 'barbican' policy was
practicable, and carefully thought out, if costly.

The reign of Henry V marked a new shift in English strategy
in France, not so much with the Agincourt campaign as with
the conquest of Normandy, which began in 1417. Agincourt was the
culmination of a march which the king decided on following the
capture of Harfleur; he was aiming at little more than returning to
England via Calais. In 1417, however, the English began the acquisition of territory in France by conquest. The aim was not to terrorise

the enemy into submission by ravaging and burning, but rather to
conquer towns and castles by means of sieges, so gaining full control
of Lower Normandy in a complex series of military operations, of
which by far the greatest was the siege of Rouen. In an astonishingly
brief time the English gained possession of the duchy, with town after
town, castle after castle surrendering. In many respects Henry V's
kingship lacked originality; despite this, however, his military strategy marked a clear break with the past, demonstrating his greatness
beyond doubt.

Castles

Defensive strategies were based on castles. Castles served many purposes; they were military strong-points, but they were also royal and
aristocratic residences, and often provided administrative centres for
royal officials, or for great estates. In strategic terms, they might
control towns, while they could also provide useful bases for military
operations. They were less valuable as a defence with which to block
invading armies than might be expected, for the short range of
medieval weaponry meant that they were usually relatively easy to
bypass. Their garrisons were too small to challenge an army in the
field. Nor, given the size of most castles, were they normally capable
of serving as a refuge to large numbers of civilians. They could often,
however, hold out with a surprisingly small garrison against a large
besieging force, and resistance would not end until castles had surrendered. It was not the battle of Evesham which ended the civil war
of the 1260s, but the surrender of the garrison of Kenilworth in
1266.

   Just as there has been doubt in general terms as to whether medieval military men were capable of devising and putting into effect
strategy in the full sense, so there has also been debate as to how far
there were considered strategies of castle-building, with controversy
centred on the Norman period. Such features of the organisation of
Norman England as the three great earldoms of Chester, Shrewsbury
and Hereford, or the compact blocks of estates forming castleries in
insecure districts, show that there was undoubtedly much thought
given to the best way in which the realm could be defended. Castles
were, perhaps, the real key to Norman success. They provided
security and defence, but were also the corner-stone of conquest and
expansion. A study of the sites chosen by the Normans for their
castle-building operations strongly suggested to one historian, J.H.
Beeler, that they were selected with a view to their strategic significance, and that they controlled the communications system of the
country. As there is no documentary evidence for this, the argument

Beaumaris (Anglesey), the last of the castles built by Edward I.

is based on the distribution of the castles.[57] The case presupposes a remarkable degree of control on the part of the Conqueror, at a time when there is no evidence that there was any system for the licensing of castle-building in England such as existed from the thirteenth century. Even when there was such a system, it was not used for strategic purposes. It was rare in warfare for castles to be used as an effective interrelated complex; rather, they served as separate and independent units.[58] The fact that most castles lay on or near lines of communication does not mean that there was some central master-plan dictating where they were built. Nor were all strategic points equipped with castles. Coventry, whose importance to the road system is stressed by Beeler, had none, nor did Dunstable, where Watling Street crosses Icknield Way. No castle controlled the crossing of the Thames at Reading.[59] The distribution pattern of the many castles built in the century after the Norman Conquest can be better explained in terms of their founders responding to the local circumstances of roads and rivers, the structure of honours and knights' fees, and the nature of the terrain itself, rather than by reference to some grand master-plan.[60]

Yet the idea that there was strategy in the planning of castle-building is not one which should be rejected. The Crown itself chose where to build its own castles, and here a strategy can be discerned. There was an obvious sense in building castles in the main towns, which were developed as military, administrative and also ecclesiastical centres. Twenty royal castles, over half of them founded in the eleventh century, were in towns. There was no strategy of controlling such a road network as existed, but all the main centres of administration and population were given castles. Most counties had a castle from which the sheriff could operate. The strategy was, perhaps, more administrative than military in a strict sense; it was a strategy of occupation rather than of conquest. Some decisions over the siting of castles were obviously dictated by military needs. It made obvious strategic sense to build castles at Dover, Pevensey and Hastings, since they controlled the Channel crossing, and there can be no doubt that the decision to build castles at Newcastle in 1080 and at Carlisle in 1092 were part of a strategy to expand royal authority in the far north. Within great marcher earldoms, and within individual lordships, it is again possible to see indications of strategic planning, with the aim of controlling of river valleys and obvious routes that raiding parties might take by building castles.[61]

Strategic considerations continued to be relevant for castle-builders in the twelfth century. Henry II's decision to build at Orford was clearly influenced by his need to provide a royal counter-weight to the power of the earls of Norfolk as expressed in their castles of Bungay, Framlingham and Walton, though interestingly mathematical ingenuity and literary symbolism provide a better explanation for the unusual form of the castle than does military need.[62] Again, Henry's acquisition of Kenilworth was clearly prompted by the strategic need, demonstrated by the rebellion of 1173, for the Crown to have a stronger power-base in the Midlands.[63] Other considerations, however, than the military might be significant. King John's castle at Odiham was situated so that the king might 'disport himself' hunting in the nearby forest, not for any reasons of military strategy.[64] Castle-building in England by the Crown for obviously strategic reasons was rare after the twelfth century, but one late exception was the construction of Queenborough on the Isle of Sheppey by Edward III, intended to defend the route up the Thames from possible French attacks.

The conquest of Wales by Edward I was accompanied by an elaborate strategic plan of castle-building. Edward's Welsh castles formed the most magnificent series of fortifications to be built in all of medieval Europe. The concept was obvious. Snowdonia was to be hemmed in by English castles, situated so that they could be easily supplied by sea. The sites were not all new. Caernarfon, for example, was built on the location of an old Norman motte-and-bailey fortress. Conwy, Harlech and Beaumaris, however, were on new sites. Plans for castle-building after the first Welsh war, that of 1277, were for two new castles, Flint and Rhuddlan, to be built in the north, with Aberystwyth and Builth further south designed to control mid Wales. The more elaborate strategy of containment of Snowdonia was developed with the castles built after the second war, that of 1282–3. Rhuddlan had clearly been intended as the main centre for English administration and control; now Conwy was equipped with elaborate royal apartments, and Caernarfon was planned with lavish internal accommodation, to house both the soldiers of the garrison and the administrative officials. Beaumaris, the finishing touch to the building programme, was added after the Welsh rebellion of 1294–5, as a necessary means of controlling Anglesey. The strategy developed as the nature of the Welsh problem became more evident to Edward and his advisers. The castle-building programme had a clear logic; it provided a network of powerful fortifications which both provided for permanent garrisons, and were sufficiently large to be used by future English armies invading Wales. Not only were the castles strong in themselves, but they were carefully sited so as to make their supply by sea an easy task. The wisdom of the strategy may be questioned. Was it necessary to build on such a scale to deal with a people who had no siege train to deploy? Would sufficient resources be available to maintain the castles in a proper state of defence? By the 1340s they were already in a sorry state of repair, and in the early fifteenth century it became clear that in time of rebellion it was necessary to divert forces, which could have been better deployed in the field, to defend the castles. Yet the magnificence of the overall concept of the castle-building programme cannot be denied.[65]

Edward I lacked the funds to build in Scotland as he had done in Wales; Master James of St George, the Savoyard master mason whose genius had dictated the form of the great castles in Wales, was reduced to building in wood at Linlithgow. New fortifications were planned in 1304, but little work was done.[66] Even so, the English-held castles in Scotland were a vital element in maintaining a military presence north of the Border, and their importance was fully recognised by Robert Bruce. The years up to 1314 saw a revolutionary campaign waged, in which Bruce avoided the traditional methods of siege warfare, but took castle after castle by escalade and surprise attack. Once captured, the castles were then slighted, 'so that the English would never again be able to dominate the land by holding the castles'.[67]

The castles of the north of England had a part to play when Robert Bruce took the war south, with the devastating raids which reached

Harlech Castle, designed by the great Master James of St George for Edward I.

into Yorkshire. There were occasional sorties made by garrison forces: on three occasions in 1315 Roger Damory led a troop from Knaresborough to assist forces further north. The Scottish demand that Harbottle should be slighted as a condition for a truce shows the value of a castle well-sited on an invasion route. In general, however, the Scots successfully demonstrated the limitations of castles in the course of their raids into northern England, by bypassing them, and avoiding their garrisons. In 1322 Edward II complained to the constable of Bamburgh castle that a Scottish raiding party had caused considerable damage, and had got away without being challenged by the garrisons of the castles in the north. Some of those living near the castle had even preferred to buy off the Scots with a blackmail payment, rather than rely on the garrison's protection. Even the rabbits in the castle warrens had been either driven off or eaten by the Scots.[68]

Intelligence

At all levels, the construction of effective strategy depended on the provision of good information. Medieval commanders faced major problems in obtaining this. News could travel surprisingly quickly, but communications were never easy. Roads were poor, and there is no evidence before the late fourteenth century for the existence of regular systems for couriers to obtain fresh horses as they rode. There were no permanent embassies overseas; individual diplomatic missions might be an important source of news, but could not provide a regular flow of information. There is no doubt that the value of proper intelligence was fully appreciated, and that every effort was made to find out all that could be discovered.[69] In 1324 one of the items in a council memorandum about the coming war in Gascony was that the earl of Kent should have spies in all the towns that were not in royal hands, to find out their attitude, to provide details of how they were furnished with stocks of food and arms, and to discover any other information about the French military preparations.[70] Intelligence was as important in medieval warfare as it was in later periods.

The vocabulary used in contemporary accounts for what is now termed intelligence can be misleading. There was no clear distinction between spies in the modern sense, scouts or even messengers. Geoffrey le Baker used the actual word 'spy' when retailing the capture of two enemy scouts (*exploratores*) in 1355.[71] References to 'secret matters' reported by messengers could concern military or diplomatic intelligence, but in most cases these were probably no more than private affairs whose purpose was not worth setting out in the documents.

Although some true spies were used, the bulk of information gleaned by military commanders came from more orthodox sources. Arrangements for a raid on the Scots to be conducted by the English constable of Edinburgh castle in 1298 laid particular stress on the need to 'spy out and cause to be spied out all the news possible about the enemies and their plans'. Those responsible for this intelligence-gathering operation, however, were not undercover agents, but were Walter de Huntercombe, an English magnate, Simon Fraser, a Scot retained as a royal household knight, the constable of Roxburgh, and the keeper and sheriff of Berwick. During Edward I's wars in Scotland much news was certainly provided by the constables of English-held castles and other officials: if letters from them were not forthcoming, they were rebuked. In the same year of 1298 the constable of Edinburgh, the household knight John Kingston, wrote to the treasurer, Walter Langton. He reported a move by the earl of Buchan, the bishop of St Andrews and other Scottish notables southwards. Simon Fraser was not to be trusted: Kingston suspected him of being in secret collusion with the Scots. The lady of Pennycuick had given refuge to her son, a supporter of the Scottish cause. The keeper of Lochmaben reported to Edward in 1301 on the whereabouts of the Scottish leaders: 'We are letting you know for sure that Sir John de Soules and the earl of Buchan with their forces are at Loudon, and Sir Simon Fraser at Stanhouses.' Of course, the constables and officials used local informants to collect news. Robert Hastang, constable of Roxburgh castle, took great care, to judge by his own account, in 1301 to send out scouts to obtain information about the Scots and their whereabouts. He arranged a meeting with a group of English commanders on 17 September, with these scouts, to organise operations.[72] Spying against the Scots continued to be important later; in 1337 William Montague spent £15 on 'sending various men to different places to discover the deeds and news of the Scots'.[73]

Some agents in the modern sense were employed. Alice of Saintonge and Alice *exploratrix* (probably the same person) was paid by King John, and was surely a true spy.[74] In August 1282 Edward I paid 10*d* to a man sent to spy on the Welsh prince Llywelyn and his brother Dafydd; no less than nine men were sent on a similar mission in October.[75] In 1338 the queen's watchman, Gerard, was sent to Paris 'to spy out secretly the doings of Philip of Valois'. He received a somewhat meagre 18*d* a day for this hazardous mission.[76] In Richard II's reign, the king retained a French squire, Nicholas Briser, for a fee of fifty marks a year, and there can be no doubt that he was a spy, recruited as an exchequer record reveals, to 'provide advice as to how the king can best proceed to harm his enemies in military expeditions'.[77]

A remarkable surviving intelligence report written in 1336, detailing French preparations for war, demonstrated the extent of information which could be gathered. Unfortunately its author is unknown, but it was written at York, though much of the information it contained must have been obtained in Paris. The support that the French proposed to give the Scots was reported; a substantial naval force had been collected in Normandy, including thirty ironclad galleys so strong that no ship could possibly resist them. The total size of the planned army was put at 40,000; it was intended to mount a double assault, with landings at Portsmouth and in Fife. The report was clearly put together from various sources, for it concluded with a section about the exploits of English troops in Scotland.[78] Such intelligence briefing papers are rare. One reason for this was given in a report by an English agent about the activities of the count of Foix in 1369 and the intrigues of the French. Once read, the document was to be burned, so as to keep the business secret. In this case, the instruction was not obeyed, but this was surely exceptional.[79]

Valuable no doubt as the report of 1336 was, it needed to be supplemented by continued observation, and the efforts made to discover the scale of French naval preparations and activity in 1339 provide a good example of English spying. In May one Potterwille was paid 45s and instructed by the king and his council to spy out the French galleys coming to the port of Zwin in the Low Countries. Jean le Clerc of Antwerp and his men were given 4s 6d as a reward for watching by night from their boats for the French galleys. Later in the year a royal sergeant went out in a boat, hired at a cost of 4s 6d, on a similar mission. In addition to these activities in the Low Countries, William de la Pole sent what the account somewhat coyly calls 'messengers' to spy on the French galleys in Normandy. Nor was spying by land neglected. The earl of Salisbury paid £33 15s to the margrave of Jülich for spies sent by him to St Quentin, Peronne and the French court, and £4 10s was spent on others sent on the advice of James van Artevelde.[80]

The arrangements for Edward III to take an expedition to France in 1369 provide a splendid example of the way in which intelligence influenced military planning. The English plans were constantly being altered and updated as new information came in about the intentions of the French. Letters on 7 August stressed that the king had recently had news of important, but unspecified, matters, and a substantial force was ordered to Sandwich on 18 August, ready to embark. On 13 August Edward wrote that he now had information that the French were about to attack the Isle of Wight and Hampshire, and arrangements were to be made for coastal defence. On the next day letters went out ordering the postponement of the Sandwich muster until 3 September. Then, later on the very same day, men were asked to go to the port immediately, because French attack by sea was imminent (it in fact took place on Portsmouth in September). On 18 August the king issued letters telling his followers that a French army had left Harfleur and was marching on the English forces to the north. Battle would follow. The English army in Normandy under John of Gaunt did indeed first come into contact with the French on 23 August, although no battle actually took place. In the end, the king himself did not go on campaign, but the troops that sailed to France provided invaluable reinforcements for Lancaster.[81] These changing plans no doubt confused many of those involved, and may give an impression of muddle and uncertainty, but it made good sense to adjust intentions in accordance with the most up-to-date information about French aims.

At the same time that every effort was made to find out what the plans and troop dispositions of the enemy were, English strategic intentions had to be kept secret. In 1297 some care was taken not to reveal English plans for a campaign on the Continent. The writs of summons that were sent out for a muster at London did not specify where the troops were to be sent. Edward I's opponents complained that without knowing where the campaign was to be, it was impossible to make proper preparations. While it may be that Edward maintained this secrecy because he knew that there would be hostility to an expedition to Flanders, he must surely also have hoped to deceive the French.[82]

In 1346 Edward III landed in Normandy. Writs had been issued forbidding anyone to leave England for eight days after his departure, so as to prevent spies communicating the news to the French.[83] The landing was certainly a surprise to the French; the destination of the expedition had been carefully kept secret. French merchants in England had been arrested in the previous years, although such precautions did not prevent the French receiving from their agents a report of preparations at Portsmouth and of discussions in a Great Council early in 1346. The destination of the expedition was not, however, revealed. Was the army intended to relieve the siege of Aiguillon in Gascony? Was Edward intending to renew operations in Brittany? These were the likely alternatives. It was very probably the advice of a French exile – and traitor – Godfrey of Harcourt that led the king to decide on a landing in the Cotentin peninsula at a very late stage in the proceedings. It is conceivable that it was no more than an accident of wind and weather that directed the fleet to St Vaast-la-Hougue; it is more likely that this was a brilliant stroke of generalship, in which the French were deluded into thinking that the landing would be anywhere but Normandy, much as the Germans were to be similarly deluded centuries later, in 1944.[84]

Another means of maintaining secrecy was to prevent enemy spies from operating. There was, of course, no counter-espionage service, but cases of espionage were certainly discovered. In 1285 it was found that Nicholas de Waltham had acted as an agent of the Welsh prince Llywelyn, and of Simon de Montfort's sons Guy and Aymer, in Edward's court. The connection was the result of Llywelyn's marriage to Montfort's daughter Eleanor.[85] The most spectacular case where a spy was caught came in 1295. One of Edward's household knights, Thomas de Turberville, who hailed from the Welsh marches, had been captured in Gascony in 1294. He reappeared in England in the following year, announcing that he had escaped. In reality, the French had let him go, keeping his sons as hostages, on condition that he reported on events in England. A letter he wrote to the Provost of Paris was intercepted. In it, he revealed the defenceless state of the Isle of Wight, reported on troops, supplies and funds to be sent to Gascony, and discussed the diplomatic efforts being made by the English. Turberville did more than report on events; he claimed to have made arrangements for the Welsh to rebel, should the Scots rise against Edward. Once the letter was discovered, Turberville was soon arrested, tried and executed for treason.[86]

Cases of spying became more frequent in the second half of the fourteenth century. In 1356 Robert de Preston was commissioned to search for, and arrest, a Scotsman whom he had reported to be in England, 'spying the secrets of the realm, and sending intelligence home'. In 1359 four men were appointed to arrest John of Cornwall and William of Derby, who in spite of their English names were said to be adherents of the French king. They had entered England secretly, and were said to be wandering around in London and elsewhere, finding out the secrets of the realm. Early in Richard II's reign the betrayal of the secrets of the realm to a Frenchman in Paris were counted among the crimes of an Italian merchant, Ugolino Gerard.[87] Many arrests of alleged spies took place; Newgate held large numbers, though in December 1380 a lot of suspects were released on royal orders.[88] In many cases, arrest was no doubt the result of popular paranoia, rather than of genuine spying activities.

In the fifteenth century spies continued to be extensively used. There was much alarm at the scale of spying during the Wars of the Roses, and evidence certainly suggests that civil war stimulated their activity. Scouts were of course much used to locate enemy forces, and had it not been for a spy in the Lancastrian army, Edward IV would have been captured in 1470. Edward as a matter of course allowed sheriffs substantial sums, up to £300, to cover their intelligence costs. In 1468 his central costs on such activities came to over £2,200. This did not approach the levels advised by Jean de Bueil in *Le Jouvencel*, whose recommendation was that princes should spend a third of their income in this way, but it was certainly a substantial item of expenditure.[89] The very end of the middle ages saw one important element of the armoury of the modern spy introduced: the earliest reference in England to the use of a cipher in intelligence work dates from 1499.[90]

Intelligence was important in the formulation of strategy; it was also important in achieving tactical success. In the Bayeux Tapestry, Duke William is shown before the battle of Hastings interrogating a

Duke William of Normandy questioning Vital, before the battle of Hastings.

Norman knight, Vital, who had been sent forward as a scout, about the position of the English troops. There are many examples of occasions when English forces obviously had good information available to them. Henry I was a man who believed to the full in the value of proper intelligence. The Tinchebray and Brémule campaigns of 1106 and 1119 were so successful, in no small measure due to the good information Henry had about the activities of his opponents. In 1123 the defeat of the rebels in Normandy at Bourgthéroulde was achieved because the earl of Chester employed spies who were able to discover the movements of the rebel forces.[91] In 1174 the king of Scots was surprised outside Alnwick and captured, thanks to information provided by a spy or scout, sent out on the advice of Ranulf de Glanville.[92] So important was intelligence that commanders might not always trust their informants, but sought to see for themselves. In 1198 Richard I almost succeeded in capturing his rival, Philip II of France. Initially he employed Mercadier and a local knight as informants, but then preferred to rely on his own acute observation. In 1202 William Marshal and the earls of Salisbury and Warenne rode out to check information given them by their scouts, that Philip II had given up the siege of Arques.[93]

The value of intelligence was again well illustrated in the civil wars of Henry III's reign. In the manoeuvrings before the battle of Evesham, Edward and his ally the earl of Gloucester had the advantage of the elder Simon in terms of information. Simon de Montfort had been trapped west of the River Severn when Edward took Worcester and destroyed the bridge there, and then moved on to seize Gloucester. The royalist forces were able to thwart him at every move. Then, thanks to a female transvestite spy called Margoth, Edward received excellent information about the troops under the younger Simon de Montfort at Kenilworth, which were camped outside the castle. Young Simon was caught completely unawares, literally with his trousers down by one account. Edward was then able to turn his full attention back to the elder Montfort. The army was deployed in three columns, and Montfort was trapped at Evesham. His intelligence was very limited, and indeed he was unaware that the troops he saw advancing towards Evesham were those of his opponents; he initially thought that they were those of his son.[94]

It would be both chauvinist and unrealistic to assume that English intelligence was consistently successful. Sometimes good information was available, but it proved impossible to make effective use of it. In 1299 Edward I was informed about the activities of Scottish ambassadors overseas, and he duly made arrangements – which did not in the end work out – to capture them at sea on their return journey.[95] Equally, there are many examples of the problems caused by a lack of good intelligence. In 1118 Henry I was engaged on the siege of Laigle, when he was informed by his chamberlain, William de Tancarville, that Rouen was threatened by his enemies. The siege was abandoned, but when Henry reached Rouen he found that the threat to the city was non-existent.[96] Far more serious was the outbreak of the Anglo-French war in 1294, which must be one of the most striking examples of a total failure of intelligence. The French publicly took a very aggressive line in negotiations over Gascony, demanding that Edward I appear before the *parlement* of Paris to answer accusations. Edmund of Lancaster and other English negotiators were persuaded that the French were prepared to enter into a secret deal. This involved a formal surrender of Gascony, which would be followed by a full restoration to the English. The surrender took place; the restoration did not. No proper military preparations were made in Gascony, and all the advantage in the early stages of the war lay with the French.[97] In 1322 Edward II marched his army north as far as Edinburgh, only to be forced to retreat south again.[98] Scouts were used to try to locate the Scots. No enemy was to be seen; the land had been emptied prior to the English advance. 'We found in our way neither man nor beast', wrote the king. The Scots had clearly good information about the English; the reverse was not the case. To be fair, Edward did receive information that the Scots were pursuing him after he had crossed the English border, for he sent for reinforcements; even so, he only just evaded capture near Byland.

Jean le Bel's account of the Weardale campaign of 1327 gives a good impression of the problems resulting from a lack of good information about the enemy's movements: the English army had little more to go on than sightings of plumes of smoke from homesteads burned by the Scots, and were constantly confused by the noises of deer and other animals.[99] Not only might intelligence be lacking; it might be available, but prove false. In 1351 there were fears of major French attacks on Calais and on the English forces in Brittany and Gascony, which it was thought would be followed up by an invasion attempt, but the threat never materialised.[100] Intelligence had its failures as well as its successes.

The idea that medieval warfare somehow took place in a strategic vacuum is plainly absurd. There were grand strategic concepts, some perhaps too grand to have been achieved; there were some campaigns that appear to the historian to have little logic and coherence. Strategic ideas became more complex and ambitious in the late twelfth century, as Richard I and John sought to nullify the French monarchy's threat to Normandy and the other lands they held in France by means of a grand alliance. With the capacity that states acquired to recruit larger armies, and to deploy much greater financial resources, such strategies looked increasingly realistic by the late thirteenth and early fourteenth centuries. It would be wrong to think in terms of a revolutionary change in strategy, but the relative failure of Edward III's plans in the initial phase of the Hundred Years War (1337–40) saw a marked shift away from the concept of achieving victory over the French by acting in concert with the princes of the Low Countries and Germany. There was a full realisation that warfare had its economic aspects, and that there were more means of putting pressure on an opponent than simply defeating him in battle. Political opportunities, such as the succession dispute in Brittany, were seized; campaigns were carefully planned and co-ordinated. Strategies were not thought through in the absence of information; medieval rulers and soldiers were fully aware of the importance of good intelligence. There may have been no medieval equivalent of the Second World War's Ultra, but the best medieval commanders no less than their modern successors understood that good strategy and effective tactics are based on sound intelligence.

9

Chivalry

It is hard to reconstruct the cast of mind of those who fought in medieval armies. Numbers of men can be calculated, their food consumption estimated, their speed of march worked out. It is not so easy to depict the cultural identity of the world in which they lived. Analogies can be suggested; in an attempt to counter excessively idealistic attitudes to medieval knighthood it has been pointed out that the rugby club bar provides a possible modern parallel for twelfth-century post-battle celebrations.[1] Even today the term 'chivalry' carries too many overtones for it to be applied with any ease to a past society with its very different values. Contradictions apparently abounded in the world of medieval chivalry. In Edward II's reign William Marmion was given a helmet with a gilded crest by his lady-love, and told to make it famous in the most dangerous place in Britain, a chivalric fancy which nearly led to his death outside the walls of Norham-on-Tweed. In 1342 in Brittany Walter Mauny charged a body of French troops, all for a vow that he would give his love a kiss.[2] Yet in 1212 William, servant of Adam Cook, brought to King John when he was at Rochester the heads of six decapitated Welshmen. After Evesham, the head of Simon de Montfort, gruesomely decorated with his genitals, was sent to Lady Mortimer. Llywelyn ap Gruffudd's head decorated the Tower of London after his death in battle in 1282. In 1306 Edward I arranged for the imprisonment of Scottish ladies of high birth in cages, so that they would be in full public view on the walls of the castles at Berwick and Roxburgh.[3] The Black Prince and his men sacked the city of Limoges in 1370: 'It was a most melancholy business; for all ranks, ages and sexes cast themselves on their knees before the prince, begging for mercy; but he was so inflamed with passion and revenge that he listened to none, but all were put to the sword, wherever they could be found.'[4] It is not easy to reconcile head-hunting, the savage mutilation of the defeated, massacres, and the mistreatment of women with the *courtoisie* of knightly cultures. For the great Dutch historian Huizinga, there was a clear contrast between the dictates of chivalry, which exercised an unfortunate influence on

military decisions, and the demands of strategy and tactics.[5]
The contradictions between the world of chivalry, and the reality
of campaigning, are not an invention of modern historians. A
mid-fourteenth-century poem, 'The Vows of the Heron', satirised
chivalric attitudes with gentle humour and some perception:

> When we are in taverns, drinking strong wine, and ladies with
> white throats and tight bodices pass and look at us, their spark-
> ling eyes resplendent with smiling beauty, nature makes our
> hearts desire to fight, looking for mercy from them as a result.
> Then we could defeat Yaumont and Aguilant, and others Oliver
> and Roland. But when we are in the field, on our trotting
> warhorses, shields hung round our necks and lances lowered, a
> great frost numbing us, limbs crushed before and behind, and
> our enemies advancing on us, then we would like to be in a great
> cellar, and never make a vow again.[6]

The concept of chivalry

The term 'chivalry' itself is not modern. It is true that it is not to be
found with any frequency in that classic of knightly behaviour, the
Histoire of William Marshal, but the word was used in the thirteenth
century. A poet described Simon de Montfort, punning on his name,
'Il est el mond et est si fort, Si ad grant chevalerie.'[7] In the fourteenth
century one of the high-priests of French chivalry, Geoffrey de
Charny, wrote a *Livre de chevalerie*. Usage of the term does not
define the chronology of the concept; as far as England is concerned,
there is a good case for seeing it as a development stemming from the
Conquest, and developing rapidly in the late eleventh and early
twelfth centuries.[8] The body of ideas encompassed in the word was
not unchanging, and there was a fresh, and much greater, emphasis
on chivalric ideas in the fourteenth century. The bulk of treatises on
the subject were written in the later middle ages, from the mid
fourteenth century, and although most of the themes they deal with
can be traced back at least into the twelfth century, it is clear that a
fourteenth- or fifteenth-century knight might realistically be expected
to have a much more sophisticated mental map of chivalric enterprise
than his twelfth-century forebear could have possessed.[9]

The concept of chivalry is not easy to define. Its horsiness needs to
be emphasised; entry to the chivalric world was confined to those
who could be expected to ride, fully armed, in war, and who at least
aspired to knightly status. 'It is best that chivalric things should be
done on horseback and not on foot', was the advice that the constable of Norham, Thomas Grey, gave to William Marmion. The

Shields drawn and painted by Matthew Paris in about 1244, from
his *Liber Additamenta*.

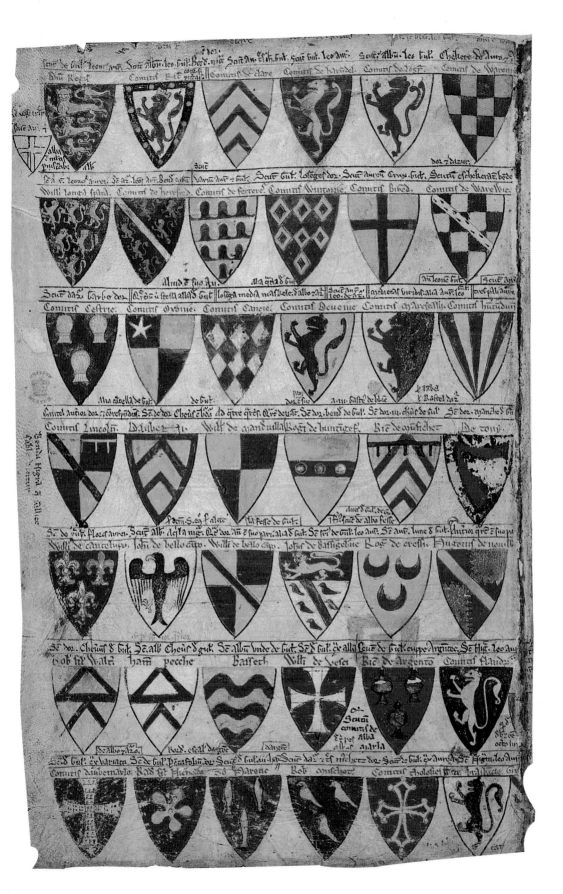

chivalric values that were stressed were those of *largesse*, or liberality, *courtoisie*, or courtesy, *prouesse*, or prowess, and *loyauté*, or
loyalty.[10] King Stephen's son Eustace was described by the author of
the *Gesta Stephani* as a model of knighthood: he was gentle, courteous, cheerful in his liberality, possessed military skills, and was
capable both of pursuing goals of peace and of confronting his
enemies with proper warlike severity. Not all of these ideals are
immediately and necessarily appropriate to the successful soldier, nor
indeed was it clear that Eustace in reality possessed them, for the
same chronicler also described the way in which he ordered his men
'to kill those who came in their way and commit indiscriminately
every cruelty he could think of'.[11] Was chivalry a distraction from the
harsh reality of warfare, a cultural construct which stressed audacity
and made it hard for men to behave with the caution, or even
trickery, that was needed for military success? Did it restrain the
excesses of soldiers, or idealise violence? Was it perhaps a set of
values for the bedchamber and the tournament field, to be discarded
where proper warfare was concerned, or did it provide the necessary
steel, the element of bravado, to give men the courage to engage in
the unpleasant business of fighting? The answers are not the same for
all periods. The life of William the Marshal, written in the early
thirteenth century, though its hero was regarded as a model of
chivalry, does not describe the same world as that which Froissart
wrote about in the late fourteenth century.

Heraldry

There were many elements to the world of chivalry. The panoply of
colour displayed in coats of arms was one of the external signs of
participation in this exotic noble culture. The origins of heraldry
appear to lie in the early twelfth century, with family devices at first
applied to banners, and then soon to shield, surcoat and horse-
trapper. Orderic Vitalis describes how, soon after the battle of
Brémule in 1119, Ralph Rufus changed arms frequently in order to
avoid recognition.[12] In the early stages, heraldic devices were only for
the great men. The young Marshal carried a shield bearing the arms
of his lord, William de Tancarville, in 1167, rather than a device of
his own. In 1136, at the siege of Exeter, no devices were worn,
making it impossible to tell friend from foe. But heraldry soon
multiplied; the need to identify men in tournaments being quite as
important as the recognition of friends and enemies in battle.
Retainers and followers adapted the designs used by their lords, and
family trees can be constructed showing the spread of particular
devices. By Henry III's reign, Westminster Abbey was being

decorated with the coats of arms of the great English magnates. The earliest roll of arms, Glover's Roll, containing 211 coats of arms, was probably drawn up in the 1250s.[13] Rolls of arms soon multiplied. Some, such as the Falkirk Roll of Arms, celebrated particular campaigns, while the Dering Roll, dating from the late 1270s and containing 324 names, was connected to the castle-guard duties owed at Dover. These rolls were the work of heralds, but were surely commissioned by nobles, proud of their arms. The entries in a straightforward roll were a straightforward heraldic record. Thus the Falkirk Roll gives for Hugh Despenser *quartile dargent et de goules et le quarter de goules frette dor od le baston de sable.* The Song of Caerlaverock was a different matter. It combined a narrative poem describing the campaign of 1300 up to the successful siege of Caerlaverock with character sketches and descriptions of the coats of arms of all the barons and bannerets participating. Here, 'the good Hugh Despenser, who loyally on his courser knows how to break up a mêlée, had a banner quarterly, with a black baston on the white, and the gules fretty yellow'.[14]

One purpose of heraldry was to aid recognition in battle or, perhaps above all, tournament – much like a modern football strip. Coats of arms came, however, to incorporate much more than that, being emblems of family pride and honour, symbolising relationships and recalling past bravery. For a coat of arms to be displayed upside down was a mark of deep disgrace, a dishonour hard to expunge. The depth of feelings is hard to recapture, but men must have felt that one purpose in campaigning was to justify and further ennoble the arms that they bore. John Charnels told a story of how he had been riding with a troop of some forty cavalry in France when he captured a French knight who bore the same coat of arms, *azure a bend or*, as William Scrope, one of his companions. Scrope wished to kill him on the spot, but his life was saved because John made him take off the coat of arms. This was told in the course of an elaborate case heard in the court of chivalry in 1386, between Richard Scrope and Robert Grosvenor, both of whom claimed the right to this particular heraldic device.[15] Important as heraldry was, with men taking much pride in their arms, it was nevertheless possible to discard them altogether, or to wear someone else's. Edward III frequently appeared incognito in tournaments, perhaps because no one would fight properly against the king in his own name. At Evesham, the future Edward I had no compunction about advancing under the captured banners of Simon de Montfort's son. At Bannockburn the earl of Gloucester did not wear a surcoat bearing his coat of arms. This led to his death; had the Scots known who he was, they would not have killed him, such would have been his ransom.[16] An alternative to the hereditary coat of arms was the use

of personal badges, which often served as a mark that a man belonged to a particular retinue. In 1335 William Montague was presented by Edward III with a crest of an eagle, as a mark of particular
favour, and of course later in the reign the Order of the Garter was
to provide a highly select group with its own special emblem and
motto. By the later fifteenth century the use of individual emblems
was coming to replace the traditional, and by now often highly
complex, coat of arms.[17]

Tournaments

The tournament was one essential form of celebration of the values
and skills involved in chivalry. Much has been written about tournaments. In the twelfth and thirteenth centuries they were virtually
small-scale battles, offering opportunities to take prisoners for
ransom as well as a means of gaining renown. Richard I licensed
tournaments in England as a means of providing the inexperienced
with a taste of something very close to real warfare. Men could learn
how cavalry forces should manoeuvre, and how to fight in a mêlée.
There might even be footsoldiers present, making the contrast between battle and tournament negligible.[18] A further distinction began
to emerge in the thirteenth century, between tournaments *à
l'outrance*, serious affairs in which men might be killed, and those *à
plaisance*, chivalric festivals sometimes taking the form of an
Arthurian Round Table celebration. In addition, tournaments might
have important political connotations, and even be regarded by the
Crown as an excuse for its opponents to plot rebellion. The pro-
hibition of tournaments was one of the means by which the minority
government at the start of Henry III's reign struggled to achieve
peace in the land. In the 1240s tournaments between the court
faction, with many of its members foreigners, and those opposed to
the king and his policies, posed an obvious threat to political stabil-
ity. Edward I attempted to regulate tournaments in 1292, and was
responsible for holding Round Tables in north Wales in 1284 and at
Falkirk in 1302 as celebrations of success in war. Yet the later years
of his reign saw the tournaments largely prohibited. From providing
essential practice for war, the tournament became all too often
an attractive alternative to the rigours of campaign, a means of
displaying chivalric skills without too much discomfort. To Edward's
fury, twenty-two knights left the army wintering on the Scottish
border in 1306–7, to go abroad for a tournament. An attempt to
satisfy demand with a tournament at Wark was abandoned.[19]

Under Edward III what had become a traditional policy of discour-
aging and prohibiting tournaments was reversed. The king was

The jousts at St Inglevert, from a fifteenth-century copy of Froissart's *Chronicles*.

himself no mean tourneyer, and whether consciously or uncon-
sciously the tournament was avidly developed as a means of exploit-
ing chivalric sentiment and encouraging support for his enterprises in
France and Scotland. The successful conclusions of campaigns were
often marked with tournaments. In 1341 a great tournament at
Dunstable saw the king himself compete, in the guise of an ordinary
knight. All the younger earls joined in with a will, and over 250
knights were said to have been present in what appears to have been
a mismanaged affair. So late did the proceedings start that it quickly
became too dark. A great Round Table at Windsor in 1344 was
followed by an attempt to create a grand Arthurian order of knights,
an over-ambitious plan which finally bore fruit, later in the decade,
on a much smaller scale with the foundation of the Order of the
Garter. The division of the Garter knights into two groups suggests
that they may have formed two tournament teams.[20] Women began
to be invited to tournaments, as spectators; at one, in 1331, the
queen and her ladies were nearly killed when their viewing stand
collapsed. At the 1344 Round Table, a special banquet was given for
all the ladies present; no men were allowed to attend, with the
exception of two fortunate French knights.[21] A play-acting element
featured in many tournaments, such as that in which one team
dressed as a pope and twelve cardinals challenged all-comers.[22] It is

Aspects of later medieval chivalry. On the right, Sir
Nigel Loring (d. 1386) is shown wearing a surcoat
powdered with the symbols of the Order of the
Garter. In reality, the garters would have been
smaller, and far more numerous. The complex
tournament scene, below, shows a mêlée in a
fifteenth-century tournament, from a treatise by
René d'Anjou. The combatants are enclosed within
the lists; ladies look on from a tall stand. The scene
opposite shows a fifteenth-century banquet with a
round table, displaying the influence of Arthurian
myth.

striking that in all the pageantry and allegory there was virtually no overt attempt at direct anti-French propaganda. The tournaments were celebrations of an international chivalric culture, and while in glorifying knighthood they undoubtedly assisted and encouraged enthusiasm for war, there was no necessity to turn them into nationalistic festivals. It is sometimes suggested that the later medieval tournament, with its specialised equipment and formalised jousts, no longer provided any real training for warfare. Yet the basic skills of horsemanship and use of weapons were surely still transferable from the tournament to the field of battle in the fifteenth century as they had been in the twelfth or thirteenth centuries.[23]

Cults and orders of knighthood

The cult of Arthur and his knights was an important part of English chivalric culture. Richard I gave the legendary king's sword to Tancred of Sicily. Edward I went so far as to excavate the tombs of Arthur and Guinevere at Glastonbury; an archaeological triumph as far as contemporaries were concerned. Whether the Round Tables he held were specifically Arthurian is not clear, and the tale of an

Arthurian masque at his second wedding is palpably unreliable. The chronicler Pierre Langtoft certainly saw Edward in Arthurian terms, though how far the king himself was convinced by such flummery is far from clear. The most spectacular chivalric occasion in the reign was probably the Feast of the Swans held in 1306 on the occasion of the knighting of his eldest son, along with some 300 other young men. The significance of the swans, upon which all present swore oaths, is unknown; there is certainly nothing obviously Arthurian about them.[24] For Edward III, the plan to found an Order of the Round Table was clearly Arthurian. In literature, the *Morte Arthure* suggests parallels between the careers of Arthur and the English king. Yet the Round Table was an abortive project. The Order of the Garter which replaced it was not obviously Arthurian. Nor was all that was Arthurian necessarily supportive of the king's campaigns; the *Morte Arthure*, for example, was critical of English war policies.

A great deal has been written about the origins of the Order of the Garter itself. It has been seen as the central device by which the king 'harnessed the idealism of chivalry to his cause and linked to himself by an obligation of honour some of the greatest names in the land'.[25] Yet its importance in the context of Edward III's reign has surely been exaggerated, perhaps in part because the Order still survives to this day. It was in fact a very small order of twenty-six knights, and while it included men such as the earls of Lancaster and Warwick, there were also some relatively obscure knights in the number. The Hainaulter Sanchet d'Aubrichecourt was not well-known, nor was the German Henry d'Enne. The earls of Northampton and Suffolk were striking omissions from the list of the first founder-members of the Garter. The establishment of the Order was clearly closely connected to the battle of Crécy; it is likely that all the members with the exception of Lancaster (who could hardly have been omitted) had distinguished themselves in the fighting there. The precise date of the foundation is unclear; the spring or summer of 1348 seems the most likely. It was on 6 August 1348 that Edward established the College of St George at Windsor, which was closely associated with the Garter. The tale that the unusual emblem of the Garter was chosen because the king picked up the Countess of Salisbury's garter at a ball, rebuking those who mocked him by saying 'Honi soit qui mal y pense' is a later myth, propagated in the sixteenth century by Polydore Vergil. Garters were in fact an article of male, not female, clothing, but why the king chose such an odd emblem is a mystery. It was probably not until the reign of Henry V that formal statutes for the Order were issued, though they probably largely followed earlier practice. Membership of the Order brought with it surprisingly few obligations and privileges, and it is interesting that the chronicler Geoffrey le Baker saw as the prime purpose not the pursuit of chivalric aims, but the maintenance of an almshouse for impoverished knights. Whether the obligation to say masses for the souls of dead Garter knights yielded effective results is a matter for the theologian, not the historian.[26]

Law and romance

Chivalry has to be seen in the context of the widely recognised legal codes which governed the practice of warfare. While the detailed evidence for the law of arms is late in date, there is sufficient to show that some at least of the central concepts were well known in the mid twelfth century. At Bedford the garrison surrendered 'in accordance with the laws of war', and at this period, as later, the unfurling of banners was regarded as a formal sign of the declaration of hostilities.[27] The law of arms as it developed by the fourteenth century has been studied with skill and perception by Maurice Keen. The laws of war were held to be internationally valid, based ultimately on the work of civil and canon lawyers. The concept of a just war was carefully worked out; a just, public war had to be declared by a sovereign prince. Such questions as the distribution of spoils, ransoming practice, the conduct of sieges were all covered by the law of arms, which was enforced in special military courts such as the English Court of the Constable. The law of arms might not do much to limit and control warfare; in 1391 one mercenary captain argued that he had fought loyally in the English cause, and that he had 'done all those things which a man can and ought to do in a just war, as taking Frenchmen and putting them to ransom, living on the country and despoiling it, and leading the company under his command about the realm of France, and burning and firing places in it'.[28] Interestingly, although there was a considerable scholarly literature on the law of arms, there was virtually no English contribution to it. There was no question of the English not accepting this law, but perhaps because of the strong common law tradition in England, this was not an attractive discipline for English legal scholars to profess.

As well as the legal background to chivalrous conduct, literary works helped to inform knightly attitudes. Such books were certainly known to a knightly audience. One of Edward I's knights, Brian FitzAlan, owned a copy of *Perlesvaus*; Fulk de Pembridge left two romances in his will; four romances were among the possessions of James Audley.[29] Various elements in warfare can be identified from the romances which did more than simply mirror the attitudes of chivalry. Equality between those fighting was important. Numbers should be equal on both sides, and although a chivalric hero might win great glory by attacking a force which greatly outnumbered his own, he might be accused of recklessness. Equality of forces was not possible where women were involved; in one romance Alexander took tribute from the Amazons rather than fight them. It was therefore wrong to assault castles which were in the hands of women. Also, 'it were not well done for to kill a man that sleeps'. Richard I, in one romance, was horrified at the suggestion that he should kill Saladin as he slumbered, though in other works there was nothing wrong in taking every possible advantage of Saracens. It was shameful to attack and fight men who were wounded, or those who had no weapons. Achilles should not have slain an unarmed Hector as he was leading prisoners from the field. An opponent who was unhorsed should be assisted to remount before the fight continued. In one case, in *Roland and Vernagu*, an exhausted knight was allowed by his opponent to rest and sleep in mid-fight. Honour was so important in the romances that there could be no question of making a tactical retreat. 'Better is it to die manly, Than to flee with shame and villainy', was how it was put in *Guy of Warwick*. As for the treatment of the populace in captured cities, when an imaginary German emperor took Bordeaux in one romance, he 'made it to be cried in every street that no man should be so hardy on pain of death to violate any woman, or deflower any maid'. The practice of taking ransoms was criticised in the *Morte Arthure*, and other romances suggest that those taken prisoner would choose death rather than captivity.[30]

It is, of course, dangerous to attempt to reconstruct the real attitudes men had towards war, or indeed any activity, from the fiction that was popular in the period. The ethos of the First World War cannot be recreated by a careful reading of the exploits of Biggles in the works of Captain W.E. Johns. There are difficulties in using the work of Froissart to illustrate chivalric practice in war, for his interpretation of events was heavily coloured by the ideals which he shared with romantic literature. Nor were the romances the only kind of literature that was read. Edward I is known to have quoted a literary work on only one occasion, when he rebuked the earl of March in 1304 for waiting until the enemy had gone before setting out himself. '*Quant la guerre fu finee, si trest Audigier sespee*' (When the war was over, Audigier drew his sword). The quotation is not exact, but the romance of Audigier is a work of the most disgusting excremental humour that can be imagined, and no doubt reduced Edward and his knights to gales of helpless laughter.[31] Another example of the type of work that no doubt proved extremely popular was one which starts in conventional enough fashion, with a knight riding out in search of fame, fortune and adventure. He was fortunate enough to meet three ladies bathing in a stream, who offered him gifts in return for their clothes, which his squire had stolen. The third lady gave him a curious gift: the ability to endow women's private parts with speech. This, as can be imagined, made for interesting subsequent adventures.[32] Such a tale is as much a part of the chivalric culture of the fourteenth century as the more orthodox romances, and it raises the question of how seriously the latter were in practice regarded. It should, however, be noted that Edward III possessed in his substantial library no fewer than fifty-nine chivalric romances, which appear to have been widely read in his immediate circle.[33]

The practice of war

It would be too simple to argue that war was a realistic affair and that chivalric concepts were wholly irrelevant to it. Ideals are important, even if they are not commonly attained. Yet it is much easier to demonstrate the importance of chivalric ideas in warfare in some periods than in others. There is, for example, surprisingly little in the conduct of Edward I's campaigns that fits a chivalric model. This was no doubt at least in part because the Welsh and the Scots were regarded as rebels, not worthy of honourable treatment; it was certainly not because chivalric concepts were unknown. The author of the *Song of Caerlaverock* tried his best to fit the 1300 Galloway campaign into a chivalric model, but did not find the task easy. He praised the gallantry of Edward's knights as they warded off the blows of the missiles hurled at them by the defenders of Caerlaverock castle. 'There I saw Ralph de Gorges, a newly dubbed knight, hit by stones and tumble and fall more than once to the ground, for he was so haughty in spirit that he would not deign to withdraw.'[34] Pierre Langtoft, in his chronicle, even criticised Edward I for a lack of chivalry in comparison to King Arthur. Above all, he was not sufficiently generous to his followers; nor did he get up as early in the morning as the legendary king.

Direct references to appeals to chivalry are not commonly recorded before the somewhat questionable evidence of Froissart becomes available. Yet clearly even so cynical a ruler as Rufus was well aware of the force of chivalric concepts when he paroled some captured knights. 'Far be it from me to believe that a knight would break his sworn word. If he did so he would be despised for ever as an outlaw.' Rufus's own word as a knight could certainly be relied upon. Orderic Vitalis noted that when he took prisoners, he 'was not cruel in his treatment of knights, but was gracious and courteous, jovial and at ease'.[35] When Stephen provided his opponent Matilda with an escort to go from Arundel to join her half-brother Robert of Gloucester, this was because it was not 'the custom of honourable knights to refuse anyone, even their bitterest enemy'.[36] Later, even in the businesslike world of indentured military service, reference to chivalric attitudes can be found. Robert Neville promised John of Gaunt that he would observe the lease of Hornby castle 'by faith as I am a loyal knight'. Simon Raly, an esquire, agreed to serve Matthew Gournay 'de son corps et gentilesse d'armes'.[37]

The chivalric worlds of the tournament and of genuine warfare came close in the incidents of single combat which often punctuated campaigning. Some were unplanned, such as Henry de Bohun's unfortunate accidental encounter with Bruce prior to Bannockburn, but more commonly they were organised in advance. Before the battle of Halidon Hill in 1333 there was a planned fight between the giant Scot Turnbull and the English household knight Robert Benhale. Many examples can be given. In 1327 when the earl of Moray and James Douglas were besieging Alnwick, there were 'grand jousts of war by covenant'.[38] In 1346 when the English and French faced each other across the Somme, a French knight challenged any English knight to have three jousts with him, 'for the love of his lady'. Thomas Colville met the challenge. The third joust was abandoned, since the French knight's shield was broken, and to have continued was considered too dangerous. Following this encounter, the two men apparently became close friends. In 1359 on Robert Knollys' *chevauchée* into central France, the English and French armies drew up opposing each other, neither side moving all day, apart from some young knights and squires who, with permission of their commanders, jousted with their equivalents on the other side. In the same year, when Edward III's great army advanced to Rheims, Bartholomew Burghersh jousted with the French, by agreement and at their request.[39] John Seton, a Scotsman fighting with the English on one of Knollys' raids in the 1370s, on one occasion vaulted the barriers of a French town, and engaged in single combat with any of the Frenchmen who wanted to test their skill on him. The French forbade anyone to kill him by archery; after a period of combat, he high-jumped the barrier, and made his way back to the English army. 'This gallant feat of Sir John Seton was highly prized by all manner of persons.' Another knight who tried, on the same expedition, to win a reputation for bravery, rode up to the barriers outside Paris, struck them as he had vowed to do, and turned his horse for home, only to be killed by a butcher in the suburbs, who, doubtless, was less appreciative of his chivalrous deed than the French knights who had cheered him on.[40]

It was not only single combat that was arranged in chivalrous fashion. An example of a high degree of chivalry is provided by the carefully organised Battle of the Thirty in Brittany in 1351, with the two sides closely matched in strength. That was exceptional, but concepts of chivalry might well be used to encourage men to fight battles when common sense pointed in a different direction. A direct appeal to chivalry was made in 1469, by Viscount Lisle, who challenged William Berkeley to battle. 'I require of you of knighthood and of manhood to appoint a day to meet me.' William agreed a date, set Nibley Green as the place, and the time as eight or nine o'clock. The battle duly took place, with Berkeley's men numbering at a contemporary estimate over 1,000. Lisle was killed, shot in the face by one Black Will.[41]

Decisions in warfare might, certainly, be prompted by chivalrous considerations. In 1147 Stephen provided the money with which the future Henry II paid off his discontented mercenary soldiers, rather than leave him at their mercy. When English troops burned Le Mans, William Marshal ordered his squires to help an old woman whose house had been set alight. Much later, at Bannockburn, the decision of the young earl of Gloucester to charge into the ranks of the Scots was motivated primarily by a chivalric desire to maintain his honour, in the face of charges of cowardice from the king, and of a dispute over his right to lead the vanguard in battle.[42] The dramatic dash by Edward III from Perth in 1336 to rescue the countess of Atholl from Lochindorb surely owed something to the king's chivalric idealism. The pages of Jean le Bel and Froissart contain many examples of chivalrous conduct in war. At the siege of Hennebont in Brittany in 1342 Walter Mauny made a sortie to destroy a powerful French siege engine. This he did, but a French cavalry force pursued him and his men as they retreated to the safety of the castle walls. 'May I never be embraced by my mistress and dear friend, if I enter castle or fortress before I have unhorsed one of these gallopers', exclaimed Mauny. A difficult action followed, but eventually Mauny was able to extricate his men, and duly all received the reward of a kiss. It is possible that the decision to turn and fight was correct, but it seems more likely that Mauny took a totally unnecessary risk to prove his qualities of knighthood.[43] Honour was one of the most important chivalric attributes. At Auray in 1364 John Chandos had great difficulty in persuading Hugh Calveley to take command of the rearguard, for this offended his sense of honour, though in this case the dispute was settled.[44] In the very last battle of the Hundred Years War, at Castillon in 1453, it seems likely that John Talbot, the hardened English commander, ordered the start of battle by unfurling his banner before he realised the strength of the French position. To have then withdrawn would have compromised his honour, even though, as events turned out, it would have saved his life.[45]

Oaths to perform chivalrous actions often prompted men to take dangerous risks. At Poitiers James Audley, with four companions, advanced deep into the French ranks and, fighting with exceptional bravery, was severely wounded. He had sworn to be the first man in any attack in battle involving the king or his sons.[46] While the oaths that men took to perform deeds of valour were serious affairs, the practice was at the same time sufficiently absurd for it to be satirised in the poem 'The Vows of the Heron', which made fun of the vows taken by Edward III and his companions in the initial stage of the war with France. According to the poem, Robert of Artois entered a banquet in London and presented a heron, most cowardly of birds, to the king, because he was too cowardly to pursue his claim to the French throne. This prompted Edward to swear to go to France, and to wait a month for Philip of Valois to come to fight him. The king's dining companions then swore to perform a range of deeds of arms in the coming war. The poem may be satirical, but it seems likely that it poked fun at a real event, and at real oaths, which probably did affect the course of campaigns.[47]

Chivalrous treatment of those who had been defeated with honour was a part of the accepted code of conduct. At a fight outside Calais in 1348 Edward III himself, fighting incognito, struggled for a long time with Eustace of Ribemont; in the end Eustace surrendered to Edward, whom he thought was simply one of Walter de Mauny's knights. At the banquet celebrating the English victory Edward declared Eustace worthy of the highest prize, gave him the fine chaplet of pearls which he was wearing, and freed him without requesting a ransom. In 1356, after Poitiers, the Black Prince served the French king John personally, praising his valour to the skies.[48] Stories should not, however, always be taken at face value. In the final stages of the civil wars of the 1260s the future Edward I defeated Adam Gurdon in single combat. The chroniclers' romanticised version is that Edward ordered his followers to stand aside while he fought Adam, and that so impressed was he with his opponent's valour that he offered him life and fortune if he surrendered. In fact, following his surrender he was handed over to the queen as a prisoner, and he had to buy back his estates for a heavy price.[49]

At an individual level the relationship between chivalry and war-fare can be illustrated from the careers of individual knights. One of the chivalric heroes of the early fourteenth century was Giles of Argentine. His record under Edward I was patchy; he was in trouble in 1302 for deserting the army in Scotland in order to fight in a tournament in Surrey, and his arrest for 'various contempts' was ordered in 1303. He fought strenuously at the siege of Stirling in 1304, and in consideration of his efforts two of his yeomen were pardoned various offences they had committed in London and in Essex. In 1306 he repeated his offence of 1302, and deserted the

Scottish campaign in favour of a tournament, this time overseas. His prowess in jousting was proven in 1309, when he was crowned 'King of the Greenwood' in a great tournament held at Stepney. He went, as a good knight should, to fight in the East, though he was unfortunate enough to be captured *en route* to Rhodes, and to be held prisoner at Salonica. At Edward II's insistence he was released, to die in suitably heroic if foolhardy fashion at Bannockburn. For Barbour, he was the third best knight in Christendom.[50] The culture of the chivalric world went too far in Giles. The sport of the tournament, the fame that could be won in combat with other knights, weighed more heavily with him than it should, while by his day the crusading venture was quixotic. His heroism was displayed in impressive fashion at Bannockburn, but his action was practical folly. His death was, for one chronicler, full of chivalric virtue, for he fell 'thinking it more honourable to perish with so great a man [as Gloucester] than to escape death by flight; for those who fall in battle for their country are known to live in everlasting glory'.[51]

What of the reverse of the coin, those actions which appear totally alien to the world of chivalry? How was it possible to equate them with the ideals? The contradictions between ideals and practice should not be overstressed. There is no doubt that William Marshal was a model of chivalry, 'the best knight in the world'. He had an early career of knight-errantry, showed himself a master of the tournament, went to the Holy Land, and had a lengthy and distinguished military record. Yet his style of warfare was one of swift, destructive mounted raids, of cunning ruses and surprise attacks, rather than one of set-piece battles, heroic cavalry charges against the odds, and protection of the civilian population. The thirteenth-century life of the Marshal suggests that effective war was chivalrous war, and the author gave no indication of any tension between the two. 'Pillage and robbery were not simply taken for granted, rather they were actually approved of as the right, the proper, the courteous way to make war.'[52] In the Hundred Years War there is the example of one of Froissart's minor heroes, Eustace d'Aubrichecourt, who performed 'many fine feats of arms, and often succeeded in knightly combat with noble men, nor could anyone stand up to him because he was young, deeply in love, and full of enterprise'. His lady-love, Isabel of Jülich, sent him horses, love-letters and tokens of her affection 'because he was so bold and courageous, and did so many great deeds of arms that everyone talked about him'. Yet, and this was not seen as inconsistent, 'he acquired much wealth in ransoms, by the sale of towns and castles, through redemptions of the countryside and of houses, and through the safe-conducts he provided'.[53] John Talbot, according to his biographer a man deeply

committed to the code of chivalry, 'seems to have constantly
subordinated notions of chivalric heroism to the overall strategic and
tactical requirements of siege and counter-siege, surprise assault
and plundering raid'.[54]

It is easy to provide examples from military practice of behaviour
which ran counter to the precepts of the idealised chivalric notions of
the romances. There was no question in 1216–17 of the rebel forces
refusing to besiege Lincoln castle because it was held by a woman,
Nicola de la Haye, or of the French not besieging Hennebont in 1342
for a similar reason. There are many cases of attacks on sleeping
enemies: the young Simon de Montfort, son of the earl of Leicester,
is said to have fled naked from his bed when Kenilworth was attacked early in the morning in 1265. Aymer de Valence successfully
surprised Bruce and the Scots at Methven while many of them slept.
Apparently unchivalrous *ruses de guerre* were common. The royalist
forces before the battle of Lincoln in 1217 succeeded in hoodwinking
their opponents into thinking that they were far more numerous than
was in fact the case. Robert FitzWalter and the earl of Winchester
went out to observe the royalist army, and reported that they were
few in number. By moving out of the city into a strong tactical
position, it would be possible to defeat them. The count of Perche,
however, with his marshal, insisted on going out to calculate the size
of the army by the French method, and reported back that it was very
large. They worked out the size by counting banners, ignorant of the

The early thirteenth-century
seal matrix of Robert
FitzWalter, lord of Little
Dunmow in Essex, one of
the rebel commanders at
Lincoln in 1217.

fact that the great men in the royalist force each had two banners. One was kept with them; the other was flown in the baggage train, which the count of Perche thought was a whole army in itself. A similar ruse was employed by Edward I in the Low Countries in 1297, when footsoldiers were sent forward bearing cavalry banners, leading Philip IV to conclude that he had a far larger and more formidable army than was in fact the case.[55] The use of captured banners by Edward before Evesham, to give Simon de Montfort the impression that reinforcements were coming to join him, is another example of the effective use of deception. At Calais in 1349 Edward III arranged a most ingenious ambush for the French, hiding troops behind a screen constructed to look like a strong stone wall, and preparing a drawbridge by sawing most of the way through its timbers so that it could be destroyed by dropping a large stone on it. This devious trap proved highly effective.[56] Such trickery was a normal part of warfare, and there is no evidence to suggest that contemporaries regarded it as beyond the pale. If the cause was just, actions taken in accordance with it were justifiable.

If opponents did not share the same set of chivalric values, then those values might be discarded. Among the many distinctions which Gerald of Wales observed between war in France and war in Wales and Ireland, was the fact that in the first case knights were taken prisoner, and in the second, they were decapitated.[57] Head-hunting was indeed a feature of the Anglo-Welsh wars, and was probably of Welsh origin. In 1233 an English troop of soldiers received a shilling a head from the Crown, as a bounty for the heads of fifty-seven Welshmen slain in the Marches, and according to Matthew Paris, when the Welsh took English towns in 1258, they decapitated all the inhabitants. Edward I had Llywelyn ap Gruffydd's head displayed for years on a pike mounted on the Tower of London. Head-hunting was also occasionally practised in the Scottish wars: the heads of Thomas and Alexander Bruce and their companions were sent as trophies to the Prince of Wales in 1307.[58] Later, in 1318, Edward Bruce's head was sent from the battlefield of Faughart in Ireland to Edward II. This was not the practice in continental warfare.

Rebellion, above all against royal authority, was regarded as a particularly serious matter. It is this, perhaps, which explains the savage retribution reported by Orderic Vitalis on English rebels defeated in 1075 by William de Warenne and Richard de Clare; all, of whatever rank, had their right foot cut off.[59] Yet attitudes shifted, perhaps as a sense of chivalry developed in the late eleventh and twelfth centuries. The Conqueror, hard man that he was, did not take as severe a view of rebels as had earlier rulers, nor did his immediate successors. After 1095 no nobleman suffered death for rebellion against a Norman ruler. Despite the bitter civil conflict of

An initial letter E in the Book of Maccabees, from the bible of about 1175 which was presented by Bishop Hugh du Puiset to Durham Cathedral.

Stephen's reign, rebels against royal authority were hardly ever executed. The case of Arnulf of Hesdin and his supporters in 1138 was the sole exception as far as the king himself was concerned. Here, the issue was not so much rebellion as the fact that Arnulf had refused to surrender Shrewsbury castle when requested to do so by the king. The rising of 1173–4 was not followed by savage reprisals, though perhaps the reluctance of rebels to fight against the king in person was one reason for this.[60] The civil war at the start of Henry III's reign was characterised by a spirit of moderation. The only notable casualty at the battle of Lincoln was the count of Perche, and as David Carpenter has noted, 'everyone was very sorry about that'. Ransoms, not executions, marked the conclusion of the war.[61] For all that Simon de Montfort was killed in a horrific moment of blood-lust at Evesham in 1265, no executions followed the battle.

Under Edward I attitudes began to change. Distinctions between different types of war were important, and helped to determine the extent to which chivalrous conduct was appropriate. A war between two equal kingdoms was straightforward enough; the laws of war should apply, and with them the whole gamut of chivalric attitudes. It was a different matter where rebellion was concerned. For Edward, the Welsh and Scottish wars were a matter of putting down resistance to his rightful authority, and so there took place at Shrewsbury the show trial and execution of Prince Dafydd after his capture in 1283. William Wallace was executed with all the gruesome ceremonies of hanging, drawing and quartering in 1305, and Bruce's rising in 1306 prompted a whole series of brutal executions. It was considered that where rebels were fighting their rightful lord, there was no just war, and the laws of war might not apply. Different, more ancient conventions were appropriate. For the Scots, however, the situation was different. Scotland in their eyes was an independent country, the war was just, and the full conventions should apply. So, Edward I could execute Scottish prisoners as rebels, with the full horrors of hanging, drawing and quartering; the Scots felt obliged to adhere to the chivalric legal conventions, and play by the rules in their treatment of knightly prisoners.[62] It is striking that the wars of Edward I were not marked by any notable chivalric acts on the part of the English; the explanation lies in the law, as well as in the king's own severe personality. Edward set clear precedents for the treatment of rebels, and under his son the end of the rebellion of the earl of Lancaster in 1322 was marked by an appalling series of executions. Pieces of dismembered traitors decorated gibbets all over the country until the prelates requested that they should be removed for proper burial. Rebellion remained a useful justification for a removal of the chivalric constraints: the Black Prince was justified in his own, if in few others' eyes, in sacking Limoges, as the city had turned against his rightful authority in rebellion, rather than war.

The execution of hostages and prisoners was a feature of medieval warfare which may seem unacceptable. The tale of how King Stephen was charmed by his hostage, the young William Marshal, and so decided to spare his life, is a good story which to modern eyes displays the king acting in a very human and attractive manner. Such an action was, however, unusual, and there are many examples of the death of hostages when terms of agreements were broken. In 1211 Robert de Vieuxpont hanged the seven-year-old son of Maelgwyn ap Rhys, and King John is said to have had twenty-eight Welsh hostages hanged in the following year. The young Thomas Seton was hanged by Edward III outside the walls of Berwick in 1333. When in 1373 Robert Knollys was besieged in his castle of Derval, the duke of Anjou had three English hostages executed since Knollys had broken the terms of an agreement not to reinforce the garrison. Knollys retaliated by executing four French prisoners he held, abandoning, as Froissart noted, the opportunity of obtaining a great ransom for them.[63] Such executions have to be seen in the context of the agreements under which hostages were handed over; they may have been inhuman, but they were not unlawful, and did not run counter to chivalric concepts. The order in the late stages of the battle of Agincourt to kill the prisoners, with the exception of the most illustrious, sits uneasily alongside Henry V's reputation for chivalry in the minds of most modern writers, but no contemporary French chroniclers criticised the king for what he did. His action could be justified not merely because there appeared to be a threat of renewed attacks from the enemy, but also because the Oriflamme, the red war-banner, had been unfurled by the French, indicating that no quarter would be given.[64] At Montereau in 1420, Henry employed men captured in the town to plead with the garrison of the castle who were still holding out. If they did not surrender, the captives would be hanged. There was much emotion and tears; Henry, unmoved, duly hanged the townspeople in front of the castle, which did not surrender for a further eight days.[65]

The scale of destruction of the property and lives of non-combatants was a feature of medieval warfare that commentators do not always find easy to equate with chivalrous attitudes. In the early thirteenth century one troubadour complained of the lowered standards of his day: 'Now honour lies in stealing cattle, sheep and oxen, or pillaging churches or travellers. Oh, fie upon the knight who drives off sheep, robs churches and travellers and then appears before a lady.'[66] Honoré Bonet, in his *Tree of Battles*, written in the late fourteenth century, berated the customs of his day in similar tones: 'In these days, all wars are directed against the poor labouring people and against their goods and chattels. I do not call that war, but it seems to me to be pillage and robbery. Further that way of warfare does not follow the ordinances of worthy chivalry.'[67] It was easy for contemporaries to argue that the standards of their own day were declining, but the practice of waging war by destroying civilian property and slaying non-combatants was a constant theme. There may be argument about the scale of disorder in Stephen's reign, but there can be no doubt that fire and sword brought chaos to many areas. Henry of Anjou, in 1149, proceeded by 'pillaging all that came in his way and setting fire to houses and churches everywhere', while Stephen's son Eustace responded by 'ordering his men to set fire immediately to the houses everywhere, to kill those who came in their way and commit indiscriminately every cruelty they could think of'.[68] The Scots had a tradition of burning, pillaging and driving off livestock on their raids into England – a tradition which in Edward II's reign became a constant habit. The technique of the *chevauchée* in the Hundred Years War relied for its effect on the damage that was done to civilian society. How could a man such as Henry of Grosmont, earl and then duke of Lancaster, on the one hand write a

An illustration from a manuscript of Honoré Bonet's late fourteenth-century *Tree of Battles*, showing the concept of the tree, surmounted by a wheel of fortune.

treatise of high moral tone, his *Livre des seynts medicines*, and on the other apparently condone the way in which war was fought?[69]

One solution is to argue that chivalrous behaviour was confined to the knightly classes. The common people were not bound by these codes, nor was it necessary to behave in a chivalrous fashion towards them. If this was so, then perhaps chivalry was no more than a cruel and hypocritical fraud, a tawdry tinsel artefact, which provided the upper classes with a spurious respectability for unacceptable behaviour. It was the case that the values of chivalry were the preserve of knights and those who fought in a knightly manner, but this did not mean that all the horrors of war faced by those of lower rank were acceptable. There was no doubt that the victims found this type of warfare totally unacceptable. The English complained bitterly in 1301 that the Scots engaged in the

> slaughter of our people without number, and in a merciless burning of monasteries, churches and villages; on all sides they

unpeopled the land, slaying children in the cradle and women lying in childbed with brutal and inhuman savagery, and terrible as it is to hear, vilely cutting off the breasts of women. Small schoolchildren of tender years, learning their first letters and grammar, they burned, in the school where they were, to the number of about two hundred.[70]

Edward I did, however, on occasion also rebuke his own men for their excesses. He reprimanded John FitzMarmaduke for his extreme cruelty and the degree of pleasure he took in the deaths of his enemies, and he was said to have been angered at the way in which the poor suffered at the hands of the Prince of Wales's army in 1306.[71] Edward III, in one of his challenges to Philip VI, argued in 1340 that all Christians, and above all princes, should avoid the destruction of people and countryside. The implication was that it was Philip who, by his unreasonable attitude, compelled Edward's troops to engage in exactly this activity.[72] Froissart was clear in his condemnation of the free companies, who lived from pillage, and of the slaughter that took place at Limoges in 1370 on the Black Prince's orders: 'I do not know why he did not take pity on the poor people, who could not have had any part in treason; but they suffered for it, and indeed suffered more than any who had been responsible for the treachery.'[73]

It can also be suggested (as it was by Froissart) that it was not the knights who were responsible for the worst of the horrors of war: at the sack of Caen in 1346, for instance, Thomas Holland and some other English knights did their best to protect the citizens from the hell launched on the town by the English common soldiery.[74] No doubt many of the worst atrocities were committed by soldiers of low rank, and no doubt it proved impossible in many cases to exercise effective discipline in the aftermath of a siege or a battle, or in plundering raids into a hostile countryside. It was not a knight who killed the earl of Hereford at Boroughbridge by skulking under the bridge, and striking up at him as he passed over. That was the work of a 'ribald'.[75]

Many of the horrors, however, were the responsibility of men of rank. Chivalry and atrocity were often proved to be close bed-fellows. This was not only so in the case of mercenaries and members of the free companies. There were men of the highest chivalric rank who were responsible for acts of extreme cruelty. In the fifteenth century John Talbot, knight of the Garter, hanged members of the garrisons of captured castles, and was responsible in 1440 for the burning of over 300 men, women and children who had taken refuge in a church at Lihons.[76] The ideology of chivalry was such that men found relatively little difficulty in accommodating the ideals of honour, piety and largesse to a hard and brutal reality. For some at least, chivalrous ideas did not outweigh the brutalising effects of war on those who fought it, but instead provided a convenient justification for them. The concepts of chivalry and the practice of warfare may not fit neatly together without any contradiction, but men do not find it hard to live in a contradictory world.

It is argued elsewhere in this book that there was what amounted to a 'military revolution' in the late thirteenth and early fourteenth centuries. It would, however, be hard to argue that there was any revolutionary change in the ideology that inspired the élite elements of English armies. The concepts underlying chivalry, the ideas of honour, generosity, prowess and loyalty, underwent some refinement in the later middle ages, and certainly received a fresh emphasis in the works of Froissart. There was by the fourteenth century a difference in the stress given to chivalric matters. Certainly, men such as Henry Grosmont, duke of Lancaster, John Chandos, or other commanders in the Hundred Years War can be shown to have acted on many occasions with quite as much realism as that displayed much earlier by William Marshal. But even allowing for Froissart's bias, it is difficult to deny that there was a new flavour, a new emphasis on chivalric practices in the warfare of the Hundred Years War. Those who followed Edward I to Wales and Scotland were not intent on fulfilling vows to perform deeds of prowess in the way that some certainly were when they disembarked in France under Edward III's banners. The ideology was not new, but it received a fresh prominence. Was it, then, the case that chivalric attitudes and behaviour were something that marked out late medieval armies and warfare, and that a significant change in the early modern period was their abandonment? Malcolm Vale has argued convincingly that ideas of honour and renown, central to chivalric culture, were most certainly not abandoned at the end of the fifteenth century, though he suggests that the absence of battles after 1534 meant that 'chivalry entered a phase of decay from which it never recovered'.[77] The developing dominance of infantry armed with arquebuses certainly cast a shadow over traditions of chivalric warfare, but many of the ideas which had influenced medieval military men continued, and still continue, to be important. 'We have one motto, "*L'audace, l'audace, toujours l'audace!*" Remember that, gentlemen. From here on out, until we live or die in the attempt, we will always be audacious.' The idea may seem to typify medieval chivalric warfare; the words, however, with all their echoes, are those of General George S. Patton, spoken in 1944.[78]

A page from a thirteenth-century French bible, showing military carts laden with provisions.

10

The Logistics of War

Armies need proper supplies. The point is self-evident, but it is often assumed that it was only in the modern period that commanders and others came to appreciate it. Modern history certainly provides spectacular examples of the failures that came from inadequate attention to the logistics of war. Napoleon's decision to invade Russia taking with him a mere twenty-four days' provisions was an obvious recipe for disaster. Rommel's fate in North Africa, starved above all of fuel as a result of his overextended supply lines, provides a more recent example of the importance of proper logistics. In contrast, excessive Allied caution with regard to the problem of supply held back the forces that invaded Normandy in June 1944, with the notable exception of Patton, whose armoured thrust ran counter to accepted wisdom.[1]

The conventional view of the advocates of the concept of a military revolution in the sixteenth and seventeenth centuries is that it was not until after the Thirty Years War that proper attention was first given to the question of supply. Whereas Gustavus Adolphus largely relied on foraging to feed his highly mobile armies, from the 1640s the French began to calculate the precise needs of their forces. Contracts were drawn up with merchants, and a system of magazines, or victualling bases, was developed. A well-organised baggage train carried sufficient reserves to ensure that an army on the march was properly provided for. Soldiers were assured of a regular supply of basic provisions.[2]

The problems of the sixteenth and seventeenth centuries were not of a different order from those of the middle ages. The use of guns might be thought to have made a substantial difference, but the evidence suggests that in the seventeenth century the rate of fire was not expected to be more than four or five rounds a day: massive supplies of ammunition were not required.[3] The size of armies did, of course, increase in the early modern period, but the contrast with the middle ages should not be exaggerated. The French army was particularly large, but the Prussian army in the late seventeenth century was no bigger than the total force deployed by Edward I in Wales in 1294–5. Marlborough's army which marched from the Rhine to the Danube in 1704 was of equivalent size.[4]

The difficulties caused by an inadequate supply of provisions were obvious. Medieval soldiers were, no doubt, hardened men, well versed in the arts of survival in hostile conditions. Even so, extreme discomfort and empty stomachs were not appreciated. A letter from one of the men in Henry III's army in north Wales, written in 1245, reveals the horrors caused by a failure to ensure adequate provisions. The men were encamped in tents around the site of the new castle at Deganwy. They were cold and frightened; their clothing was inadequate, and they feared that the Welsh might attack at any moment. A halfpenny loaf of bread cost five pence. An Irish ship had arrived with a cargo of foodstuffs; it had been left stranded by the tide, where it lay open to Welsh attack. A fight resulted, with many casualties on both sides. The army was left with only one tun of wine, and food prices were exorbitant.[5]

Edward II's letters explained the failure of his 1322 expedition to Scotland, when he had marched north with an army 'such as never had been seen in our time, or in the times of our ancestors', by arguing that although he had met no resistance, he had to retreat from the Forth because Flemish pirates had prevented his ships from bringing food supplies to him.[6] The Scots had cleared the country of all fodder. The story was that all the English foragers managed to find was a single lame cow. Earl Warenne quipped 'This is the dearest beast I have ever yet seen; it must have surely cost £1,000 or more.'[7] Jean le Bel's account of the English campaign against the Scots in Weardale in 1327 vividly reveals the problems and discomforts that resulted from inadequate provisions. All the men had to eat were loaves of bread which had been tied to their saddles; these were soaked with the horses' sweat. A few had drinking bottles; the majority had to drink from the river. There was no forage or litter for the horses. Eventually, some supplies were brought from Newcastle. There were rich profits to be made from badly baked bread and poor quality wine; Le Bel's view was that a jug of wine which should have been worth no more than 4*d* was being sold for two shillings and more.[8]

Even when food was in sufficient supply, there might still be problems. When the Angevin forces invaded Normandy in 1136, they had insufficient cooks and bakers with them. The men, according to Orderic Vitalis, ate uncooked food, and a result suffered dysentery.[9] A note on an account drawn up in the mid 1360s explained the low price put on bread 'because those loaves were for most part rotten and of low value because they had been kept a long time'.[10] Inadequate care taken with the preparation of food, together with generally insanitary conditions, seem the most likely explanation for the appalling dysentery which affected Henry V's army at the siege of Harfleur.[11]

Food requirements

The essential needs of a medieval army were for food and drink. Bread was, of course, the staple diet; pottage made from beans, peas and perhaps oatmeal might supplement it. The grain was often poorly milled, with simple handmills. Abrasive grit was left in the flour, with the result that teeth might be worn down flat, as was shown by careful examination of Bartholomew Burghersh's skeleton.[12] Fresh or salted meat, and dried or salted fish were another requirement. Local water supplies could not be relied upon; ideally, ale or wine were needed if dysentery and other infections were to be avoided. The quantities of barley often provided suggest that impressive amounts of ale were consumed; drunkenness among soldiers could cause considerable problems, as when the Welsh infantry rioted on the eve of the battle of Falkirk in 1298.[13] Nor was it just the men who needed food and drink. In the same way as a modern army requires oil for its transport and its armoured assault vehicles, so a medieval force needed oats and water for the horses. All this entailed organisation of a high order.

Attempts have been made to calculate the food requirements of a medieval army on a largely theoretical basis. Despite the fact that the numbers of men and horses assembled for William I's invasion of England are not known, Bernard Bachrach has made heroic attempts to calculate their consumption of food (4,000 tons a month) and drink, and even the mountains of equine excrement (three million pounds) that had to be dealt with. The figures are not easy to work out, and have attracted some criticism (one problem was that the horses appeared to excrete more than they consumed), although they are clearly of the right order.[14] The quantities of food required for a substantial army were nevertheless immense, and there are contemporary estimates that give a reasonable indication of what was needed. It was easier to calculate food requirements for the relatively small forces in castle garrisons than it was for a whole army. The accounts of Humphrey de Bohun for the Clare lands in Glamorgan, entrusted to him in 1262 after the death of Richard de Clare, earl of Gloucester, reveal that consumption was worked out on a weekly basis. At Neath, a force of fifty-two men with thirteen horses were to receive three quarters of wheat each week, with two quarters of malted wheat and four quarters of malted oats. Just over five and a half quarters of provender was allocated for the horses. One pound six shillings was set aside for *companagium*, relish to go with bread.[15] Similar calculations exist for English garrisons in Scottish castles during Edward I's attempted conquest, one suggesting that twenty men would need one quarter of wheat a week, and two of malt, along with substantial quantities of meat and fish. Horses required a peck of oats every night. As is the case with much medieval evidence for food consumption, the calorific value of such a diet, at over 5,000, was far in excess of what would be regarded today as appropriate.[16] If these estimates are multiplied to show the needs of an entire army, very impressive figures are attained. A large army of 30,000 men would need some 4,500–5,000 quarters of grain each week (perhaps around 800 tons). If there were 5,000 horses (a low estimate), about 2,000 quarters of oats or fodder would have been needed every week. A campaign lasting two months would, on this basis, entail providing over 50,000 quarters of grain. The average yield per acre of cereal crops was perhaps one quarter per annum. These are, of course, crude theoretical figures, but they can be seen in the context of Edward I's demand that 100,000 quarters of grain should be provided for his troops in Gascony in 1296. Although the exchequer protested that this was an impossible quantity, orders were nevertheless issued for the collection of 63,200 quarters.[17]

At the very least, the Crown needed to ensure that there were sufficient supplies for the royal household on campaign; in practice, a wise commander would need to be confident that there was no danger that the entire army would run out of foodstuffs. A calculation of the needs of Edward I's household during his Scottish wars was that the pantry department would need ten quarters of wheat a day, or 1,830 quarters from April to September, while the same quantity of malt was needed to make ale. So far as meat was concerned, 1,500 oxen, 3,000 sheep, 1,200 pigs and 400 bacons were required. Yet more cereal had to be provided for the royal horses, who were thought to need 3,000 quarters of oats.[18] Another indication of the quantities required is provided by an estimate in the late 1330s of the supplies needed by the 4,000 men in the fleet from the Thames to the north, for a four-month period. This listed 5,400 quarters of wheat, 8,250 of barley, 2,400 of beans and peas, sixty tuns of ale, 12,960 bacons, forty-five lasts of herring, 32,400 stockfish, and 9,072 stones of cheese.[19] That would give twenty men 1.7 quarters of wheat, 2.5 quarters of barley, and 0.75 quarters of beans and peas each week: figures rather more generous than those for early fourteenth-century English garrisons in Scotland.

The collection of food supplies

There were various ways in which armies could be supplied. The Crown could make elaborate arrangements to supply victuals, using all the resources of sheriffs and local officials to collect goods, which were taken to the campaign bases. Men could also be expected to take their own supplies with them; magnates had the resources to organise their own provisioning system. Merchants could be encour-

Supplies being carried to the Norman ships in 1066, from the Bayeux Tapestry.

aged to support English armies. Lastly, armies might well succeed in feeding themselves, by foraging as well as fighting their way through enemy territory.

There is little surviving evidence about military victualling before the late twelfth century. The Bayeux Tapestry provides a pictorial record of the loading of William's invasion fleet with arms, equipment, barrels of drink and sacks of food. Pipe Roll evidence from Henry II's reign provides a good indication of what was done, but the focus of the picture is limited to the shires and counties; there are no central records of what foodstuffs were collected. No accounts for the armies themselves survive. For the 1165 expedition to Wales the Pipe Rolls show that corn was provided from Gloucestershire, Lincolnshire, Oxfordshire, Berkshire and Worcestershire; malt, oats, beans and peas, bacons and cheeses were among the commodities collected for the army. Similar details can be extracted from the Pipe Rolls for the provision of foodstuffs from the English counties for Henry II's expedition to Ireland in 1171. A substantial 6,424·5 measures (probably quarters) of wheat, 2,000 of oats, 584 of beans, with 4,106 bacon pigs, 160 quarters of salt and 840 weys of cheese were provided.[20]

Documentation from John's reign provides more detail of the logistics of war. In 1205 an expedition to France was prepared, but did not sail: one chronicler commented that an incalculable sum had been spent on the fleet, the provisions and all the miscellaneous equipment needed.[21] In the next year, an expedition to Poitou was successfully organised. Some hints about the provisioning arrangements are provided by the Pipe Roll for 1206. The Somerset account reveals that eighty quarters of flour and 243 quarters of oats were sent to Portsmouth. Twenty oxen and forty sheep were driven there. Grain also came from as far away as Colchester in Essex, and iron was brought from the Forest of Dean.[22] For the Irish expedition of 1210 the Pipe Roll for John's twelfth year records that he took from Yorkshire 200 bacons, thirty-eight quarters of wheat, 127 quarters of oats, thirty-three quarters of malt, and three tons of wine. In addition, hurdles and pontoons were loaded at Whitby. All these supplies were taken by sea to Pembroke, ready for the crossing of the Irish Sea. The overall totals of supplies mentioned in this roll may not seem particularly impressive: 669 quarters of oats, 631 quarters of wheat, 152 quarters of barley, and thirty-three quarters of malt.[23] However, the next year's accounts add details for the bishopric of Durham, which was in the king's hands. From the Durham estates alone 1,784 quarters of wheat and 1,725 quarters of oats were sent to Ireland, along with eighteen quarters of beans. Twenty-five ships were hired to take these supplies, along with hurdles, bridges, salmon, salt and iron. The account of Brian de Lisle, custodian of Knaresborough and Pontefract, in the same roll, reveals that 177 quarters of wheat and flour, ninety-four quarters of malt, thirty-three quarters of salt, 500 bacons, 109 cheeses, 1,040 horseshoes and five pairs of hand-mills were all sent to Ireland. Moreover, 180 hurdles and 155 bridges were sent from the manor of Cawood to Pembroke.[24] This can represent only a fraction of the full victualling effort made by John's government. The bulk of what was needed was probably bought by officers of the royal household who did not account in the Pipe Roll for their activities. That such quantities should have been provided from counties as distant from Ireland as Yorkshire and Durham is remarkable. It was a very considerable enterprise to bring grain supplies by sea from the north-east to Pembroke, and the fact that this was done suggests that substantial quantities of food must in addition have been drawn from western counties, even though these are not recorded on the Pipe Rolls.

It would be tedious to provide a catalogue of all the requests for foodstuffs that can be found in the records: a few examples should suffice. The siege of Kenilworth in 1266 at the close of the Barons' Wars occasioned particularly heavy demands on the sheriffs of the midland counties; it was the length of the operation, rather than the number of troops, that caused the problem.[25] There was a real quantitative change with the second Welsh expedition undertaken by Edward I in 1282, for many more troops needed to be fed over a longer period than in the past. In planning the war, one of the first questions that the council considered was victualling. Markets were prohibited in the Marches, so as to force merchants to bring their goods to the army, much as John had ordered. A permanent supply base was set up at Chester, and John de Maidstone, who had charge of it, had at his disposal over 23,000 quarters of grain. In order to meet the army's needs, 1,100 cattle were brought together, and 6,600 tuns of wine were acquired. Large numbers of carts were collected from monastic houses to ease the problems of transport.[26] Edward had learned his lesson from the first Welsh war, when royal clerks and officials had been sent to no less than six counties to buy up provisions in an operation costing only £406, and it had been necessary to send harvesters to Anglesey, partly no doubt to put pressure on the Welsh by depriving them of food, but also to obtain grain for the English army.[27]

In the 1290s demands for foodstuffs reached even higher levels, with campaigning taking place in Wales, Scotland, Gascony and Flanders. In the spring of 1296 the exchequer ordered 26,500 quarters of grain, and in November no less than 63,200 quarters. In the following year, thirty-eight ships took almost 17,000 quarters of wheat and oats to Gascony, and 8,700 quarters were taken to Flanders. Some of these supplies had been collected in the previous year, but in 1297 at least 10,300 quarters of wheat, 6,700 quarters of oats, 2,400 quarters of barley and malt, and 1,000 quarters of beans and peas were collected by the sheriffs and their agents. Even with these amounts, once the campaign had begun, it still proved necessary for the Crown to buy some food locally in the Low Countries in the autumn.[28]

The Scottish wars ensured that demand remained high for the rest of Edward I's reign. Royal instructions went into great detail about the way in which the supplies were to be prepared: 'You shall have the wheat well ground and properly sifted, so that there is no bran left in it, and you shall put the flour into good strong clean casks, so that the flour can be closely packed and pressed down, and in each tun you should put three sticks of hazel, and some salt at the bottom of each, to prevent the flour from going bad.'[29] When grain was stored, it had to be turned regularly to prevent it becoming damp and rotten. All sorts of problems might arise. Wine casks might leak, or their contents evaporate, but the problem which occurred at Berwick in 1300 was surely unexpected. The wine began to freeze in its casks, and thirty-two quarters of coal were burned to prevent this disaster.[30] Permanent victualling bases were established at Berwick in the east, and at Skinburness, near Carlisle, in the west. In 1303, to take one sample year, the royal victuallers had about 1,800 quarters of wheat flour, 6,500 quarters of wheat, 1,500 quarters of malt and barley, 6,000 quarters of oats, 1,300 quarters of beans and peas, and 1,366 tuns of wine, along with other commodities, at their disposal.[31] The operation of the victualling system was a major preoccupation for Edward's administrators. A letter, written from Dunbar by one anonymous royal clerk to another, near the end of the reign, gives some impression of the mundane problems that these men faced:

> Greetings. I am very surprised that you have not yet sent ahead the ship loaded with victuals to Stirling, with Benedict of Canterbury, as was agreed between us, and which you said was ready before I left. So I ask you, as you care for the honour and reputation of the king and his army that as soon as you have read this letter, that you should send all the victuals that you have, such as flour, wine and other things. And hasten the flour that is coming from Roxburgh. And get the ale made that I ordered, and send it on. And if you have not got enough tuns, get canvas from the wardrobe and put the flour in it, as I instructed you. And do not neglect any of this in any way.[32]

It was not normal Crown policy to provide free food for all those serving in its armies. Many of the victuals taken on campaign by the government were sold to the troops, often at a profit, though it was also a common practice to make gifts of food and drink to the troops. On occasion food might be handed out in lieu of wages; on the Flanders campaign in 1297 Welsh infantry were given bread worth almost £100 in place of four days' pay.[33] Normally, issues of victuals were carefully accounted. The account of James de Dalilegh, royal victualling officer at Carlisle in 1300, included details of 118 quarters of malted oats, delivered to the royal household, 133 quarters of milled malt sold to the men of the garrisons of Dumfries and Lochmaben, and 102 quarters of malt made over and charged to John de St John and Peter of Dunwich. On one occasion 170 quarters were lost, when the house in which they were stored at Skinburness was flooded in a storm.[34] The amount each man received was recorded; thus in 1304 Ralph de Monthermer, earl of Gloucester by marriage, received the following from different victualling officers:

Oats – 95 quarters, @ 3s each
Wheat – 36 quarters, @ 8s
Malt – 20 quarters, @ 6s 8d each
Wine – 17 tuns, @ £4 each
Herrings – 3,000, cost 16s 6d
Cod – 160, cost 36s 8d
Beef – 6 carcasses, @ 10s
Wax – 56 lbs

The total value came to £114 12s 2d, which was duly charged to Ralph.[35]

The requests for food for troops in Scotland in the early fourteenth century must have seemed incessant, especially to men who lived in the grain-producing counties of eastern England. Even when there were no full campaigns in Edward II's initial years on the throne, demands did not cease, for campaigns were planned if not carried through. In 1309 the government ordered 5,200 quarters of wheat, the same quantity of oats, 4,100 quarters of malt, and 1,300 quarters of beans and peas. In the following year, much larger quantities were requested: 11,300 quarters of wheat, 6,400 quarters of malt and barley, 9,200 quarters of oats, 1,600 quarters of beans and peas, along with 1,300 beef carcasses and a considerable amount of salt. A further purveyance was then requested in 1311, at about the 1309 level. Even in 1316, a year of appalling famine resulting from incessant rain, demands did not cease. The Crown demanded 4,600 quarters of wheat, 2,400 of malt and barley, and 4,700 quarters of oats, as well as other goods.[36]

The account of Henry Shireoaks, royal victualler at Newcastle upon Tyne in 1322–3, shows considerably smaller quantities than had been needed to support Edward I's Scottish wars. He had charge of 3,611 quarters of wheat, 3,807 quarters of barley and 3,137 quarters of oats. Wine, however, was in substantial supply, with no less than 1,546 tuns received from Gascony. There was no permanent royal accommodation available that could serve as the victualling base in Newcastle; money had to be spent on hiring cellars and granaries in the town. Much of the food was provided by the sheriffs in the traditional manner, but interestingly just over 1,000 quarters of wheat came from Gascony, and a further 1,258 were provided by an Italian merchant, Manentius Francisci.[37] In 1336 the royal victualler at Newcastle, Robert Tong, was purchasing most of his grain from the bishop of Durham; out of a total of 1,284 quarters of wheat, the bishop provided 1,000 quarters. The victuals were still stored in rented property; William de Embleton provided one cellar, two granaries and a bolting house; thirty-three other men also rented property to Tong.[38]

The requirements for supplies for the English forces in France in the Hundred Years War were not so great as those for the armies which had fought for Edward I in Wales and Scotland. It was part of the English strategy that the troops should live off the land, and for the most part the land was fruitful. Even at the start of the war, Edward III's officials were not collecting supplies on the scale that his grandfather's had done. The accounts of the royal wardrobe no longer included details of victualling costs, which makes it harder to assess the overall scale of operations, but sufficient evidence survives to show what was happening. The account of William Dunstable, buyer and provisioner in seventeen counties from Yorkshire to Essex, in the spring and early summer of 1338, shows that he obtained almost 2,000 quarters of wheat, almost 2,400 of malt, a mere seven quarters of oats, 226 of beans and peas, some 120 cattle and 650 sheep, along with quantities of bacon, cheese, salt, horseshoes, horsenails and caltrops. The administrative effort involved in collecting these supplies was still considerable. Granaries had to be rented in Great Yarmouth, King's Lynn, Aylesbury and elsewhere. Flour, stockfish and caltrops were stored in a cellar rented in Sandwich. Balances to weigh the flour milled from the wheat had to be bought, as did a bushel measure.[39] Yet Dunstable did not have the quantities of foodstuffs to look after that Richard de Bromsgrove had in Berwick in the early years of the fourteenth century.

Estimates for the victualling needs of an expedition to France in the 1340s put to the royal council were that 4,000 quarters of wheat, 6,000 of oats, and 1,000 of malt were required, while quantities of ale, cheese, salt meat and other commodities were also needed. These were very substantially less than the demands imposed on the country under Edward I.[40] Even so, the requirements placed on the English counties might be considerable. An account submitted by the sheriff of Lincoln for victualling operations in 1356 shows that the county provided 685 quarters of wheat, 615 quarters of oats, and 105 quarters of beans and peas, along with 135 bacons, eleven beef carcasses, and quantities of cheese. Interestingly, almost all of the oats were bought from a single merchant, rather than from individual growers. There were considerable other costs involved. Sacks, wooden tuns and weighing balances had to be bought, and there were costs in milling some of the grain into flour. Indeed, the purchases of food came to £185, and the miscellaneous costs to £53.[41]

Prise and purveyance

The Crown relied on a prerogative right, that of prise, in collecting foodstuffs. This right of compulsory purchase was of long standing in so far as it permitted royal officials to take goods for the use of the king's household. Castle constables also had limited rights of prise. The issue was not at the forefront of complaints against Angevin government, but there was a new article included in the eyre in 1208 about compulsory prises taken by sheriffs, and in Magna Carta it was laid down that no constable or other royal bailiff should take anyone's corn or other goods without cash payment, or the agreement of the seller that payment might be delayed. Prises were a matter of complaint in 1258, though the context is that of purveyance for the king's household, not for his armies.[42]

The inquiry into local government recorded in the Hundred Rolls, which took place in 1274–5, clearly shows that sheriffs had been taking foodstuffs to provide for royal armies in the closing stages of the Barons' Wars without prompt payment, or indeed any payment at all. In the first Statute of Westminster of 1275 the government responded with a clause forbidding prises to be taken without consent, though the king reserved his ancient rights, and the clause was not enforced.[43] With the Welsh war of 1282–3 the government began to make extensive use of the right of prise as a means of supplying the army, commissioning sheriffs and royal clerks to collect the goods that were needed. The Crown specified how much was wanted from each county, leaving the detailed local arrangements to the sheriff. The country was not equally burdened with demands: the problem of transporting victuals meant that those regions with good waterway systems and access to convenient ports, and of course those near to the campaigning areas, were afflicted most. During the Scottish wars the counties of the east of England – Yorkshire, Lincolnshire, Cambridgeshire, Essex and Huntingdon – were called upon most frequently. Ireland was much used to supply armies operating in the west of Scotland.

The supply of materials for armies has surely always been fertile ground for corruption. The wide boys of medieval England found ample opportunity in the system of prise, or purveyance as it came to be known, to exercise their talents for extortion. In some cases, assessments of how much food men could provide were made fairly by local juries, or by some form of communal decision, but more frequently a sheriff's official simply demanded quantities of goods on an arbitrary basis.[44] Nation-wide inquiries in 1298 into the misdeeds of officials in the years since the start of the French war in 1294 yielded, at least in Lincolnshire, more complaints about the system of collecting victuals than anything else. Grain was taken for the officials' own use; food was seized and no receipt or tally provided; money was extracted in return for unauthorised exemptions.[45] In Ireland in 1304 purveyance was seriously obstructed when the royal official entrusted with the task came to Dublin, only to find that all the goods in the market had been removed and hidden in nearby houses. The mayor's sergeant refused to arrest those responsible, and was himself imprisoned as a result of his contumacy.[46] The most common offence revealed by an inquiry made in 1341 was the extortion of money or goods; the illegal seizure of foodstuffs and other goods was the second most frequent. A former sheriff was even charged with failing to send 300 bacons and 500 quarters of wheat to Scotland, though he was acquitted of this charge. One collector of victuals was accused of taking twenty cattle from one village, and

holding them until he had been paid £5; he then went on to take 200
cattle together with salted meat from other places, returning them
only when £40 had been paid. A typical entry in the inquiry record
revealed that three deputies of the victualling officer William of
Dunstable had taken forty quarters of wheat, oats and peas from the
vicar of Sleaford in Lincolnshire, and nine quarters from the villagers, which they took to Boston. They then imprisoned the vicar
and the parson, releasing them only after a fine of £2 11s had been
paid.[47] Examples of malpractice are numerous. In 1339 a former
sheriff of Nottingham was even accused of taking seventy-six eggs
without payment. The abbot of Ramsey paid £7 13s 4d to have his
lands spared the attentions of the royal purveyors.[48] The burden of
purveyance did not fall equally on all social classes: the evidence
shows that the well-off were often able to avoid the Crown's demands. If they could not do so, they were in a position to pass the
burden on to their tenants. Royal officials whose grain was taken
received better prices, and almost certainly more prompt payment,
than other men.[49]

The scale of corruption and malpractice greatly added to hatred of
an unpopular system. In 1297 prise was a central issue in the
opposition's case against the Crown; in the aftermath of the political
crisis of that year the Crown made what were little more than
cosmetic changes to the system. Orders for the collection of foodstuffs now went out from the chancery, not the exchequer, and the
precise requirement from each county was set out in detail. The
reasons for the Crown's demands were explained, largely by abusing
the Scots, and the word 'prise' began to be replaced by 'purveyance'.
Such cosmetic changes were not convincing. In 1300 it was decreed
that the system should be used only to supply the royal household
with food; as a result, in the next year 'loans' of food supplies were
requested from the counties.[50] Purveyance, however, could not be
abandoned; the troops had to have food. In 1311 the king's baronial
opponents, the Ordainers, expressed their fear that purveyance might
lead to popular rebellion. All prises were to cease, except for those
justified by traditional rights.[51] This was obviously impractical, as
armies had to be fed. The requisitioning of transport to carry the
victuals to the armies was a further unpopular element. In 1333 the
abbot of Crowland protested vigorously that his house could not
accept the burden of providing a cart with five horses for the muster
at York. The Prior of Spalding likewise refused; he had already
provided horses and carts for Eblo le Strange, the patron of the
house.[52] Purveyance continued to be regarded as a major abuse.

A popular poem written in about 1340 condemned the king who
ate off silver, and paid in wooden tallies; how much better to pay in

silver, and eat off wood![53] Commissions to inquire into the misdeeds of royal officials, notably those of 1298 and 1341, did little to ease the complaints of those who had suffered loss. Parliament in 1339 witnessed fierce complaints against purveyance. The Commons asked that anyone who took goods without payment should be arrested. William Wallingford, who had been in charge of receiving supplies for the royal army in Flanders, was made a scapegoat and arrested.[54] Purveyance continued to be an issue; no parliament sat between 1343 and 1355 without complaints from the Commons on this issue.[55]

In January 1350 the government, fearing a large-scale French attack on Calais and other English-held territory in France, ordered purveyance by the sheriffs in association with specially nominated commissioners. This resulted in demands for 7,700 quarters of wheat, 9,320 quarters of barley, 2,400 quarters of oats, 2,130 quarters of beans and peas, 1,750 quarters of rye, 5,220 beef carcasses and 10,530 bacons. Parliament protested at these quantities, arguing that a dearth of corn was threatening. The government responded in February, reducing its demands substantially; only 4,140 quarters of wheat were requested, and the quantities of other commodities were similarly cut back.[56] This was the last major request for victuals on a national scale. In 1351 demands for victuals for Calais prompted protests that they were contrary to statute and did not have parliamentary consent. Feeding Calais, or rather the large garrison stationed there, was a major problem. Parliament complained that payment was not being made for goods purveyed for the port.[57] Perhaps in response to this pressure, in 1353–5 the task was performed not by purveyors or sheriffs, but by the keeper of victuals in the town himself. Thereafter, victualling was largely in the hands of great merchants, such as John de Wesenham, who were commissioned by the Crown to buy foodstuffs and supply them to Calais. In 1355, when there was a severe shortage of grain in Calais, the Crown ordered proclamations in every seaport from Southampton to the north-east, asking merchants to take corn there.[58] Purveyance did not wholly cease, however, and there were strong complaints in parliament in 1362, when it was said that the 'heinous name of purveyor should be changed and named buyer'. These were largely directed at the way in which food was obtained for the royal household, and no longer at the provision of army victuals. Edward III responded with a statute which made any return to the kind of victualling system operated by Edward I virtually impossible. It is no longer fashionable to argue that Edward III made concessions which irrevocably weakened the English monarchy, but in this respect at least, the case has some justification.[59]

Merchants

The changing pattern of victualling at Calais was a microcosm of what was happening more widely. Hostility to the purveyance system led to a much greater dependence on merchants for army food supplies.[60] The use of merchants was not, of course, new. The early evidence comes from 1212, when royal orders went out preventing the holding of ordinary food markets throughout England during the king's planned expedition to Wales. Merchants were instructed to follow the army with all the goods that they could provide. Similar methods were used by Edward I during his Welsh wars, and on at least two occasions in Scotland he was thankful for the presence of merchants, as royal supplies had run out. In 1314 merchants were forbidden to export victuals to Flanders or elsewhere; they were strongly encouraged to come to support the campaign in Scotland. In 1327 the king, on campaign in Weardale, wrote to the sheriff of Yorkshire and the mayor of Newcastle to try to encourage merchants to bring foodstuffs for sale to the army. In 1339 the Crown turned to merchants, above all to Thomas Melchebourne of Lynn, to provide by purchase or purveyance the foodstuffs that were needed by the English garrisons and forces in Scotland. Dependence on merchants increased in the 1350s as the Crown counted the political cost of purveyance. For the Burnt Candlemas campaign in Scotland of 1356, Edward asked the ports of the east coast to provide food, rather than organising purveyance through the sheriffs. The task of victualling was, in effect, handed over to the merchants.[61] The government had discovered that it was not necessary for it to make the same efforts as in the past to supply troops with food. As well as depending on merchants, there must also have been greater reliance on men bringing their own supplies with them.

Accounts submitted by an Italian, Manentius Francisci, provide a good example of the provision of food supplies by a merchant. In 1322 he and a companion, three horses and four serving boys were sent from York to buy grain for the Scottish campaign. He went first to Lincolnshire, to Louth and Boston, and then to King's Lynn, and on to Kent, Essex and London. In all, the mission took 168 days, and he succeeded in buying almost 2,500 quarters of wheat, about 1,100 quarters of barley, 790 quarters of beans, 620 quarters of oats and 140 quarters each of malt and mixed grain. Most of the grain was handed over to the sheriffs for shipment north; Manentius had some difficulty since they were reluctant to accept more than they could get milled into flour. Only 1,258 quarters of wheat collected by him was sent directly to the royal victualling office at Newcastle.[62]

Some supplies were, of course, provided by magnates and others who took part in royal expeditions. In 1277 the earl of Gloucester's men brought provisions from as far away as Lincolnshire to Wales, and in 1282 the earl of Norfolk arranged for grain and meat to be sent to him from his Irish manors. Robert FitzWalter also acquired supplies in Ireland. In 1301 the earl of Lincoln employed two ships from Poole to take some of his supplies to Scotland, and in 1314 arrangements were made to take the earl of Hereford's supplies north in four vessels. In 1316 the earl of Pembroke's men were given permission to buy victuals in the liberty of Richmond, as their lord was on his way north to Scotland. In 1319 Roger Damory sent a ship loaded with victuals from Norfolk to support him at the siege of Berwick.[63] The decline in royal purveyance must have placed more stress on individual initiative in organising supplies. Henry V required his captains to have sufficient foodstuffs for two months when the troops first mustered, and they were expected to make their own arrangements for further supplies. Much trade, no doubt highly profitable, was done by merchants bringing their goods to Normandy. The mayor of London made arrangements for shipping to be provided for those who had victuals to take to the army, and many letters of protection and safe-conducts were issued to merchants coming to Normandy. In 1417 proclamations were issued declaring that anyone shipping victuals to Caen for the army need not pay any customs duties. In the next year the king wrote to London. The siege of Rouen had just begun, and he was anxious that 'yet wille do arme as manie smale vessels as ye may goodly with vittaille, and namely with drinke, for to come to Harfleur, and thennes as fer as they may up ye river of Seyne to Roan'.[64] Articles drawn up for the duke of York in 1440 concerning the conduct of the war in France included a request that every effort be made to ensure that the Seine estuary was kept secure by English naval forces, so as to enable supplies to be easily brought to Harfleur. There was no question, however, of reliance upon royal purveyance of foodstuffs at this period. Instead, the duke requested that he should have full licence to export wheat and other victuals from England. [65]

Foraging

Living off the land was a normal method for armies to feed themselves. It was not necessarily an easy solution to the problems of victualling, for foraging parties had to be well organised, with arrangements made for the supplies they found to be distributed fairly among the men. A proper foraging system could be a vital element in military success, as Sherman demonstrated in Georgia during the American Civil War. If a force was moving quickly through enemy territory, then it could normally feed itself without too much difficulty; immobility spelled problems, as local resources were rapidly used up. This was why sieges often presented major logistical problems, as the royalists discovered when encamped round Kenilworth in 1266, exhausting the resources of ten counties.[66] Much, of course, depended on terrain. There was little problem in living off the land for Edward III's army which invaded fertile Normandy in 1346; in contrast, the host which marched to Scotland in 1322 found a deserted land, already cleared by their opponents.

The process of foraging is not well-documented. There was no reason to account for goods that were simply pillaged from the enemy, and little reason for chroniclers to record quite ordinary events. In Wales, Edward I sent harvesters equipped with scythes to Anglesey in 1277. In part this was no doubt intended as a move to starve out the Welsh, but it also provided a way of feeding his own army.[67] On Edward III's expedition in Scotland in 1336, the army came to the abbey of Kinloss in Moray. 'In the said abbey was wine and ale, and salt fish, grain and other necessities, on which our men dined, and were considerably cheered up.'[68] In the Hundred Years War the *chevauchée* was intended to put pressure on the enemy by ravaging and burning; foraging for supplies was an essential element in the strategy. Froissart's account of Edward III's unsuccessful expedition of 1359–60 to France, in which he marched to Rheims and on eastward into Burgundy, makes it clear that foraging was the main source of food, even though a very substantial baggage train accompanied the army. Lack of supplies and forage forced the army to leave Rheims: the countryside could not support a large host for a lengthy stay. At Tonerre, however, the army stayed for five days, because they found so much good wine there. In almost every case where Froissart mentions the capture of a town, he wrote about the food and drink that was taken. At Flavigny in Burgundy sufficient was apparently taken for a month. During Lent fresh fish was provided, caught in rivers and lakes from light leather boats, providentially included in the baggage train.[69]

The care which had been taken by the Crown to ensure that forces were adequately provided with food supplies in the days of Edward I was no longer evident by the fifteenth century. Henry V did not bring sufficient quantities with him to France in 1415. When he began the siege of Harfleur, one of the first things on which he took advice was how 'detachments might be sent out to obtain food for men and horses for the sustenance of the army'. On the march to Agincourt, food supplies ran out, but in exchange for not burning Boves in Picardy, sufficient bread and more than enough wine was obtained to keep the army going a little longer. Before the battle, the troops were hungry for food as well as for victory. Later, the English garrison forces in Harfleur were compelled to engage in extensive foraging raids in order to survive, as supplies were not being sent

Looting a house during the Hundred Years War, from a late fourteenth-century manuscript.

from England.[70] Henry V's military ordinances show the importance of foraging to his armies. The men were ordered, for example, not to take more than was needed for their own use. Any additional food supplies should be shared with the others in the army. Later in the fifteenth century, in 1450, it is striking that when John Fastolf drew up advice for a force to relieve Caen, he argued that its commander must ensure that he was well supplied with 'speres, bowes, arowes, axes, malles, gonnes, ridbaudekins, and alle other stuffe necessarie', but did not specify victuals. All that he suggested in that context was that the sea should be kept open.[71] As in other respects, the evidence of victualling suggests that fifteenth-century armies were not as well organised as their predecessors.

The careful organisation of military victualling was not an innovation of the so-called Military Revolution of the early modern period. The elements were all firmly in place in England by 1300. There was an elaborate nation-wide system for collecting foodstuffs, there were established victualling bases for the supply of both field armies and garrisons, and there was a planning system capable of making realistic assessments of needs. This system was not, however, maintained. Prise, or purveyance, was extremely unpopular, and political factors led to its eclipse in the course of the fourteenth century. The use of contract merchants provided a possible alternative, but by the fifteenth century the Crown was no longer attempting to make victualling arrangements for English armies on the scale, or in the detail, that had been characteristic of Edward I's day. The circumstances of the French war, which meant that policy as well as necessity dictated that armies should live off the land, were another important element in the change. The problem of how to provide adequate logistic support for armies was one which needed to be approached afresh in the sixteenth and seventeenth centuries. What was required, however, was not the invention of the wheel, but its reinvention.

11

The Navy

Naval warfare in the medieval period bears only slight comparison with that of more modern times. Ships demonstrated the relative technological poverty of the age. Vessels were small, with limited carrying capacity and scant manoeuvrability. The strategies of blockade and the sophisticated tactics of the Napoleonic period were far beyond the reach of medieval sailors. Whenever possible, ships stayed within sight of land and safety. Battles in the open sea were a near-impossibility; when fleets did engage, it was normally in harbour, or close in-shore. The concept of 'control of the sea' is one which it is hard to apply to the medieval period. Ships could not remain at sea for lengthy periods, and were too much at the mercy of tides and winds to exercise really effective control.[1] Yet the importance of ships, and of the sailors who manned them, was immense. Without naval support, English medieval armies could have achieved little. Not only did armies, with their horses and supplies, need to be transported by sea to fight in France, the Low Countries and Ireland; naval support was also essential for campaigning in Wales and Scotland. The capture of Anglesey was an important element in English strategy in Wales under Edward I, and in Scotland the role of ships bringing supplies north to Berwick, and then on to Leith and further north was vital, as Edward II discovered in 1322 when for want of such support he had to abandon his Scottish campaign. Providing transport was no doubt the major occupation of most English ships on naval service. It was also necessary to provide defence for English coastal ports against foreign naval activity. The French and their allies presented a very real threat at some periods. Naturally, it made sense for the English not merely to defend their coasts, but to try to take the war to their enemies. The scale of naval operations was such as to impose a very considerable burden on England's seaports. The demands of the Crown on manpower were very heavy, and the needs of a major campaign removed ships for long periods from more profitable employment in trade.[2]

The warship (*right*) is taken from the seal of Dover of 1284, that below from the Luttrell Psalter of *c*. 1320–40. Both feature fighting castles of permanent construction, but the later vessel is more advanced with a stern rudder rather than a steering oar. The scene of fourteenth-century naval warfare (*facing page*) is from the lower margin of a page in a volume of papal decretals, and shows ships of the cog type.

Ship types

In broad terms, ships were of two types. There were galleys, and more substantial sailing ships. The Mediterranean galley, with its carvel (planks laid edge to edge, not overlapping) construction, was rare in northern waters; the English galleys were descendants of the Viking type of vessel, with overlapping clinker planking. Galleys, relatively light in construction and slender in build, were not suited to the waters of the Bay of Biscay and the North Sea, and their life-span was short. One of two built in London in 1295 had to return for repairs after her maiden voyage, and another built at Newcastle in the same year needed a major refit after a mere six months in service.[3] Not surprisingly, galleys were not commissioned or used by the English after the thirteenth century, but smaller oared vessels were of value. Balingers were of similar design to galleys: oared vessels which usually had a single mast and sail. Accounts and inventories from the early years of Henry VI's reign suggest that balingers might be of anything from twenty-four to 120 tons, with perhaps up to forty oars. Such ships were important for fighting; they were not designed for transport purposes. Barges were probably similar in design, but were larger and broader in build, and might be used for carrying cargoes.[4]

Cogs, hulks, carracks and ships were different types of sailing vessels. The distinctions between them, no doubt self-evident to medieval mariners, are far from clear. The cog was flat-bottomed, with an angular stern; the ship probably had a more rounded stern. All were broad-beamed, with good carrying capacity and poor manoeuvrability. The replacement of the old-style steering oar with the sternpost rudder from the late twelfth century was important, for it made it easier to build taller ships as well as improving steering. In

the fourteenth century the addition of the whipstaff was a further advance, providing greater leverage on the tiller and enabling the steersman to be stationed higher in the superstructure of the vessel. Castles were added to bow and stern for military purposes. Initially these were temporary structures, but by the fourteenth century they were often permanent. Their height was essential for fighting, but they had the disadvantage of adding to the ship's windage. By Edward III's reign the Crown was using some very substantial vessels. In the early 1340s the *George* had a crew of two masters, two constables, a clerk, four carpenters, 130 sailors and twenty-six pages, while the *Cog Thomas* and *La Dyonys* had complements almost as numerous.[5] Still larger vessels came into royal service in the form of carracks. These were a very distinctive ship type. They were Mediterranean vessels, and those in English service, as under Henry V, were captured from the French or their allies. Much larger than most northern ships, they were carvel-built, and rode high out of the water. For most of the medieval period, no ships had more than a single mast, rigged for a great square sail. The sailing qualities of such a rig were obviously very limited; running before the wind was easy, while reaching might be possible, but there was surely little question of any ability to tack, even with a small spar, the *lof*, used as a kind of wooden bowline.[6] Multi-masted ships first appeared in the Mediterranean. The great dromon captured by Richard I on crusade was three-masted. Yet it was not until the early fifteenth century that English experiments began with multi-masted ships; the immense 1,400-ton *Gracedieu* of 1420 probably had three masts and a bowsprit, and though she proved to be something of a white elephant, she pointed the way forward for naval architecture.[7]

One calculation is that in the most favourable conditions, with a strong following wind, a medieval cog was capable of as much as ten knots.[8] Conditions, however, could not be relied upon. The difficulty of sailing ships with a simple rig of a single mast and square sail is demonstrated by the account of a new galley built at Winchelsea in 1337. She had a double crew, of forty-four men, and it took them twenty-six days to go from Winchelsea to London. The weather kept her in port for eight days, and then, once at sea, contrary winds meant that she stayed for seven days off Dover, unable to make her way up the Thames estuary.[9] Such problems were not uncommon. Reinforcements sent to Brittany in the autumn of 1342 failed to arrive, as a result of autumn gales, and when the king himself returned from Brittany to England early in the following year he and his men suffered five weeks of storm-tossed misery.[10] Edward III's 1346 expedition was delayed in setting out for France for two weeks as his fleet sailed fruitlessly from Portsmouth to Yarmouth and back. In the autumn of 1372 a very substantial fleet, under the command of the king himself, sailed from Sandwich and succeeded in reaching no further than Winchelsea before the expedition was abandoned: a miserable anti-climax to the last expedition in which Edward himself took part.

The size of ships naturally varied considerably. In 1301 the largest ship used to transport Irish troops to Scotland was 195 tons, while ten others were over 100 tons. Just over a century later there were some very much larger ships in service. Under Henry V the *Gracedieu*, built at Southampton, had a keel some 125 feet long, and her beam approached 50 feet. In addition to this huge ship the Crown owned the 1,000-ton *Jesus* and the 760-ton *Holighost de la Tour*. A ship under construction at Bayonne in 1419 would have been 186 feet in total length. By way of comparison, the late eighteenth-century forty-four gun frigate USS *Constitution* had a keel about 160 feet long, a waterline length of about 175 feet, and a beam of 43 feet.[11]

The costs of building the king's ships were considerable. The Pipe Roll for 1212 reveals that over £600 was spent on the king's great ship, the *Deulabeneie*, and the building of nine new galleys along with sixteen smaller boats, and the repair of other vessels. The bishopric of Durham, then vacant, contributed £44 towards the building of another new galley.[12] The galleys ordered by Edward I in 1294 cost between £205 and £355 each.[13] Shipbuilding accounts are, inevitably and unfortunately, not particularly informative about the actual design of the vessels, though they provide impressive evidence for the technical terms used by medieval shipbuilders. The building of the 1294 Southampton galley was a major enterprise. There was clearly some unfamiliarity among local shipbuilders with the problems of building a galley, and expert assistance was provided by a Gascon from Bayonne. Materials came from Portsmouth, Poole and the Isle of Wight. A plot of land had to be hired as a yard, houses were rented for workshops and stores. The operations lasted seventeen weeks. When complete, it was crewed by a master, three constables and 120 men. It bore twenty-five banners when it sailed, a symbol perhaps of civic pride as well as of warlike readiness.[14] The account for the *Philippe*, built at Lynn in 1336, shows that the exchequer provided £666 13s 4d to cover the cost. Construction took some fifty men about fifteen weeks. The ship was made seaworthy by caulking her with moss, and the liberal application of thirty-seven barrels of pitch. The great single mast cost £10, a substantial sum, and £37 2s 5d went on Spanish iron to make the three main anchors. The sail was red and black, presumably in stripes, and measured some ninety feet in height, with a width, allowing for seams, approaching sixty feet. Eighty oars were also available for propulsion. The ship, which probably resembled her Viking predecessors to some extent, was protected from the elements when in harbour by a huge red and white cloth awning.[15] In the 1370s an eighty-oar barge was built in London at a cost of £621.[16]

The acquisition of ships

At times, there was a substantial core of royal ships for the navy, as individual monarchs built or bought a number of vessels. There was, however, no permanent tradition of a royal navy. John made great efforts to establish a fleet of galleys in 1205; there is a list of fifty-one on the Close Roll. In that year £968 1s 8½d was spent on the royal fleet, excluding payments to sailors.[17] His son, Henry III, in contrast made no efforts to build or maintain a royal fleet. Edward I, as in many other things, copied his grandfather in ordering the construction of a fleet of galleys in 1294. Thirty were ordered, large vessels of 120 oars, but evidence of building costs survives solely for two built at London, and one each at Newcastle, Southampton, York, Ipswich, Dunwich and Lyme Regis.[18] Edward III, in the late 1330s, had eleven ships based at the Tower of London, and between 1344 and 1352 over fifty royal ships have been identified. In the last years of his reign numbers approached forty. One, romantically and perhaps unsuitably, was called the *Alice* after the royal mistress, Alice Perrers.[19] Henry V was very well aware of the importance of the navy. The build-up to his invasion of France in 1415 saw great ships constructed, and other vessels purchased or requisitioned for royal service. By 1418 Henry owned as many as thirty-nine ships, many of them won from the king's enemies in naval engagements.[20] The captains of these royal ships were permanently engaged by the Crown, but the crews were composed of impressed men.

In addition to royal ships, the Crown could count on the naval equivalent of feudal service, owed by the Cinque Ports of southeast England (originally Dover, Hastings, Hythe, Romney and Sandwich). The total number of ships due was fifty-seven, and service was for a mere two weeks. A total of 1,254 men were expected to man the ships, and by the early fourteenth century, when ships were much larger than they had been when the levels of service had been established, the Crown was content with half, or less, the original quota of ships, provided that the number of sailors was not reduced. The obligation of the Ports was not forgotten even when feudal service had been abandoned. In 1372 they were required to provide six vessels for a month's service, and in 1387 to provide ten, crewed by 600 men, for twenty days.[21]

The great majority of ships used by the Crown in war were ordinary merchant vessels, requisitioned by royal officials. Sheriffs

The seal of Sandwich, one of the Cinque Ports, dating from 1238.

might be entrusted with the task; commissioners might be appointed to negotiate with seaports; responsibility might be given to the admirals; or writs might be sent to civic authorities requesting that they should supply a given number of ships. The task was not easy. In 1301 twelve south coast towns which had promised to supply vessels failed to do so, for a variety of excuses. The men of Poole claimed that the earl of Lincoln had requisitioned their ships, while it was argued that the only suitable ships Sleaford possessed were both in Gascony. In 1302 two ships were obtained from Bristol, but the royal constable of the castle had to use force to recruit crews for them. In the north it required all the authority of the keeper of the palatinate of Durham, then in royal hands, to compel the co-operation of Hartlepool, Wearmouth and Jarrow. In 1303 three men were appointed to inquire into the fact that some ships selected from east coast ports, from Essex to Northumberland, had not appeared, and into the desertion of sailors from those which had.[22] An agreement made by the civic authorities of Exeter in 1310 shows some of the difficulties involved in obtaining shipping. They had consented to provide one ship for the Scottish war, but a lack of suitable vessels, contrary winds, and a want of co-operation from Exeter's subsidiary ports meant a month's delay. Part of the wages was paid promptly; the rest was held back until the ship returned to port, so as to prevent the crew deliberately delaying their return.[23]

There were considerable difficulties in obtaining ships in the initial stages of the Hundred Years War, prior to the battle of Sluys. Lack of ships, indeed, meant that Edward was unable to sail for Flanders in the spring of 1340, and it was not until June that he was able to embark his troops.[24] Ships once seized by the king's agents might be kept in port for lengthy periods, and while sailors were paid wages, shipowners received no compensation for the loss of trade. Ships arrested in September 1374 had to wait to sail for France until April of the following year. There is evidence from 1344 for the payment of compensation to men whose ships were lost or damaged in royal service, but this was a rare act of generosity on Edward III's part. Exceptionally, the owners of three ships burned at La Rochelle in 1372 were each granted a royal ship as a replacement. In the 1380s pressure in parliament led the Crown to grant payments, usually at 2s a ton, to shipowners whose vessels were pressed into royal service.[25]

Detailed study of the port of Great Yarmouth in the fourteenth century has demonstrated how serious the effects of naval impressment might be on the local economy. In 1347 the townsmen claimed that under Edward II Yarmouth's fleet numbered ninety substantial vessels, but fifty-four had been lost, and only twenty-four were left in a decent state of repair. Compensation for losses was scant, and the town's trade suffered when its ships were arrested for lengthy periods. In 1338, for example, the port had lost the use of forty ships for an entire year.[26]

Commandeered merchant vessels needed to be converted for war purposes. 'Castles' could be added to bow and stern, and a fighting top fitted to the mast: in 1349 Nicholas Pyke received an advance of £8 so that he might construct a 'hindercastle' on the *Passagiere*. These castles gave archers a high vantage point, but their additional bulk must have made poor manoeuvrability worse. Indeed, in 1317 Eustace the Monk had a castle constructed on a ship at Dover 'so big and so marvellous that all would wonder at it'. It overhung the bulwarks of the ship, which needed to be towed by boats, for it could no longer be sailed.[27] In addition, it was necessary to convert ships so that they could carry horses. The Bayeux tapestry provides vivid pictorial evidence that the Normans brought horses across the Channel in 1066, but the artist's impression of how this was done probably bears little relation to reality. The Normans had some expertise in this, for at the same period they were also transporting horses by sea in the Mediterranean, from the Calabrian mainland to Sicily. Later accounts show that stalls were constructed from hurdles or planks, but precisely how the horses were confined so that they could not injure themselves is not explained by the sources. It may well be that, as in the Mediterranean *taride* and galleys, they were supported and even raised off their feet by a system of canvas slings. Gangways were needed so that the animals could be embarked, in itself a

Horses transported across the Channel, as depicted in the Bayeux Tapestry. In practice, it would have been necessary to fit the ships with wooden stalls to restrain the horses.

hazardous operation.[28] When horses were taken on long voyages, as to Gascony, providing sufficient fodder and fresh water must have been a major problem. It is not likely that any single ship would have carried very large numbers of horses; evidence shows that when mounts were shipped from Ireland to Scotland in 1303, the minimum number in any ship was ten, and the maximum thirty-two.[29]

The use of the navy

In the Norman period, shipping was vital in providing the link between England and Normandy, with the English Cinque Ports performing a central role in supplying vessels. On occasion, substantial numbers of ships were needed to take entire armies across the Channel; on others the king might travel, as Rufus did in 1099, with a single vessel. The lack of documentary evidence presents severe problems for this period, but it seems likely that there was at least one royal ship, an *esnecca*, with a master who was obliged to maintain her and provide a crew. Problems appear to have been few, save for the celebrated disaster of the loss of the White Ship in 1120, when Henry I's son William and his companions were drowned off Barfleur. This was a wholly exceptional incident; disaster may have threatened many who crossed in stormy weather, but there were no other notable casualties.[30]

Under Henry II fleets played a vital role in warfare. Henry fully appreciated the importance of naval support for his Welsh campaigns, even obtaining ships from Dublin in 1165. The king's own intervention in Ireland was possible only because sufficient shipping could be mobilised to take a substantial expedition across the Irish Sea in 1171; some 400 vessels were assembled at Milford Haven. The problems of relying on a navy were, however, brought home to the king when severe winter storms meant that he was for a time isolated from England, with no means of communication.[31] The importance of shipping was also very clear during the rebellion of 1173–4, when the movement of troops across the Channel was an essential element in royal strategy. The defence of Normandy under Richard I and John also required the use of ships on a substantial scale.

The loss of Normandy in 1204 transformed England's naval situation. No longer did the Channel offer a convenient, if occasionally dangerous, connection between the lands of the English monarchy. It became a stretch of water disputed between English sailors, notably those of the Cinque Ports and Yarmouth, and their Norman rivals. It is not surprising that it was under John, shortly after Normandy was lost, that naval activities received a powerful emphasis. Under William of Wrotham, naval administration was reorganised, and great efforts went into both shipbuilding and the impressment of merchant shipping. In April 1206 orders went out to seize all ships capable of transporting at least eight horses in a number of ports from Yarmouth round to Portsmouth. The Cinque Ports were instructed to send the ships that they owed by way of service. Almost 2,000 sailors were employed by the Crown in sailing 206 ships to Poitou, the voyage taking ten days. In addition to the royal efforts, individual magnates also provided ships: William Brewerre went with three, Henry FitzCount and Reginald de Mohun with two. The entire fleet must have been most impressive.[32] Naval efforts a few years later, in 1212, were again on a large scale. The cost of shipping for forces going to Gascony and Ireland approached £2,000. One thousand three hundred sailors were sent to sea in twenty galleys and forty ships, and another 1,200 in six galleys and ninety-one ships. A further 862 sailors received payment for time spent in harbour at Portsmouth in seventy-five ships.[33] In 1213 the navy proved its value, when a substantial French fleet was destroyed at Damme, near Bruges.

Fleets could be very large. In 1230 Henry III sailed for Poitou with 288 ships, allowing another 131 to return to their home ports as they were not needed. Edward I's Flanders expedition of 1297 required the use of about 300 ships. The Scottish wars, however, did not call for such numbers, as the ships were not needed to carry troops and horses northwards from England; they were wanted to bring supplies and, in 1303–4, to act as pontoons for a bridge across the Firth of Forth. In 1301, to give the example of one year's campaigning, fifty-three ships were employed in taking victuals up the east coast. Most were fairly small vessels with crews of twenty or thirty men, though the *Nicholas* and *Michael* of Yarmouth had a complement of sixty, as did the *Navis Dei* of Hartlepool. On the west coast another fleet supported the Prince of Wales's army in Galloway. Forty-seven ships were used, over twenty of them from Ireland. Six ships, indeed, had sailed from Waterford to Dublin only for it to be found that they were not needed.[34] Towards the end of Edward II's reign, problems in Gascony meant that a reluctant government had to assemble men and shipping so that the inadequate English forces in the duchy could be reinforced. In 1325 a fleet of eighty ships manned by some 1,650 sailors was brought together to transport a small force of about 300 cavalry and almost 1,800 infantry to Bordeaux.[35]

The main function of fleets in the early fourteenth century was not glamorous. Transport of men, horses and victuals was above all what was needed. Carriage by sea was far more cost-effective than transport by land, and in Edward I's Welsh and above all his Scottish wars naval transport played an essential role, not to move troops (save to Anglesey), but to bring them supplies. Some voyages were surprising. In the summer of 1300 there was a need to take grain from Kirkcudbright, and deliver it, ground into flour, to the army at Ayr. One vessel went to Workington, where the grain was milled, and returned north to Ayr. Two went to Whitehaven, while a fourth, remarkably, sailed to Dublin, and then returned north to Ayr. This latter voyage took fifteen days, at an average speed of three-quarters of a knot an hour.[36] That was much faster than the *Nicholas* of London, which took eight days to travel from Newcastle to Berwick in 1301, averaging roughly a third of a knot an hour.[37] Long voyages might see cargoes go rotten. Early in 1304, 1,125 quarters of wheat, and quantities of other victuals, arrived in seven ships at Berwick, all the way from the Isle of Wight and Southampton; all were hopelessly decayed. A further ship had been wrecked before it could reach its destination. When supplies from England reached Gascony in 1325, the bulk of the grain was found to be rotten. It had lain in store in English granaries for six months before being shipped, so it was probably already in poor condition before the voyage across the Bay of Biscay saw it decay to worthlessness.[38]

The Hundred Years War brought far greater requirements on English shipping, for men and horses needed to be transported to the Low Countries and to France, along with supplies, on a regular basis. In 1338 Edward III made use of 361 ships to transport his army to

Antwerp, and for miscellaneous services in support of his enterprise in the Low Countries. About 12,500 sailors were involved in these operations. The *Cog Edward*, with a crew of seventy, was employed from 13 July to 2 August 1338 in taking the king himself to Flanders. A second voyage with a much smaller crew of twenty-nine was made with royal wool from Yarmouth to Flanders, and a third, again with a cargo of wool, in November with a crew of forty-eight. The king's expedition of 1346–7, which culminated in the siege of Calais, made much larger demands on the country's naval resources, and required 738 ships in all. There had been considerable delays in assembling this fleet, with frequent postponements.[39] It could, of course, be difficult to obtain sufficient shipping for a major campaign. In 1359 the great expedition to France was substantially delayed by want of ships, though the situation was eased by sending the duke of Lancaster ahead of the main army, and by using the short crossing to Calais. Many of those on the expedition had to hire their own transport, receiving in consequence allowances to pay for the transport of horses.[40]

Manpower and wages

Demands for naval manpower were heavy. The largest ship from the Cinque Ports in the fleet which took Edward I to Flanders in 1297 had a crew of forty-nine, but one vessel from Bayonne was manned by a hundred sailors. Edward III's *Cristofre* of the later 1330s had a crew of 106 sailors and fourteen pages, while the *Cog Thomas* had 119 sailors and sixteen pages. A large balinger in the early fifteenth century, the *Nicholas* of 120 tons, usually had a crew of 107 men.[41] It is easy to understand why galleys needed large crews, but perhaps not so evident as why such numbers were required on sailing ships with just one mast and sail. It has been estimated that a medium-sized vessel, a cog of 136 tonnes loaded displacement, would have needed five men to operate a capstan so as to raise anchor. Four men were needed to loose the sail, and another four would have been required to man the braces. Securing the clews and sheets would have needed another four. In addition, the ship needed a master, a helmsman, a boatswain, a carpenter and a sailmaker, making a total minimum complement of twenty-two. A large ship, with a huge square sail, would have required many more men. As a result of the intensive manning of the ships, it took startlingly large numbers of sailors to transport an army. In 1297 about 5,800 sailors were needed to take a force of some 9,000 men to Flanders, and that was a relatively economical use of sailors.[42] In 1345 the earl of Lancaster sailed for Gascony with a force of around 2,000 men. His fleet consisted of 152 ships, manned by 2,484 sailors with 306 boys or servants. The voyage from Falmouth to Bordeaux lasted from 23 July to 10 August, a total of forty-two days. The 738 ships which transported the great army of 1346–7, numbering some 30,000, were manned by 15,000 sailors.[43] The demands of the king for naval support bore much more heavily on the seaports of England than his requests for soldiers bore on the inland towns and counties, and it is hardly surprising that the impressment of men was very unpopular.

Where true naval expeditions were concerned, as opposed to the transport of armies to France, substantial numbers of soldiers as well as sailors were still recruited. In 1373 the earl of Salisbury sailed with about 2,500 sailors and 2,400 soldiers, and this was the normal proportion. In 1378 the earl of Buckingham's force of some 8,000 was made up of roughly equal numbers of soldiers and sailors.[44] The soldiers in naval expeditions at this period were normally composed of equal numbers of men-at-arms and archers; thus the earl of Warwick contracted in 1373 to provide 200 men-at-arms and 200 archers. By Henry V's reign it was usual in naval service for archers to outnumber men-at-arms by two to one, as against the normal three to one for service on land.[45] In 1416 two separate forces were organised, one of 350 men-at-arms and 700 archers, the other of 200 men-at-arms and 500 archers. True naval patrols were set up under Henry. In 1417 three magnates commanded a total of 616 men-at-arms and 1,232 archers at sea, operating out of Dartmouth and Winchelsea. In 1420 the earl of Devon agreed to take a force of 500 men-at-arms and 1,000 archers to sea between the end of April and the beginning of November. His force consisted of five ships and ten balingers. These patrols were not intended to wait in port until an enemy fleet appeared. In 1419 the earl of Devon had been ordered to stay at sea for three months, and not to put to shore save in bad weather, or to take on water. He was to patrol the region between Dieppe and Cherbourg. The importance of such naval activity under Henry V was immense; a combination of the capture of the Norman ports and patrolling by sea ensured in his reign as effective a control of the Channel as was possible in this period.[46]

Wages for naval service were paid at similar levels to service on land. Under Edward I a shipmaster was paid 6d a day, and an ordinary sailor 3d, and like soldier's wages, these rates did not change substantially for the rest of the medieval period. The 'pages', perhaps ship's boys, who feature in some accounts were paid $1\frac{1}{2}d$ a day.[47] Soldiers who served at sea received the same wages as they would on land, though in the fourteenth century the regard offered to them was lower, presumably because their service was not on horseback.

Command

Naval command went, as a rule, not to men with lengthy experience of the sea, but to soldiers. Appointments were not permanent, but were usually made for a specific campaign or season. In 1294, when Edward I faced the threat of French galleys raiding the south coast, two household knights, William Leyburne and John Botetourt, were appointed as captain and sub-captain of the fleet. In the following year they were described as admirals – the first use of the term in England. In 1300 Gervase Alard, the leading man of the Cinque Ports, an experienced shipmaster, was appointed to command the fleet, but the office of admiral continued to be given more often to men of rank rather than of seafaring experience. The lists of naval commanders are full of names of men who must have felt far more at home on dry land. John Perbroun was an exception: a Yarmouth man, he served as admiral on several occasions between 1317 and 1333. No doubt a man such as John Botetourt, whose final naval appointment was made in 1315, did acquire some expertise in ships and the sea, but for the most part these medieval fleet captains and admirals must have relied heavily on the advice of the professional mariners under their command, such as Hugh Fastolf of Yarmouth who served as an admiral's deputy and did notably well as a recipient of royal patronage.[48] At the start of the Hundred Years War the earls of Suffolk, Salisbury, Huntingdon and Arundel, along with Bartholomew Burghersh and Walter Mauny, featured as admirals; the sole professional sailor was Peter Bard of Winchelsea. By the end of Edward II's reign it had become normal to divide the fleets and their command into two: one from the Thames northwards and the other from the Thames to the west. It was not until Henry V's reign that the single position of Admiral of England emerged; the first holder was Thomas Beaufort, duke of Exeter.[49]

Fighting at sea

Although most of the time men spent at sea was devoted to the transport of goods and men, there was some fighting at sea. The battle of Sluys in 1340 was a notable victory which deserves its place alongside Crécy, Poitiers and Agincourt. Naval warfare was a matter of close engagement and hand-to-hand fighting. The aim was to grapple enemy ships, and board them; sinking them from long range as in more modern naval warfare was not possible, and the ships did not have the momentum to fight in classical fashion, aiming to sink opponents by ramming them. The main weaponry available was provided by archers and crossbowmen; installing converted siege

An artist's reconstruction of the battle of Sluys, 1340.

machinery was not a practicable proposition. Exceptionally, the *All Hallows Cog* was provided with a single gun in 1337–8 at a cost of a mere 3*s*. Not until the fifteenth century is there evidence for ships being regularly equipped with guns. In the 1420s the *Holigost de la Tour* was fitted with six guns, with two chambers each, while the *Thomas de la Tour* had four guns, each with three chambers.[50]

Naval battles were few, in part at least because of the lack of manoeuvrability of the ships themselves. The battle of Sandwich in 1217, however, was one engagement where tactical skill on the part of the English sailors may have been a decisive element. A substantial French fleet set out across the Channel from Calais with reinforcements for the French forces in England in the final stages of the civil war which began at the end of John's reign. The English fleet set out from Sandwich under the command of Hubert de Burgh, and initially passed in front of the French fleet, sailing out towards Calais. The English then turned, and with the wind behind them, came up on the French from astern. It is not clear whether the tactic was deliberate, and it worked only because some of the French, eager for a fight, clewed up their sails so as to slow down. The French flagship, commanded by Eustace the Monk, lay low in the water, heavily laden with thirty-six knights, horses, and even a massive stone-throwing engine, a trebuchet. The English, from the height of the castles on their one tall cog, hurled pots of lime, so temporarily blinding their opponents. Victory was then easily achieved, though the bulk of the French fleet escaped safely to Calais.[51]

Edward III's greatest naval victory took place at Sluys in 1340. Edward sailed on 22 June from Orwell, and approached the Flemish coast early in the morning of the next day. He received information that a French fleet was blocking the mouth of the Zwin, making it impossible to reach Bruges. A small reconnaissance force landed, and took careful note of the position of the French ships. The attack was set for high tide in mid afternoon on the next day, 24 June. Both fleets were organised into three groups, just as if it were a land battle. The English, with the wind and sun behind them, sailed down upon the lines of French ships, which were chained together. The French commanders had argued bitterly with their Genoese ally, Barbavera. He had wanted to take the French fleet out to sea, from where they could attack the English from the windward side, rather than to try to fight in the enclosed waters of the estuary, where there would be no opportunity to manoeuvre. As it was, the English had all the tactical advantage. By pretending to prepare to turn about, the English gave the impression that they were about to retreat; the French unchained their ships, leaving the way open for the English attack. English archers wrought havoc, their weapons proving more effective than the French crossbows. When the ships crashed together, the English men-at-arms soon gained the advantage. The first line of French ships was taken, and then the second, as panic overtook their defenders. Some fighting continued through the night, and one small group of French ships succeeded in escaping to the safety of the open seas. The English had taken no less than 190 out of an estimated 213 French ships. The price the French paid in lives was immense. The great majority of those slain were ordinary sailors, mostly Normans; there had been few knights and experienced men-at-arms in the French fleet – an important factor in its defeat.[52] The battle was of great importance, giving the English if not true control of the seas, at least a considerable degree of mastery for many years to come.

The English were not invariably victorious at sea. One important naval duty was the maintenance of a secure route between Gascony and England (merchant fleets normally sailed in convoy for fear of French attack). The vulnerability of English shipping was demonstrated in 1372 when a force under the earl of Pembroke was resoundingly defeated by Castilian galleys off La Rochelle, a defeat which had an initially devastating effect on English morale, but which provided the incentive to put much more effort into subsequent naval activity. Pembroke's fleet was a small one, with perhaps no more than three substantial ships equipped with castles on fore

The defeat of the earl of Pembroke at La Rochelle in 1372.

and stern, and possibly only some twenty vessels in all. The forces being transported to Gascony were small, consisting of the earl, twenty-four knights, fifty-five squires and eighty archers. The Castilian ships were fewer still in number, but were formidably equipped, even possessing canon. The battle was won by the Castilian tactic of spraying oil on the decks of the English ships, and firing it by means of flaming arrows, as well as in hand-to-hand fighting.[53] In relation to Sluys, La Rochelle was no more than a minor skirmish, but it was of great importance in destroying any myths of English invincibility, and giving the French new heart. Yet French naval projects on a vast scale in the mid 1380s, aimed at achieving a full-scale invasion of England, came to nothing. There was even an ambitious and highly novel concept of creating a vast prefabricated town which was to serve as the base camp for the invasion force, having been brought in its component parts in seventy-two ships from Brittany and Normandy to Sluys. It was, perhaps predictably, the autumn weather rather than English seamanship that prevented these plans from being carried out.[54]

One naval function of intermittent importance was the need for ships to defend England against possible French attack. Hardly surprisingly, the French took such opportunities as they could to retaliate against the English ravages of their land by doing all

possible damage to English ports. There was justified concern under Edward I, and in 1295 the sheriffs were ordered to assemble ships at Portsmouth, Harwich, Orwell and Ravenser, and accounts show that the coast from King's Lynn to Berwick was duly guarded by a squadron of eight ships. A naval attack on Hythe was thwarted by ships from Yarmouth, but Dover was assaulted. In 1296 larger fleets were organised; John Botetourt commanded ninety-four ships taken from ports between Harwich and King's Lynn, the great majority from Yarmouth. In the following year ships were sent to watch the French coast, to warn of any attack, while two small squadrons defended the English shore.[55] Arrangements for naval defence were once again made during the Hundred Years War. The need for them was emphasised when first Portsmouth and then Southampton suffered very severely from a naval raids in 1338 by the French and their Genoese allies. Southampton was virtually destroyed by fire. Trade ceased for at least a year, and rental values did not recover for many years.[56] The lesson of the dangers of a failure to provide naval protection was a hard one. In 1342 the king ordered ships to be ready at Sandwich at Easter, 'for he thinks that if a fleet is collected at a suitable time it will prevent his enemies from making attacks on the sea coast'.[57]

The navy had an essential role in English warfare in the medieval period, if rarely a glamorous one. The technical deficiencies of medieval shipping meant that a sophisticated naval strategy could never be adopted; the tasks of the navy were essentially those of providing transport of men, horses and victuals. There was no 'military revolution' in naval matters; there was a gradual improvement in shipbuilding, but although some fifteenth-century vessels were impressively large, their seaworthiness and general capability were probably little advanced from the ships which had served to bring William I to England. Such naval fighting as there was mostly took place in enclosed coastal waters, for it was very hard for fleets to engage on the open sea. The navy's importance should not, however, be underestimated. The scale of manpower involved in naval affairs was startlingly large; in any assessment of the burden of war on England, the impact on the seaports was surely disproportionately great. Above all, without transport by sea, English armies in Wales and Scotland could have achieved little, while shipping obviously provided an essential underpinning for the campaigns in France. Seasick and uncomfortable troops probably gave few thanks to the mariners, but the skills of seamanship were as important for English success in war as those of handling horse, lance, sword and bow.

12

Siege Warfare

Sieges dominated medieval warfare in a way that battles never did. That great warrior Richard I fought no more than two or three battles in his entire career, but he was constantly involved in siege warfare, and indeed even died from an injury sustained when attempting to capture a castle. The battle of Crécy in 1346 was dramatic, but it was the subsequent siege of Calais that brought lasting gains to the English. It was the hard, long grind of sieges that gave Normandy to Henry V, not the single dramatic victory at Agincourt.

Sieges often played a major part in civil war, for it was important to establish and maintain control over territory, and castles were the obvious instrument for this purpose. The civil war of Stephen's reign was dominated by sieges; even the battle of Lincoln can be seen as an incident of siege warfare. Lincoln castle was besieged by King Stephen; Robert of Gloucester then came to the city to relieve the siege, and battle ensued. A typical snapshot of warfare may be taken from 1145. The earl of Gloucester's son Philip was heavily engaged in fighting royalist troops based at Oxford. He advised his father to deal with the royalists 'by building castles in the most suitable places to check more carefully the sallies of those who served the king'. A new castle was duly built at Faringdon, which proved highly effective for a time, but the royalists sent messages to King Stephen, who brought up troops and laid siege to Faringdon. Eventually the garrison, tormented by stone-throwing machines and archery, abandoned the struggle. No battle took place, but these moves in this game of military chess placed Stephen at a temporary advantage.[1] The struggle at the end of John's reign and the beginning of that of his son provides another demonstration of the importance of sieges. Although it was said that after the siege of Rochester in 1215 men lost their faith in castles, the campaigning was dominated by castles and the need to capture them.[2] Once again, a battle at Lincoln was provoked by a siege, while the fortunes of the French prince Louis depended to a considerable extent on whether or not he could take Dover. By 1322, however, the position was very different. Siege warfare played little part in the rebellion of Thomas of Lancaster. Rather than attempt to hold out in Pontefract, he and his followers marched north towards Scotland, only to find their route blocked at Boroughbridge. There were sieges during the Wars of the Roses, notably that of Harlech which held out for some four years in the 1460s, but castle warfare did not dominate the campaigns.[3]

Siege warfare played a lesser part in the Welsh wars, and in fighting in Ireland, for the obvious reason that the Welsh and Irish did not themselves rely on castles in the way that the English or French did. In border warfare the Welsh, when conducting their damaging raids, were frequently able to bypass the many castles held by the English. The Welsh did engage in castle-building in the thirteenth century, but they did not have any castles of great strength. They began the war of 1282–3 with surprise attacks on castles held by the English, at Hawarden, Aberystwyth, Carreg Cennen and Llandovery, but in his campaign Edward I did not have to conduct any lengthy sieges of fortresses such as Dolwyddelan or Castell-y-Bere. The latter held out for no more than ten days. Castles were one of the weapons used by the English in their conquest of Ireland, but many were simple structures, largely dependent on earthworks for defence. Lengthy sieges were not a feature of warfare in Ireland, but the destruction and rebuilding of frontier castles was a regular occurrence. The Irish view was summed up in a description of Aedh O'Neill, who died in 1230. He was 'the person of the Gaidhil that most killed and pillaged the Foreigners, and destroyed castles'.[4]

In Scotland, where there were some major stone castles by the early fourteenth century, siege warfare was more important. All that was achieved in Edward I's expedition of 1300 into Galloway was the taking of Caerlaverock castle. In 1301 Bothwell was captured by the use of a great wooden movable siege tower, or belfry. The capture of Stirling after a costly and lengthy siege in 1304 brought one stage of Scottish resistance to an end, in a way that the English triumph at Falkirk had failed to do, and it was the siege of Stirling by the Scots in 1313 that led to the English expedition of the following year and the disaster at Bannockburn, for surrender had been offered by the English garrison of Stirling provided that no relieving army appeared before Midsummer 1314. Robert Bruce's strategy of destroying castles when they were taken from the English did much to ensure that the war proceeded in such a way that it was not so much dominated by sieges as it might otherwise have been.

In their campaigns in France, the English had no advantage when it came to siege warfare. This helps explain why a central element of their strategy in the fourteenth century was the use of the *chevauchée*. This was not designed to capture territory or castles, but rather to ravage the countryside as the mounted force moved rapidly

Siege warfare in the fifteenth century. This illustration shows a wooden siege tower, a cannon with a complex range-finding and elevation system, and an attempt to scale the defences.

through French territory. Swift raids, as the Scots demonstrated in northern England, could make a detour around defended strongpoints. There was no time for lengthy sieges during the great raids into France though lesser castles might be captured by assault or a brief show of force. It would, for example, have been impossible to take the elaborate equipment needed for major sieges on the Black Prince's *chevauchées* of 1355 and 1356. Not all campaigns took this form, however. Calais was captured in 1347 after a major siege, and Edward III attempted to capture Rheims by siege in 1360. From Harfleur in 1415 to Rouen in 1419, Henry V showed himself to be as adept at siege warfare as Agincourt showed him to be at battle. Siege warfare also had its very significant place in the campaigning in south-western France. Gascony was a land of castles, and the defensive war fought by the Gascons and the English against the Valois kings was one of a multitude of sieges and counter-sieges.

Siege warfare made quite different demands upon armies from mobile campaigning or open battle. Cavalry was of little use in a siege, though, as at Lincoln in 1217, a somewhat misguided sense of what was honourable might induce men to attack stone walls on horseback.[5] There was little value in sheer weight of numbers in a siege. Expertise in archery was important, but the main advantage that the longbow had in battle, its rapid rate of fire, was not so significant when opponents had strong defences to shelter behind. The crossbow, with its power and accuracy, was an ideal weapon for siege warfare. Considerable expertise was needed for the specialised operations involved in attacking fortifications, such as mining and the use of the great siege engines such as belfries and trebuchets. Sanitation and food supply presented quite different problems in a long-drawn-out siege from those of a swift mobile campaign.

Despite these obvious requirements, the composition of armies was normally dominated by the needs of battle rather than of sieges. In 1144 the forces Stephen had at Winchcombe do not seem to have been capable of any sophisticated form of siege warfare. He gave orders that his forces should arm themselves, and storm the castle. Some were to advance shooting arrows, others would crawl up the motte, while the remainder rushed around the castle hurling whatever they could at the defenders. These methods proved effective, but perhaps only because the garrison was small.[6] A striking example of an ill-prepared army is provided by the English campaign of 1319 against the Scots. The expedition was prompted by the shameful loss through treachery of Berwick to Robert Bruce, and the recovery of the town was the prime objective. Yet there is no evidence to show that siege equipment was brought north on any scale; all that the substantial English force were able to do was to dig themselves in around the town, while a naval blockade prevented any relief from the sea. No effective assault was mounted, no siege engines were brought into operation, and Berwick remained firmly in Scottish hands. As the Scots chose to launch a diversionary attack into Yorkshire, rather than challenge the English army directly, the entire campaign closed in confusion and disagreement.[7]

Siege engineers

At the siege of Caerlaverock in 1300, the value of experts in siege warfare was well demonstrated. Nothing was done until ships arrived bringing supplies and siege engines. Edward I's army initially attempted a straightforward assault. The infantry was beaten back by a hail of missiles from the defenders. The men-at-arms then hurried forward, displaying considerable folly as well as bravery, some acting 'as if fired up and blinded by pride and despair'. Shields were battered and broken, and successive waves of attackers were driven back. John de Creting even galloped up to the castle walls in his haste to win honour. Adam de la Forde attempted to bore through the walls. Eventually it was the siege engines, almost certainly great stone-throwing trebuchets, erected by the master engineer recruited for the campaign, Brother Robert of Ulm, that won the day for the English. One of these machines was brought not by sea, but manually from Lochmaben, the short journey taking a total of seven men a week. A yard or throwing beam for the machine then had to be made at Caerlaverock. Stones from this and other siege engines landing in the castle caused many casualties, and forced the Scots to offer surrender. For all his importance in achieving this success, Brother Robert received no more than wages at the rate of 9d a day, in contrast to the 4s paid to the bannerets. In addition to Robert, Adam of Glasham and five other master carpenters were with the army, along with a hundred ordinary carpenters. A small troop of a dozen miners was probably not much use at Caerlaverock, but was an essential element in a force prepared for siege warfare.[8]

Robert of Ulm was a member of a profession of military experts whose contribution to military history is too often undervalued. Contemporaries valued knights with their chivalric reputation far more highly than professional engineers, though it is interesting that a poet in the early thirteenth century, Guiot of Provins, condemned the way in which the 'artists' of war, the chivalrous class, found their supremacy usurped by miners, engineers and other experts in siege warfare.[9] Robert de Bellême at the turn of the eleventh century had made good use of such men; Orderic Vitalis referred to the stone-throwing machines built for him at the siege of Bréval by an ingenious engineer.[10] It is, however, from the late twelfth century that the names and, in some cases, the outlines of the careers of military engineers can be worked out in adequate detail. Many of those described as *ingeniatores* appear in the records largely as castle-builders, such as Maurice the Engineer who was responsible for the keeps at Newcastle upon Tyne and Dover under Henry II. Master Elias of Oxford was extensively engaged in building and repair work on the royal castles in the 1190s, and in 1194 brought the royal siege engines from London for the siege of Nottingham. In 1201 John retained Master Urric specifically to construct siege engines for the campaigns in Normandy. In 1210 he was in charge of the siege train that the king took with him to Ireland, and was accompanied by Master Osbert and three other men, masons who cut the ammunition for the stone-throwing machines, and a small troop of miners and carpenters. Most engineers began their careers as builders, but Urric seems to have started his as a crossbowman. King John granted him lands in Essex held as knight's fees, and his status was further demonstrated by his receipt of financial reward at the same level as the king's household knights.[11] Master Bertram had a lengthy and distinguished career as a military expert under Henry III and Edward I (assuming that the name was borne by one man, not two). His career ranged from Gascony to Wales. Records testify to his activity in Gascony in the 1250s, notably at the siege of Bénauges in 1253; he then reappeared in royal service in England in 1276, when he was engaged on constructing siege engines in the Tower of London. It is possible that he was responsible in 1277 for the initial laying-out of the sites of the new castles built by Edward I in Wales at Flint and Rhuddlan. Edward also made use of his expertise in siege warfare in Wales at Dolwyddelan and at Castell-y-Bere. Almost certainly a Gascon in origin, Bertram was one of the many foreigners who provided the English government with the expertise it needed.[12] Thomas of Houghton was the most important of the royal carpenters in the second half of Edward's reign, and was also termed an engineer. His duties ranged from constructing a pile-driver for the foundations of St Stephen's chapel, and creating the wooden screen round Queen Eleanor's Westminster tomb, to making siege engines for the siege of Stirling in 1304, where he was the senior of seven master-carpenters. Curiously, he was not present on the Caerlaverock campaign of 1300, when his place was taken by Robert of Ulm.[13] It would be easy to extend such a list of those employed as experts in castle-building and castle-breaking.

Despite the vital part that the engineers played in warfare, their role was not recognised in the way that Guiot de Provins had expected. Glory remained with the bannerets, knights and men-at-arms, and the contribution of the technical experts was not fully acknowledged. Master James of St George received exceptional rewards, for he was appointed as constable of Harlech castle, and was granted a pension of 3s a day in recognition of his good service. Yet even he never received as much as a banneret, whose daily wage was 4s,[14] nor did he obtain rewards in land. No other engineer was as highly regarded as Master James. This lack of contemporary recognition for the men who constructed the siege engines and, no doubt, supervised their operations with a designer's affection for his product, is hardly surprising. Military engineers have rarely achieved the fame they deserve, and a man such as Vauban under Louis XIV was anomalous indeed. It is the fighting men who achieve high rank and fame, and no engineer carries a field-marshal's baton in his rucksack.

With the advent of artillery a new form of expertise was required. The first known use of gunpowder in Britain was during Edward I's Scottish campaign of 1304. A Burgundian, Jean de Lamouilly, used sulphur and saltpetre, two of the main ingredients of gunpowder, probably to make what was termed 'Greek fire' to burn the houses within Stirling castle. This was a potent incendiary mixture, used to spread fire and usually containing pitch; it was not used to propel projectiles. Two shillings was spent on earthenware pots, which were perhaps filled with the mixture and then hurled into the castle.[15] The earliest guns known to have been made in England were the work of the royal smith, Walter, in co-operation with one of the king's carpenters, Reginald of St Albans; they made the guns used in the Crécy–Calais campaign of 1346–7. It was not, however, the makers of the guns who took charge of them during the campaign, but rather a royal clerk, Thomas of Rolleston. Twelve artillers and gunners who manned the novel weapons in the siege of Calais are named in the pay accounts. Instructions were given that all the saltpetre and sulphur that could be found were to delivered to Rolleston, who in 1346 had charge of approaching 1,000 lbs of each. Gunnery expertise ran in families. In the second half of the fourteenth century three members of the Byker family were engaged as royal artillerymen, making guns and other weapons. In the fifteenth century gun manufacture at the Tower of London was dominated by members of the Clampard family.[16]

Below the ranks of the expert engineers were the craftsmen and workmen. Miners, usually recruited from the Forest of Dean, had an important role in siege warfare. Thirty miners were at the siege of Bedford in 1224, and following the success of the operation, to which they contributed notably, their leader, John de Standon, was rewarded with twelve acres of land, and his three chief associates eight apiece. In 1301 there was a small troop consisting of one master miner, and twenty-one men under his command in the royal army in Scotland.[17] Carpenters were essential, to work on siege engines. Masons cut ammunition, and ditchers were important in constructing siege works. The overall numbers of such men in English armies were, however, never large; important as siege warfare was, its needs did not dictate recruitment policy to the extent that might have been expected.

Siege equipment

Much has been written about the engines which the engineers built and serviced; these devices have a strange fascination.[18] The largest were the great siege towers, or belfries. These had been used by the

Romans, and knowledge of them had not been lost. They were much used in the Norman period. Robert de Bellême had one built at Courcy in the late eleventh century, and at St Audemer in 1123 Henry I personally gave instructions to the carpenters building such a tower. At the siege of Lisbon during the Second Crusade the English built one ninety-five feet high, but when it was moved toward the walls of the city, it became firmly stuck, and had to be abandoned. A second, eighty-three feet high, was protected with hides and mats of osier to guard it from stones and fire. It proved to be of more use than the first.[19] It is not always clear from the sources whether siege towers were stationary structures, built to enable attackers to overlook the defences of a castle, or whether they were intended to be wheeled up to the walls to effect an assault. The tower built by the English crusaders at Lisbon in the second crusade was certainly mobile. Edward I had a prefabricated belfry built at Glasgow, and taken on thirty carts to Bothwell castle, where it was erected and moved towards the walls on a road made from logs. The operation was a triumphant success, unlike the Scots' attempt to use a similar belfry to effect an entry to Carlisle in 1315.[20] The 'somercastell' built by John Crabbe for the siege of Dunbar in 1338 at a cost of £47 4*s* 10*d* is, in contrast, more likely to have been a stationary tower than a movable device.[21]

Siege towers have not fascinated as much as the great stone-throwing engines. These so intrigued the emperor Napoleon III that he had full-scale replicas constructed. Modern reconstructions have been built in the 1980s in Denmark and Czechoslovakia, and in the 1990s in France and in Kalamazoo, Michigan.[22] English documentary sources detailing the construction of these siege machines are, unfortunately and inevitably, tantalisingly uninformative about the way they actually worked. Quantities of wood, some metal, ropes, leather for slings: these were the usual components. One account shows that copper and tin were used in substantial quantities, apparently for axles. Lead was the normal material for the counterweights, but the keeper of Berwick's 1298 account shows that iron was used for this purpose in a great siege engine called *Forester*. This machine had a massive iron nail as the central pivot for the main beam or yard.[23] At the siege of Stirling in 1304 the greatest of the machines constructed by Edward's men was called the *Warwolf*. Accounts survive which show that it took some three months, with at one time as many as five master carpenters and forty-nine others, to make what was clearly a gigantic engine, but there is no clue as to how it actually operated.[24] The terminology used by chroniclers was very varied, and is often unhelpful. *Petraria* were obviously stone-throwing machines, but the term could probably cover a number of very different devices. Mangonels are also often referred to, but again it is not clear whether the word was used with precision.

The main account of the siege of Exeter in 1136 refers to the use of engines, but it is clear that these were either towers, or shelters concealing the activities of those undermining or boring into the walls. Throwing engines are referred to in a description of the siege of Faringdon in 1145, but they do not seem to have been common during the Anarchy. They were used by the English at the siege of Lisbon in this period, when two machines were operated by teams of a hundred men working in rotation.[25] References in the Pipe Rolls to siege engines during the rebellion of 1173–4 are surprisingly rare. Yvo the engineer was paid one mark to hire carpenters to make engines when the king came to Huntingdon in 1174, and a mangonel was bought at a cost of one mark for Dover.[26] By the end of the twelfth century, the use of such machines was more commonplace. In 1194 both mangonels and petraries were provided for the sieges of Marlborough and Nottingham, but the records do not reveal what the differences between these machines were. A slightly later reference to 'Turkish mangonels' suggests an eastern origin for some.[27] The normal assumption is that there were two basic techniques, torsion and lever. Torsion machines were known in the ancient world, and derived their power from twisted skeins of rope or leather. Their use in the medieval period, at least before the fourteenth century, is not well documented or illustrated, and the petraries and mangonels of the late twelfth and early thirteenth centuries were probably all devices which used a lever and a sling to cast stones. The lever could either be operated manually, by a gang of men pulling it by means of ropes, or by fitting a heavy counterweight, which when released pulled a long beam rapidly from a horizontal into a vertical position, releasing the projectile from its sling. The machine which the Scots used at Wark in 1174, whose first stone barely came out of the sling, and landed on one of the Scots' own men, was very probably powered manually.[28]

A major change came with the adoption of the counterweight at the start of the thirteenth century, creating the type of machine known as the trebuchet. The *Malvoisin* brought to England in 1216 by Prince Louis was probably a huge counterweight engine. The *petraria* and mangonels used at the siege of Bedford in 1224 seem to have had similar components: large cables, ropes, hides for slings, and quantities of tallow. Some were presumably counterweight machines, with other lighter ones operated manually.[29] Trebuchets with counterweights could launch a far larger projectile than a manually powered machine, and were capable of considerable accuracy. The modern reconstructions suggest that a range of 200 yards with a projectile weighing 33 lbs was well within their capability. There were problems, however, in deploying these great machines. Siege engines were made so that they could be dismantled, but they were too large to be a part of the baggage train of a normal field army. It

(*Right*) A modern reproduction of a trebuchet, standing outside the walls of Chinon (dép. Indre-et-Loire). (*Below*) An illustration from Walter of Milemete's treatise of 1327, showing a trebuchet at the moment of release. The yard has just been unhooked; the counterweight will swing the yard upwards, and with it the sling, loosing off the stone ammunition.

took ten days to take the siege engines needed for the siege of Bytham in 1221 in twelve carts all the way from London, at an average speed of about ten miles a day.[30] Where possible, siege engines were transported by sea; this might not be quicker, but it was much easier. In 1304 the preparation of the siege train for the siege of Stirling took place at Berwick, with some machines being brought from Brechin and even Aberdeen. They were then sent up the Forth estuary by ship. Church roofs were pillaged by the English troops to provide lead for the counterweights. Robert Bruce, then on the English side, presumably bringing equipment from Carrick, could not send it by sea. He found difficulty in transporting the frame of one great engine, as he could not find any cart suitable for the task. The king ordered John Botetourt to assist him.[31]

There were many other devices used in siege warfare. Springalds were machines like huge crossbows, mounted on wheeled frames and firing massive darts or quarrels. They were as much a part of the armoury of the defenders in a siege as of the attackers. Battering rams might be used to good effect, or miners might work at the walls under the protection of a 'cat' or 'sow', a movable protective shed which was wheeled up to the walls. No doubt there were improvements in the design of this type of equipment over time, but there was no sudden technological innovation transforming their potential in the way that the introduction of the counterweight revolutionised the effectiveness of the throwing engines.

Fire was often the easiest way to reduce a castle; even a stone keep would contain more than enough combustible material to make it impossible to resist an incendiary attack. Fire was used to destroy the empty castle at Cirencester in 1142. At Devizes in 1149 the first act of Stephen's son Eustace was to set fire to all the houses around the castle and in its outworks.[32] Pitch and sulphur were bought in 1194 for use in sieges, no doubt making a form of 'Greek fire'.[33] At the siege of Bedford in 1224 it was the use of fire at the end that forced the small defending force out, to surrender and execution.[34] Kildrummy fell in 1306 when a traitor set fire to the stores of corn kept in the hall.[35] Defenders might also make use of fire. At the siege of Berwick in 1319 the Fleming John Crabbe prepared incendiary bales of wood, tar, pitch and brimstone, bound together with iron loops. These were dropped from a tall crane on the protective 'sow' used by the English to approach the walls, after this had already been dealt a destructive blow by a stone-throwing engine. 'The sow has farrowed', shouted the delighted Scots.[36]

There was much other equipment that was needed for the conduct of a successful siege. Thirty picks, twenty shields and twelve scaling ladders were sent to Marlborough in 1194 from Hampshire; 12,000 quarrels for crossbows came from London.[37] The siege of Stirling in

1304 saw large quantities of crossbows, longbows, bolts, quivers and arrows collected from London, Lincolnshire and Northumberland. The sheriff of Lincoln sent thirty-six crossbows, 286 longbows, 1,200 quarrels and a hundred dozen arrows, at a cost of £27.[38] In addition to the offensive equipment, besiegers needed to have protection from the missiles hurled or shot by their opponents. Hurdles, 'bretasches' and protective screens were required in large numbers. In a lengthy siege, the encampment of the besiegers developed into a substantial fortification itself.

Guns

It was many years from the introduction of guns before they began to transform warfare. It is interesting that they did not attract similar condemnation from the ecclesiastical authorities as crossbows had earlier: their death-dealing potential was not immediately appreciated. The first known picture of a gun dates from early 1327, and is contained in a source close to the Crown, the treatise presented to Edward III by an obscure Chancery clerk, Walter Milemete. The illustration probably derived from a pattern-book in the workshop of a London illuminator; it does not prove that the Crown itself possessed any guns at that date. Guns were almost certainly used, apparently to some effect, at the siege of Berwick in 1333. The guns used at Crécy were probably covered with wood and bound with

The earliest known picture of a cannon, taken from Walter of Milemete's treatise written early in 1327. The ammunition is a bolt rather than a ball. Unfortunately the artist had little idea of what sort of carriage a cannon required.

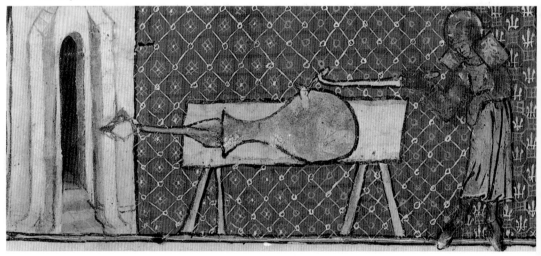

iron hoops. They were simple light weapons, almost as dangerous to those firing them as to those at whom they were fired. They may have been multiple-barrelled 'ribalds', mounted on simple carts. One rather surprising advantage of these early guns was that they were cheap: in the early 1350s a cannon cost 13*s* 4*d*, whereas a springald cost £3 6*s* 8*d*. By the late fourteenth century, however, guns had developed into formidable siege weapons, capable of casting a large, heavy projectile a considerable distance. The gunpowder revolution was beginning to take effect. Some guns were cast from a copper alloy, using similar technology to that used for casting bells: this was probably the earliest form. Larger weapons were fabricated from long strips of wrought iron, bound round with iron hoops. At Cherbourg in 1379 the English possessed seven guns which fired stones two feet in circumference, and three which used fifteen-inch ammunition. The average weight of a great cannon at this period was still less than 400lbs, but little more than a quarter of a century later an account shows that one of the great guns at the siege of Aberystwyth, the *Messenger*, weighed 4,480lbs. Henry V 'played at tennis with his hard gune-stones'. At the siege of Harfleur in 1415 the guns were clearly the most potent weapons in the English armoury. It was cannon-fire which reduced the barbican to such a state of ruin that the English were able to set fire to such of the structure as still stood. The French were forced to surrender. According to a near-contemporary poem, the great cannon *London* established a fifteen–love lead, *Messenger* brought the score to thirty–love, and *King's Daughter* won the game.[39] The guns of the late fourteenth and fifteenth centuries undoubtedly made a major difference to siege warfare, tilting the balance in favour of the attackers. In Gascony in 1437 the castle of Castelnau-de-Cernès was besieged by the English, and 'broken down during the said siege by cannon and engines, and a great part of the walls of the same thrown to the ground'. In 1442 Dax fell to the French after a siege of only three weeks, and St Sever was surrendered after less than a month. In England, Bamburgh fell rapidly to the earl of Warwick's forces in 1464, once 'all the king's guns that were charged began to shoot upon the said castle'. Cannon had speeded up the previously leisurely pace of siege warfare very markedly.[40]

Defence

The growing sophistication of the means of attack were, of course, countered by the development of more sophisticated defences. The appearance of the trebuchet was an important factor in persuading men that they should build their curtain walls higher. Mining techniques rendered sharp angles vulnerable, as was demonstrated at

Cannon were used for defence as well as offence; this is an interior view of one of the gunloops at Raglan Castle in Gwent.

Rochester in 1215, when one whole corner of the rectangular keep was brought down when pit-props made combustible with the fat from forty pigs were set alight. The thirteenth century saw round towers used in place of the square ones of the past. The greater use of flanking towers threatened besiegers with effective fire from well-sited arrowloops. By the time that Master James of St George was designing the great castles of North Wales, defenders had many advantages. The use of concentric lines of defence, as at Rhuddlan, Harlech and, in its most developed form, Beaumaris, presented successive obstacles to attackers. The relatively slender outer walls were pierced with ample arrow-loops, to enable defenders to shoot devastating volleys of arrows at any besiegers. At Caernarfon the site did not allow for concentric defences, but there were triple tiers of arrowloops built into the southern curtain wall, and massive mural towers each provided the strength that formerly had been confined to a single keep. Twin-towered gatehouses were designed to impress, and provided a feature of strength, not weakness. Care was taken to ensure that supplies could easily be brought in by sea.

Although castle-builders seem to have responded effectively to previous changes in the technology available to besiegers, the introduction of cannon was not met with an immediate response on the part of the master masons and their patrons. No doubt this was at

Orford Castle in Suffolk, built by Henry II. The circular plan of the keep, with the three rectangular turrets and a forebuilding to defend the entry, was unique, and was developed more for symbolic than for military reasons.

least partly because the early cannon were not particularly powerful, but in the first half of the fifteenth century the style of defences which had proved effective against stone-throwing engines began to show its weakness against artillery. The addition of gunloops to existing and new castles from the later fourteenth century was not an adequate response, for it was possible only to use small guns from them, while the noise and smoke must have meant that only a very few rounds could be fired before conditions became intolerable. It was not until the sixteenth century in England that the massive squat bastion was built as an effective response to siege ordnance.

It would be a mistake to assume, however, as has often been done, that all developments in military architecture bore a clear relationship to military necessity. The ingenious circular keep built by Henry II at Orford in Suffolk, which features projecting rectangular towers, may appear to represent an early solution to the weaknesses of the square keep. The design, however, was more probably the result of a combination of considerable mathematical ingenuity and a desire to express in stone imperial and even religious symbolism by means of a circular hall. The thirteen corbels which support the roof may represent the number of Christ and the Apostles, or that of Charlemagne and his twelve knights. A better-known example of symbolism in castle architecture is that of Caernarfon, where the polygonal towers and dark bands in the masonry, together with eagles on the turrets, provided a deliberate parallel with the walls of Constantinople, an intriguing echo of imperialism in distant Wales.[41]

Siege tactics

Siege tactics did not undergo such major changes in the course of the medieval period as did those of battle. The basic techniques of encirclement and blockade to starve an enemy out, of the use of siege equipment to reduce the strength of defences, and of assault, could not change much, though the development of new weapons of attack, and of improved defences, did result in some shifts in the balance between defending and attacking forces. The siege of Pont Audemer late in 1123 provides a good example of an early siege. The town and castle were held by the rebel Waleran of Meulan, with French assistance. Henry I's army first of all attacked and entered the town, plundered it and set it alight. The castle, which had a substantial garrison, was encircled, and the surrounding countryside ravaged for twenty miles around. A great belfry was constructed, which stood twenty-four feet higher than the walls. This was dragged up close, and archers and crossbowmen loosed arrows and bolts at the garrison, while rocks were hurled down on them. After seven weeks of blockade and bombardment, the garrison offered to surrender. They were allowed to leave with their equipment and honour intact, and to go where they wished.[42]

In the mid twelfth century, under Stephen, relatively minor castles succeeded in holding out with surprising success; besiegers appear to have been capable of little more than blockading castles, often by building rival defensive structures. Assault by men crawling up the steep sides of a motte was a last and somewhat desperate resort. By the thirteenth century, the balance had shifted, and it was only the greatest of castles, such as Dover, that offered much hope of lengthy resistance. The French prince Louis began a major siege of Dover in 1216. The castle was blockaded by sea, and surrounded by land. Stone-throwing machines were set up to bombard the gate and the curtain walls; a great wooden siege tower was erected, and a 'cat' used to protect men as they moved up to the walls. Miners worked in the moat to dig under the fortifications. Though the barbican fell to assault, the siege was eventually unsuccessful.[43] Maurice the Engineer had done his work well when he built the great keep. Nevertheless, the vulnerability of castles was demonstrated in the early thirteenth century, not only at Rochester but also at Bedford in 1224, and it is striking that the civil war of the 1260s, even though it ended with the great siege of Kenilworth, was much less dominated by sieges than the Anarchy of Stephen's reign or the civil war of 1215–17 had been.

The most satisfactory methods of gaining castles were those that involved no military action at all. In 1143 Robert FitzHildebrand won Portchester castle by his skill in the bed, not the battlefield. He seduced the castellan's wife, and then imprisoned her husband.[44] It might be possible to negotiate the surrender of a castle by more straightforward methods, avoiding open conflict. Castellans would be well aware of the futility of attempting to hold out against impossible odds, though a sense of honour and a fear of how their own side might react were strong deterrents to swift surrenders. When Hubert de Burgh consulted the garrison of Dover in 1216 as to whether he should surrender, it was agreed that he should not, 'lest by shamefully surrendering the place he should incur the mark of treason'. When he was impeached in parliament in 1376, William Latimer faced charges in parliament relating to the surrender of St Sauveur in Normandy, a castle whose constable was one of his esquires.[45]

If surrender could not be negotiated without fighting, there were still ways of avoiding the time and expense of mounting a full-scale siege. Henry de Tracy in 1139 captured Torrington in Devon, evading the guards at night, and forcing those in the keep to surrender by throwing lighted torches through the loopholes, setting the interior on fire. In the next year, again at dead of night, Robert FitzHubert, a Flemish mercenary, captured Devizes castle by using leather scaling ladders. He and his men entered the castle unnoticed, and captured all but a few of the sleeping garrison. A small number were able to take refuge in the keep, but were soon forced to surrender as they had no food supplies with them.[46] Gerald of Wales told the remarkable story of a very small Welshman who entered Cardiff castle by night, using a ladder, in 1158, and succeeded in kidnapping the earl and countess of Gloucester, with their young son, without alerting the garrison. In 1175 the Welsh made a night assault on Abergavenny castle, and captured the constable and his wife, though some of the garrison were able to find safety in the keep.[47]

In the early fourteenth century Robert Bruce and his followers proved to be past masters at the art of escalade and surprise attack. The Scots did not have the forces or the equipment for siege warfare of the traditional type, and innovation proved highly effective. Sudden night attacks, using simple equipment, were more than a match for traditional defences. The fullest details of the equipment come from one of the few unsuccessful attempts, when the Scots tried to take Berwick in 1312. Scaling ladders were used, but the night assault was noticed, for a dog barked and warned the garrison. The Scots left their equipment behind, and it was laid out in the town for inspection. The rope ladders had rungs made of boards measuring two feet six inches by six inches, and a fender was attached to every third rung to hold the ladder away from the wall. At the top there was an iron hook, and the whole ladder was lifted up to the wall with a long lance.[48] Shortly afterwards Perth fell to a night attack. Bruce himself led his men, wading first through the icy waters of the moat, and then climbing the walls by means of scaling ladders. The king was the second man over the ramparts. At Roxburgh in 1314 James Douglas and his men camouflaged in black used similar ladders to scale the castle by night. At Edinburgh too a night escalade succeeded in placing an apparently impregnable fortress in Scottish hands.[49] Bruce and his men had carried through a small-scale revolution in siege warfare, by the simplest of means.

A full-scale siege was a highly complex operation. When time was little object, and relief unlikely, encirclement and blockade were an easy option for besiegers, and the strategy was widely adopted. At Exeter in 1136 Stephen surrounded the castle with siege towers and other structures. He was unable to prevent some reinforcements entering the castle, for, dressed all in mail, they were indistinguishable from his own men. Yet eventually, with the hot weather, the castle wells dried up. Stores of wine ran out, and the garrison was compelled to surrender. A couple of years later Bedford likewise surrendered, its defenders exhausted and starving. Stephen was not always successful. At Tetbury in 1144 his men initially reduced the surrounding countryside by fire and sword, and then stormed the outer defences of the castle, driving the garrison into a narrow inner redoubt, perhaps a keep. Siege engines were then set up, and preparations made for a close blockade. The operation would no doubt have worked had it not been for the intervention of the earl of Gloucester.[50] Such operations could be both costly and lengthy. The siege of Exeter was said to have cost Stephen 15,000 marks and lasted nearly three months. A well-supplied force could last out for much longer: the English at Stirling were able to hold out for most of the year 1299, until, with even their war-horses eaten, they were compelled to abandon their resistance.[51] Nor was it easy to maintain a tight blockade: a determined man might slip through the besiegers' lines and succeed in bringing reinforcements. In Edward I's reign Piers de Kirkoswald made his way out of Berwick when it was under siege by the Scots, and swam the Tweed, with letters asking for help tied in his hair. Still naked, he then made his way to Norham. He then returned to Berwick, once again swimming to the castle, with the welcome news that help was on its way.[52]

Normally, besiegers would not rely solely on blockade to achieve results, but would bring into operation the full range of equipment at their disposal. At Bedford in 1224 a tall wooden tower was constructed, so that the king's crossbowmen would have full view of the defences. A 'cat' was used to protect the miners as they worked to bring down the walls, and stone-throwing engines battered the defences. The outer defences probably fell to simple escalade. The castle was taken in four separate stages; first the barbican, then the outer bailey, followed by the inner bailey and then the keep itself. When the miners succeeded in setting fire to the keep, the garrison sent out all the women and prisoners, along with messengers to try to obtain surrender terms. None were obtained. The exhausted men spent the night in the keep, and came out to face the gallows. The expenses and wages of the knights, sergeants, engineers and others operating the siege engines and undertaking duties at the siege in 1224 came to an impressive £1,311 18s 2d.[53]

The scale of preparations for a major siege is demonstrated by the operations to provide for the king's forces at Kenilworth in 1266. Siege engines were prepared in the Forest of Dean, and 4,000 quarrels sent from St Briavel's castle there in June. In July a further 6,000 quarrels were ordered. Thirty thousand quarrels were to come from Lincoln, and a further 30,000 were ordered from London. Three hundred sheaves of arrows were brought from Surrey and Sussex. A great belfry was taken from Gloucester to Kenilworth. The sheriff of London even sent a whale; it is to be hoped that the meat did not go bad during the journey. Fourteen carts were used to carry the royal wine to the siege, and 4*s* was spent on horsehair, needed for the siege engines. Iron was short at the siege, and the sheriff of Gloucester was told to buy ten marks' worth. Ropes and hemp came from Bridport. A great many hurdles were needed to protect the besiegers, and the sheriffs of Buckingham and Bedford, Gloucester, Worcester and Warwick were all ordered to see to their construction. In all, the requisitions of materials and foodstuffs to support the siege exhausted the revenues of ten counties, whose sheriffs were unable to bring in any cash to the exchequer in 1267.[54]

Another major siege was that of Stirling in 1304. The castle was held by William Oliphant. His request that he should be allowed to consult his lord, John de Soules, to see if he would authorise surrender, was rejected by Edward I. The king had determined on a show-piece siege as a means of imposing his authority on Scotland. No less than thirteen siege engines were brought to Stirling, one from as far away as Bridgwater, and a heavy bombardment was mounted. Forty quarriers worked to prepare the ammunition for the great trebuchets. A belfry was set up. The mayor of Newcastle upon Tyne sent four men and one woman to make ropes for the royal siege engines, as well as twenty-nine crossbows, fifty-nine longbows and other equipment. Seventy-five carpenters at one stage were engaged in building defensive mantlets. The English did not have things all their own way; one shot from an springald passed between the king's thighs, almost miraculously not wounding him. The Scots, however, could do little in face of an overwhelming English superiority. Within the castle there was only one large siege engine, and its yard broke. Edward ordered the construction of two new machines at Stirling, one a battering ram which proved worthless, and the other the *Warwolf*, a 'horrible engine'. The proceedings were all watched by the ladies of the court, for whom a special viewing gallery with an oriel window was constructed. Eventually, after some ninety days, the garrison offered surrender. The *Warwolf* was almost ready, and the king, plainly anxious to try out his new toy, refused to let anyone leave or enter the castle until it had been tried out. It proved successful, bringing down a large section of wall, and the dejected garrison were duly allowed to make their exit.[55]

The Hundred Years War had both its major sieges and a great many minor incidents of assaults on towns and fortified castles. The advantages which the English so clearly had on the battlefield were far less evident when it came to siege warfare. The duke of Lancaster began a lengthy siege of Rennes in October 1356, which lasted until the following July. Lancaster, for all his merits, was no innovative commander, and he used all the traditional techniques of siege warfare: mining, a belfry (which was set on fire by the defenders), siege engines and blockade. The duke was ordered by Edward III to abandon the siege, which he should have done according to the terms of a truce. In what may seem a farcical ceremony Lancaster agreed terms which allowed him to enter the town with ten knights. His honour was saved, for he had earlier sworn not to leave Rennes until his banner flew from battlements, and this was done for a brief period. The duke then withdrew.[56] The deficiencies of the English in conducting sieges had been evident earlier, as for example at Tournai in 1340, and were to be seen again when Edward III failed in what should have been the culmination of his French war: the siege of Rheims in 1359.

Some sieges conducted by the English during the Hundred Years War were successful, notably Edward III's siege of Calais in 1346–7, and Henry V's siege of Rouen in 1419. The latter began in August, and from the outset was envisaged as a blockade, with English encampments right round the walls. A ditch and bank were constructed by the English, and chains across the river completed the encirclement. As starvation set in within the city, the besieged pushed out the old and ill, in the hope that the English would feed them. Henry would not oblige, and would not allow the pathetic refugees passage through the English lines. They were left to starve in the no man's land between the walls and the besiegers. Negotiations were eventually successful in January 1420. The English were to take eighty hostages, and receive a substantial payment. The townspeople were also to build a new palace for the English king in Rouen.[57]

The style of many English campaigns in France, taking the form of the swift *chevauchée*, was not appropriate for lengthy sieges. A highly mobile force would not be able to take with it heavy siege equipment, though on occasion a swift assault might be successful. The Black Prince's capture of Romorantin in 1356 provides a good example of what could be achieved on such an expedition, for it was a rapid affair, which delayed the progress of his army by no more than a few days. A powerful donjon or keep was the obstacle facing the English. Initial assaults were ineffectual, and siege engines were prepared. The use of Greek fire led, according to Froissart, to the thatched roof of the keep being set ablaze.[58] Surrender soon followed.

Siege conventions

Sieges were normally protracted affairs. This meant that there could be careful consideration of what should be done, and how. Actions could be properly thought out, and it was even possible to find time to consult academic authorities.[59] There was also often ample time for negotiations with the besieged garrison to take place, as efforts were made to persuade them to surrender. The very deliberate pace and character of much siege warfare meant that the ground was fertile for the growth of conventions and the establishment of customs. These are best known and documented from the fourteenth century, when the conduct and laws of war were the subject of academic analysis.[60] There are sufficient references, however, from earlier periods to suggest that most were of long standing.

There were differences in types of sieges; one conducted by a king was especially serious. During the revolt of the young Richard Marshal in 1233, Henry III besieged the castle of Usk, but because his food supplies began to run out, he was forced to abandon the operation. So shaming was this that Henry sent some bishops to negotiate with Richard, asking him to preserve the royal honour by surrendering the castle, on the understanding that it would be returned to him in fifteen days. Henry's sense of honour, unfortunately for the Marshal, was not so strong that he felt it necessary to keep this latter part of the bargain.[61] Much later, the distinction between royal and other sieges was formally recognised in indentures. Richard de Grey and Stephen Scrope agreed in 1400 to keep Roxburgh for three years, and Henry IV promised that if they were subjected to a royal siege, he would rescue them within three months. Presumably if he did not do so, they were at liberty to surrender to the Scots.[62]

The first essential was that the besieging force should demand the surrender of the garrison, offering terms. Once a shot was released from a siege engine or fired from a cannon, the siege in formal terms had begun. If no terms were offered by the besieger, there were no legal restrictions on the pillage and slaughter that could take place. Provided, however, that the captain of a beleaguered garrison made a reasonable effort to resist, he was free to treat with the besieging force, so as to avoid the brutal consequences of assault or unconditional surrender. Indentures might set out the position for the constable: when Richard Tempest agreed to take charge of Berwick in 1352, he was allowed to negotiate surrender terms only when he had been besieged for three months without relief.[63] Different rules applied to the process of pillaging a captured town or castle if a negotiated surrender had taken place, as against those that applied in cases of assault.

A very common arrangement was for a suspension of hostilities to be agreed at the start of a siege; the garrison would concede that they would surrender if no relieving force appeared. At Newbury, during Stephen's reign, John FitzGilbert bought time from his besiegers by handing over his son William as a hostage, but he promptly put the boy's life at risk when, contrary to the terms agreed, he reinforced the castle with men and supplies. William was threatened with death, but the king could not bring himself to give the final order.[64] In 1173 Roger de Stuteville negotiated a forty-day period during which he could try to find a relieving force for Wark castle; if he failed, he promised to surrender the castle. He was successful, though in most cases it was the besiegers who gained from such bargains. At Stirling in 1304 Edward I refused the constable of the castle, William Oliphant, when he asked to be allowed to send a message to his master, John de Soules, who was in France, to ask whether or not he should surrender. Clearly Oliphant had rejected the king's initial request for the surrender of the castle, on the excuse that he should consult his lord. Edward's reaction was typical: 'If he thinks it safer to defend the castle than to surrender it, let him see.'[65]

When a castle garrison surrendered and made their mournful exit, it was normal for the victors to sound trumpets in triumph. Odo of Bayeux tried to insist that this should not be done when he surrendered Rochester early in William Rufus's reign, but his pleas were not accepted.[66] If surrender was unconditional, this would be emphatically symbolised by the clothing and manner of the defeated garrison. At Stirling in 1304 Oliphant's men came out of the shattered castle barefoot, with ashes on their heads; the burghers of Calais in 1347 were forced by Edward III to make their way out of the town with halters round their necks. This was all in accordance with the laws of war, for these were men surrendering unconditionally. In contrast, when the English garrison of Stirling surrendered late in 1299, this was under terms, and they were given safe-conducts to go to English-held Berwick.[67]

Siege warfare may have been governed by conventions, but these often did little to ameliorate the horrors of war. Conditions were often insanitary, and starvation for the besieged the order of the day. It would be possible to produce a lengthy catalogue of accounts of starving and exhausted men driven by hunger, disease and despair to put themselves at the mercy of their enemies. Some instances were exceptional. In the siege of Rochester early in William Rufus's reign, the besieged garrison was plagued by flies that bred in the rotting corpses of men and horses. They could eat only if their companions drove the insects away from their mouths with fly-whisks, and hardly surprisingly were forced to offer surrender.[68] Letters from the garrison at Berwick in the winter of 1315–16 testify to the appalling suffering resulting from a combination of nation-wide famine, blockade by the Scots, and a failure on the part of the government to provide assistance. Even the horses, when they died, were eaten, their boiled carcasses being given first to the cavalrymen, with the footsoldiers left to pick over the bones.[69] At Harfleur in 1415 dysentery killed far more, among both besieged and besiegers, than died as result of the actual fighting.[70]

Descriptions of sieges suggest that the essential techniques of negoti-
ation, blockade, bombardment and assault did not change markedly
during the medieval period. While this may be true in a very general
sense, there was a constant dialectic of development between the arts
of defence and attack. The introduction of the trebuchet around
1200 gave attackers an advantage, soon negated by higher curtain
walls and flanking towers; the development of powerful siege cannon
by the early fifteenth century began to transform siege warfare, as no
effective defences were introduced until much later in the century.
The scale of siege warfare expanded as the state developed new
capacities to direct resources to meet its military ends. The siege of
Kenilworth of 1266 was conducted with a lavishness which could
scarcely have been possible a century previously, and the siege of
Calais showed how effectively Edward III could mobilise the resources of his kingdom on a huge scale. Henry V further demonstrated the way in which late medieval armies could conduct major,
lengthy sieges with operations such as those at Harfleur and Rouen.
In the final stages of the Hundred Years War it was the French who
showed how effective organisation combined with skilful use of
improved artillery could bring about the speedy surrender of English
garrisons.

13

Battle

The purpose of war was not to achieve victory by fighting battles. Rivals might be brought to terms by other means. The destruction of enemy territory by fire and sword could be, and often was, achieved without fighting a major battle. Land could be won by besieging towns and castles. Sometimes, but not as frequently as might be expected, battle was the culminating point of a campaign, the object to which so much of the work of recruiting and organising armies was ultimately directed. According to the chronicler Geoffrey le Baker, the Black Prince sought battle at Poitiers in 1356 because it was only through battle that peace could be achieved.[1] The battle of Auray in 1364 was fought, said Froissart, because each side wanted to put an end to the war in Brittany, and saw this as the best way to do so. Some English knights emphasised another motive when they begged John Chandos before the engagement not to listen to overtures of peace, for they desperately needed the money from booty and ransoms that victory would bring.[2]

Medieval battles have been much studied, for all too often in the past the history of warfare has been seen as the history of battles. There are great dangers, however, in attempting to reconstruct events on the battlefield. The number of chroniclers who had first-hand military experience of any kind was small. William of Poitiers, chaplain to the Conqueror, had been a soldier before entering the Church. Jordan Fantosme was present at Alnwick in 1174. Jean le Bel was an eyewitness of the 1327 Weardale campaign which he described so vividly, but when it came to the battle of Crécy, he had to rely on information given him by John of Hainault and a dozen knights of his household, and from a number of English knights. They had all been present, and could give a good account only of the preparations and the aftermath of the battle, but not of the fighting itself. Henry V's chaplain was at Agincourt, though not in the front line.[3]

The majority of chroniclers had to rely on second-hand information. Newsletters, relatively common by the fourteenth century, were rarely informative on the details of fighting in battle. Returned soldiers might provide some information, but all too often medieval writers had to rely on their imagination, sometimes adapting other accounts to suit what they knew of the circumstances of a particular conflict. The chronicle accounts of the battle of Falkirk in 1298 provide a good example of how difficult it is to reconstruct a battle. According to the fullest account, by Walter of Guisborough, after the cavalry failed to dislodge the Scottish defensive formations, or schiltroms, the infantry successfully opened them up with archery and stone-throwing. A St Albans chronicle, however, suggests that a cavalry attack on the Scots from the rear was the decisive move in the battle.[4]

Often, battle must have been literally indescribable. Lacking good means of communication, commanders must have found it impossible to know what was taking place in all parts of the battlefield, and no one would have been in a position to piece together all the stories of the combatants in order to reconstruct events. It is not surprising that historians are frequently faced with irreconcilable chronicle accounts. A further problem is that the precise location of many battles is unknown; without knowledge of the terrain, it is not possible to make full sense of the events. Much effort has gone, for example, into attempting to identify the site of Bannockburn, but absolute certainty is not possible. Such problems should not, however, lead historians to assume that battles were disorganised affairs, waged by men who could not control their troops and who could do little more than encourage the outbreak of chaos.

Full-scale battles were not frequent. Hastings was very probably the Conqueror's sole experience of command in a major set-piece battle.[5] Henry II was not present at a single one. In his youth Edward I experienced the trauma of defeat at Lewes, and the heady pleasure of victory at Evesham, but after he became king, for all that his military career took him to the Holy Land, to Wales, to Flanders and to Scotland, he took part in only one true battle, that at Falkirk in 1298. Edward III experienced full-scale battle on land on only two occasions, at Halidon Hill in 1333, and at Crécy in 1346. The infrequency of battles means that it is dangerous to assume a rational development of tactics from one battle to another. There can have been very few who fought at the thirteenth-century battles of Lincoln in 1217 or Lewes in 1264 who had previous experience of major battle. In the Hundred Years War, however, the situation was different, for although the major battles were few, experienced soldiers would certainly have built up considerable knowledge of how to fight in smaller-scale encounters.

There are many reasons why battles were relatively few. The paucity of battles during the English campaigns in Wales is hardly surprising, for the Welsh did not have troops who could challenge English armies effectively on equal terms. It was with distinct surprise that the writer of a newsletter noted that in 1295 the Welsh leader Madog and his men 'awaited our men on open ground . . . they were the best and bravest Welsh that anyone has seen'.[6] The risks involved were considerable, and a wise commander would seek to achieve advantage over his enemy by other means, notably by ravaging and destroying his lands. For the Scots, it was even preferable to destroy their own lands as a means of weakening the enemy, rather than risk battle. In 1322 the country through which the English host advanced was cleared of crops and herds. Edward II could achieve nothing, and was forced to withdraw: 'we found in our way neither man nor beast'. Only six Scottish prisoners were taken on the campaign, which was a disaster for the English. It was not always the case that the English sought battle and their opponents avoided it. In Ireland in 1318 it was the Irish who looked for battle against Richard de Clare, while he tried not to fight.[8] Alternatives were preferable to battles, even though the latter were regarded as potentially decisive. In 1340 Edward III received a report from someone fighting for him in Scotland: 'A certain secret matter which was discussed in the king's presence in Sir Henry de Ferrers' chamber could not be explored until now because the enemy host has always lain in the forest, but if it could be accomplished, it could have as great an effect on the war as a battle.'[9] It is not clear what this plan was, but it clearly provided an attractive alternative to a full-scale field engagement. Sir Thomas Grey, commenting on the wars against the French under Edward III, noted that 'several times during this war the French came before the English, and departed without fighting'.[10]

There was no shame in a sensible decision not to fight. Henry II was described by Gerald of Wales, rightly, as a man of valour, 'yet in war he always feared the uncertain outcome of battles, and in his great wisdom "tried all other means before he had recourse to arms"'.[11] In 1187 Henry marched to relieve his sons Richard and John who were besieged in Chateauroux by Philip II of France. Philip duly raised the siege, but rather than retreat, arrayed his troops ready for battle. Henry II did the same. All was ready for battle, but a papal legate threatened those on both sides with anathema. Negotiations began, and although it was not possible to conclude a peace, a truce was agreed.[12]

The consequences of failure in battle might be serious indeed, and help to explain the comparative rarity of full-scale engagements. The 'decisive battles' theory of history is hardly popular, but for Harold in 1066 Hastings was indeed decisive. In 1214 the defeat at Bouvines spelled disaster for the English king John and the German ruler Otto IV. Defeat in battle went hand-in-hand with death for Simon de Montfort in 1265, as it did for Llywelyn ap Gruffudd in 1282. Two kings of Scots were captured in battle by the English: William the Lion in 1174 and David II in 1346. The French king John suffered a similar fate at Poitiers in 1356. There were excellent reasons to avoid full-scale engagements.

Battle might be regarded as a form of trial before God. The outcome was determined, in these terms, not by the relative strength of the two sides, their skill and tactical ability, but by the moral force of their cause. It required a great deal of faith to be ready to submit to divine judgement in this way: far better to win a war by other means. Edward III in one of his justifications for his actions explained that Philip of France had refused any peace overtures and so 'the king judges it better to make a speedy passage and place himself in the hands of God'. This was propaganda; in reality, hard calculation must have been behind Edward's decision to mount an expedition to France in 1346, rather than a desire to accept a divine verdict on the justice of his cause. The intention was to raid, ravage and burn French territory; battle, when it came at Crécy, may not have been deliberately sought by the English.[13]

If there were such good reasons to avoid battle, it is legitimate to ask why any were ever fought. Battle undoubtedly often appeared to offer a final resolution to one or both sides, which might have attractions. Sometimes it was a virtually unavoidable consequence of negotiations. In 1314 Bannockburn was fought because Edward Bruce, King Robert's brother, had arranged in the previous year with the English commander of Stirling castle that the garrison would surrender unless it was relieved by the following midsummer. The challenge was one which Edward II had to meet; if he failed to do so, he would have lost what limited credibility he had as king. Robert Bruce equally had little option but to fight. Halidon Hill in 1333 saw the situation reversed. Following negotiations for the surrender of Berwick to the English, the Scots had no alternative but to try to relieve the town.

Pride, a sense of honour and perhaps obstinacy might also lead men to battle. At Monmouth in 1233 the young Richard Marshal was advised by his companions to flee rather than face the far more numerous troops of Baldwin de Gynes; his response was to say that he had never turned his back upon his enemies.[14] Wiser commanders might have taken a different view, but commanders were not always wise. Battle was sometimes the last resort of a desperate man. Simon de Montfort both at Lewes in 1264 and at Evesham in the following year was placed in a position where he had no effective alternative but to fight. On the first of these occasions a powerful feeling of mission, spiced with religious conviction, may well have helped convince him that it was right to fight. On the second, he may even have been driven by a sense of impending martyrdom. In Edward I's

Richard Marshal's fight with Baldwin de Gynes at Monmouth in 1233, as depicted by Matthew Paris.

liroif denorssuer occif

An imaginary mid-thirteenth-century battle scene, taken from a life of Edward the Confessor, illustrating the ferocity of the mêlée.

Welsh wars, Llywelyn ap Gruffudd was defeated at Irfon Bridge in 1282 when he took a desperate gamble in breaking out of the stranglehold which the English king was imposing on him in north Wales. In the final days of rebellion in 1322, the earl of Lancaster's men at Boroughbridge were faced with the option of surrender to an implacable enemy, or of fighting. The earl of Hereford chose to fight; Lancaster to surrender. In both cases death was the outcome.

In some cases it is hard to be sure whether battle was intended or not. The great battles of the Hundred Years War are open to varied interpretations. The English armies at Crécy, Poitiers and Agincourt can all be seen as having been effectively caught by the French. Yet it can also be suggested that in all three instances the English hoped to bring the French to battle. In 1346 there was much posturing by both sides, and the English, according to their own official account, delayed crossing the Seine at Poissy for three days waiting for the French to give battle.[15] Prior to the battle of Poitiers the Black Prince did not hurry to move his army rapidly back to Gascony when he became aware of the approach of the French royal host. Lengthy negotiations preceded the battle, and it is hard to believe that if the English had wanted to avoid fighting, they could not have succeeded in doing so. As for Agincourt, Henry V determined on the march from Harfleur knowing that he might well have to fight a major battle, and did so 'piously reflecting that victory consists not in a multitude but with Him from Whom it is not impossible to enclose the many in the hand of the few and Who bestows victory upon whom He wills', and no doubt making more practical calculations in addition.[16]

Battles might take very different forms. There was a major contrast between those that resulted from a surprise attack on an unsuspecting enemy, and set-piece battles, in which both sides had ample time to prepare their positions and decide on their tactics. The surprise attack was obviously highly effective, with the resulting engagement often more of a rout than a true battle. In July 1174 the Scots army under King William the Lion was encamped outside the walls of Alnwick. An army of northern magnates, mostly from Yorkshire, mustered at Newcastle. There was debate as to what to do; Bernard de Balliol counselled boldness. A scout was sent ahead to report on the position of the Scots, and the army advanced by night towards Alnwick. In the morning there was a thick mist. Hidden in a wood, the commanders heard the report of the scout. The mist cleared, and before them lay Alnwick and the Scots army. The Scots thought that the force approaching them was another Scottish force, until the English charged. The small English army, consisting, some said, of no more than 400 knights, routed the Scots and captured their king.[17] A similar early-morning attack on an unsuspecting Scottish army was effective at Methven in 1306, when Aymer de Valence achieved a rare triumph over Robert Bruce. Henry of Derby's success over the French at Auberoche in 1345 was gained largely by means of a sudden and unexpected charge on an unprepared enemy, who were more concerned with preparing dinner than looking out for the English.[18] Surprise attacks were not always successful. In 1388 the English attacked the Scottish encampment at Otterburn at dusk, with disastrous consequences. The English themselves suffered from surprise attacks. In 1157 part of Henry II's army was caught in ambush in wooded country by the Welsh. Eustace FitzJohn and Robert de Curcy were killed, and there were rumours that the king himself had been slain.[19] The disaster of Stirling Bridge in the autumn of 1297 took place because the Scots were able to attack an unsuspecting English army under earl Warenne while it was crossing the Forth at Stirling; the narrow bridge constricted the movement of the English troops, making a Scottish victory a certainty. There was nothing in the code of conduct of medieval warfare that excluded surprise as a means of achieving victory with a knock-out blow. It was rare, however, to be able to catch an enemy completely off his guard. Competent commanders took the trouble to send out scouts to discover where their opponents were, and gained sufficient time to prepare for battle. Surprise might, however, be achieved by trickery. At Evesham in 1265 Prince Edward advanced, with his vanguard bearing the banners of the Montfortian troops that had been recently captured at Kenilworth. Not until Montfort sent his barber, a man expert in heraldic matters, up the tower of Evesham abbey to view the approaching forces was the truth discovered.[20]

Preparation for battle

Battle was sometimes planned and fought virtually by agreement. Both sides were normally well aware of the situation they faced, and had ample time to prepare their forces. Before the battle of Lewes in 1265 the rival armies, royalist and Montfortian, had good intelligence of each other's movements. The king had established himself in a strong base at Lewes; the Montfortians were some eight miles away. Negotiations between the two sides took place, but came to nothing. Montfort marched closer to Lewes, and sent a letter of defiance to the king. Henry, his brother Richard and son Edward, responded with a letter of their own, defying Montfort and his supporters. This probably took place on 13 May. According to undoubtedly biased reports, the royalists spent the night carousing and enjoying the company of 700 strumpets. Montfort, in contrast, used the darkness to advance his troops on to the Downs. He addressed his troops, who prayed for victory. In the minds of the chroniclers, at least, he established a strong moral advantage before the conflict began.[21] There are obvious similarities with the well-known scenes on the eve of Agincourt, when the French spent the night gambling for the prisoners they hoped to take, while the English, having made confession, kept silence through the wet night.[22] Conditions might be very hard while men waited for dawn. Before the battle of Falkirk in 1298 the English army was halted in open country near Linlithgow. They slept in the open, with shields for pillows and armour for beds. The horses were kept bridled, each near its rider; the king's charger, ill-guarded by its groom, put its foot on the sleeping Edward I, fortunately without seriously injuring him. It is scarcely surprising that the host made an early start, advancing through Linlithgow at dawn. But even in the haste to locate the Scots in the early morning of 22 July 1298, Edward I halted so that he and the bishop of Durham could hear mass.[23] Froissart explained how, in preparation for the abortive fight at Buironfosse in 1339, 'the two armies got themselves in readiness, and heard mass, each lord among his own people and in his own quarters: many took the sacrament and confessed themselves'. Before Crécy, at about midnight, Edward III 'went to his bed; and, rising early the next day, he and the prince of Wales heard mass, and communicated. The greater part of the army did the same, confessed, and made proper preparations.'[24]

Prayer might help to build up morale, but it was not the only method. Speeches to the troops before the armies engaged were a conventional means of trying to whip up enthusiasm. There were obvious problems in addressing a large body of men; probably relatively few could actually hear what was said, even when the commander rode up and down the ranks, as Edward III did on several occasions. Edward I, a man of few words, could scarcely have addressed his whole army, which was some 24,000 strong, at Falkirk in 1298. In some cases chroniclers included a speech as a literary device, rather than a true record of events. The earl of Arundel's speech of 1173 at Breteuil (where no battle in fact took place) was copied by Roger of Howden from Henry of Huntingdon's account of a speech before the battle of the Standard.[25] Froissart's brief account of the address to the troops by Queen Philippa before the battle of Neville's Cross in 1346 is pure fiction, as the queen was not present.[26] In other instances, however, the accounts seem more plausible. Before the battle of the Standard in 1138 either the bishop of Orkney, or Walter Espec, lord of Helmsley and Wark, appealed to the warlike traditions of the Normans. Ailred of Rievaulx provides a long text, attributing the speech to Walter. Although he was writing much later, some touches suggest that the account was more than

Baldwin FitzGilbert (*left*) addressing the troops on behalf of King Stephen, prior to the battle of Lincoln in 1141.

mere literary artifice.[27] Before the battle of Lincoln in 1141 there were, according to Henry of Huntingdon, speeches by the earl of Chester and the earl of Gloucester in the Matildine army. King Stephen did not address the royalist army, as his voice was not strong enough to be heard. Baldwin FitzGilbert therefore made the speech on his behalf, but before he could finish, the din of the enemy, with shouts, neighing of horses and blowing of horns, drowned his words.[28] At Bannockburn, there is no record of any speech by Edward II or his commanders, but Bruce is supposed to have urged his men on with inspiring talk of liberty and religion.[29] On the Weardale campaign of 1327, the young Edward III was led on horseback along the lines of troops, encouraging them. Though no more than a youth, he showed his appreciation of the demands of war by also telling his men that they were not, under pain of death, to advance before they received orders to do so. At Halidon Hill in 1333 he dismounted like his men, and went forward in front of the army to encourage them. Before the abortive battle at Buironfosse he rode along the lines of men ready for battle, asking that they should do all they could to help him preserve his honour. Before the battle of Crécy he moved right round the English lines, laughing and persuading all to do their duty, so that cowards were made into brave men – or so the chronicler Jean le Bel believed. He sensibly followed this up by giving orders that all were to eat and drink, until the trumpet sounded for battle.[30] Interestingly, the Black Prince is recorded as making two speeches before the fighting began at Poitiers in 1356: one to the knights, the other to the archers. This seems a realistic touch. The message of death or glory is plausible, even if the splendid Latin phrases used by Geoffrey le Baker for the speeches reflect the literate skills of the chronicler rather than the oratorical ingenuity of the prince.[31] Before Agincourt Henry V, mounted on a small grey horse, went along the ranks of his men, encouraging them with talk of the justice of his cause, their English heritage and previous victories over the French. He also told the archers that the French threatened to cut three fingers off the right hand of every one of them, to prevent them killing man or horse in the future.[32]

The display of standards was another part of the preliminaries of a formal encounter. In the civil war of the 1260s, Henry III used the raising of his dragon standard as a formal declaration of the opening of hostilities. This standard was a magnificent piece of work. The dragon had jewelled eyes, and was designed in such a way that its tongue appeared to flicker. In 1321 when the royal forces were pursuing Thomas of Lancaster and the rebels northwards, there was a move at Burton to unfurl the royal banner, as a signal of the start of open conflict, but the younger Despenser argued successfully that this should not be done, and no battle took place. At the same period it cost the English administration in Ireland £2 15s 4d to have a war banner made.[33] At Crécy the French unfurled the celebrated Oriflamme, which was countered by the English order to display their Dragon standard. Both were symbols of all-out war, in which no quarter would be given.

Occasionally, the start of general hostilities might be preceded by single combat, as a result of specific challenges. Before Halidon Hill, one of Edward III's household knights, Robert Benhale, worsted a gigantic Scottish champion. However, the most famous of all encounters before battle proper – the pre-Bannockburn skirmish between Robert Bruce and Henry de Bohun in which the latter was killed – was the product of an accidental meeting, not of the issue of formal challenges. Jousting before battle between knights on either side became a common feature during the Hundred Years War.[34]

Even when all the troops were arrayed in their allotted places, prayers said, speeches made and banners unfurled, battle might still not take place. Towards the end of Stephen's reign, in 1153, the king's forces were arrayed facing those of the future Henry II on two occasions. The more notable was in August, close to Wallingford. Although Henry was anxious to fight, the barons on both sides were nervous about the possible outcome of battle. Some, undoubtedly, were afraid of losing, while others had a vested interest in the war continuing, and feared the peace that success for either party might

bring. Both Stephen and Henry complained about the treachery of
their supporters. The two armies, after facing each other for some
time across the river, simply drew back, and their commanders were
compelled to enter into negotiations instead of letting their differences be determined by the outcome of combat.[35] Henry was something of a specialist in battles which did not take place. At Breteuil in
1173 he drew up his force in battle array, but both his men and the
French had cold feet, and no fighting took place. This was the case
again in 1187.[36] In 1214 John came close to engaging the French
prince Louis near La Roche-au-Moines, but his Poitevin supporters
were unwilling to fight. Louis was no keener on battle, and according
to Roger of Wendover both armies fled, saluting each other from the
rear.[37] At Buironfosse (also known as La Capelle) in 1339 Edward
III's forces, augmented by those of his allies in the Low Countries,
faced a French host for a whole day. There was much debating in
each headquarters; eventually those who favoured caution won the
arguments, and there was no battle.[38] In 1359 Robert Knollys made
a *chevauchée* into central France. He was shadowed for some time by
the French army, and the two hosts prepared for battle. Nothing
happened all day. At night, the French prepared to move, to gain the
advantage of surprise by attacking from an unexpected angle.
Knollys, however, was told of their plans by a prisoner who escaped,
and the English moved off hastily, to avoid conflict.[39] In 1369 English
forces under John of Gaunt faced the French at Tournehem in
Normandy for a week, with no more than skirmishing taking place.
Two knights from each side even met to determine a suitable battle
site, but to no avail. The arrival of reinforcements under the earl of
Warwick then persuaded the French that it would be best to withdraw; a Burgundian spy in the English camp revealed Warwick's
determined attitude, which contrasted with that taken by Gaunt.[40]

Tactical dispositions

The most important preliminaries of battle were the tactical decisions
taken when the troops were arrayed in position ready to fight. In
particular, the question of whether or not men were to fight on
horseback or on foot was of crucial importance. It is likely that
commanders had their plans ready long in advance, though details of
the terrain would obviously need to be taken into account. Nor were
such plans of much value if a force was caught by surprise. Most
armies were divided into three or four main units, usually termed
acies in Latin, and perhaps most easily translated as divisions or
battles. In the Norman period, it was common practice for these to
be lined up one behind the other. At Tinchebray, Henry I seems to

have had only two divisions, with one cavalry troop held in reserve at a distance. The two main divisions fought on foot; the king himself and most of his knights and barons were dismounted. At Brémule, Henry's troops were divided into three or perhaps four divisions, ranged in successive lines of defence, and mostly dismounted. At Lincoln in 1141 the forces ranged against Stephen were organised in three divisions, with Ranulph of Chester's troops in the front, those magnates who had been disinherited by Stephen in the second, and Robert of Gloucester's troops in the third. The sources are unfortunately very uninformative on the question of how the archers were arrayed, but one account of the Battle of Standard suggests that they were interspersed with dismounted knights in the front line.[41] In all these conflicts the Anglo-Norman forces showed quite as much tactical awareness as the English were to do in the great battles of the Hundred Years War. The defensive potential of dismounted knights and men-at-arms was fully appreciated, as was the effectiveness of a cavalry charge in achieving the final rout of an enemy. Wace described a fictional battle in terms which set out the ideal tactical disposition of this period. The best soldiers were placed in the front rank, with crossbowmen and archers on either flank. The majority of the army dismounted, and drew up their ranks in good order. They advanced with cut-down lances at a slow pace as one body, ready for the mêlée. Odo Borleng, one of Henry I's household knights who

commanded the royalist troops at Bourgthéroulde in 1124, summed up the best tactical thinking of the day superbly: 'the best plan is for one section of our men to dismount ready for battle and fight on foot, while the rest remain mounted ready for the fray. Let us also place a force of archers in the front line and compel the enemy troops to slow down by wounding their horses.'[42] In the event, the rebels under the young Waleran de Meulan, ignoring the sensible advice of Amaury de Montfort, charged. The royalist archers were positioned so as to be able to shoot at the knights on their unshielded right sides, and brought down their horses. Henry I's troops carried the day. At the battle against the Scots near Northallerton in 1338, the best English troops dismounted, and formed up in the front line intermingled with archers. The majority of the English force fought on foot, tightly packed around the Standard from which the battle would take its name. The horses and the mounted knights were led some distance away, according to Richard of Hexham, so that the animals would not be terrified by the sound of the Scottish war cries.[43]

It became increasingly difficult to persuade knights to fight on foot. It was clearly thought remarkable that in the battle of Arsuf during the Third Crusade, 'knights, whose horses had been slain, fought, when compelled thus to dismount, 'mid the archers'.[44] By the time of the Barons' War in the mid thirteenth century, there was no question of knights fighting other than from the saddle. At Lewes three divisions faced each other, the Montfortians having the advantage of holding a fourth division in the rear. There were no successive defensive lines in the manner of Brémule, though it seems likely that the cavalry were placed in front of the infantry forces. At Evesham the élite forces on both sides were mounted, though when Simon de Montfort's horse was killed and he was compelled to fight on foot, his enemies followed suit.[45] There is nothing to indicate that Edward I's knights and men-at-arms ever dismounted to fight. In 1295 the earl of Warwick, according to one account, combined crossbowmen and knights in a single line at the battle of Maes Moydog, but there is no indication that the latter dismounted. The fact that the pay-roll mentions a mere thirteen archers and crossbowmen in the English force casts some doubt on the chronicler's story.[46]

Change came as a result of the tactics developed above all by the Scots. At Bannockburn the English fought in traditional manner, their cavalry not integrated with the infantry, the archers to the rear rather than on the flank.[47] According to a much later Scottish source, Barbour's life of Robert Bruce, the English cavalry were divided into ten separate bodies. If so, this was highly unusual. The army would normally have been organised into three or four main battles, and it is likely that this was what was done. The Scots prepared the ground by digging pits to hamper any cavalry charges, and organised their

Dismounted twelfth-century knights, as depicted on a gilt-bronze pyx of English or German origin.

troops in four strong defensive circular formations, or schiltroms. They were triumphant, forcing the English to fight on a narrow front, and so minimising their numerical advantage. The English should have been prepared: they had encountered schiltroms at Falkirk, where they had eventually been broken; and at Loudoun Hill in 1307 Aymer de Valence had been defeated when Bruce succeeded in narrowing the front by taking advantage of boggy ground and digging defensive ramparts.[48] The first hints that the English could develop tactics capable of dealing with the Scots came in 1318 at Faughart in Ireland, where Anglo-Irish forces under John de Bermingham defeated and slew Robert Bruce's brother Edward. Accounts of what happened are unclear and inconsistent, but archers clearly played a significant part in the battle.[49] A much clearer indication that the English had learned from the Scots came at Boroughbridge in 1322. Andrew Harclay, a veteran of border warfare, drew up his men in schiltroms, in the Scottish manner. He also made highly effective use of archers. This should not be seen as a full anticipation of the later tactical dispositions of the Hundred Years War, for it is not clear that Harclay ordered knights and men-at-arms to dismount, but he did show an appreciation of the potential of fighting on foot. Boroughbridge was scarcely a battle, for Thomas of Lancaster's forces failed to cross the River Ure to engage Harclay's royalist forces. Perhaps the most decisive blow was struck by the 'ribald' who, skulking strategically under the bridge, was able to kill the earl of Hereford: he 'fiercely with a spear smote the noble knight into the fundament, so that his bowels came out there'.[50]

It was not until 1327 that someone (it is not known who) realised that English knights should be ready, as in the past, to fight in battle on foot. Writs summoning forces in that year laid down that the cavalry should come prepared for conflict in this way. The writ of summons stressed that no one was to delay coming on campaign because they lacked a destrier, or warhorse; what was needed were swift rounceys for the pursuit of the Scots. So whether it was because of a suspected lack of trained warhorses, or because it was appreciated that the best way to combat Scottish tactics was to dismount, is not clear. The initial plan, indeed, was for the order of battle to consist of three large divisions or battles on foot, each with two wings of mounted troops. No engagement actually took place on the Weardale campaign, for the Scots refused to leave the security of strong hilltop positions, but when the English arrayed themselves in three divisions ready to fight, all were ordered to dismount.[51] The new tactics of fighting on foot were first put into effect at Dupplin Moor in 1332, when a small English force, acting without explicit royal approval, achieved a resounding victory over the Scots. They established a position in a narrow site, which prevented the Scots taking advantage from their greater number, and by use of archery and dismounted knights were able to cut the enemy to pieces as they advanced. Such was the press of men that hideous heaps of dead and dying men were formed, up to a spear's length in height. In the following year Edward III himself achieved victory at Halidon Hill; once again the English were able to array their troops ready for battle in a strong defensive position. They were again prepared to fight on foot, 'contrary to the old ways of their fathers', reserving their horses for the rout.[52] The pattern was established for the great battles of the Hundred Years War. The normal plan for battle was to set out the army in three divisions, side by side, with the baggage and the horses kept in the rear. Archers were placed so as to provide flanking fire as the enemy approached the lines of heavily armoured infantry. At Buironfosse in 1339 'our lord the king got off his charger, and made all his men dismount, and he arrayed his army, the archers to the side of the men-at-arms, and the Welsh with their pikes next to them, organising his squadrons in the best way he knew'. Edward III also placed a mounted division on one flank, to act as a rearguard and to prevent any disorganised retreat.[53]

The first battle in France in which the English proved the value of their new tactics was the small engagement at Morlaix in Brittany in 1342, at which the English were heavily outnumbered. The earl of Northampton dismounted his troops, and had trenches and pits dug to halt the enemy cavalry. The preparations for the battle were sound, and led to ultimate, if hard-fought and limited, success in which the archers played a major role.[54]

Similar tactics to those used at Morlaix were employed on a much larger scale at Crécy in 1346; it is surely relevant that Northampton was one of the commanders of the second 'battle' there. There has been much argument about the way in which the archers were positioned. In his account Froissart describes them as being organised *en herce*, in a harrow formation. This has normally been interpreted as meaning that they were set in triangular hollow wedges, between or slightly forward from the divisions of men-at-arms. Harrows, however, were not all the same shape, and the most obvious feature of a harrow is less its overall shape than the grid pattern formed by the wooden bars used to make it, very like that of a portcullis. The term may have been used by Froissart to suggest the way the archers were arranged in ranks, but it is impossible to know precisely what he meant. *Herce* may not even have meant harrow; the word could have been derived from *hericius*, a hedgehog.[55] The implication of Froissart is that the archers were placed on the flank of each of the battles. Jean le Bel's account makes archers a part of each battle, which supports this interpretation. Geoffrey le Baker's account, in contrast, suggests that they were positioned on each side

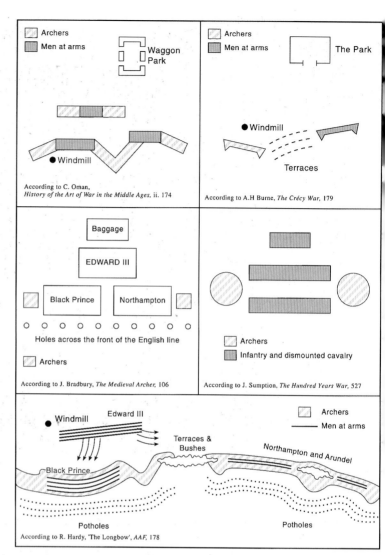

Archers

Men at arms

Waggon Park

According to C. Oman,
History of the Art of War in the Middle Ages, ii. 174

Archers

Men at arms

The Park

● Windmill

Terraces

According to A.H Burne, *The Crécy War*, 179

Baggage

EDWARD III

Black Prince   Northampton

○ ○ ○ ○ ○ ○ ○ ○ ○ ○
Holes across the front of the English line

Archers

According to J. Bradbury, *The Medieval Archer*, 106

Archers

Infantry and dismounted cavalry

According to J. Sumption, *The Hundred Years War*, 527

● Windmill   Edward III

Terraces & Bushes

Northampton and Arundel

Black Prince

Potholes   Potholes

Archers

Men at arms

According to R. Hardy, 'The Longbow', *AAF*, 178

Alternative suggestions for the disposition of the English troops at Crécy, 1346.

of the whole army, like wings, so that their arrows would fall on the enemy from the flank, and this seems a highly plausible arrangement. He also mentions the small pits, about a foot square, which were dug to hinder the French cavalry. The baggage carts were formed up in the rear; the horses were kept with them, ready for use at the end of the battle.[56] Another suggestion is that the archers were formed up within two circles made up of baggage carts for their protection, but this is hard to justify from the sources. At Crécy the English used, perhaps for the first time in battle, an additional long-distance weapon, in the form of some cannon. These had some effect against the Genoese crossbowmen in French service, but they were too few in

The battle of Crécy, 1346, from a fifteenth-century manuscript of Froissart's *Chronicles*.

number, and would have taken so long to load and fire, that their role cannot have been decisive.[57] The figure opposite shows the varied interpretations that historians have put on the evidence for the organisation of the army. None of the proposed plans carries total conviction; the evidence is not sufficient to enable such reconstructions to be made. All but one share a common implausibility, for it is striking that although archers certainly outnumbered men-at-arms in the English force, only in Robert Hardy's plan are they allocated sufficient space. There can be no certainty as to the precise disposition of the English at Crécy, but the basic principle adopted was clearly that of forming up dismounted men-at-arms with archers on the flanks, in a strong defensive position.

At Poitiers in 1356 the English tactics followed these tried and tested methods. The three divisions, with archers on the flanks, were drawn up making use of a hedge to provide protection. A body of archers was detached, under the command of the earl of Oxford, so

that they could engage the French from the side. The baggage was
held in the rear. An element which was to prove very important was
the cavalry force under the Gascon Captal de Buch, which was held
in reserve. The French appear to have caught the English somewhat
by surprise, attacking the rear of the columns, but the Black Prince
was able to regroup his men swiftly. If the English tactics were well-
tried, the French were experimenting. They had tried copying the
English technique of fighting on foot in some small-scale battles in
1351 and then at Mauron in 1352, and now, advised by the Scot
William Douglas, they dismounted the bulk of their cavalry. They
could, however, emulate English fighting methods only to a limited
extent. The tactic of dismounting men-at-arms was effective primarily as a defensive gambit; if troops were expected to march forward
to engage the enemy, they would be tired before the fighting started.
Furthermore, the use of archers was an integral and essential element
in English battle tactics, and the French had no longbowmen to
deploy.[58]

The first hint that the English tactic of drawing up troops in
defensive formation, with archers in support, was not invincible
came in the same year as the battle of Poitiers, in a small-scale
engagement near Coutances in Normandy. Godfrey de Harcourt,
with a force of English and Navarrese soldiers, was defeated, for the
French formed up using large shields as a protection against the
ferocious English archery. The archers emptied all their quivers, to
little effect, and fell back. An important cause of Godfrey's defeat
was that his men failed to maintain their ranks.[59] At Auray in 1364
the French again displayed intelligence in combating the English
tactics. This battle was fought between Charles of Blois, Bertrand du
Guesclin and Breton forces on the one side, and John de Montfort
aided by John Chandos, Robert Knollys, Hugh Calveley and other
experienced English veterans. The English archers loosed their flights
of arrows as was normal; but the Breton and French forces were well
prepared, with proper protection. You could not, claimed Froissart,
have thrown an apple in the French ranks without it landing on a
helmet or a spear. The battle was fought at close quarters, with
a fierce mêlée; success went to the English largely because their
formations held tight, in contrast to Charles of Blois' army. The
rearguard, under Calveley, was not initially brought into the action,
but served an essential purpose in shepherding back into the fight
those who left the English ranks.[60]

When the war with France reopened in 1369, the English did not
continue to enjoy the tactical advantage that they had demonstrated
at, above all, Crécy and Poitiers. There were now no large-scale
battles; for the most part the war followed a pattern of sieges and
raids. There were many skirmishes; some went one way, some the

other. It was not until Henry V's invasion in 1415 that a large-scale battle once again took place, and the old pattern briefly reasserted itself. At Agincourt in 1415 the English once again prepared to fight from a strong defensive position. The army was not a large one, so only one line of battle was set. The main force was in the centre, with the vanguard placed on its right, as a wing, and the rearguard brought forward on the left to make another wing. The archers were arranged in wedges (*cuneos*) set between these divisions. They were now equipped with stakes as an additional defence against cavalry attack. The French had their battle plans prepared, and intended to use lightly armed cavalry to attack the English from the flanks and rear, while dismounted men-at-arms engaged from the front. Archers and crossbowmen were to be deployed on the wings. Events, however, rarely follow plans, and the wooded, boggy terrain did not allow the French to deploy their forces as they had wanted. In the battle, the French, mindful no doubt of the disasters of the past, stood their ground and did not advance, until eventually, late in the day, Henry ordered his men to move forward, halting, well within bowshot, before they reached the French lines. French cavalry attacks were driven off, and the scene was set for the men-at-arms to fight it out in the mêlée.[61]

Strong defensive positions proved to be a key to English success. One element in the tactical dispositions prior to battle was to place the supply train in a secure position. At Verneuil in 1424 the duke of Bedford ordered the wagons with the horses, all linked together, to take up a defensive position, supported by 2,000 archers. They were not only able to repulse a French attack, but were able, still relatively fresh, to join in the main battle at a decisive point.[62] Ironically, in the last engagement of the Hundred Years War, the battle of Castillon of 1453, it was the French who had established themselves within strong defensive lines, and the English who were mown down (by artillery rather than archery) as they attacked.

Fighting in battle

When fighting began, there was no doubt much confusion. It is possible, however, to distinguish some elements of battle. There was the use at the outset of long-distance weapons, above all archery; the cavalry charge; the mêlée; and the final rout. The opening of battle was extremely noisy. Jordan Fantosme remarked on this at the start of William the Lion's attempt to take Carlisle in 1173: 'Great was the noise as the battle began; there was the ring of iron, and the clash of steel'.[63] Henry of Huntingdon, describing an imaginary battle, wrote of the thunder of war, the sound of weapons and blows, and the shouting which burst out.[64] Noise served as a weapon to terrify the enemy. In 1234 Richard Marshal routed royalist forces under John of Monmouth, charging out of a wood making as much din as possible, with trumpets blaring.[65] At the outset of the battle of Crécy drums and trumpets added to the din. It was said that the noise of battle in 1356 was so great that it echoed from the walls of Poitiers itself, seven miles distant from the fighting.[66] Battle cries were important, in part as a means of recognition, in part to frighten the enemy, and perhaps also in part as a means of reinforcing a collective identity, and of supporting friends in the fight. The French shouts of 'Montjoie St Denis' were answered by English yells of 'St George for Guyenne'. The battle cry, of course, remains to this day an important element in the armoury of the football supporter.

It was not normal for there to be any lengthy equivalent to the artillery exchanges which preceded the battles of the First World War: long-distance weapons were not used as a means of softening up the enemy prior to an advance. Heavy artillery weapons were not very practical on the field of battle. Guns and heavy siege engines were hard to manoeuvre, and had an extremely slow rate of fire. The English used guns at Crécy, but these were small and ineffective, more noisy than lethal. At Agincourt the French used some catapults, but after an initial volley they were withdrawn under the hail of English archery.[67] In 1453, at Castillon, the value of artillery in battle was proved, but that was an unusual engagement, in which the English under Talbot attacked a heavily defended French camp, prepared long in advance. The advent of effective field artillery was much later. It was surprisingly rare that a long-distance archery duel took place in the initial stages of a battle. On the second day at Bannockburn there was a brief exchange of archery fire when fighting began, but most of the English archers were held in the rear, and were brought into action only at a fairly late stage.[68] At Neville's Cross in 1346, however, the initial English move was to fire flights of arrows at the dense Scottish formations, and in the same year the first English response to the French advance at Crécy was to bring their archery into play.[69]

The crucial role of archery was to deter, slow, and even halt an enemy advance. Once the English developed in the fourteenth century their tactics of fighting from a defensive position, archery frequently proved devastating, and the longbow was a true battle-winning weapon. Horses were especially vulnerable to arrows, but the Scots discovered to their cost at Neville's Cross that archery was also effective against their massed defensive formations on foot, compelling them to take the fight to the English, with disastrous results. When the French decided to counter English methods by advancing on foot, as at Poitiers, the English bowmen were still able to wreak havoc. One well-informed chronicler remarked, however, that whereas in the past men knew after the first three or four – or at the most six – volleys of arrows which way the battle would go, at Poitiers there was still uncertainty after a hundred.[70] At Auray in 1364 Bertrand du Guesclin appeared to have evolved a solution, by advancing well-armoured men in a very tight formation which offered no easy targets. The English archers threw their bows away and joined in the mêlée, fighting with hand weapons.[71] Auray, however, was an exception. Agincourt, above all, was to show that as late as the fifteenth century the English longbow was still a weapon of quite exceptional capabilities.

The cavalry charge is traditionally regarded as the classic weapon of medieval warfare. The Byzantine princess, Anna Comnena, had commented that a fully armed western knight could smash his way through the walls of Babylon itself. The potential shock effect of fully armoured troops, mounted on heavy horses, lances couched, was immense. The visual effect of brightly coloured surcoats and trappers, and the noise of rattling armour and neighing horses, must have combined to terrorise even before the charging cavalry thudded into the lines of their opponents. The charge, however, was not easy. It must surely have required much training to co-ordinate a force of knights effectively, to ensure that some did not arrive at the enemy lines long in advance of the others. Manoeuvring such a force, wheeling it or halting it, must have presented great problems. Medieval commanders did not normally have troops at their disposal which had trained together for long periods; even a magnate's own retinue would contain many men specifically recruited for a particular campaign, each unused to riding with his new colleagues. In some periods the royal household provided a core of experienced knights used to campaigning together; at others its composition changed too rapidly. Knights were, of course, normally well-trained in the individual skills of their military calling, and often well-practised through taking part in tournaments, but it cannot have been easy to persuade them to act in unison. These are matters which the sources do not discuss, and which are not included in the manual so much used in the middle ages, Vegetius's *De re militari*.[72] It is likely that developments in armour made the co-ordinated cavalry charge more difficult in the course of time. With the conical helmet and simple nasal of the Norman period, vision and hearing were not much impaired. Orders could be given and understood. For the cavalryman of the later middle ages, with his fully visored bacinet, the problem must have been much greater.

It is therefore not surprising to find that the full-scale cavalry charge was not used as extensively as might be expected. It has rightly been remarked of the battle of Hastings that 'There is no suggestion in the evidence of what can be called the "classic" use of cavalry – that is to say a massed charge of heavily armed horsemen, riding knee to knee, using their mounts to overwhelm their opponents, and then attacking with lances and swords.'[73] The terrain was not suitable, with the English massed at the top of a hill. It is more likely that the Norman cavalry operated in small units, rather than a massed charge. Hastings is often seen as the inevitable success of the mounted knight against the anachronistic English infantry, but the battle was a close-run thing, and the Norman triumph far from inevitable. Indeed, it may have been that the Norman archers were at least as decisive as the cavalry in breaking the close formations of the English.[74] In the battles in Normandy under Henry I, the English tactics of fighting largely on foot precluded the use of the cavalry charge as a weapon, save in the final stages of battle. At Lincoln in 1141 Stephen sent forward a line of footsoldiers and knights with the aim of preventing his opponents crossing a ford, but Robert of Gloucester's men 'rushed on them violently' – not quite the vocabulary of the organised charge. According to the author of the *Gesta Stephani*, the charge featured again at Wilton in 1143. Stephen arrayed his army in squadrons ready for close combat, while the earl of Gloucester divided his men into three formations, described as wedges, and charged with great effect. This, however, may be little more than literary invention, for another more circumstantial account presents a different picture. According to Gervase of Canterbury, Robert of Gloucester caught Stephen by surprise when he was resting in the nunnery at Wilton.[75] Charges were hard to co-ordinate, as Raymond le Gros found outside Dublin in 1171. He and his men charged the Irish, but by the time he reached their lines he was far in front of the others, and single-handed transfixed two of the enemy with his lance.[76]

The charge was a rarity in twelfth- and early thirteenth-century warfare. That great soldier, William Marshal, if his biographer is to be believed, took part in only two cavalry charges, one early in his career at Drincourt in 1167, and the other as an old man at Lincoln in 1217.[77] On the Third Crusade, at Arsuf in 1191, the desperate charge of the Hospitallers, followed by that of the rest of the knights, proved to be a battle-winning weapon. This was, however, highly exceptional, and took place contrary to Richard I's orders. Had these been followed, victory might in fact have been achieved more easily.[78] In the Baron's Wars of the mid thirteenth century, cavalry charges certainly featured. At Lewes, Prince Edward routed the Londoners who were facing him: this was a classic use of cavalry against a force largely fighting on foot. That charge, however, did not win the battle, for Montfort's other forces, well-positioned on high ground, were able to attack the division commanded by the king's brother, Richard of Cornwall. When Edward returned from an undisciplined rout of the Londoners, the battle was effectively lost. The speed of his cavalry proved his undoing. Evesham again was largely a cavalry battle, though it is not clear to what extent there were true charges. There was an initial advance by Montfort's men with, presumably, the desperation of those cornered and outnumbered, and then the forces of Edward and the earl of Gloucester closed in from the flanks forming a dense mêlée.[79]

The problems involved in cavalry charges were well illustrated by the English defeat at Bannockburn. The Scots had ample time to prepare their positions, and the natural obstacle presented by boggy ground was reinforced by pits, dug and camouflaged so as to bring down the English horsemen. Ill-discipline as much as the careful Scottish preparations were the foundations of the English downfall. Henry de Bohun's lone charge at Robert Bruce in the preliminaries to the fighting was the first example of the excess of individualism which was typical of Edward II's army. That was followed by an engagement which saw the earl of Gloucester unhorsed, and, according to one account, the cowardly flight of Robert Clifford.[80] The same day saw a charge by Thomas Grey and William Deyncourt, following a vigorous exchange of views between Grey and Henry de Beaumont; Grey was wounded, and Deyncourt killed. The two men clearly had inadequate support in an unplanned, impetuous action. Worse was to come on the following day. A quarrel between the earl of Gloucester and the earl of Hereford over who had the right to lead the vanguard ended with a suicidal charge by Gloucester. Again he had insufficient support; charges of treachery were levied against one of his knights, Bartholomew Badlesmere. It was said that had the Scots known who Gloucester was (he was not wearing his coat of arms), they would not killed a man worth an immense ransom.[81] At the close of the battle, Giles of Argentine charged, apparently alone, into the mass of Scottish spearmen, an action which says much for his sense of chivalry, but nothing for his common sense or the discipline of the English army. The battle showed all too clearly that, in the wrong hands, the cavalry charge, rather than being a devastating weapon, might lead to disaster. Well-organised infantry, fighting from a prepared defensive position, were more than a match for ill-organised and badly disciplined armoured cavalry.

It is hardly surprising that after the experience of Bannockburn, the cavalry charge was not high on the list of tactical expedients used by English commanders. A central part of the tactical revolution that the English carried through in the Scottish wars of the 1330s, and in the early stages of the Hundred Years War, was the abandonment of the cavalry charge as the initial move in a set-piece battle. It still, of course, had its place in surprise attacks and was used to good effect in 1345 at Auberoche, and doubtless featured in many a skirmish.

By its nature, the mêlée was the hardest part of battle for chroniclers to describe, though some accounts provide an impression of the horrors of close hand-to-hand fighting. Jordan Fantosme in his description of the battle at Alnwick provides some good details of the nature of the mêlée in the twelfth century. The immense vulnerability of a knight once he lost his horse is very clear. The Scots King William charged into the fight, hurling to the ground the first man he struck. A sergeant, presumably on foot, thrust his spear at the king's horse. William fell, the dying horse on top of him; he could do no more than surrender to Ranulf de Glanville. One knight on the Scottish side, Richard Maluvel, did as much single-handedly as the thirteen knights with him. 'As long as he was on his horse he feared nothing; he had a splendid horse and he was splendidly accoutred'; but once his horse was slain, he promptly surrendered.[82]

The sheer press of men and horses in the mêlée could create scenes of appalling horror. Friendly troops advancing from the rear could cause almost as much damage as hostile forces. At Dupplin Moor in 1332 the Scots pressing from behind, on a narrow front, piled up on one another. Suffocation killed many, as the heaps of bodies rose ever higher.[83] There were similar scenes at Agincourt in 1415. The French attacked in three columns, directed at the three main English standards. When those in the front of the columns were killed in the initial clashes, others pushed from behind. Men clambered up on the bodies of their fallen comrades, only to fall themselves. Macabre heaps of suffocating men and corpses were formed, up to six feet in height.[84] The duke of York was unlucky enough to fall in the front line, and die from the lack of air as men tumbled on top of him. He was the most notable casualty on the English side.

The duration of battles varied very considerably. Hastings was an extraordinarily long fight, continuing through most of the day. Bannockburn lasted for two days. Tinchebray, in contrast, was probably settled in about an hour.[85] The mêlée, if the fight was extended, was exhausting. At the battle of Morlaix in 1343, when according to Geoffrey le Baker the French fought harder than at any time in the war up to the battle of Poitiers, there was a break in the battle on three occasions, so tired and out of breath were those on both sides.[86] At Crécy in 1346 the fighting began in the late afternoon, and was largely finished by dusk. At Neville's Cross in the same year the battle started in the morning, soon after nine; it ended in the evening, at Vespers. The effort of fighting for so long was great, and there were two or three rest-periods taken by mutual agreement in the course of the struggle.[87] Agincourt, in contrast, was a relatively short battle. The two armies had faced each other, neither making a move, for

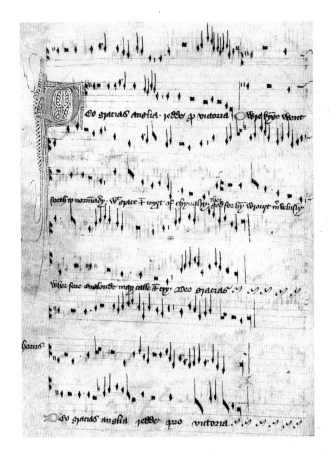

A song, complete with musical notation, written in celebration of the English triumph at Agincourt in 1415.

much of the day, and the real fighting took little more than two or three hours.[88]

The end of the mêlée often came when one side introduced a new force, which decisively tipped the balance. It could be infantrymen. At Falkirk in 1298 the archers were brought up, and succeeded where the cavalry had failed to break the strong defensive schiltroms of the Scots. The Welsh foot, however, refused to take part in the battle, until the very end when it became clear that the English had won the day.[89] More commonly, it was the introduction of a fresh cavalry force, rather than infantry, that was decisive. At Poitiers, the Captal de Buch's men delivered the decisive hammer-blow in the late stages of the battle, when, in a brilliantly planned move, they attacked the French from the rear.[90]

Casualties and the rout

The last stage of battle was the rout. At Hastings, the English eventually

turned to flight and made off as soon as they got the chance,
some on looted horses, many on foot; some along the roads,
many across country. Those who struggled but on rising lacked
the strength to flee lay in their own blood. The sheer will to
survive gave strength to others. Many left their corpses in the
depths of forests, many collapsed in the path of their pursuers
along the way. The Normans, though not knowing the terrain,
pursued them keenly, slaughtering the guilty fugitives and bringing matters to a fitting end, while the hooves of the horses
exacted punishment from the dead as they were ridden over.[91]

The rout might take longer than the battle itself. Poitiers was fought
in a morning; the pursuit of the enemy took until the evening. It was
in the course of the many minor individual engagements that took
place as the French fled the battlefield that Thomas Berkeley surprisingly suffered the ignominy of being captured by a squire – the only
Frenchman to make a fortune on a day of disaster for his king and
fellow countrymen.[92]

It was normally during the rout that the bulk of casualties
occurred. Drowning was a common form of death in the aftermath
of battle, as those fleeing from the field attempted to cross rivers.
Many of the Londoners routed by Prince Edward at Lewes were
drowned in the Ouse, and after Evesham, a good many of Montfort's
infantry suffered a similar fate in the Avon. Walter of Guisborough
noted that many Scots were drowned after their disastrous defeat at
Falkirk in 1298. At Stirling Bridge, Marmaduke Tweng was advised
to try to reach safety by crossing the river rather than by fighting his
way through the Scottish forces. He, however, preferred to hew a
way with his sword rather than to risk death by drowning, and was
successful. Only one knight succeeded, with great difficulty, in swimming the river with his horse.[93] A considerable number of English
suffered the same fate in the Bannock Burn in 1314, and it was noted
that more were drowned in the Swale than were killed by the Scots
at the battle of Myton in 1319.[94]

The evidence for the casualty rates in medieval battles is contradictory. The battle of Blore Heath in Cheshire in 1459 witnessed heavy
casualties, to judge by chronicle evidence, but careful reassessment of
the evidence reveals that a mere nine men of note can be proved to
have died there. Contemporaries did try to calculate how many men
died in battles. Peter Langtoft's chronicle gives a very precise number
for those slain at Dunbar in 1296: 10,054, 'I have the number by
tally.' The exactitude of the calculation may seem convincing, but
another text of the chronicle gives the figure as 22,000, and explains
'Peter tells you this, who has tallied it all.' A third version raises the
number to 30,000. Walter of Guisborough's figure is 'about 10,000'.

In the aftermath of Crécy, Reginald de Cobham was ordered by the king to collect together all the heralds who could recognise coats of arms, and draw up a roll of the dead. No such document survives, and the figures given by chroniclers are not trustworthy. Jean le Bel gives the totals as nine princes, 12,000 knights, and 15,000 or 16,000 others, and states that only three English knights died, but little credence should be given to his calculations. A more plausible figure is given by Geoffrey le Baker, who gave the total of nobles and knights slain at over 4,000, but again such estimates are hardly to be relied upon. At Poitiers, one estimate put the deaths of men-at-arms at a not-implausible 2,500; it was noted that casualties among the ordinary foot had not been numbered.[95] Attempts were certainly made in the aftermath of battle to count the dead, but the task cannot have been an easy one, and the temptation to exaggerate considerable.

It might be expected that as armour improved, with the adoption of plate in place of mail, casualty rates would fall, at least among the knights. The evidence points in the opposite direction. Orderic Vitalis noted that at Brémule in 1119 only three knights were killed: this is explained in terms of the mail they wore, and the fact that the victors were keener to capture than to kill their enemies.[96] At the battle of Lincoln in 1217 the French count of Perche was killed, but there appear to have been virtually no other casualties. At the battle of Lewes knightly deaths could be counted on the fingers of one hand. Evesham was a very different story: there a savage blood-lust was displayed by Prince Edward's troops, typical of the bitterness of civil war. Yet the fact that only eighteen sword-belts 'of enemies of the king' were delivered into the royal wardrobe suggests that knightly casualties may not have been all that high. A recent calculation is that 'we can only be sure of the deaths of thirty or so knights'.[97] The fact that casualties were normally of this order helps to explain the shock when at least sixteen knights, and many men of lesser rank, were drowned in the disaster at the Anglesey pontoon bridge in 1282.[98] At Bannockburn in 1314 there were notable casualties. Henry de Bohun died in single combat with Robert Bruce. The earl of Gloucester and Giles of Argentine, acclaimed as the third-best knight in Christendom, were killed when they made their suicidal charges into the Scottish ranks. From chronicles, the names of almost forty English knights killed in the battle can be drawn – an uprecedentedly high figure.[99] Boroughbridge, the conflict which saw the end of Thomas of Lancaster's rebellion in 1322, was little more than a skirmish, but it was the occasion of one very notable death, that of the earl of Hereford.

With the Hundred Years War, casualty levels rose sharply. One estimate puts the losses among the French cavalry at Poitiers and

Agincourt at about 40 per cent.[100] A famous and poignant story is told by Froissart which hints at the horror of the deaths at Crécy. The blind king of Bohemia begged his companions to lead him into battle. His knights did so, with their horses' reins tied together so that they would not lose him; he was put in the front rank so that he could strike at least one blow with his sword. On the next day he and his companions were all found dead, their horses still tied together.[101] The practice of ransoming prisoners should have reduced the level of knightly casualties, particularly as ransom figures rose sharply in the course of the Hundred Years War, but the situation of the English, fighting against heavy numerical odds at Crécy, Poitiers and Agincourt, necessitated a policy where quarter was not always given. The official English estimate of the French death toll at Poitiers was two dukes, one bishop, sixteen bannerets and no less than 2,326 other men-at-arms.[102] Agincourt was a slaughter on an astonishing scale. Henry V's chaplain noted the deaths of three dukes, five counts, over ninety barons and bannerets, and 1,500 knights and between 4,000 and 5,000 gentlemen. He noted on the English side, one duke, one earl, two knights and nine or ten others killed, though no attempt was made to calculate the number of archers who fell. Other estimates also suggest that English losses were surprisingly small, while one indication of the level of French losses is that five grave-pits were dug, with over 1,200 men buried in each.[103] At Neville's Cross in 1346 casualties were perhaps not so high as in the French wars: Baker in his chronicle listed two earls and twenty-one knights killed on the Scottish side, noting that many more were killed in the succeeding rout.[104] Otterburn in 1388 was a different story. Chronicles suggest heavy casualties in this extraordinary night battle, and excavations at the church at Elsdon revealed the burial of some 1,200 men killed in the fighting.[105]

There is surprisingly little information on the wounds incurred in battle. The injuries of David of Scotland at Neville's Cross are attested to; he was struck in the face by an arrow, and needed the attention of two barber-surgeons from York to extract the barb.[106] Some battle injuries were horrific; in a fight against the Norwegians one English knight had his hip-bone cut away with a single blow from a battle-axe.[107] James Audley was badly wounded at Poitiers, but as in many other cases, no precise details of his injuries are recorded. At Lussac, soon after the resumption of the Hundred Years War in 1369, the celebrated John Chandos was fatally wounded when he and his troops were advancing on the French on foot. He stumbled on his long surcoat and slipped on the icy ground. He had omitted to lower his visor, and a French squire succeeded in thrusting his lance into his face. Chandos fell on to the weapon, which penetrated his skull. He died twenty-four hours later.[108]

The aftermath of battle must have been appalling. Bodies lay unburied; the grisly task of heralds counting the dead must have been accompanied by the much more unpleasant activities of scavengers trying to profit as best they could, pillaging the corpses. After Robert of Gloucester's capture at Stockbridge in 1141, 'You could have seen chargers finely shaped and goodly to look upon, here straying about after throwing their riders, there fainting from weariness and at their last gasp; sometimes shields and coats of mail and arms of every kind lying everywhere strewn on the ground.'[109] How the cleaning up process was done is best left to the imagination.

Relatively few battles had their memorials. Battle Abbey is the most notable commemoration combined with atonement, founded by the Conqueror following Hastings. The abbot of St Mary's, York, petitioned to be allowed to build a chantry chapel at Myton, for the souls of those slain in the battle there in 1319. It may be that the cross on the battlefield of Crécy really does represent the spot where the king of Bohemia died, but the concept of the battlefield war memorial was a not widespread one in the medieval period. It was, for example, not until 1845 that an obelisk was erected to commemorate the battle of Evesham, very possibly in the wrong place.[110] That, however, is no reason not to honour those who fought and died in horrific circumstances.

The evidence for the way in which individual battles was fought is often contradictory and confusing, and caution is needed in suggesting clear lines of development. It was not always easy for men to learn from one battle, and apply the lessons to the next. The argument for a military revolution in battle tactics is obvious. The devastating impact of footsoldiers, above all of archers, hinted at in 1322 at Boroughbridge, demonstrated at Dupplin Moor and Halidon Hill in 1332 and 1333, and proved beyond all doubt at Crécy and Poitiers, is a familiar theme. There is no doubt that the tactics used by the English against the French in the fourteenth century were devastating, and the testimony of Jean le Bel shows that they were regarded as novel. The case, however, is not quite so straightforward. The battles of the early twelfth century had seen the efficacy of a combination of archers and dismounted knights demonstrated with abundant clarity. The scale of the fourteenth-century battles was doubtless much greater than that of Tinchebray or Brémule, but the tactics employed by Odo Borleng at Bourgthéroulde were very similar to those that Edward III would adopt over 200 years later. Norman warfare was quite as revolutionary in its battle tactics as was that of the English in the fourteenth century.

14

Conclusion: A Military Revolution?

One of the themes of this book has been the ways in which the armies recruited by English kings were transformed in the course of the medieval period. It was not simply a question of changes in equipment and tactics, though such traditional aspects of military history were significant. There were many other important elements, and this book has aimed to examine the development of medieval armies in a much broader sense, ranging from the initial stages of obligation and recruitment, through the problems posed by the logistics of war, to the practice of warfare in siege and battle, and to the difficult questions of the ideology of chivalry. In this way it may be possible to assess whether or not the changes that took place amounted to a 'military revolution'.[1]

The concept of a 'military revolution' has found broad acceptance among historians of the early modern period. Michael Roberts was the first to advance the theory; he argued that in terms of the size of armies, tactics and strategy, finance and logistics, there was a decisive leap forward made during the early seventeenth century. Tactical changes and the development of drill made possible a revolution in strategy. Armies grew in size, to meet the new needs. Expenditure on war rose to fresh heights, and military activity imposed a far greater administrative load on society than in the past. Novel financial techniques, especially as regards the provision of credit, were important in facilitating change. For Roberts, the prime example was the reign of Gustavus Adolphus in Sweden; as a historian of Sweden, his choice was predictable.[2] Since he wrote, other scholars have suggested modifications to his position. The dates of the military revolution have moved, and further examples have been added. Geoffrey Parker has stressed the importance of the conflict in the Netherlands, and emphasised the developments of the later sixteenth century. He has also brought the question of fortification into the argument. More recently, Jeremy Black has taken issue with the emerging orthodoxy. He questioned the significance of the tactical innovations that provided one of the foundations of Roberts's argument, and suggested that change in the period 1560–1660 was limited in character. He argued that there was much greater innovation in the late fifteenth century, and above all in the period 1660–1760. Change then was both qualitative and quantitative. There was the technological advance of the replacement of matchlocks and pikes by flintlocks and bayonets. Under Louis XIV Vauban built defensive fortifications on a quite new scale. Armies increased massively in size: in 1667 the French army numbered 85,000, and by 1678 it was almost 280,000 strong.[3]

There is no reason why the early modern period should have a monopoly of military revolutions, and indeed one of the main proponents of the concept, Geoffrey Parker, pointed to developments similar to those in early modern Europe which took place in China in the third century BC, and have left a vivid memorial in the form of the terracotta army.[4] There are many parallels much closer at hand, and medievalists, consciously or otherwise, have pointed to resemblances between the early modern military revolution and changes in their period. Not all suggestions have held up under scrutiny. Lynn White Jr put forward a celebrated thesis, arguing that the introduction of the stirrup to western Europe in the seventh or early eighth centuries made possible the development of feudal heavy cavalry. The stirrup helped the rider to stay on his horse; the argument, however, fell, for it was based on inadequate and unconvincing evidence.[5] Another technologically based military revolution is claimed for the fourteenth century, with the great successes of the English longbow; a case can also be made, suggesting that the development of guns by the early fifteenth century prompted significant change.[6] Many historians have propounded another revolution, one in which the key to change was the replacement of unpaid feudal forces by more professional paid troops. This idea has proved so popular that it has been argued that such a move took place in virtually every period of the middle ages, from the days of King Alfred, who is said to have spent a sixth of his annual revenue from taxation on the wages of his fighting men, to the fourteenth century. The importance of pay in the Anglo-Norman armies of the late eleventh and early twelfth centuries was pointed out by J.O. Prestwich. His pupil Sir James Holt found that King John 'was being compelled increasingly to ensure the performance of his liege men by the provision of cash rewards'. J.E. Morris considered that pay was at the heart of the transformation of English armies in the reign of Edward I.[7] The argument that pay effected a revolutionary transformation does not convince, when there is such uncertainty as to when this took place. Andrew Ayton has constructed a very different case for a military revolution in the fourteenth century, by concentrating not on pay, but on the overall composition of the army. The core of his argument is that the emergence of the mounted archer and the mixed retinue, which combined men-at-arms and archers, transformed English armies between 1330 and 1360.[8]

The most plausible arguments are those based on the total experience of war, so following Roberts's exposition of his case. The evidence of the size of English armies points to a very significant increase under Edward I. He was capable of putting up to 30,000 men in the field, notably in Wales in 1294, and in Scotland in 1298. The figures may not compare with the huge forces, some ten times bigger, that the French could deploy by the late seventeenth century, though that was the total force spread over many fronts. The medieval figures look more impressive when set against the numbers of the forces that Parma assembled in Flanders for the planned invasion of England in 1588, which were on an optimistic estimate 26,000 strong. They also compare reasonably with the forces ranged at Breitenfeld in 1631, when 10,000 Imperialist horse and 21,400 infantry were opposed by 13,000 Swedish cavalry and 28,000 foot.[9] The large numbers achieved under Edward I were to be seen again in 1346–7, but most of the armies sent to fight in France in the Hundred Years War were much smaller. Armies were rarely more than 8,000 strong.

Drill was important in enabling early modern armies to manoeuvre efficiently, and to use firearms to good effect. Here there is much less by way of a medieval parallel. The evidence for drilling and training medieval armies is not impressive. Infantry troops were, however, well organised in their hundreds and twenties, and there were standard-bearers and men charged with shouting orders. The speed of march could be controlled, for an army could be told to march forward at *le petit pas*. Given the nature of the weapons used, there was much less need for synchronised drill than with forces armed with muskets. It was important that archers could be ordered to shoot their flights in unison. As far as cavalry were concerned, there is no reason to suppose that medieval knights were any worse at maintaining their position in a charge than their more recent counterparts.

Tactics in the middle ages were more sophisticated than is often allowed. Geoffrey Parker has written of the early modern tactical revolution when 'the feudal knights fell before the firepower of massed archers or gunners'. The French at Crécy were already falling before impressive firepower, a couple of centuries too soon according to this view. There was a tactical revolution in the early fourteenth century, when the English developed the technique of using dismounted men-at-arms with archers in support on the flanks. This may not seem so novel when considered alongside the battles of the early twelfth century, when dismounted knights and archers had proved so successful in Henry I's campaigns in Normandy. There was no continuity, however, between the battle tactics of the twelfth and the fourteenth centuries. In the twelfth century it was customary to line up the main divisions of the army one behind the other; in the great battles of the Hundred Years War the dispositions of troops were more complex. It may not often be clear from the sources precisely how the archers were placed in relation to the men-at-arms, but what is evident is that commanders were able to articulate the various elements of armies with considerable skill.

In terms of strategy, there can be no doubt that medieval rulers and commanders had highly ambitious plans, based on sound strategic understanding. It is impossible to agree with Roberts that there was 'a new strategy of devastation' in the early modern period, though there may be some doubts as to whether devastation was always intended as an alternative to battle.[10] Fire and sword were used by William I to ravage wide tracts of territory; the Scots used such techniques when invading England in the early fourteenth century, and the *chevauchées* of the English in the Hundred Years War were intended to put pressure on the Valois monarchy by destroying the prosperity of the land. There was also strategy on a grand scale, with the creation of grand alliances intended to encircle the French from Flanders to the Pyrenees; there were elaborate campaign strategies, with different armies acting in concert to carry out a single plan. Such strategies were first developed under Richard I and John, and put into effect again by Edward I and Edward III. There were changes and shifts of emphasis in strategy, as with the development of the 'barbican' strategy in the 1370s. Henry V's approach to the conquest of Normandy was very different from the type of strategy employed previously in the French war. It is not possible to argue that there was any one single military revolution in English strategy in the medieval period, but there was certainly complexity and sophistication in the ideas that were developed. There is no justification for regarding the medieval period as the dark ages of strategy. On a small scale, the strategy that Edward and his allies used to entrap Simon de Montfort at Evesham in 1265 was both well conceived and brilliantly executed. On a broader canvas, Edward III showed imagination and flexibility in devising strategies that achieved far more than could have been expected in his French war from 1337 to 1360.

An important factor in the military revolution of the early modern period was, it has been claimed, the ability of states to keep the large armies of the period properly supplied. Under Cromwell, 'Scotland and Ireland were conquered by timely provisions of Cheshire cheese and biscuit.' This was perhaps the area in which the early modern military revolution was least effective, for starvation frequently decimated armies. There was very considerable reliance on the ability of soldiers to live off the land by foraging. From the 1640s, however, the French began to calculate the precise needs of their forces. They drew up contracts with merchants, and established a system of magazines, or victualling bases.[11] The medieval parallels are obvious; the English relied on their bases at Chester, Berwick and Carlisle for campaigns in Wales and Scotland. They calculated carefully the needs of men and horses so that the quantities required could be worked out. The administrative machinery of sheriffs and local officialdom was used to collect huge quantities of supplies for military purposes. All of this demonstrates the capacity of the medieval state to organise itself efficiently for war. Wheat, barley, oats, beans and peas, salt fish, beef and bacon, if not necessarily Cheshire cheese and biscuits, were all provided in substantial quantities. The evidence for this is clear as early as the twelfth century from the Pipe Rolls of Henry II's day. Under Edward I the pressures of war necessitated the development of victualling systems on a massive scale, which can certainly be regarded as revolutionary. There were difficulties, as in 1322 when Edward II's army in Scotland did not receive the expected supplies by sea, but no English medieval force faced the appalling losses through lack of proper victualling arrangements that are known to have occurred in the seventeenth century. In 1643 Turenne's force of 16,000 men (no larger than many a medieval army) lost two-thirds of its number to starvation when retreating towards the Rhine.[12]

The medieval period did not witness a single revolution in techniques of fortification that can be compared with the introduction of the defences against artillery of the early modern period, when low, squat bastions replaced the tall walls and towers of the medieval period. It was not until the reign of Henry VIII, with the building of such coastal fortifications as Walmer and Deal, that the implications of artillery began to be fully realised. Yet a case can be made for the existence of military revolutions in castle-building in the medieval period. The introduction of the castle in the eleventh century was, of course, revolutionary in itself. The effective abandonment of the great rectangular stone keeps in the late twelfth and early thirteenth centuries, when new castles were built, showed a striking capacity for innovation when faced with demonstrations of the efficacy of mining, and with changing weapons technology in the form of the introduction of the trebuchet. Under Edward I the Crown engaged in a massive and extensive project with the creation of the great chain of castles ringing north Wales, from Flint round to Harlech. The extensive use of concentric lines of defence, the abandonment of the keep after the building of Flint, the use of mural galleries to increase greatly the potential fire-power, as at Caernarfon, marked these castles as being at the leading edge of contemporary military technology, but it was perhaps the speed and scale of the building programme, rather than the architectural detail, that marked Edward's castle-building programme as radically new. The cost came to over £90,000 – an unprecedented sum.[13]

The power of states to collect massive resources and deploy them in the pursuit of military ends made the military revolution of the early modern period possible. It was essential to have financial mechanisms available so that wars could be fought on credit. The availability of American bullion assisted the Habsburg monarchy; the Dutch borrowed money on the security of future taxes. Ultimately, it was success in trade that gave them the ability to raise the funds they needed to fight.[14] In England, it has been suggested that the 1690s saw the emergence of the 'fiscal–military state', with heavy taxation, extensive borrowing, and the foundation of the Bank of England in 1694.[15]

The financing of war has not been part of the central subject-matter of this study; however, it needs to be sketched briefly, for it is an important part of the case for an early modern military revolution. The claims for that period find ready parallels in the middle ages. The late twelfth and early thirteenth centuries saw unprecedented pressures on the English state as a result of Richard I's crusade and ransom, together with the eventually unsuccessful defence of Normandy and John's attempts to regain it. A mixture of loans and taxes, culminating in the collection of a thirteenth of the assessed value of movable goods and rents, enabled the demands to be met. Contemporaries were clear that the demands made by Richard I were unprecedented, and John's thirteenth raised almost £60,000. It has been argued that the resources that the French monarchy had available to it were greater than those that the English could deploy, but even if this was so (and the case is not proven), the fact remains that impressive sums were collected by Richard and John. Huge sums of money were available to John, stored up in castle treasuries. After the dismissal of the army recruited in 1212 to fight in Wales, the king sent 120,000 marks to Bristol, from where it was to be divided between various castles.[16]

The cost of warfare rose substantially under Edward I. The first Welsh war probably cost no more than about £20,000. That of 1282–3 lasted much longer, and saw more forces deployed, at a cost to the exchequer of some £150,000. The total of military expenditure between 1294 and 1298, with campaigns in Wales, Flanders and Gascony, probably amounted to £750,000. The bills for campaigns during the Hundred Years War were massive. Edward III's unsuccessful campaigns in the Low Countries between 1338 and 1340 cost some £400,000. War wages alone in 1359–60 came to £133,000. The costs of war from 1369 to 1375 have been calculated at over £670,000.[17]

With costs of this magnitude, the scale of warfare under Edward I and his grandson Edward III was possible only because of improved methods of raising money and, above all, credit mechanisms. Direct taxation, in the form of parliamentary subsidies, was one part of the answer. It provided an effective means of raising substantial sums. Taxes could be levied frequently, when there was acute military need. These parliamentary taxes were levied annually from 1294 to 1297, yielding over £190,000, and there were successive taxes for three years from 1337, providing the Crown with over £100,000. These direct taxes, assessed on a valuation of movable goods, had their precedents, notably in John's thirteenth, but between 1237 and the end of his reign Henry III had been unable to gain consent to levy any such taxes. In contrast, Edward I levied seven between 1290 and 1307, Edward II six in the course of his reign, and Edward III six before 1340. Since these taxes had to be individually negotiated, and because there was no fixed assessment before 1334, it was only after that date that they could provide the stable, regular income needed to guarantee security for loans. In addition to these general taxes, there was taxation of the Church. From 1294 to 1297 almost £130,000 was paid in taxes by the clergy, while the three years of taxation agreed in 1337 yielded some £45,000.[18]

Another part of the solution to the financing of war lay with indirect taxes, specifically levies on the export of wool and hides, which provided much better security for loans than direct taxes. John had introduced customs duties in 1202, but the experiment had not lasted. A permanent system was introduced in 1275, according to one account on the advice of an Italian merchant.[19] The grant of 6s 8d on every sack of wool exported from England was made in perpetuity, and the yield was substantial. The initial purpose was not to finance war, but almost certainly to pay off the debts that the king had incurred on his crusade. However, it soon became clear that the heavy financial demands of a campaign could be met more easily if money was borrowed on the security of the customs. In 1294 Edward I set a further important precedent, when he succeeded in raising the level of export duties during the period of the French war to 40s a sack, in place of an initial plan to seize all the wool in the country for the Crown. The pattern was similar under Edward III, when wool subsidies were a central feature of royal war finance. In the 1350s income from the taxation of overseas trade approached an average of £90,000 a year.[20]

Customs revenue provided good security for loans. The great lenders were the Italian bankers; Richard I and John had already turned to them before 1200. Under Edward I the great Italian merchant-banking houses came to dominate Crown credit finance. The

Riccardi of Lucca were the first of a series of Italian lenders; they were succeeded by the Frescobaldi of Florence, who were expelled from England by the Ordainers in 1311. Antonio Pessagno of Genoa advanced substantial funds to Edward II in the central years of his reign, but far more important were the Bardi and Peruzzi of Florence who dominated credit finance in the early years of Edward III's reign. Large sums were involved. The aggregate debt to the Riccardi, who were bankrupted in 1294, was some £392,000. Edward III owed huge sums to the Bardi and Peruzzi: they advanced over £82,000 between September 1336 and December 1337, and over £70,000 by Michaelmas 1338. At the time of their bankruptcy in the 1340s, the Bardi were owed £103,000 and the Peruzzi £71,000. As these companies failed, so English lenders emerged, of whom the earliest major figure was William de la Pole of Hull. It was syndicates of English merchants who provided the financial backing needed for the campaign of 1346–7; English wool, as well as English arrows, helped to win the battle of Crécy.[21]

The financial methods of the period 1270–1350 were of course not identical to those at the time of the early modern military revolution. Given the attitude of the Church it was not possible to offer good rates of interest openly, although the Crown did the best it could by rewarding lenders with grants and payments in compensation for damages. The English Crown in the middle ages was not able to guarantee interest and eventual full repayment of loans in the way that the Dutch could in the sixteenth and seventeenth centuries. Yet it was possible for Edward I and above all Edward III to raise very substantial sums from foreign lenders, much as the Dutch were able to do. According to Parker, the advent of Dutch financial techniques to Britain meant that under Queen Anne it was possible to borrow 31 per cent of the money needed to finance war between 1702 and 1713.[22] Certainly Edward I's borrowings did not reach such heights; loans probably covered about 12 per cent of his total war expenditure during the years 1294–8.[23] In the early years of the Hundred Years War, however, the percentage was very much higher. Edward III raised some £400,000 in the Netherlands between December 1337 and March 1340. This compares with total outgoings of £410,292 from July 1338 to May 1340 recorded by the wardrobe, the department which met most of the costs of the war. Very little cash was sent from England; the only significant sum was £5,865 taken by the keeper of the wardrobe in July 1338.[24] Other funds were transferred less directly, through seizures in England of wool which was then sold abroad, which amounted to a form of credit operation. Virtually all of Edward's military expenditure in these years was based on credit; it would not be unreasonable to suggest that as against the 31 per cent of expenditure borrowed by Queen Anne's government, Edward III's borrowings in the initial years of the Hundred Years War amounted to some 90 per cent.

It is of course true that not all of the elements of the early modern military revolution are to be found in the medieval period. Although gunpowder was known and used as early as Edward I's reign, guns were of little use save as siege weapons, and even here developments were slow. The technological advances did not match the improvements in muskets and guns of the sixteenth and seventeenth centuries. While there were treatises on the laws of war produced, in France and Italy but not England, there were no military academies set up to train an officer corps. The naval dimension of English medieval warfare does not bear comparison with the advances in the sixteenth and seventeenth centuries, in large measure because there were no comparable technical advances. Yet the increase in the size of armies, the efficiency in supplying them with victuals, the elaborate nature of strategy and the extended scale of warfare, the tactical developments of the use of archers and men-at-arms in an integrated force, and the development of financial mechanisms to support such military efforts, all provide very close parallels to the case that has been argued by Roberts and his disciples.

Why then, if there were such important developments in the medieval period, above all perhaps under Richard and John, and then in the late thirteenth and early fourteenth centuries, was there a 'military revolution' in the early modern period? One answer is that the changes of the period 1270–1350 were not sustained. The scale of the resources that the state could put into war declined: the economy of the era after the Black Death of 1348 was not capable, in the long term, of maintaining the kind of military and financial effort that had been made in the 1290s and late 1330s. The 32,000 at the siege of Calais formed the last large English medieval army; thereafter, numbers were much smaller. Henry V probably took some 10,500 men to France in 1415, but that was a highly exceptional effort. Very large armies proved to be of limited value; the introduction of the mounted archer in the 1330s was one of the factors that contributed to a decline in the size of armies, for such men could not be recruited in the numbers that ordinary footsoldiers might be. 'The traditional system of paying each soldier his due in person was gradually abandoned in favour of some form of administrative devolution, by which the governments paid private contractors and entrepreneurs to supply the military services that they could no longer afford to organise for themselves.'[25] The words are Geoffrey Parker's, describing one of the effects of the early modern military revolution; they could equally well have been written of the shift from direct management of armies by the Crown to the contractual indenture system in the fourteenth century. The move to recruiting both men-at-arms and archers by indenture coincided with a reduction in the size of armies. The financial structures did not endure. The mechanisms operated by the Italian bankers were built on shaky foundations; the collapse of the Bardi and the Peruzzi in the 1340s spelled an end to the system of credit finance devised under Edward I, and large-scale military enterprises became harder to finance. Attempts to introduce new methods of taxation, notably with the three poll taxes starting in the late 1370s, were a conspicuous failure. The financial structure was not changed to take account of the way in which exports of raw wool declined, and those of cloth rose. Loans from syndicates of English merchants, particularly Londoners, were not on the scale of those from the Italians earlier. Henry V was fortunate in being able to turn to Bishop Henry Beaufort for substantial loans. In 1421 alone Beaufort advanced £17,666.[26] It is clear that the financial strains which resulted from Henry's success in France were very considerable, and that it would have been very hard to sustain such a level of military activity.

There was a striking failure to innovate in the late fourteenth and fifteenth centuries. Henry V's great triumph at Agincourt bore a startling resemblance to the previous major English triumphs in the French war, and although his conquest of Normandy was characterised by new strategic thinking, there was little that was novel in the actual methods of fighting, or in the organisation of the troops in his day. War normally acts as a catalyst for rapid technological change, but this was not the case in this late medieval period. Personal armour became more complex and ingenious, but there was no fundamental change after plate largely replaced mail in the first half of the fourteenth century. Guns became larger, but not more sophisticated. Many of the earlier achievements of the government in organising war were, if not forgotten, at least neglected by the fifteenth century. The increasing abandonment of direct recruitment by the Crown, and the use instead of a contract system meant a loss of direct government control of the recruitment system, and this may have hampered innovation. The attempts that were made in the early fourteenth century to provide better armed infantry, and lightly armed cavalry, were not paralleled later. The systematic victualling programmes which had been so characteristic of Edward I's campaigns had been abandoned. Purveyance by sheriffs and their officials had been undeniably unpopular, and the use of contract merchants offered an attractive alternative. However, the practice of leaving it to individual magnates and military contractors to make their own arrangements for provision of supplies was not as satisfactory as the earlier systems had been. Henry V's troops were starving by the time Harfleur fell in 1415.

It is fashionable to argue that the relative failure of the late medieval state should not be stressed. Society as a whole was capable of finding other solutions to the problems that faced it; arbitration, for example, provided a very acceptable alternative to the use of the royal law courts. Government and the maintenance of order at a local level could be provided by the complex mesh of local relationships of clientage and kinship, and there was less need for elaborate central mechanisms. The great magnates are no longer seen by historians as having been perpetually at odds with the Crown and central government, but are viewed rather as providing an alternative and effective means whereby society might be ordered. Yet the history of the English armies of the later part of the Hundred Years War suggests that the weakening of the central control, and the decrease in royal bureaucracy, did contribute to an evident stagnation, which was characterised by an unwillingness to experiment with different forms of military organisation. The needs of the defence of Normandy after Henry V's conquest demanded a very different approach from that required by the expeditionary forces of the past, but as Anne Curry has pointed out, change was hampered by 'the inability of the fifteenth-century English mind to conceive of anything other than a personal system'. Indentures made in 1430 with English captains in Normandy indicate the level of conservatism. They were not to recruit more than half their retinues locally; all the archers were to be from the British Isles or Gascony, and the ratio of three archers to every lance was to be maintained.[27] The extensive use of the system of muster and review indicates a desire for efficiency, but does not suggest any imagination in the approach adopted by English commanders. Sir John Fastolf was one man who did think hard about the problems of the war and how to win it, but his advice was hardly novel, nor was it accepted.[28] The striking reduction in the proportion of bannerets and knights in English armies, first evident after the reopening of the French war in 1369, and abundantly evident in the armies of the final phase of the conflict, is no doubt a reflection of a growing disenchantment with the war. It also reflects the inability of the state to compel or persuade some of its most important subjects to perform what was once regarded as their undoubted duty.

The French responded much more effectively than the English to the changing circumstances of the fifteenth century. The problems they faced were similar; indeed, the proportion of bannerets (at 0.3 per cent) and of knights (at 1.9 per cent) in the French armies of 1418–20 was much lower than the figure in England. French artillery was superior to that possessed by the English. In 1445 the French began a major reform of the military structures, systematising what had already been achieved. The six-man cavalry unit, or lance, was established. In 1448 the *franc-archers* were set up, recruited parish by parish in much the way that English infantry had been recruited 150 years previously. In 1450 the French were able to put a force of almost 20,000 men in the field, half of them mounted. By the 1470s they were establishing a proper national victualling system for the armies.[29] There was, too, a change of attitude. The extraordinary career of Joan of Arc instilled a new fervour, and Charles VII adopted a systematic approach to the problems of war which was lacking among the English. By Louis XI's reign the French were beginning to establish a true permanent army.

The early modern military revolution has become less and less convincing as its chronological limits have expanded. Black, in his criticism of the Roberts thesis, suggested that 'innovation and development were concentrated in the late fifteenth and then again in the late seventeenth centuries'.[30] It is hard to accept transitions over so long a period as a revolution. Nor is it surprising to find similar changes taking place earlier, in the medieval period. Equally, however, while there is a good case for arguing that the developments of the early modern period were anticipated in the medieval period, the chronology of change was such as to make it difficult to apply the term 'revolution'. The years up to and around 1200 witnessed a significant transformation of warfare. Highly developed strategies both for the crusade and for the conflict with the Capetian monarchy of France evolved, and the period saw the decline in the importance of knight service combined with the widespread use of mercenaries. These were years that also saw military architecture develop rapidly, in response to improvements in siege techniques. Equally, many of the elements considered to typify the early modern military revolution also featured in the late thirteenth and early fourteenth centuries: the increased size of armies, elaborate supply arrangements, complex strategy and effective tactics. These were all made possible by credit finance. Yet although this weakens the case for the early modern military revolution, it does not make an alternative case for gradual, steady evolution. Rather, it demonstrates that in different periods, when similar problems presented themselves, closely comparable solutions were developed. Change was not even-paced.

There was no single medieval military revolution, but there was experiment and change, and considerable sophistication. Two periods can perhaps be picked out as particularly important. First, there was that which spanned the late twelfth and early thirteenth centuries, when war was organised and financed by the state on a new dimension, when elaborate strategies were devised on an international scale, and when traditional forms of military obligation

were reassessed and revised. The second period, from the late
thirteenth century to the 1340s, again saw major changes. War was
fought with a new intensity, and military resources were deployed on
a yet more massive scale. There were important experiments in
recruitment methods, which were increasingly dominated by contract and pay. Victualling was well organised by the state, with
careful calculation of need, elaborate systems for collecting foodstuffs in the country, and supply bases set up. Commanders
developed highly effective battle tactics, with dismounted men-
at-arms and archers dominant. The parallels to the early modern
periods are obvious.

War had its glamour in the middle ages: the splendid colours of the
banners, the glitter of armour, the magnificence of the horses, the
sound of the trumpets. The glowing colours of manuscript illustrations present one side of the story, but there was also another side:
the mud, brutality and misery. There were glorious deeds inspired by
chivalrous feelings of honour and loyalty, but there was also fear and
terror, and acts of sheer savagery. Defeated opponents might be
treated with honour, or their heads might be used to adorn the
Tower of London. Men had to campaign and fight in appalling
conditions, often when exhausted by hard marching, and suffering
from starvation and disease. There were heroes and there were
villains, but above all there were the ordinary men who had to
endure the misery and pain of campaigning. This book began with
three sketches of warfare. There was the heroic individual, Richard
Marshal, achieving fame with notable feats of arms, fending off his
enemies with mighty blows from his sword. Then there was the
chivalrous host marching into Scotland in 1300, banners born aloft
in a splendid display of colour and pageantry. While there is truth
underlying these descriptions, rather than conclude this book on a
glorious note, it is more apposite to end by returning to the third
sketch, that of the English army in 1327: the men huddled together,
wet, cold and hungry as they spent the night by the banks of the
Tyne.

Glossary

Aventail	A mail garment protecting the neck.
Banneret	A military rank, superior to that of a knight. Bannerets bore square banners, rather than long pennons.
Bacinet	Relatively light helmet with a rounded or pointed top. It might be fitted with a visor.
Balinger	Small oared vessel with single mast and sail.
Barbican	Outerwork of a castle, providing additional defence for the gatehouse. Also used to describe the strategy developed by the English in the late fourteenth century.
Barded horse	Horse equipped with a covering, usually cloth over thick padding, or armour.
Battle	A main division of the army; usually there were three or four battles in an army.
Belfry	Large movable wooden tower used in sieges.
Bracers	Plate armour for the arms.
Bretasche	Protective wooden screen used in siege warfare.
Caltrop	A small spiked device, intended to impede horses.
Cat	See **sow**.
Chanfron	Armour for a horse's head.
Chevauchée	Mounted raid into hostile territory.
Cog	A type of substantial sailing ship.
Conroi	Squadron or detachment of cavalry.
Cuisses	Plate armour pieces protecting the thighs.
Destrier	Charger, warhorse.
Falchion	Broad-bladed cutting weapon.
Fief	Land held in return for military (and other) service.
Fyrd	Anglo-Saxon army.
Gorget	A piece of plate armour protecting the neck.
Greaves	Plate armour pieces protecting the legs.
Greek fire	Incendiary mixture used primarily in siege warfare.
Habergeon	Mail coat, smaller than a hauberk.
Haketon	Leather jacket, probably reinforced with mail.
Hackney	A type of horse of no great value.
Hauberk	Mail coat.
Hide	A measure of land, not consistent in size, but often c. 120 acres.

Hobelar	Lightly armed cavalrymen, Irish in origin. First appeared in Edward I's reign in his Scottish wars.
Indenture	A contract, drawn up in two parts, one to be kept by each party. The two were written on a single piece of parchment, which was then divided by a jagged or indented cut.
Jupon	Tightly fitted garment worn over armour in the fourteenth century.
Knight's fee	Land from which the service of one knight was due.
Mangonel	Stone-throwing siege engine, often thought to have operated on the torsion principle.
Palfrey	A riding horse.
Poleyns	Small pieces of plate armour protecting the knees.
Prest	An advance, usually against wages.
Regard	A form of bonus, paid quarterly, the normal rate being 100 marks for the service of thirty men-at-arms.
Rouncey	An ordinary horse.
Sallet	A type of late-medieval, open-faced helmet.
Schiltrom	Scottish formation of closely packed footsoldiers, highly effective against cavalry.
Sow	Protective movable shed, enabling besiegers to approach close to a castle's walls.
Surcoat	Long flowing garment worn over armour.
Trapper	Cloth worn over armour or padding by a horse.
Trebuchet	Stone-throwing siege engine operated by means of a counterweight.
Vintenar	Man in charge of a group of twenty footsoldiers.

Note on money

Two different systems of account were used in medieval England. The most usual employed the pound sterling: there were twenty shillings in the pound, and twelve pennies in the shilling. Alternatively, marks might be used. The mark was two-thirds of the pound, so one mark consisted of thirteen shillings and four pence.

Abbreviations

AAF	*Arms, Armies and Fortifications in the Hundred Years War*, ed. A. Curry and M. Hughes (Woodbridge, 1994)
ANW	*Anglo-Norman Warfare. Studies in Late Anglo-Saxon and Anglo-Norman Military Organisation and Warfare*, ed. M. Strickland (Woodbridge, 1992)
Baker	*Chronicon Galfridi le Baker de Swynebroke*, ed. E.M. Thompson (Oxford, 1889)
BIHR	*Bulletin of the Institute of Historical Research*
CCR	*Calendar of Close Rolls*
CDS	*Calendar of Documents Relating to Scotland*
CPR	*Calendar of Patent Rolls*
EHR	*English Historical Review*
Froissart	*Chroniques de J. Froissart*, ed. S. Luce, 15 vols (Paris, 1869–1975)
Le Bel	*Chronique de Jean le Bel*, ed. J. Viard and E. Déprez (Paris, 1904)
Orderic Vitalis	*The Ecclesiastical History of Orderic Vitalis*, ed. M. Chibnall, 6 vols (Oxford, 1969–80)
PRS	Pipe Roll Society
RS	Rolls Series
TRHS	*Transactions of the Royal Historical Society*

Manuscript references, unless otherwise indicated, are to documents in the Public Record Office.

Notes

1 The Nature of Medieval Warfare

1 *Chronica Rogeri de Wendover*, ed. H. Hewlett (RS, 1889), iii, 61–2, 72, 85–6.
2 *The Siege of Carlaverock*, ed. N.H. Nicolas (1828), 3, 65.
3 BL, MS Cotton Nero C.VIII, f. 54.
4 *Le Bel*, i. 42–74.
5 *Gesta Henrici Quinti*, ed. F. Taylor and J.S. Roskell (Oxford, 1975), 58–9, 66–7, 76–7, 80–81.
6 C. Tyerman, *England and the Crusades 1095–1588* (Chicago, 1988), provides a full survey.
7 'Gesta Edwardi de Carnarvan', in *Chronicles of the Reigns of Edward I and Edward II*, ed. W. Stubbs (RS, 1883), ii, 75; *The Red Book of the Exchequer*, ed. H. Hall (RS, 1896), iii, 926. See also ibid., 918.
8 *The Wardrobe Book of William de Norwell 12 July 1338 to 27 May 1340*, ed. M. Lyon, B. Lyon, H.S. Lucas (Brussels, 1983), 327.
9 M. Roberts, *The Military Revolution, 1560–1660*, reprinted in his *Essays in Swedish History* (1967); G. Parker, *The Military Revolution: Military Innovation and the Rise of the West, 1500–1800* (Cambridge, 1988); J.M. Black, *A Military Revolution? Military Change and European Society 1550–1800* (1991).
10 *Chronicle of William of Rishanger of the Barons' Wars*, ed. J.O. Halliwell (Camden Soc., 1840), 45.
11 *The Chronicle of Walter of Guisborough*, ed. H. Rothwell

(Camden Soc., 89, 1957), 305.
12 *Adae · Murimuth, Continuatio Chronicarum. Robertus de Avesbury, De Gestis Mirabilis Regis Edwardi Tertii*, ed. E.M. Thompson (RS, 1889), 358.
13 *CCR 1346–1349*, 30. For a list and map of these places, see H.J. Hewitt, *The Organisation of War under Edward III* (Manchester, 1966), 128–9.
14 Parker, *The Military Revolution*, 75–7; Black, *A Military Revolution?*, 37–8, 42–4; M. Van Crefeld, *Supplying War* (Cambridge, 1977), 17–19.
15 J. Gillingham, 'Richard I and the Science of War in the Middle Ages', *War and Government in the Middle Ages*, ed. J. Gillingham and J.C. Holt (Woodbridge, 1984), 81.
16 *Calendar of Documents relating to Scotland*, v, ed. G.G. Simpson and J.D. Galbraith (1986), no. 715.

2 The Military Elite

1 *Le Bel*, i. 57–8. It is often suggested that Luttrell was armed for a tournament, not for war, but see R. Marks, 'Sir Geoffrey Luttrell and some Companions: Images of Chivalry c. 1320–50', *Wiener Jahrbuch für Kunstgeschichte*, 46–7 (1993–4), 351. I owe this reference to the kindness of Mark Ormrod. Parts of this chapter are based on my 'Miles in armis strenuus: the Knight at War', *TRHS*, 6th ser., 4, 1995.
2 William of Newburgh in *Chronicles of the Reigns of Stephen, Henry II and Richard I*,

ed. R. Howlett (RS, 1884–89), i. 46. J.F.A. Mason, 'Barons and their Officials in the Later Eleventh Century', *Anglo-Norman Studies*, 13 (1990), 249, 254, notes that there is no evidence of constables on honours worth less than £1,000 in Domesday terms, and gives Roger of Montgomery's constable as an example of one who may have commanded his lord's household knights.
3 D. Crouch, *Image of Aristocracy 1000–1300* (1992), 114–15; N. Denholm-Young, *History and Heraldry* (Oxford, 1965), 22–5.
4 *L'histoire de Guillaume le Maréchal*, ed. P. Meyer (Paris, 1891–1901), i. ll. 4771–6.
5 *Historical Documents relating to Scotland*, ed. J. Stevenson, ii. 222–4.
6 *CPR 1345–48*, 226, 273; N. Saul, *Knights and Esquires: The Gloucestershire Gentry in the Fourteenth Century* (Oxford, 1981), 8.
7 E 101/28/70.
8 *Froissart*, vii. 34. The incident is also described by the Chandos Herald in *La Vie du Prince Noir by Chandos Herald*, ed. D.B. Tyson (Tübingen, 1975), 134.
9 Crouch, *Image of Aristocracy*, 118–19.
10 The most recent discussion is J. Scammell, 'The Formation of the English Social Structure: Freedom, Knights and Gentry, 1066–1300', *Speculum*, 68 (1993), 591–618.
11 *Lestoire des Engles solum la translacion Maistre Geffrei Gaimar*, ed. T.D. Hardy (RS, 1888), i. 259–60; *Gesta*

Stephani, ed. K.R. Potter and R.H.C. Davis (Oxford, 1976), 208–9. Dubbing is discussed by Coss, *The Knight in Medieval England*, 52–3.

12 Distraint of knighthood is discussed by M. Powicke, *Military Obligation in Medieval England* (Oxford, 1962), 71–81.

13 For the controversy over the economic status of knights in the thirteenth century, see P.R. Coss, 'Sir Geoffrey de Langley and the Crisis of the Knightly Class in Thirteenth-Century England', *Past and Present*, 68 (1975); D.A. Carpenter, 'Was there a Crisis of the Knightly Class in the Thirteenth Century? The Oxfordshire Evidence', *EHR*, 95 (1980), 721–52; and most recently P.R. Coss, *Lordship, Knighthood and Locality: a Study in English Society c. 1180–c. 1280* (Cambridge, 1991), 264–304.

14 *Catalogus Baronum*, ed. E. Jamison (Rome, 1972); D. Matthew, *The Norman Kingdom of Sicily* (1992), 256–7.

15 *Historie militaire de la France, I – Des origines à 1715*, ed. P. Contamine (Paris, 1992), 89.

16 *Pipe Roll, 20 Henry II* (PRS, 21, 1896), 94, 132.

17 *Pipe Roll, 5 Richard I*, ed. D.M. Stenton (PRS, ns 3, 1927), 132; *Rotuli de Liberate ac de Misis ac Praestitis regnante Johanne*, ed. T.D. Hardy (1844), 6.

18 *Pipe Roll, 4 Henry III*, ed. B.E. Harris (PRS, ns 85, 1987), 135.

19 *Liber Quotidianus Contrarotulatoris Garderobae*, ed. J. Topham et al. (Soc. of Antiquaries, 1787), 232.

20 M.C. Prestwich, 'Cavalry Service in Early Fourteenth Century England', *War and Government in the Middle Ages*, ed. Gillingham and Holt, 155.

21 *The Wardrobe Book of William de Norwell*, 335–6, 339, 352.

22 'Private Indentures for Life Service in Peace and War', ed. M. Jones and S. Walker, *Camden Miscellany*, 32 (Camden Soc., 5th ser., 3), 63.

23 This is a necessarily brief summary of a highly complex process of social evolution. For an excellent discussion, see Saul, *Knights and Esquires*, 14–26.

24 The development of armour is ably discussed by C. Blair, *European Armour* (1958), and by K. DeVries, *Medieval Military Technology* (Peterborough, Ontario, 1992), 56ff. Armour of the Conquest period is discussed by I. Peirce, 'The Knight, his Arms and Armour in the Eleventh and Twelfth Centuries', *The Ideals and Practice of Medieval Knighthood*, ed. C. Harper-Bill and R. Harvey (Woodbridge, 1986), 152–64.

25 For discussion, see N.P. Brooks and H.E. Walker, 'The Interpretation and Authority of the Bayeux Tapestry', *Proceedings of the Battle Conference 1978*, ed. R.A. Brown (Ipswich, 1979), 19–20.

26 I. Peirce, 'The Knight, his Arms and his Armour c. 1150–1250', *Anglo Norman Studies*, xv (1992), 251–66.

27 *Expugnatio Hibernica: the Conquest of Ireland by Giraldus Cambrensis*, ed. A.B. Scott and F.X. Martin (Dublin, 1978), 76–7.

28 Peirce, 'The Knight, his Arms and his Armour', 258.

29 *Select Cases of Procedure without Writ under Henry III*, ed. H.G. Richardson and G.O. Sayles (Selden Soc., 60, 1941), 56; *Select Cases in the Court of King's Bench, Edward I*, iii, ed. G.O. Sayles (Selden Soc., 58, 1939), cv, n. 5.

30 *Calendar of Inquisitions Miscellaneous, 1307–49*, nos 527, 797; BL Stowe Charter, 622.

31 *Le Bel*, i. 156.

32 *Foedera*, III (ii), 388.

33 *Pipe Roll, 2 John*, ed. D.M. Stenton (PRS, ns 12, 1934), 209; *Pipe Roll, 9 John*, ed. M.A. Kirkus (PRS, ns 22, 1944), 31.

34 *Cal. Liberate Rolls, 1251–1260*, 380.

35 BL. Cotton MSS., Nero C. VIII, f. 57.

36 E 101/376/7.

37 E 101/16/5.

38 E 101/393/11.

39 *Cal. Inquisitions Miscellaneous, 1307–1349*, no. 797.

40 E 101/20/37.

41 BL. Stowe Charter 622; Saul, *Knights and Esquires*, 24.

42 Personal experience, when teaching a seminar, of wearing a reproduction fifteenth-century Burgundian sallet, provided by Mr Keith Bartlett suggests this most strongly.

43 *L'Histoire de Guillaume le Maréchal*, ll. 16597–604.

44 'I never spoke with an English lancer who had been engaged in the late Sikh wars that did not declare the lance to be a useless tool, and a great incumbrance in close conflict.' L.E. Nolan, *Cavalry; its History and Tactics* (1853), 127.

45 *L'Histoire de Guillaume le Maréchal*, i. ll. 8845–9.

46 *Froissart*, v. 168.

47 M.G.A. Vale, *War and Chivalry: Warfare and Chivalric Culture in England, France and Burgundy at the End of the Middle Ages* (1981), 118.

48 *Select Cases in the Court of King's Bench, Edward I*, ed. G.O. Sayles, iii (Selden Soc, 58, 1939), 102.

49 The history of the sword is a complex matter. See R.E. Oakeshott, *The Archaeology of Weapons* (1960), 200–252, 301–36; R.E. Oakeshott, *The Sword in the Age of Chivalry* (1981); I. Peirce, 'The Development of the Medieval Sword', *The Ideals and Practice of Medieval Knighthood*, 3 (1990), 139–58.

50 *Chronicles of England, France, Spain and the Adjoining Countries by Sir John Froissart*, trans. T. Johnes (1839), 535.

51 *The Historia Novella by William of Malmesbury*, 49; *Expugnatio Hibernica*, 176–7; above, 1–2.

52 St Anselm, quoted by Coss, *The Knight in Medieval England*, 24.

53 *The Black Prince's Register*, iv, A.D. 1351–1365 (1933), 67–8.

54 *Diplomatic Documents preserved in the Public Record*

Office, i. *1101–1272*, ed. P. Chaplais (Oxford, 1964), 1–4.
55 E 101/3/10; T.F. Tout, *The Place of the Reign of Edward II in English History* (2nd edn, 1936), 250–53.
56 *The Account Book of William de Norwell*, 386.
57 R.A. Newhall, *The English Conquest of Normandy* (Yale, 1924), 191, 194n. A. Ayton, *Knights and Warhorses. Military Service and the Aristocray under Edward III* (Woodbridge, 1994), 219, argues on the other hand from falling valuations that the evidence of the 1359 campaign points clearly to a 'decline in the English warhorse'. The price of horses may have fallen; their numbers did not. Evidence of the same sort for the value of horses is unfortunately not available for the fifteenth century.
58 R.H.C. Davis, *The Medieval Warhorse* (1989), 22–3, 66–7.
59 K. Thompson, 'Robert of Bellême Reconsidered', *Anglo-Norman Studies* 13 (1990), 284.
60 *Rotuli Litterarum Clausarum*, ed. T.D. Hardy (1833–4) i. 171; *Documents Illustrative of English History in the Thirteenth and Fourteenth Centuries*, ed. H. Cole (1844), 238, 251.
61 Prestwich, *Edward I*, 163.
62 Prestwich, *Edward I*, 163; H.J. Hewitt, *The Horse in Medieval England* (1983), 25; W.R. Childs, *Anglo-Castilian Trade in the Later Middle Ages* (Manchester, 1978), 120–21.
63 E 101/105/2.
64 Hewitt, *The Organisation of War under Edward III*, 88. It should be noted that the argument put forward there about the acquisition of horses in France in 1359 does not stand up to analysis; see below, 369, n. 40.
65 *Rotuli de Liberate ac de Misis et Praestitis*, 140; *Documents*, ed. Cole, 244; Davis, *Medieval Warhorse*, 83–4, gives details of de la Lande's career and activities.
66 There is some discussion of these matters in Prestwich, *Edward* I, 162–3.

67 E 101/99/6.
68 E 101/104/30; E 101/107/3.
69 *Orderic*, v. 242.
70 E 101/104/30. For a valuable discussion of other accounts from this period, see Hewitt, *The Horse in Medieval England*, 10–25. The cost of maintaining military horses has remained high. According to *The Times*, 6 February 1995, the last twenty operational army horses were to be formally retired on 1 April 1995, so as to save £500,000 a year, or £25,000 per horse.
71 Davis, *Medieval Warhorse*, 90–92, elaborates on this point. His argument relies, however, simply on the survival of *equitia* accounts, rather than on a detailed analysis of the accounts themselves. The survival of accounts was haphazard, and Davis's graph on p. 87 has to be interpreted with greater care than he intended.
72 *Rotuli de Liberate ac de Misis et Praestitis*, 150.
73 Davis, *Medieval Warhorse*, 82; *Rot. Lit. Claus.*, i. 171b; *Pipe Roll, 5 Richard I*, 99; *Documents Illustrative of English History*, ed. Cole, 238, 251. The *livre* of Anjou was worth about a quarter of the pound sterling.
74 *Pipe Roll, 12 John*, ed. C.F. Slade (PRS, 1951), 9, 200–201; *Pipe Roll, 11 John*, ed. D.M. Stenton (PRS, 1949), 198; *Pipe Roll, 13 John*, ed. D.M. Stenton (PRS, 1953), 200; *Pipe Roll, 16 John*, ed. P.M. Barnes (PRS, 1962), 155.
75 *Pipe Roll, 12 John*, 8–9, 93, 139, 160.
76 Davis, *Medieval Warhorse*, 82; *Rot. Lit. Claus.*, i. 171; Cole, *Documents*, 238; BL Add. MS. 7965, ff. 15v, 18; *The Account Book of William de Norwell*, 213, 216, 310–11; *Liber Quotidianus*, 179; Ayton, *Knights and Warhorses*, 194–256. See also his 'The Warhorse and Military Service under Edward III' (Hull Ph.D., 1990).
77 *Histoire militaire de France*, i, ed. P. Contamine (Paris, 1992), 85.
78 P. Binski, *The Painted*

Chamber at Westminster (1986), plates X, XXV.
79 E 101/16/5.
80 Davis, *Medieval Warhorse*, 97.
81 G. Tylden, *Horses and Saddlery* (London, 1965), 117. Gerald of Wales commented on the awkwardness of the high, curved saddle, which made swift mounting and dismounting impossible: *Expugnatio Hibernica*, 246– 7.
82 A. Hyland, *The Medieval Warhorse from Byzantium to the Crusades* (Gloucester, 1994), 7–8.
83 R.P. Abels, *Lordship and Military Obligation in Anglo-Saxon England*, 138, 167–8; Barlow, *Edward the Confessor*, 170.
84 J.O. Prestwich, 'The Military Household of the Norman Kings', *ANW*, 93–127.
85 Below, 149; *Pipe Roll, 20 Henry II*, 59; *Expugnatio Hibernica*, 168–9; Roger of Howden, *Gesta Regis Henrici Secundi*, ii. 5.
86 S.D. Church, 'The Knights of the Household of King John: A Question of Numbers', *Thirteenth Century England IV. Proceedings of the Newcastle upon Tyne Conference 1991*, ed. P.R. Coss and S.D. Lloyd (Woodbridge, 1992), 151–62; *Foreign Accounts Henry III*, 35.
87 My calculations from the 1225–6 list, C 72/2, m. 20, differ slightly from Dr Church's 'The Knights of the Household of King John'. The knights who appear in all three lists are Reginald Basset, Herbert Bozun, Roger Bigod, Henry FitzReginald, William des Montz, John de Neville, Hugh Saunzavoir, Gerard Talbot, John Talbot and Robert Tregoz.
88 R.F. Walker, 'The Anglo-Welsh Wars, 1217–67' (Oxford University D.Phil. thesis, 1953), 66–7.
89 Prestwich, *Edward I*, 147–8; M.C. Prestwich, *War, Politics and Finance under Edward I* (1972), 47, 52. For a detailed study, see R.L. Ingamells, 'The Household Knights of Edward I',

(Durham Ph.D., 1993).

90 For a convenient tabulation, see C.J. Given-Wilson, *The Royal Household and the King's Affinity: Service, Politics and Finance in England 1360–1413* (1986), 205.

91 *The Wardrobe Book of William de Norwell*, xci–ii, 301–6. I have excluded from my calculation three clerks, Kilsby, Norwell and Charnels, who received robes at the bannerets' rate.

92 Given-Wilson, *The Royal Household and the King's Affinity*, 204–12, 221–2.

93 *Documents Illustrating the Crisis of 1297–8*, ed. M.C. Prestwich (Camden Soc., 4th ser., 24, 1980), 157; *The Siege of Carlaverock*, 3–11; Walker, *Lancastrian Affinity*, 14; A. Goodman, *John of Gaunt. The Exercise of Princely Power in Fourteenth-Century Europe* (1992), 213; N. Denholm-Young, *Seignorial Administration in England* (Oxford, 1937), 166–7.

94 Prestwich, *War, Politics and Finance*, 66; *Liber Quotidianus Contrarotularis Garderobae*, 195, 197, 200; BL MS Stowe 553, ff. 56–62; E 36/204, ff. 99–100; E 101/393/11, ff. 79–81, 84v; J.W. Sherborne, 'Indentured Retinues and English Expeditions to France, 1369–1380', *EHR*, 79 (1964), 738; C.T. Allmand, *Henry V* (1992), 210.

95 For recent discussion, see S.L. Waugh, 'Tenure to Contract: lordship and clientage in thirteenth-century England', *EHR*, 101 (1986), 811–38; P.R. Coss, 'Bastard Feudalism Revised', *Past and Present*, 125 (1989), 27–64; D. Crouch, D.A. Carpenter and P.R. Coss, 'Debate: Bastard Feudalism Revised', *Past and Present*, 131 (1991), 165–203.

96 H. Gough, *Scotland in 1298* (Paisley, 1898), 207, 209, 213; C 67/2; C 81/1720, no. 107; E 101/612/12, 6.

97 P. Morgan, *War and Society in Medieval Cheshire, 1277–1403* (Chetham Soc., 3rd ser., 34, 1987), 138, 150–51.

98 BL Add Roll 64320.

99 F.M. Stenton, *The First Century of English Feudalism* (Oxford, 1932), 140, 273–4; *Orderic Vitalis*, ii. 260–62.

100 Cited by J.M.W. Bean, *From Lord to Patron: Lordship in Late Medieval England* (Manchester, 1989), 144.

101 *Histoire de Guillaume le Maréchal*, ii. 312–13.

102 Bean, *From Lord to Patron*, 157; S.K. Walker, *The Lancastrian Affinity* (Oxford, 1990), 11.

103 Stenton, *First Century of English Feudalism*, 176–89.

104 J.C. Holt, *The Northerners* (Oxford, 1961), 51.

105 D. Crouch, *William Marshal. Court, Career and Chivalry in the Angevin Empire 1147–1219* (1990), 138.

106 Waugh, 'Tenure to Contract: Lordship and Clientage in Thirteenth-Century England', 826; D. Williams, 'Simon de Montfort and his Adherents', *England in the Thirteenth Century*, ed. W.M. Ormrod (Grantham, 1985), 173.

107 Saul, *Knights and Esquires*, 69–71, 83; Walker, *Lancastrian Affinity*, 27; Morgan, *Medieval Cheshire*, 150–51.

108 C81/1722/74; C 67/16.

109 Prestwich, *War, Politics and Finance*, 64–5; Saul, *Knights and Esquires*, 83; C 67/15.

110 Morgan, *War and Society in Medieval Cheshire*, 154; Walker, *The Lancastrian Affinity*, 48–50.

111 A.J. Pollard, *John Talbot and the War in France 1427–1453* (1983), 83–101.

112 *Histoire de Guillaume le Maréchal*, i. ll. 3381–423.

113 Prestwich, *War, Politics and Finance*, 46–7; K.B. McFarlane, 'An Indenture of Agreement between two English Knights of Mutual Aid and Counsel in Peace and War, 5 December 1298', *BIHR*, 38 (1965), 200–10.

114 P. Chaplais, *Piers Gaveston, Edward II's Adoptive Brother* (Oxford, 1994), 6–22.

115 K.B. McFarlane, 'A Business Partnership in War and Administration, 1421–45' *EHR*, 78 (1963), 290–310; J.C. Bridge,

'Two Cheshire Soldiers of Fortune of the XIV Century: Sir Hugh Calveley & Sir Robert Knollys', *Journal of the Chester Archaeological Society* 14 (1908), 161, for the tomb, but not this conclusion about it. For other examples of Cheshire knights entering into brotherhood agreements, see Morgan, *War and Society in Medieval Cheshire*, 166–7.

116 *Liber Quotidianus Contrarotulatoris Garderobae*, 200, 207; E 101/393/11, f. 85v.

117 *Siege of Carlaverock*, ed. Nicolas, 4; *Baker*, 82.

118 M. Chibnall, 'Military Service in Normandy before 1066', *ANW*, 29, 35–6; M. Bennett, 'Wace and Warfare', *ANW*, 243, 247; Bennett, '*La Règle du Temple* as a Military Manual, or How to Deliver a Cavalry Charge', *Studies in Medieval History presented to R. Allen Brown*, ed. C. Harper-Bill, C.J. Holdsworth and J.L. Nelson (Woodbridge, 1989), 14–15; *Histoire des ducs de Normandie et des rois d'Angleterre*, ed. F. Michel (Paris, 1840), 173. For a broader discussion of *conrois* and retinues, see J.F. Verbruggen, *The Art of Warfare in Western Europe during the Middle Ages* (Amsterdam, 1977), 72–6.

119 J.H. Round, *Feudal England* (1895), 206–8. A.L. Poole, *Obligations of Society in the XII and XIII Centuries* (Oxford, 1946), 50–51, argued against Round. He suggested that the term *constabularia* might apply to any body of men, but that in military terms it, and *constabularius*, applied solely to substantial bodies of infantry. His case is confused and unconvincing; there is no reason why there should not have been *constabularia* of cavalry just as there were of infantry.

120 *Pipe Roll, 20 Henry II*, 34, 56, 63, 125; *Expugnatio Hibernica*, 168; T.K. Keefe, *Feudal Assessments and the Political Community under Henry II and his Sons* (Berkeley and Los Angeles, 1983), 70.

121 S.D. Church, 'The Earliest English Muster Roll, 18/19

December 1215', *Historical Research*, 67 (1994), 2, 8–17; E 101/13/35, no. 16.

122 *Adae Murimuth, Continuatio Chronicarum*, 206.

123 M. Bennett, '*La Règle du Temple* as a Military Manual, 15; R.C. Smail, *Crusading Warfare* (Cambridge, 1956), 109.

124 For the identification problem, see Marks, 'Sir Geoffrey Luttrell and some Companions: Images of Chivalry', 345.

125 M. Mallett, *Mercenaries and their Masters* (1974), 148; *Chronique de Jean Froissart*, v. 36, 46.

126 P. Contamine, *Guerre, état et société à la fin du moyen âge. Etudes sur les armées des rois de France 1337–1494* (Paris, 1972), 278.

127 J.E. Morris, *The Welsh Wars of Edward I* (Oxford, 1901), 159, 163.

128 *Liber Quotidianus Contrarotolatoris Garderobae*, 195ff.; BL MS Stowe 553, f. 56ff.; E 101/20/25.

129 E 36/204, ff. 102v, 103.

130 E 101/393/11, f. 79.

131 Sherborne, 'Indentured Retinues and English Expeditions to France, 1369–1380', 722, 729–30, 732. The problems Gaunt faced in recruiting bannerets and knights is noted by Walker, *The Lancastrian Affinity*, 52.

132 Sherborne, 'Indentured Retinues and English Expeditions to France, 1369–1380', 738.

133 Figures calculated from N.H. Nicolas, *The History of the Battle of Agincourt* (1827), 333ff.

134 Allmand, *Henry V*, 206.

135 A. Curry, 'English Armies in the Fifteenth Century', *AAF*, 47; M.G.A. Vale, *English Gascony, 1399–1453* (Oxford, 1970), 110; M. Jones, 'John Beaufort, duke of Somerset and the French expedition of 1443', *Patronage, the Crown and The Provinces*, ed. R.A. Griffiths (Gloucester, 1981), 92, 100.

136 S.M. Wright, *The Derbyshire Gentry in the Fifteenth Century* (Derbyshire Record Soc., viii, 1983), 8.

137 See below, 65–6.

138 J.E. Morris, 'Mounted Infantry in Medieval Warfare', *TRHS*, 3rd ser., viii (1914), 77–84.

139 *The War of Saint-Sardos (1323–1325)*, ed. P. Chaplais (Camden Soc., 3rd. ser., lxxxvii), 161.

140 *Diplomatic Documents preserved in the Public Record Office*, i. 1–4; Prestwich, 'Military Household of the Norman Kings', 103.

141 *Expugnatio Hibernica*, 92–3.

142 R.F. Walker, 'Hubert de Burgh and Wales, 1218–1232', *EHR*, 87 (1972), 475, 481.

143 Prestwich, *War, Politics and Finance*, 68.

144 A.E. Prince, 'The strength of English Armies in the Reign of Edward III', *EHR*, 46 (1931), 357, 361, 364, 368; A. Ayton, 'The English Army and the Normandy Campaign of 1346', *England and Normandy in the Middle Ages*, ed. D. Bates and A. Curry (1994), 267; Sherborne, 'Indentured Retinues and English Expeditions to France, 1369–1380', 729–30; Allmand, *Henry V*, 210. For a careful criticism of the reliability of pay rolls, see Ayton, *Knights and Warhorses*, 138–55.

145 E 101/68/5.

146 E 101/10/13.

147 *The Controversy between Sir Richard Scrope and Sir Robert Grosvenor in the Court of Chivalry*, ed. N.H. Nicolas (London, 1832), i. 51, 53, 57, 74, 181–2.

148 *Documents illustrating the Crisis of 1297–8*, 7.

149 Powicke, *Military Obligation*, 174–5.

150 A.E. Goodman, 'Responses to Requests in Yorkshire for Military Service under Henry V', *Northern History*, 17 (1981), 240–52.

3 Military Obligation

1 F.H. Russell, *The Just War in the Middle Ages* (Cambridge, 1975), provides a full analysis.

2 S. Reynolds, *Fiefs and Vassals* (Oxford, 1994), provides a very important critique of ideas about 'feudalism'.

3 This is the theory of, most notably, C.W. Hollister, *Anglo-Saxon Military Institutions* (Oxford, 1962).

4 N.P. Brooks, 'The development of military obligations in eighth- and ninth-century England', *England before the Conquest*, ed. P. Clemoes and K. Hughes (Cambridge, 1971), 82.

5 *Domesday Book*, i. 56, 172. R.A. Brown, *Origins of English Feudalism* (1973), 50–51, argues that the difference in penalties reflects the different social status of those involved, but it is not clear that this was the case.

6 My argument owes much to the work of Abels, *Lordship and Military Obligation in Anglo-Saxon England*. See also below, 62, for some further discussion of the Berkshire Domesday entry.

7 *Select Charters and other Illustrations of English Constitutional History*, ed. W. Stubbs, revised by H.W.C. Davis (9th edn, Oxford, 1921), 97.

8 J.H. Round, *Feudal England* (1895), 238. For an excellent recent summary of the issues regarding the introduction of knight service, see B. Golding, *Conquest and Colonisation. The Normans in Britain 1066–1100* (1994), 119–45.

9 *The Red Book of the Exchequer*, ed. H. Hall (RS, 1896), i. 412.

10 Ibid., 206, 208.

11 Brown, *Origins of English Feudalism*, 66–71, discusses the five-hide unit. An attempt was made in the late thirteenth century on the Worcester estates to rationalise service on this basis, but it is clear that even here the five-hide unit was not standard.

12 J. Gillingham, 'The Introduction of Knight Service into England', *ANS*, 5 (1982), 53–87.

13 Simeon of Durham, *Symeonis Monachi Opera Omnia*, ed. T. Arnold (RS, 1882–5), i. 131.

14 J.C. Holt, 'The Introduction

of Knight-Service in England', *ANS*, 6 (1983), 89–96.

15 C.W. Hollister, *The Military Organisation of Norman England* (Oxford, 1965), 210–11.

16 M. Chibnall, 'Military service in Normandy before 1066', in *Anglo-Norman Warfare*, ed. M. Strickland (Woodbridge, 1992), 28–40. For a recent discussion of scutage rates, see Keefe, *Feudal Assessments and the Political Community*, 37–40, and see also his useful table on 30.

17 Stenton, *First Century of English Feudalism*, 177.

18 F. Barlow, *William Rufus* (1983), 370.

19 *Select Charters*, ed. Stubbs, 119.

20 *Chronicles of the Reigns of Stephen, Henry II and Richard I*, 193, 202; Round, *Feudal England*, 223–4.

21 Ibid., 46–7; *The Historical Works of Gervase of Canterbury*, i. 447.

22 Keefe, *Feudal Assessments and the Political Community*, 13–15.

23 Ibid., i. 275–6, 299, 308–10, 329, 369–71, 431.

24 Ibid., 288–91.

25 Ibid., 239–40.

26 Ibid., 301.

27 The *muntatores* are fully discussed by Suppe, *Military Institutions on the Welsh Marches*, 63–87.

28 Holt, 'Introduction of Knight Service', 104–5.

29 Stenton, *First Century of English Feudalism*, 175.

30 S. Harvey, 'The Knight and the Knight's Fee in England', *Past and Present*, 49 (1970). D.F. Fleming, 'Landholding by *Milites* in Domesday Book: a Revision', *ANS*, 13 (1990), 83–98, provides valuable comments and criticisms.

31 Stenton, *First Century of English Feudalism*, 168.

32 Poole, *Obligations of Society*, 57–76.

33 J.H. Round, *The King's Sergeants and Officers of State* (1911), 17.

34 *Chronica Rogeri de Houe-*

den, iv, ed. W. Stubbs (RS, 1871), 40.

35 S.K. Mitchell, *Studies in Taxation under John and Henry III* (Oxford, 1914), 97, 110; J.C. Holt, *Magna Carta* (2nd edn, Cambridge, 1992), 427. Part of the evidence for the new reduced quotas is provided by what Holt terms a 'roll of summonses' for the Poitou expedition of 1214, printed in *Pipe Roll, 17 John and Praestita Roll 14–18 John*, 101–3. This resembles later records of feudal musters.

36 N. Vincent, 'A Roll of Knights Summoned to Campaign in 1213', *Historical Research*, 66 (1993), 89–97.

37 *Pipe Roll, 12 John*, ed. C.F. Slade (ns xxvi, 1951) 14, 35; *Pipe Roll, 16 John*, ed. P.M. Barnes (ns xxxv, 1962), 112, 114.

38 Ibid., 74.

39 Curiously, Stubbs in his *Select Charters* (9th edn, 1921), 173–4, printed as a sample return to the 1166 inquiry the one example where service is stated to be *ad custum vestrum*, at the Crown's expense.

40 *Pipe Roll, 17 John and Praestita Roll, 14–18 John*, 77–80, 98.

41 For example, *Pipe Roll, 4 Henry III*, ed. B.E. Harris (PRS, 1987), 111–12; *Receipt and Issue Rolls, 26 Henry III*, ed. R.C. Stacey (PRS, 1992), 1, 9, 12, 39, 41, 50.

42 *Select Charters*, ed. Stubbs, 295 (Clause 16).

43 Mitchell, *Studies in Taxation*, 182–3.

44 J.S. Critchley, 'Summonses to Military Service early in the reign of Henry III', *EHR*, 85 (1971), 79–95. For the new quotas, I.J. Sanders, *Feudal Military Service in England* (Oxford, 1956), 59–90, 134.

45 *Close Rolls, 1261–4*, 276–7, 302–5, 377.

46 M.C. Prestwich, 'Cavalry Service in Early Fourteenth Century England', *War and Government in the Middle Ages*, ed. Gillingham and Holt, 148; Prestwich, *War, Politics and Finance*, 79–80; *Parliamentary*

Writs, ed. F. Palgrave (1827–34), II. i, 401–8.

47 C47/5/7; C47/22/3, no. 64.

48 C47/5/7.

49 Prestwich, 'Cavalry Service in Early Fourteenth-Century England', 149.

50 Prestwich, *War, Politics and Finance under Edward I*, 81; *Documents and Records Illustrating the History of Scotland*, ed. F. Palgrave (1837), 218–20.

51 Prestwich, 'Cavalry Service in Early Fourteenth Century England', 151–2; *War, Politics and Finance*, 75–6.

52 For example, in 1333 William La Zouche was summoned to come with as many men as he could provide, in fealty and homage: *Rotuli Scotiae*, i. 240.

53 M.C. Prestwich, 'Colonial Scotland', *Scotland and England 1286–1815*, ed. R.A. Mason (Edinburgh, 1987), 9.

54 R.F. Frame, 'Military Service in Ireland', *Medieval Frontier Societies*, ed. R.A. Bartlett and A. MacKay (Oxford, 1989), 105–7; R.A. Newhall, *The English Conquest of Normandy* (New Haven, 1924), 209–12; A. Curry, 'English Armies in the Fifteenth Century', *AAF*, 64.

55 The 1385 summons has been the subject of some controversy. See N.B. Lewis, 'The Last Medieval Summons of the English Feudal Levy, 13 June 1385', *EHR*, 73 (1958), 1–15; J.J.N. Palmer, 'The Last Summons of the Feudal Army in England', *EHR*, 83 (1968), 771–5.

56 *Select Charters*, ed. Stubbs, 184.

57 *Close Rolls, 1261–4*, 274.

58 *Parliamentary Writs*, i. 327.

59 *Documents Illustrating the Crisis of 1297–8*, 122.

60 Cited by Powicke, *Military Obligation*, 69.

61 For distraint, see above, 16.

62 Prestwich, *Edward I*, 197; Powicke, *Military Obligation*, 107–8.

63 Prestwich, *Documents Illustrating the Crisis of 1297–8*, 6–7, 108–9; *War, Politics and Finance*, 84–6; Powicke, *Military Obligation*, 111–12.

64 Prestwich, *War, Politics and Finance*, 88–90.
65 D.W. Burton, 'Requests for Prayers and Royal Propaganda under Edward I', *Thirteenth Century England III*, ed. Coss and Lloyd, 25–35.
66 Prestwich, 'Cavalry Service in Early Fourteenth-Century England', 154–6.
67 Ayton, 'The English Army and the Normandy Campaign of 1346', 24–5; Powicke, *Military Obligation*, 195–9.
68 *Pipe Roll, 16 John*, xv, 139; Holt, *Magna Carta*, 192–3.
69 *CDS*, ii, no. 1801.
70 Prestwich, *War, Politics and Finance*, 76.
71 *The Treatise of Walter of Milemete*, ed. M.R. James (Roxburghe Club, 1913), xvii, ff. 27b–30.

4 Rewards

1 M. Bennett, 'Wace and Warfare', *ANW*, 241.
2 *Gesta Stephani*, 204–7. See also the examples cited by Crouch, 'Debate: Bastard Feudalism Revised', 169.
3 *Expugnatio Hibernica*, 134–7; Round, *Feudal England*, 215–16; Prestwich, 'Military Household of the Norman Kings', 100; *Rotuli Normanniae in turri Londonensi asservati*, ed. T. Duffus Hardy (1835), 54.
4 *Documents Illustrative of English History in the Thirteenth and Fourteenth Centuries*, ed. Cole, 264, 266.
5 *Roll of Divers Accounts for the Early Years of the Reign of Henry III*, ed. F.A. Cazel, Jr (PRS, ns 44, 1982), 36.
6 R.C. Stacey, *Politics, Policy and Finance under Henry III, 1216–1245* (Oxford, 1987), 186; A. Lewis, 'Roger Leyburn and the Pacification of England, 1265–7', *EHR*, 54 (1939), 204.
7 *Historical Letters and Papers from Northern Registers*, ed. J. Raine (RS, 1873), 249.
8 See for example Walter de Mauny's pay, set out in *The Wardrobe Book of William de Norwell*, 331. He was paid as a banneret at 4s until 21 July 1338, and then at 8s until 16 November 1339. For wages tied to horse numbers, ibid., 353.
9 Prestwich, 'Cavalry Service in Early Fourteenth-Century England', *War and Government in the Middle Ages*, ed. Gillingham and Holt, 149.
10 Prince, 'Indenture System under Edward III', 292–3.
11 S.K. Walker, 'Profit and Loss in the Hundred Years War: the subcontracts of Sir John Strother, 1374', *BIHR*, 58 (1985), 103–4.
12 *Pipe Roll, 20 Henry II*, 67.
13 *Rotuli de Liberate ac de Misis et Praestitis*, 182–5; see above, 69.
14 *Book of Prests 1294–5*, ed. E.B. Fryde (Oxford, 1962).
15 *The Wardrobe Book of William de Norwell*, 425.
16 E 159/75, m. 5d.
17 Prestwich, *War, Politics and Finance under Edward I*, 166.
18 E 101/7/11.
19 E 101/20/25.
20 E 36/204, ff. 123, 138; E 101/25/19.
21 Walker, *Lancastrian Affinity*, 69.
22 J.W. Sherborne, 'The Cost of English Warfare with France in the Later Fourteenth Century', *BIHR*, 50 (1977), 145.
23 Nicolas, *Agincourt*, appendix, 16–17.
24 Pollard, *John Talbot*, 109, 111.
25 *Liber Quotidianus Contrarotulatoris Garderobae*, 199.
26 S.D. Lloyd, 'The Lord Edward's Crusade, 1270–2: its setting and significance', *War and Government in the Middle Ages*, ed. Gillingham and Holt, 126–7; H.G. Richardson and G.O. Sayles, *The Governance of Medieval England* (Edinburgh, 1963), 463–5. The translation given there is unfortunately inaccurate.
27 Prestwich, *Edward I*, 148–9.
28 'Private Indentures for Life Service in Peace and War', ed. Jones and Walker, 35–6.
29 D. Crouch, 'A Norman "conventio" and bonds of lordship in the middle ages', *Law and Government in Medieval England and Normandy*, ed. Garnett and Hudson, 315–18.
30 See the references given above, 353 n. 95. As is often the case in such debates, much in the argument hinges on the precise definition of terms.
31 Morgan, *War and Society in Medieval Cheshire*, 18–19.
32 'Private Indentures for Life Service', ed. Jones and Walker, 37–8, 51–3, 54–5; N.B. Lewis, 'An Early Indenture of Military Service, 27 July 1287', *BIHR*, 13 (1935), 85–9; Denholm-Young, *Seignorial Administration in England*, 167–8; J.M.W. Bean, *From Lord to Patron: Lordship in Late Medieval England* (Manchester, 1989); and for a useful recent summary, Coss, *The Knight in Medieval England 1000–1400*, 114–17.
33 *Documents Illustrating the Crisis of 1297–8 in England*, ed. Prestwich, 146; Bean, *From Lord to Patron*, 47–8; Saul, *Knights and Esquires*, 96–7.
34 B.D. Lyon, *From Fief to Indenture* (Cambridge, Mass., 1957), 206.
35 Lyon, *From Fief to Indenture*, argues forcibly that the resemblance between the *fief rente* and the indenture was not coincidental. For him, the *fief rente* provided the link between feudal service and later contractual service. For a recent discussion, see Bean, *From Lord to Patron*, 131–48.
36 *Scotland in 1298*, ed. H. Gough (Paisley, 1888), 64–5; Prestwich, *War, Politics and Finance under Edward I*, 68–9, 73, 76.
37 E 101/68/1, nos 11, 12.
38 J.R.S. Phillips, *Aymer de Valence, Earl of Pembroke 1307–1324* (Oxford, 1972), 148–50, 312–15.
39 N.B. Lewis, 'Recruitment and Organisation of a Contract Army. May to November 1337', *BIHR*, 37 (1964), 1–19.
40 E 101/68/3, no. 45.
41 *Wardrobe Book of William de Norwell*, 325–6, 331. The

record makes it clear that in these cases service was according to a *convencionem indentatam*. The belief of the editors of the account book (p. xcv) that all who served did so under contract seems unwarranted.

42 M.C. Prestwich, 'English Armies in the Early Stages of the Hundred Years War: a Scheme in 1341', *BIHR*, 56 (1983), 102–13.

43 E 101/68/3, no. 49. Lump sum contracts were entered into by John de Coupland for the custody of Berwick and Roxburgh castles in 1356 and 1361: E 101/68/3, nos 75, 81.

44 Ayton, *Knights and Warhorses*, 110–11; A.E. Prince, 'The Indenture System under Edward III', *Historical Essays presented to James Tait*, ed. J.G. Edwards, V.H. Galbraith, E.F. Jacob (Manchester, 1933), 293; E 101/68/3 no. 62.

45 E 101/25/33.

46 E 101/68/4, no. 90. Prince, 'The Indenture System under Edward III', 293–4.

47 E 101/404/24.

48 Walker, *The Lancastrian Affinity*, 39–80.

49 E 101/68/5/107.

50 A. Goodman, 'The Military Subcontracts of Sir Hugh Hastings, 1380', *EHR*, 95 (1980), 114–20; Walker, 'Profit and Loss in the Hundred Years War: the subcontracts of Sir John Strother, 1374', 100–106.

51 K. Fowler, *The King's Lieutenant, Henry of Grosmont, First Duke of Lancaster 1310–1361* (1969), 57.

52 E 101/32/30, mm. 1, 6.

53 E 101/38/27.

54 M. Jones, *Ducal Brittany* (Oxford, 1970), 154.

55 Pollard, *John Talbot*, 73.

56 E 101/68/3, no. 64. The practice was not, of course, unknown on the Continent.

57 *Diplomatic Documents preserved in the Public Record Office*, i, *1101–1272*, ed. P. Chaplais (1964), 2.

58 *Pipe Roll, 5 Richard I*, 92, 132.

59 Waugh, 'Tenure to Contract', 827; Jones, 'An Indenture

between Robert, Lord Mohaut and Sir John Bracebridge', 389.

60 E 101/68/3, no. 66.

61 E 101/101/14.

62 Ayton, *Knights and Warhorses*, 74–5, discusses this problem.

63 E 101/28/70.

64 *CDS*, iii, no. 1378. Ayton, *Knights and Warhorses*, 104–5, argues that *restor* was dropped from the terms of service in 1334 and 1335.

65 Ayton, *Knights and Warhorses*, 120–37; 'Indentures of Retinue with John of Gaunt, Duke of Lancaster, enrolled in Chancery 1367–1399', ed. N.B. Lewis, *Camden Miscellany 22* (Camden Soc., 4th ser., 1, 1964); E 101/68/5, nos 101, 103, 106; E 101/32/30.

66 I have argued this case more fully in *War, Politics and Finance under Edward I*, 68–76.

67 Prestwich, 'Cavalry Service in Early Fourteenth Century England', 153.

68 *Le Bel*, i. 155.

69 *Pipe Roll, 4 Henry III*, ed. B.E. Harris, xii–xiii; *Roll of Divers Accounts for the Early Years of Henry III*, 34; *Pipe Roll, 5 Richard I*, 148; *Rotuli de Liberate ac de Misis et Praestitis*, 223.

70 *The Treatise of Walter of Milemete*, ff. 27b–30.

71 Jones, *Ducal Brittany*, 49.

72 *Pierre de Langtoft: le Règne d'Edouard Ier*, ed. J.-C. Thiolier (Créteil, 1989), 282–3.

73 M.C. Prestwich, 'Royal Patronage under Edward I', *Thirteenth Century England I*, ed. P.R. Coss and S.D. Lloyd (Woodbridge, 1986), 47.

74 R.R. Davies, *Conquest, Coexistence and Change: Wales, 1063–1415* (Oxford, 1987), 363, 371.

75 I have discussed Edward's land policy in Scotland in a little more detail in 'Colonial Scotland: the English in Scotland under Edward I', *Scotland and England 1286–1815*, ed. Mason, 6–17.

76 Prince, 'Indenture System under Edward III', 295; E 101/68/4, no. 75; E 101/68/5, nos 95ff.

77 C.T. Allmand, *Henry V*,

198–204; R. Massey, 'The Land Settlement in Lancastrian Normandy', *Property and Politics: Essays in Later Medieval English History*, ed. A.J. Pollard (Gloucester, 1984), 76–96.

78 *Black Prince's Register*, iv. 196–8, 291.

79 *CCR 1346–1349*, 453.

80 *Gesta Stephani*, 94–5.

81 C.J. Neville, 'A Plea Roll of Edward I's Army in Scotland, 1296', *Miscellany of the Scottish History Society*, xi (1990), nos 50, 80, 149, 179, 181, 185.

82 Nicholson, *Edward III and the Scots*, 174.

83 *Rot. Pat.*, i. 17, 21, 24.

84 Prestwich, *War, Politics and Finance*, 263–4.

85 D. Hay, 'The Division of the Spoils of War in Fourteenth-Century England', *TRHS*, 5th ser., 4 (1954), 95–9, 108–9.

86 E 101/68/3, no. 66; Hay, 'The Division of the Spoils of War', 94.

87 Ayton, *Knights and Warhorses*, 129–30; 'Indentures of Retinue with John of Gaunt, Duke of Lancaster', ed. Lewis, 88.

88 E 101/334/2, schedule attached.

89 Hay, 'The Division of the Spoils of War', 107; G.A. Holmes, *The Good Parliament* (Oxford, 1975), 37.

90 *CCR 1346–1349*, 81; *CPR 1345–1348*, 337.

91 F.M. Powicke, *The Loss of Normandy* (2nd edn, Manchester, 1960), 363.

92 *Documents illustrating the Crisis of 1297–8 in England*, ed. Prestwich, 182, 190.

93 H.S. Lucas, *The Low Countries and the Hundred Years War, 1326–1347* (Ann Arbor, 1929), 364; *Foedera, Conventiones, Litterae etc.*, ed. T. Rymer, rev. A. Clarke *et al.* (1816–69), II, ii. 1123. For diplomatic reasons, Guy was released in 1340 without the king demanding a ransom from Flanders.

94 G.L. Harriss, *King, Parliament and Public Finance in Medieval England to 1360* (Oxford, 1975), 490; M. Jones, 'The ran-

som of Jean de Bretagne, count of Penthièvre', *BIHR*, 45 (1972), 10, 25.

95 'The Ransom of John II, 1360–70', ed. D.M. Broome, *Camden Miscellany*, xiv (Camden Soc., 1926), provides details of the payment of the ransom.

96 *Foedera*, III, i. 467.

97 *Black Prince's Register*, iv. 339, 379, 381.

98 *Oeuvres de Froissart*, ed. Kervyn de Lettenhove (1867–77), xviii, 484.

99 P.-C. Timbal, *La guerre de cent ans vue à travers les registres du parlement (1337–1369)* (Paris, 1961), 307–15.

100 E. Perroy, 'Gras profits et rançons pendant la guerre de Cent Ans; l'affaire du comte de Denia', *Mélanges d'histoire du Moyen Age dédiés à la mémoire de Louis Halphen* (Paris, 1951), 574–80; A. Rogers, 'Hoton versus Shakell: a ransom case in the court of chivalry, 1390–5', *Nottingham Medieval Studies*, vi (1962), 74–108; vii (1963), 53–78.

101 *Rotuli de Liberate ac de Misis et Praestitis*, 118.

102 *Northern Petitions*, ed. C.M. Fraser (Surtees Soc., 194, 1981), 179.

103 *Oeuvres de Froissart*, ed. Kervyn de Lettenhove (1867–77), xviii, 554–6.

104 *The Complete Peerage*, ed. G.E. Cockayne, rev. V. Gibbs *et al.* (1910–57), vi, 618–19.

105 *CDS*, iii. no. 611; Soc. of Antiquaries MS 121, p. 63; BL Stowe MS 553, f. 69.

106 Pollard, *John Talbot*, 113–14.

107 J.A. Tuck, 'War and Society in the Medieval North', *Northern History*, 21 (1985), 48, 50.

108 Jones, *Ducal Brittany*, 166–8.

109 Timbal, *La guerre de cent ans vue à travers les registres du parlement*, 283–302. This incident led to a very complex lawsuit.

110 Holmes, *Good Parliament*, 38.

111 E 101/8/4, m. 2.

112 *CCR 1346–1349*, 83. For the exclusion of certain types of action, see ibid., 85.

113 E 101/32/39.

114 J.S. Critchley, 'The Early History of the Writ of Protection', *BIHR*, 45 (1972), 196–213; S.D. Lloyd, *English Society and the Crusade 1216–1307* (Oxford, 1988), 164–6.

115 *CPR 1346–1349*, 314–15; Morgan, *War and Society in Medieval Cheshire*, 155.

116 SC1/39, 174.

117 *Documents Illustrating the Crisis of 1297–8*, ed. Prestwich, 141–2; *Documents Illustrative of the History of Scotland*, ed. J. Stevenson (Edinburgh, 1870), ii. 222–4.

118 P. Dixon, *Aydon Castle* (1988), 7–14.

119 K.B. McFarlane, 'The Investment of Sir John Fastolf's Profits of War', *TRHS*, 5th ser., 7 (1957), 91–116.

120 Pollard, *John Talbot*, 102–21.

121 *The History of Parliament. The House of Commons, 1386–1421*, ed. J.S. Roskell, L. Clark and C. Rawcliffe (Stroud, 1992), iv, 67–8.

122 *Pipe Roll, 17 John and Praestita Roll 14–18 John*, 79; Morris, *Welsh Wars of Edward I*, 68; H.J. Hewitt, 'The Organisation of War', *The Hundred Years War*, ed. K. Fowler (1971), 78.

123 *Orderic Vitalis*, vi. 294.

5 Infantry

1 *The Holkham Picture Bible Book*, ed. W.O. Hassall (1954), f. 40. It is irrelevant, but intriguing, to note from his comment on another picture, showing Noah's Ark with a drowned couple in the foreground, that an earlier editor, M.R. James, could not distinguish between naked male and female bodies.

2 *Orderic Vitalis*, vi, 348, 470.

3 *Expugnatio Hibernica*, 140–41.

4 *Pipe Roll, 5 Richard I*, 99, 148; *Pipe Roll, 7 Richard I*, ed. D.M. Stenton (PRS, ns 6, 1929) 205.

5 *Chancellor's Roll, 8 Richard I*, ed. D.M. Stenton (PRS, ns 7, 1930), xvii–xviii. 60, 88.

6 Morris, *Welsh Wars of Edward I*, 131–2, 160, 175, 188, 190.

7 Ibid., 209; Prestwich, *War, Politics and Finance*, 92–3.

8 Ibid., 94–9.

9 G.W.S. Barrow, *Robert Bruce and the Community of the Realm of Scotland* (1965), 293–4.

10 BL Stowe MS 553.

11 Ayton, 'The English Army and the Normandy Campaign of 1346', *England and Normandy in the Middle Ages*, 266–7.

12 Prince, 'The Strength of English Armies in the Reign of Edward III', 361, 363, 369–70; Sherborne, 'Indentured Retinues and English Expeditions in France, 1369–1380', 722, 724, 728–9.

13 Allmand, *Henry V*, 210; Newhall, *The English Conquest of Normandy*, 192; *Letters and Papers illustrative of the Wars in France during the reign of Henry VI*, ed. J. Stevenson (RS, 1861), 403–14; M. Jones, 'John Beaufort, duke of Somerset and the French expedition of 1443', *Patronage, the Crown and the Provinces in Later Medieval England*, ed. R.A. Griffiths (1981), 92, 99.

14 Above, 58.

15 Hollister, *Anglo-Saxon Military Institutions*, 29.

16 Abels, *Lordship and Military Obligation*, 176–8; *Select Charters*, ed. Stubbs, 98.

17 *Rotuli Scotiae*, i. 422, cited by Prince, 'The Army and Navy', 355.

18 Powicke, *Military Obligation*, 39–41; F. Barlow, *William Rufus*, 78, 80; *Select Charters*, ed. Stubbs, 109. For a sceptical view, see H.G. Richardson and G.O. Sayles, *The Governance of Medieval England* (Edinburgh, 1963), 54.

19 *Gesta Stephani*, 32–4.

20 Round, *Feudal England*, 223–4; P. Latimer, 'Henry II's campaign against the Welsh in 1165', *Welsh History Review*, 14 (1989), 547–51.

21 *Select Charters*, ed. Stubbs, 182–4. The assize is discussed by Powicke, *Military Obligation*, 54–6. The text puts the wealth qualification at sixteen marks, but this is surely an error for fifteen, as suggested by Richardson and Sayles, *The Governance of Medieval England*, 95n., 439n.

22 Powicke, *Military Obligation*, 58–60.

23 *Close Rolls 1237–42*, 482–3; *Select Charters*, ed. Stubbs, 363–5; Powicke, *Military Obligation*, 82–95.

24 *Select Charters*, ed. Stubbs, 355; Powicke, *Military Obligation*, 86, 92–3.

25 Hollister, *Anglo-Saxon Military Institutions*, 31–7.

26 Suppe, *Military Institutions of the Welsh Marches*, 125–42, provides the fullest account of Welsh military obligation.

27 *Select Charters*, ed. Stubbs, 463–6.

28 Prestwich, *War, Politics and Finance*, 99–100.

29 Ibid., 101–2; J.R. Maddicott, *The English Peasantry and the Demands of the Crown 1294–1341* (*Past and Present*, Supplement 1, 1975), 42–3.

30 Prestwich, *Three Edwards*, 69, citing SC1/28, 107; *Cal. Chancery Warrants*, 437.

31 *CCR 1341–3*, 369–70.

32 C 47/2/44.

33 *Select Cases in the Court of King's Bench, Edward III*, ed. G.O. Sayles (Selden Soc., 82, 1965), vi, 17–18.

34 B.W. McLane, *The 1341 Royal Inquest in Lincolnshire* (Lincoln Record Soc. 78, 1987), nos 686, 689–90, 692; *CPR 1345–8*, 112–13.

35 Lewis, 'The Recruitment and Organization of a Contract Army, 1337', 12; *Wardrobe Book of William de Norwell*, 356–62.

36 E 101/393/11, f. 115–115v.

37 The point is rightly emphasised by Ayton, *Knights and Warhorses*, 17.

38 *Vita Edwardi Secundi*, ed. N. Denholm-Young (1957), 94.

39 Prestwich, *War, Politics and Finance*, 104–5; *CPR 1345–8*, 224; Wrottesley, *Crécy and Calais*, 261.

40 For 1322, see BL Stowe MS 553, f. 81.

41 M.J. Bennett, *Community, Class and Careerism: Cheshire and Lancashire Society in the Age of Sir Gawain and the Green Knight* (Cambridge, 1983), 164, 174.

42 *Giraldi Cambrensis Opera*, ed. J.F. Dimock (RS, 1868), vi, 53–4, 180–81.

43 Neville, 'A plea roll of Edward I's army in Scotland, 1296', nos 111, 121.

44 *Pipe Roll 5, Richard I*, 99.

45 *The Wardrobe Book of William de Norwell*, 360; E 101/23/22; E 101/393/11, f. 115v.

46 *Liber Quotidianus Contrarotulatoris Garderobae*, 184, and see entries in later accounts, such as E 101/11/15.

47 Prestwich, *War, Politics and Finance*, 95–8; *Liber Quotidianus Contrarotulatoris Garderobae*, 253; SC1/61/63.

48 BL MS Stowe 553, ff. 80–81.

49 *The Wardrobe Book of William de Norwell*, 356; E 101/393/11, f. 115.

50 J. Bradbury, *The Medieval Archer* (Woodbridge, 1985), 27–57, provides an excellent discussion of the role of infantry, and above all archers, in this period.

51 P. Contamine, *War in the Middle Ages*, trans. M. Jones (Oxford, 1984), 71–2.

52 *Pipe Roll, 7 John*, xxii, xxv.

53 *Pipe Roll, 8 John*, xxvii; R. Payne-Gallwey, *The Crossbow* (2nd edn, 1958), 60, 62–4, 73–5.

54 Morris, *Welsh Wars of Edward I*, 90, 188.

55 Bradbury, *English Archer*, 81–2; 'Extracts from the Coram Rege Rolls and Pleas of the Crown, Staffordshire, of the reign of Edward II, a.d. 1307 to a.d. 1327', ed. G. Wrottesley, *Collections for a History of Staffordshire*, 10 (Staffordshire Record Soc., 1889), 16–17.

56 See for example BL Cotton MS Nero C.VIII, f. 54v., for the purchase of 180 dozen bows of Spanish yew in Edward II's reign, at a cost of £36.

57 The best evidence for the longbow is provided by the surviving examples from the sixteenth-century wreck of the *Mary Rose*. The estimates of draw weights and rate of shooting have been kindly provided by Robert Hardy. For the manufacture of bows, and other technical details, see R. Hardy, *Longbow* (revised edn, 1982), 173–236. See also for recent comment, C.J. Rogers, 'The Military Revolutions of the Hundred Years' War', *Journal of Military History*, 57 (1993), 250.

58 Black, *A Military Revolution?*, 61.

59 I write from limited practical experience. The first time I fired a .303 Short Model Lee Enfield, fitted with aperture sights, I achieved a score of 34 out of 35; my only attempt to shoot with a bow was too disastrous to be worth setting out in detail.

60 Morris, *Welsh Wars of Edward I*, 15–16, 32–4; Bradbury, *Medieval Archer*, 15–16, translates Gerald of Wales. I am indebted to the arguments he puts elsewhere, notably 83–4, against Morris's thesis.

61 Archers from the Weald were specifically noted in one of the accounts for Edward I's second Welsh war, E 101/3/30.

62 E 101/12/17 is the infantry payroll for this campaign. For an account of the battle, see *The Chronicle of Walter of Guisborough*, ed. H. Rothwell (Camden Soc., 89, 1957), 325–8.

63 BL Add. MS 8835, f. 73. Five slingers from Nottingham were present on the 1359 campaign in France; E 101/393/11, f. 116.

64 Prestwich, *War, Politics and Finance*, 101.
65 BL Stowe MS 553, ff. 80v–81; J.E. Morris, 'Mounted Infantry', 89.
66 These measures are conveniently summarised by Powicke, *Military Obligation*, 142–7.
67 C47/2/48, no. 26.
68 Morris, 'Mounted Infantry', 91.
69 M.C. Prestwich, 'English Armies in the Early Stages of the Hundred Years War: a Scheme in 1341', *BIHR*, 56 (1983), 108, 112; C47/2/31.
70 *Expugnatio Hibernica*, 50–51, 248–9, 298.
71 Powicke, *Military Obligation*, 53; *Pipe Roll, 5 Richard I*, 148; *Pipe Roll, 3 John*, 137. The term for archer used here is *archerius*, rather than *sagittarius*, as was usual later.
72 Bradbury, *Medieval Archer*, 50.
73 R. Nicholson, *Edward III and the Scots* (Oxford, 1965), 175–6; Prince, 'The Strength of English Armies in the Reign of Edward III', 355.
74 *Foedera*, II, ii. 705.
75 For hobelars, see above, 52.
76 Prince, 'The Strength of English Armies', 364, 366; Goodman, *Wars of the Roses*, 175–6.
77 *Gesta Henrici Quinti*, 70–71; Nicolas, *Agincourt*, 42; Bradbury, *Medieval Archer*, 131; *Chroniques par Waurin*, ii. 212; M. Bennett, 'The Development of Battle Tactics in the Hundred Years War', *AAF*, 15.
78 *The London Eyre of 1276*, ed. M. Weinbaum (London Record Soc., 1976), no. 18; *Foedera*, III, ii, 79; C.G. Cruickshank, *Elizabeth's Army* (2nd edn, Oxford, 1966), 105.
79 *Philippe de Commynes Memoirs*, trans. M. Jones (Harmondsworth, 1972), 72.
80 C47/2/58.
81 W. Hudson, 'Norwich Militia in the Fourteenth Century', *Norfolk and Norwich Archaeological Society*, xiv (1901), 284, 290, 294, 306–7, 312–14.

82 Maddicott, *The English Peasantry and the Demands of the Crown 1294–1341*, 38–41.
83 *CCR 1243–46*, 538; *CPR 1358–61*, 221–2; Hewitt, *Organisation of War*, 69; E 101/385/35; *Foedera*, III, ii. 911.
84 Newhall, *The English Conquest of Normandy*, 259, 261.
85 Prestwich, *War, Politics and Finance*, 101; Morris, *Welsh Wars*, 97; Prestwich, *Edward I*, 195; A.E. Prince, 'The Army and Navy', *The English Government at Work, 1327–1336*, i, ed. J.F. Willard and W.A. Morris (Cambridge, Mass., 1940), 362–3; G. Wrottesley, *Crécy and Calais* (1898), 148; H.J. Hewitt, *The Black Prince's Expedition of 1355–1356* (Manchester, 1958), 15–16; Nicolas, *Agincourt*, appendix, 35; A. Goodman, *The Wars of the Roses: Military Activity and English Society, 1452–97* (1981), 146; Cruikshank, *Elizabeth's Army*, 91.
86 *Liber Quotidianus Contrarotulatoris Garderobae*, 257–9, 266; E 101/393/11, ff. 115v–17.
87 Powicke, *Military Obligation*, 59–60, 92–3; Prestwich, *War, Politics and Finance*, 139.
88 *Chronicon Henrici Knighton*, ii. 109; *The Anonimalle Chronicle 1333 to 1381*, ed. V.H. Galbraith (Manchester, 1970), 185–6.
89 For a detailed discussion, see Hewitt, *Organisation of War under Edward III*, 1–27; J.R. Alban, 'English Coastal Defence: some Fourteenth-Century Modifications within the System', *Patronage, the Crown and the Provinces in Later Medieval England*, ed. R.A. Griffiths (Gloucester, 1981), 57–78.
90 E 101/385/35.
91 Prestwich, *The Three Edwards*, 102–3.
92 Bridge, 'Two Cheshire Soldiers of Fortune of the XIV Century: Sir Hugh Calveley & Sir Robert Knollys', 170.
93 Morgan, *War and Society in Medieval Cheshire, 1277–1403*, 134.
94 *Letters and Papers Illustrative of the Wars of the English in*

France during the Reign of Henry the Sixth, ed. J. Stevenson (RS, 1861), 421–2.

6 Mercenaries

1 Roger of Howden, *The Chronicle of the Reigns of Henry II and Richard*, ed. W. Stubbs (RS, 1867), ii. p. cviii.
2 See, for example, Hollister, *Military Organisation of Norman England*, 167, where the definition of mercenary is deliberately broadened to include all who fought for pay. See also M. Chibnall, 'Mercenaries and the *Familia Regis* under Henry I', *ANW*, 84–92.
3 J.O. Prestwich, 'War and Finance in the Anglo-Norman State', *ANW*, 59–83.
4 Richardson and Sayles, *The Governance of Medieval England*, 75; Simeon of Durham, *Gesta Regum*, ii. 310; *Gesta Stephani*, 112–13, 130–1, 154–5, 188–9.
5 *Gesta Stephani*, 232–3.
6 Round, *Feudal England*, 221–2; Richardson and Sayles, *The Governance of Medieval England*, 72.
7 *Jordan Fantosme's Chronicle*, ed. R.C. Johnston (Oxford, 1981), 73.
8 J. Boussard, 'Les mercenaires au xiie siècle: Henri II Plantagenet et les origines de l'armée de métier', *Bibliothèque de l'Ecole des Chartes*, 106 (1945–6), 189–224.
9 *Pipe Roll, 20 Henry II*, 135; Boussard, 'Les mercenaires', 218–20. Boussard's figures were derived from later Mediterranean evidence about the number of men ships could carry, and he dismissed the view that northern vessels were much smaller. In 1297, however, almost 340 ships were needed to transport an army of some 9,000 men, with equipment and horses, across the Channel, an average of about twenty-six men per ship.
10 *Pipe Roll, 20 Henry II*, 8.
11 Containe, *War in the*

Middle Ages, 244–5.
12 Gillingham, *Richard the Lionheart*, 101, 300.
13 S. Painter, *The Reign of King John* (Baltimore, 1949), 299.
14 *Rotuli Litterarum Patentium in Turri Londonensi asservati*, ed. T.D. Hardy (1835), 12, 26.
15 *Ibid.*, 15, 17, 20–21, 24. These men are also discussed by Powicke, *The Loss of Normandy*, 337–43.
16 *Pipe Roll, 8 John*, xix.
17 *Rotuli de Liberate ac de Misis ac Praestitis*, 177–228. In some cases this record identifies men as Flemings, but in others it does not do so. Nor is it clear that all mentioned were knights, though this seems probable.
18 Church, 'The Knights of the Household of King John', 160; *Documents Illustrative of English History in the Thirteenth and Fourteenth Centuries*, ed. Cole, 238, 242, 266; Church, 'The Earliest English Muster Roll, 18/19 December 1215', 6–17.
19 S. Brown, 'The Mercenary and his Master: Military Service and Monetary Reward in the Eleventh and Twelfth Centuries', *History*, 74 (1989), 35.
20 *Orderic Vitalis*, vi. 28.
21 *Gesta Stephani*, 105.
22 Boussard, 'Les mercenaires', 206.
23 The quotation is from Caxton's translation of Christine de Pisan's reworking of Vegetius, *The Book of Fayttes of Arms and of Chyvalrye*, ed. A.T.P. Byles (Early English Text Soc., 1932), 26.
24 *Gesta Stephani*, 204–5.
25 Roger of Wendover, *Flores Historiarum*, ii. 150.
26 H. Géraud, 'Les routiers au douzième siècle', *Bibliothèque de l'Ecole des Chartes*, 3 (1841–2), 128–9.
27 Contamine, *War in the Middle Ages*, 243–4; *Chronicles of the Reigns of Stephen, Henry II and Richard I*, i. 209–10; Walter Map, *De Nugis Curialium*, ed. M.R. James (1914), 56–7.
28 Brown, 'The Mercenary and his Master', 20–38, argues the point at some length.

29 Holt, *The Northerners*, 32–3; *Histoire des ducs de Normandie*, 161.
30 Carpenter, *The Minority of Henry III*, 20–1, 78–9; *Histoire des ducs de Normandie*, 173, 180–81.
31 Prestwich, *Edward I*, 39–41.
32 *Le Bel*, i. 81.
33 *Wardrobe Book of William de Norwell*, 350, 355.
34 Fowler, *The King's Lieutenant*, 204; *Foedera*, III, ii. 745; *CPR 1361–4*, 317–18; *CPR 1367–70*, 12; J.A.F. de Larrea Rojas, *Guerra y sociedad en Navarra durante la Edad Media* (Bilbao, 1992), 144.
35 *The History of Parliament. The House of Commons 1386–1421*, ii. 729–33.
36 *Oeuvres de Froissart*, ed. Kervyn de Lettenhove, xviii. 340–41.
37 *Froissart*, v. 190, 195.
38 *Foedera*, III, ii. 50; *Society at War: the Experience of England and France during the Hundred Years War*, ed. C.T. Allmand (Edinburgh, 1973), 92.

7 Command

1 Prestwich, *Edward I*, 193.
2 *Guillaume de Poitiers, Historie de Guillaume le Conquérant*, 251–7. William's reception at Rouen on his return to Normandy after Hastings is here equated to a Roman triumph, but this is more a demonstration of William of Poitiers' classical learning than anything else.
3 *Chronicles of Edward I and Edward II*, 3–21.
4 Prestwich, *Edward I*, 51.
5 *Ibid.*, 58.
6 *Le Bel*, ii. 105–6.
7 Suppe, *Military Institutions on the Welsh Marches*, 111.
8 Barlow, *William Rufus*, 397.
9 *Black Prince's Register*, iv. 143–5; E 101/63/3, no. 87.
10 Sherborne, 'Indentured Retinues and English Expeditions to France, 1369–1380', 733, 736.
11 *Scalacronica*, 187; E 101/393/11, ff. 79, 87; M.R. Powicke, 'Lancastrian Captains', in *Essays*

in Medieval History presented to Bertie Wilkinson, ed. T.A. Sandquist and M.R. Powicke (Toronto, 1969), 371–82.
12 *Froissart*, v. 33; vi. 159; vii. 43; Goodman, *John of Gaunt*, 224.
13 *Foedera*, III, i. 37, 83.
14 *The Black Prince's Register*, iv. 143–5.
15 The argument is put by, among others, C.T. Allmand, *The Hundred Years War* (1988), 71–3. A very different line was taken by K.B. McFarlane, *The Nobility of Later Medieval England* (1973), 40.
16 It is now becoming customary to train some academics in the arts of 'management'. In my own case, this included being instructed on how to lie on the floor and breathe regularly ('stress management'); if academics can be taught to 'manage', surely medieval magnates could be trained to command? My thanks are due to the University of Durham for sending me on such a management course.
17 See above, 150–51.
18 Prestwich, *Edward I*, 192, 193. One version has it that the army at Irfon Bridge was commanded by John Giffard and Roger Mortimer the younger.
19 Prestwich, *Edward I*, 477; *Documents Illustrative of the History of Scotland*, ed. Stevenson, ii. 222–4.
20 *Ibid.*, ii. 467–8. The quote about Audigier replaced a proverb about canine excrement. For the Audigier poem see below, 230.
21 Prestwich, *Edward I*, 381–5, 506.
22 Maddicott, *Thomas of Lancaster*, 167–70.
23 *Froissart*, vi. 156–7.
24 C47/2/29.
25 *Chronicles by Sir John Froissart*, trans. Johnes, 456, 465; *Foedera*, III, ii. 897; Sherborne, 'Indentured Retinues and English Expeditions to France', 723–5.
26 *Wars of the English in France*, II (ii), 596.
27 Goodman, *Wars of the Roses*, 125–7.

28 *Orderic Vitalis*, v. 214; vi. 230, 246; J.O. Prestwich, 'The Military Household of the Norman Kings', *ANW*, 107, 112.
29 *Rot. Lit. Claus.*, i. 71.
30 A. Lewis, 'Roger Leyburn and the Pacification of England, 1265–7', *EHR*, 54 (1939), 193–210.
31 Prestwich, *War, Politics and Finance*, 57; *Edward I*, 510.
32 Sherborne, 'Indentured Retinues and English Expeditions to France', 738.
33 Richard of Hexham, *Chronicles of the Reigns of Stephen, Henry I and Henry II*, iii. 174; Russell, *The Just War in the Middle Ages*, 109.
34 The Norwich crusade is well summarised by M. McKisack, *The Fourteenth Century, 1307–1399* (Oxford, 1959), 431–3.
35 J. Sumption, *The Hundred Years War: Trial by Battle* (1990), 502.
36 *Chron. Guisborough*, 327–8.
37 Prestwich, *Edward I*, 498.
38 T. Madox, *The History and Antiquities of the Exchequer* (1769), i. 41; the early constables are usefully discussed in *Regesta Regum Anglo Normannorum 1066–1154*, ii, ed. C. Johnson and H.A. Cronne (Oxford, 1956), xv–xvi, and iii, ed. H.A. Cronne and R.H.C. Davis (Oxford, 1968), xix–x; for an older view, Round, *The King's Sergeants and Officers of State*, 76–81.
39 E.B. Fryde, 'Magnate Debts to Edward I and Edward III', *National Library of Wales Journal*, 27 (1992), 277.
40 Round, *King's Sergeants*, 85; Prestwich, *Edward I*, 146–7.
41 G.E.C., *Complete Peerage*, x. 91–8; *Select Cases in the Court of King's Bench, Edward III*, ed. G.O. Sayles (Selden Soc., 82, 1965), 6; Sumption, *The Hundred Years War*, 509.
42 Round, *The King's Sergeants*, 79–80; J. Green, *The Government of England under Henry I*, 25–6.
43 *Gesta Stephani*, 169.

44 S. Painter, *William Marshal, Knight Errant, Baron, and Regent of England* (repr. 1971), 104; Crouch, *William Marshal*, 207. The marshal's role in supervising feudal service is suggested by his receipt of some fines for non-performance, *Roll of Divers Accounts* (PRS, ns. xliv, 1982), 32–3.
45 *The Chronicle of Benedict of Peterborough*, ed. W. Stubbs (RS, 1867), ii. 131, where there is reference to 'constables and justices and marshals of the army'.
46 Powicke, *The Loss of Normandy*, 368–9.
47 *Rot. Lit. Claus.*, i. 164.
48 J.E. Morris, *Welsh Wars of Edward I*, 156–8, discusses this.
49 Morris, *Welsh Wars*, 173, 190.
50 Ibid., 251; Prestwich, *War, Politics and Finance*, 249.
51 *Chron. Guisborough*, 246.
52 Ibid., 327.
53 Prestwich, *Edward I*, 482–3.
54 Prestwich, *War, Politics and Finance*, 267.
55 The tract on the Marshal and Constable is to be found in BL Cotton MS Nero D. VI, a volume possibly compiled for Thomas Mowbray in the 1380s; the tract on the Marshal is in BL Cotton Vespasian B. VII. In these and other manuscripts these tracts are frequently found together with the *Modus Tenendi Parliamentum*, as for example in Durham Dean and Chapter Muniments Reg. 1.
56 See Prestwich, *War, Politics and Finance*, 263n.; BL Cotton MS, Vesp. B VII, ff. 105v–107; BL Cotton MS, Nero D. VI, f. 85; Durham Dean and Chapter muniments, Reg. 1. F. Grose, *Military Antiquities respecting a History of the English Army* (1801), i. 193–7, provides a translation of the tract on the Marshal and Constable. In the present century the Earl Marshal receives no perquisites: 'I believe you have a salary of £20 a year as Earl Marshal.' 'So the papers say.' 'You don't actually get it?' 'No.' *Sunday Times* (13 June,

1965).
57 *Acta Imperii Inedita Seculi XIII*, ed. E. Winkelman (Innsbruck, 1888), i. 762.
58 *Vita Edwardi Secundi*, 53; *Rot. Scot.*, i. 249.
59 Pollard, *John Talbot*, 37–8.
60 *Wars of the English in France*, II (ii), 596–7.
61 *Chronicles, Stephen, Henry II and Richard I*, 108; *The Chronicle of Jocelin of Brakelond*, ed. H.E. Butler (1949), 70–71.
62 *Rotuli de Liberate ac de Misis et Praestitis*, 177, 187, 189, 192, 210, 214.
63 *Wardrobe Book of William de Norwell*, 338.
64 T.F. Tout, *Chapters in the Administrative History of Mediaeval England* (Manchester, 1920–33), iv, 139–42.
65 Prestwich, *War, Politics and Finance*, 161–2.
66 Tout, *Chapters in Administrative History*, v, 346; E 101/404/24.
67 *Le Bel*, i. 55, 65. The same phrase, 'le petit pas', was used earlier by Wace: Bennett, 'Wace and Warfare', *ANW*, 248, 250.
68 Ambroise, *Crusade of Richard Lion-Heart*, 258; *Froissart*, vii. 18; Monstrelet, translated by N.H. Nicolas, *Agincourt*, 256.
69 *Willelmi Rishanger Chronica et Annales*, ed. H.T. Riley (RS, 1865), 441–2. The chronicler's account of this skirmish is unfortunately far from clear; see, for a fuller analysis, H. Johnstone, *Edward of Caernarvon*, 52.
70 *Adae Murimuth, Continuatio Chronicarum*, 214.
71 *Chroniques par Waurin*, iii. 242.
72 Robert de Torigni, 132.
73 *Chron. Guisborough*, 325.
74 *Le Bel*, i. 44–5.
75 *The War of Saint-Sardos*, ed. Chaplais, 220–21.
76 Morillo, *Warfare under the Anglo-Norman Kings*, 63.
77 *Benedict of Peterborough*, ii. 110–11, 131; *The Chronicle of*

Richard of Devizes, ed. J.T. Appleby (1963), 16, 22.
78 *Rot. Lit. Claus.*, i. 164.
79 *Foedera*, iii. 89.
80 Nicolas, *Agincourt*, appendix 8, 31–40.
81 *Gesta Henrici Quinti*, 69, 81.
82 Newhall, *The English Conquest of Normandy*, 226, 228.
83 Neville, 'A Plea Roll of Edward I's Army in Scotland', 7–133; the particular cases referred to are nos 10, 19, 20, 23, 38, 48, 74, 80, 99, 101–3, 111, 116, 121, 129, 184.
84 Henry of Huntingdon, 241; Simeon of Durham, *Historia Regum*, ii. 308.
85 *Expugnatio Hibernica*, 178–81.
86 *Chronicles by Sir John Froissart*, trans. Johnes, 219.
87 Ambroise, *Crusade of Richard Lion-Heart*, 260; *Chron. Guisborough*, 252.
88 *Chroniques par Froissart*, iv. 91–2.

8 Strategy and Intelligence

1 *Letters and Papers Illustrative of the Wars of the English in France during the Reign of Henry VI*, ed. J. Stevenson, II (ii) (RS, 1864), 575–85. For a valuable commentary on Fastolf's proposals, see M.G.A. Vale, 'Sir John Fastolf's "Report" of 1435: a New Interpretation Reconsidered', *Nottingham Medieval Studies*, 17 (1973), 78–84. This criticises the views of R. Brill, 'The English Preparations before the Treaty of Arras: a New Interpretation of Sir John Fastolf's "Report", September, 1435', *Studies in Medieval and Renaissance History*, 7 (1970), 213–47.
2 There are, of course, notable exceptions to this statement. See for example Verbruggen, *The Art of Warfare*, 249–300.
3 F.M. Stenton, *Anglo-Saxon England* (2nd edn, Oxford, 1947), 585.

4 Richardson and Sayles, *The Governance of Medieval England*, 366.
5 H.G. Richardson, reviewing *The History of the King's Works*, EHR, 80 (1965), 556.
6 H.J. Hewitt, *The Black Prince's Expedition 1355–1357*, 13; C. Oman, *A History of the Art of War in the Middle Ages* (rev. edn, 1924), ii. 111.
7 R.V. Jones, *Most Secret War: British Scientific Intelligence, 1939–1945* (1978), 245–6; George S. Patton, Jr, *War as I Knew It* (Boston, 1947), 92, cited by D.H. Fischer, *Historian's Fallacies: Towards a Logic of Historical Thought* (New York, 1970), 158–9.
8 C.R. Shrader, 'A Handlist of Extant Manuscripts containing the *De Re Militari* of Flavius Vegetius Renatus', *Scriptorium*, 33 (1979), 280–305; Prestwich, *Edward I*, 123.
9 J. Bradbury, *The Medieval Siege* (1992), 86; R. Rogers, *Latin Siege Warfare in the Twelfth Century* (Oxford, 1992), 238–9. It is possible, as A. Murray, *Reason and Society in the Middle Ages* (Oxford, 1978), 128–9, suggests, that the count was reading a revised and expanded version of Vegetius's original text.
10 For some sceptical comments, see Morillo, *Warfare under the Anglo-Norman Kings*, 118.
11 J.O. Prestwich, 'Richard Coeur de Lion: *Rex Bellicosus*', *Richard Coeur de Lion in History and Myth*, ed. J.L. Nelson (1992), 6–13.
12 C. Tyerman, *England and the Crusades 1095–1588* (Chicago, 1988); Prestwich, *Edward I*, 75.
13 Prestwich, *Edward I*, 329–32.
14 *Expugnatio Hibernica, the Conquest of Ireland*, 244–9.
15 *Giraldi Cambrensis Opera*, vi. 218–22.
16 *Murimuth, Avesbury*, 205–12.
17 C 47/2/29, m. 5.
18 C 47/2/31.

19 Prestwich, 'English Armies in the Early Stages of the Hundred Years War', 111–13.
20 C 47/2/29.
21 J. Black, in *European History Quarterly*, 24 (1994), 266.
22 *Documents Illustrative of the History of Scotland*, ed. Stevenson, ii. 28–30.
23 Barlow, *William Rufus*, 385; S. Morillo, *Warfare under the Anglo-Norman Kings*, 114; H. Ellis, *Original Letters*, 3rd ser. iv (1846), 34–9; *Oeuvres de Froissart*, ed. Kervyn de Lettenhove, xviii. 27–9.
24 The itinerary is described in some detail by Johnstone, *Edward of Caernarvon*, 49–54.
25 *Baker*, 255–7, 293–6, provides itineraries with distances.
26 A.H. Burne, *The Agincourt War* (1956), 70–1. I am grateful to Dr H.J. Harris for advice about Sherman's march.
27 A.L. Poole, 'Richard the First's Alliances with the German Princes in 1194', *Studies in Medieval History presented to F.M. Powicke*, ed. R.W. Hunt, W.A. Pantin, R.W. Southern (Oxford, 1948), 90–9; Gillingham, *Richard the Lionheart*, 283.
28 The former case is put forward by Prestwich, 'Richard Coeur de Lion: *Rex Bellicosus*', 11 and n. 36; the latter is argued by J. Gillingham, 'Richard I and the Science of War in the Middle Ages', *War and Government in the Middle Ages*, ed. Gillingham and Holt, 90.
29 *Pierre de Langtoft*, 268–9. For the origins of this war, see M.G.A. Vale, *The Angevin Legacy and the Hundred Years War 1250–1340* (Oxford, 1990). For a much earlier parallel example of a king taking advice before making war, see *Orderic Vitalis*, v. 238–40, for Rufus being told by his barons to invade Maine.
30 For a fuller account, see Prestwich, *Edward I*, 386–98.
31 See for example C 47/30/4, nos 16, 18. The fullest account of the diplomatic aspects of the early stages of the Hundred Years War

is H.S. Lucas, *The Low Countries and the Hundred Years' War, 1326–1347* (Ann Arbor, 1929).

32 The financial aspects of the alliances are fully covered by E.B. Fryde, 'Financial Resources of Edward III in the Netherlands, 1337–40', in E.B. Fryde, *Studies in Medieval Trade and Finance* (1983).

33 See A. Curry, *The Hundred Years War* (1993), 122–50, for a discussion of the international context of the Hundred Years War.

34 Latimer, 'Henry II's Campaign against the Welsh in 1165', 534–7.

35 Morris, *Welsh Wars of Edward I*, 155–6.

36 Prestwich, *Edward I*, 189–96.

37 Douglas, *William the Conqueror*, 227.

38 Prestwich, *Edward I*, 470, 494.

39 J. Scammell, 'Robert I and the North of England', *EHR*, 73 (1958), 385–403.

40 *Guillaume de Poitiers, Historie de Guillaume le Conquérant*, ed. R. Foreville (Paris, 1952), 90.

41 Simeon of Durham, *Historia Regum*, ii. 188; *Gesta Stephani*, 186–7.

42 D.M. Palliser, 'Domesday Book and the "Harrying of the North"', *Northern History*, 29 (1993), 1–23; E.M. Amt, 'The meaning of waste in the early pipe rolls of Henry II', *Economic History Review*, 44 (1991), 240–8.

43 *Jordan Fantosme*, ll. 440–51.

44 J. Scammell, 'Robert I and the North of England', *EHR*, 73 (1958), 388–9; *Historical Letters and Papers from Northern Registers*, ed. J. Raine (RS, 1873), 270, 274, 279–82; C. McNamee, 'Buying Off Robert Bruce: An Account of Monies paid to the Scots by Cumberland Communities in 1313–14', *Transactions of the Cumberland and Westmorland Antiquarian and Archaeological Society*, 92 (1992), 83; R.A. Lomas, *North-East England in the Middle Ages*

(Edinburgh, 1992), 54–72.

45 J.T. Glatthaar, *The March to the Sea and Beyond: Sherman's Troops in the Savannah and Carolinas Campaigns* (New York, 1986), 141.

46 Gillingham, 'Richard I and the Science of War', *War and Government in the Middle Ages*, ed. Gillingham and Holt, 85.

47 *Murimuth, Avesbury*, 304, 307; *Baker*, 65; Hewitt, *Organisation of War*, 115, 124–5; *Oeuvres de Froissart*, ed. Kervyn de Lettenhove, 18, 93.

48 *Anonimalle Chronicle*, 35, 45; *Baker*, 131–2.

49 For a recent survey, M. Jones, 'War and Fourteenth-Century France', *AAF*, 103–20; see also R. Boutrouche, 'The Devastation of Rural Areas during the Hundred Years War and the Agricultural Recovery of France', *The Recovery of France in the Fifteenth Century*, ed. P.S. Lewis (1971), 23–36.

50 *Murimuth, Avesbury*, 358–9.

51 Ibid., 442.

52 For recent discussion, see Curry, *The Hundred Years War*, 61–6.

53 K.A. Fowler, 'News from the Front in the XIVth Century', *Guerre et société en France, en Angleterre et en Bourgogne XIVe–XVe siècle*, ed. P. Contamine, C. Giry-Deloison, M.H. Keen (Villeneuve d'Ascq, 1991), 78–9, 84.

54 Fowler, *The King's Lieutenant*, 154–6.

55 Goodman, *John of Gaunt*, 232–4.

56 *Rotuli Parliamentorum* (1783–1832), iii. 36; the policy is explained by Jones, *Ducal Brittany*, 84.

57 J.H. Beeler, *Warfare in England, 1066–1189* (Ithaca, 1966), 53–6. His arguments are set out more fully in his 'Castles and Strategy in Norman and Early Angevin England', *Speculum*, 31 (1956), 581–601.

58 C. Coulson, 'Freedom to Crenellate by Licence – An Historical Revision', *Nottingham Medieval Studies* 38 (1994), 86–

137; M. Strickland, 'Securing the North: Invasion and the Strategy of Defence in twelfth-century Anglo-Scottish Warfare', *ANW*, 212.

59 D.J. Cathcart King, *The Castle in England and Wales* (1988), 11.

60 The idea that there was a licensing system for early castles is discussed and firmly rejected by C.H. Coulson, 'The Castles of the Anarchy', *The Anarchy of Stephen's Reign*, ed. E. King (Oxford, 1994), 67–92. The counting of castles is a difficult task, for definition of a castle can be problematic, and many earthwork structures cannot be dated with precision. N.J.G. Pounds, *The Medieval Castle in England and Wales* (Cambridge, 1990), 68, suggests that no more than 900 can be attributed to the period before 1154.

61 Pounds, *The Medieval Castle in England and Wales*, 57–8; R.G. Eales, 'Royal Power and Castles in Norman England', *The Ideals and Practice of Medieval Knighthood*, iii, ed. C. Harper-Bill and R. Harvey (1990), 63–9.

62 T.A. Heslop, 'Orford Castle, nostalgia and sophisticated living', *Architectural History*, 34 (1991), 36–58, provides a recent, controversial interpretation of Orford.

63 R.A. Brown, 'A Note on Kenilworth Castle: the Change to Royal Ownership', *Archaeological Journal*, 110 (1953).

64 R.A. Brown, H.M. Colvin, A.J. Taylor, *The History of the King's Works*, i (1963), 68.

65 Prestwich, *Edward I*, 207–15 for a brief account; the castle-building programme is fully analysed in *The History of the King's Works*, i. 293–408.

66 *History of the King's Works*, i. 413, 419.

67 *Chronicon de Lanercost*, 223.

68 *CDS*, iii, nos 779, 783; M.C. Prestwich, 'English Castles in the reign of Edward II', *Journal of Medieval History*, 8 (1982), 165, 167.

69 For a discussion of the

importance of intelligence in the twelfth and (to a lesser extent) the twentieth centuries, see J.O. Prestwich, 'Military Intelligence under the Norman and Angevin Kings', *Law and Government in Medieval England and Normandy*, ed. G. Garnett and J. Hudson (Cambridge, 1994), 1–30.

70 *The War of St Sardos (1323–1325)*, ed. P. Chaplais (Camden Soc., 3rd ser., 87, 1954), 67.

71 *Baker*, 131 ('spies', scilicet exploratores).

72 *Documents Illustrative of the History of Scotland*, ed. Stevenson, ii. 302–4, 339–40, 417, 431, 434–5.

73 BL MS Nero C.VIII, f. 214.

74 *Rotuli de Liberate ac de Misis et Praestitis regnante Johanne*, ed. T.D. Hardy (1844), 111, 141, 250.

75 E 101/359/9.

76 *The Account Book of William de Norwell*, 228.

77 J.R. Alban and C.T. Allmand, 'Spies and Spying in the Fourteenth Century', in *War, Literature and Politics in the Late Middle Ages*, ed. C.T. Allmand (Liverpool, 1976), 79–80, 86–7.

78 *Original Letters*, ed. H. Ellis, 3rd ser., iv (1846), 30–33.

79 *Oeuvres de Froissart*, xviii. 505.

80 *The Account Book of William de Norwell*, 215, 253, 268, 279.

81 For a splendid full account of these events, see J.W. Sherborne, 'John of Gaunt, Edward III's Retinue and the French Campaign of 1369', *Kings and Nobles in the Later Middle Ages*, ed. R.A. Griffiths and J. Sherborne (Gloucester, 1986), 49–50. See also below, 315.

82 *Documents Illustrating the Crisis of 1297–8 in England*, ed. Prestwich, 4.

83 Alban and Allmand, 'Spies and Spying in the Fourteenth Century', 90.

84 Sumption, *The Hundred Years War*, 493–500, provides an excellent exposition of the background to the Normandy landing of 1346.

85 Prestwich, *Edward I*, 175; F. Pollock and F.W. Maitland, *The History of English Law* (2nd edn, Cambridge, 1898), ii. 507n.

86 Prestwich, *Edward I*, 383; J.G. Edwards, 'The Treason of Thomas Turberville, 1295', *Studies in Medieval History presented to F.M. Powicke*, 296–309.

87 *CDS*, iii, no. 1614; *Foedera*, III, i, 442; Alban and Allmand, 'Spies and Spying in the Fourteenth Century', 93–4.

88 Ibid., 98–9.

89 I. Arthurson, 'Espionage and Intelligence from the Wars of the Roses to the Reformation', *Nottingham Medieval Studies*, 35 (1991), 138.

90 Ibid., 149.

91 J.O. Prestwich, 'Military Intelligence under the Norman and Angevin Kings', 12–13.

92 *Jordan Fantosme's Chronicle*, 128, 130.

93 Gillingham, 'William the Marshal', 9.

94 Prestwich, *Edward I*, 50–51; D.A. Carpenter, *The Battles of Lewes and Evesham 1264/5* (1987), 38–59, provides a detailed analysis.

95 *Documents Illustrative of the History of Scotland*, ed. Stevenson, ii. 372–4.

96 *Orderic Vitalis*, vi. 198–200.

97 Prestwich, *Edward I*, 378–81.

98 This campaign has been analysed by N. Fryde, *The Tyranny and Fall of Edward II* (Cambridge, 1979), 119–33.

99 *Le Bel*, i. 53, 56.

100 *CFR 1347–56*, 273.

9 Chivalry

1 Crouch, *William Marshal*, 32.

2 *Scalacronica*, 145; *Chroniques de Froissart*, ii. 152.

3 *Documents Illustrative of English History in the Thirteenth and Fourteenth Centuries*, ed. H. Cole (1844), 231; Prestwich, *Edward I*, 508–9.

4 *Chronicles by Sir John Froissart*, trans. Johnes, i (1839), 453–4; *Froissart*, vii. 250.

5 J. Huizinga, *The Waning of the Middle Ages* (1924; cited from 1968 reprint), 95–7.

6 *Political Poems and Songs*, ed. T. Wright (RS, 1859), i, 21. I follow in part the translation given by Keen, *Chivalry*, 223.

7 *Political Songs*, ed. Wright, 61. This can be translated as 'He is strong and has great chivalry.'

8 Gillingham, '1066 and the Introduction of Chivalry into England', *Law and Government in Medieval England and Normandy: Essays in honour of Sir James Holt*, ed. G. Garnett and J. Hudson (Cambridge, 1994).

9 The fullest recent discussion of the topic as a whole is provided by M.H. Keen, *Chivalry* (New Haven, 1984).

10 *Scalacronica*, 146; Keen, *Chivalry*, 2. He adds to the qualities that of *franchise*, the bearing that is born of a combination of good lineage and virtue.

11 *Gesta Stephani*, 208–9, 222–3.

12 *Orderic Vitalis*, vi. 242; *Histoire de Guillaume le Maréchal*, i. l. 1478. For recent discussions of early heraldry, see Crouch, *The Image of Aristocracy*, 220ff., and A. Ailes, 'The Knight, Heraldry and Armour: The Role of Recognition and the Origins of Heraldry', *Medieval Knighthood*, iv, ed. C. Harper-Bill and R. Harvey (Woodbridge, 1992), 1–22.

13 N. Denholm-Young, *History and Heraldry* (Oxford, 1965), 41.

14 Gough, *Scotland in 1298*, 143; *Song of Carlaverock*, 28.

15 *The Scrope and Grosvenor Controversy*, i. 211–12.

16 Ailes, 'The Knight, Heraldry and Armour', 3–5.

17 Nicholson, *Edward III and the Scots*, 205; Vale, *War and Chivalry*, 97.

18 J.R.V. Barker, *The Tournament in England 1100–1400* (Woodbridge, 1986), 17, 25. My comments on tournaments are heavily dependent on this important study.

19 Ibid., 45, 48, 66–7; Carpenter, *Minority of Henry III*, 50;

Prestwich, *Edward I*, 509–10. Prohibitions on tournaments are discussed by R.W. Kaeuper, *War, Justice and Public Order. England and France in the Later Middle Ages* (Oxford, 1988), 199–211.

20 J. Vale, *Edward III and Chivalry: chivalric society and its context 1270–1350* (Woodbridge, 1982), 56–75, 88; Murimuth, 124.

21 Murimuth, 63, 155.

22 Ibid., 146.

23 Later tournaments are discussed by Vale, *War and Chivalry*, 80–87.

24 Gillingham, *Richard the Lionheart*, 159. Vale, *Edward III and Chivalry*, 16–24, provides a good summary of Edward I's Arthurian interests. See also Prestwich, *Edward I*, 120–22.

25 M. McKisack, *The Fourteenth Century 1307–1399* (Oxford, 1959), 252.

26 The fullest recent discussion of the Order of the Garter is D'A.J.D. Boulton, *The Knights of the Crown. The Monarchical Orders of Knighthood in Later Medieval Europe 1325–1520* (Woodbridge, 1987), 96–166, but see also L. Jefferson, 'MS Arundel 48 and the Earliest Statutes of the Order of the Garter', *EHR*, 109 (1994), 356–75.

27 C. Holdsworth, 'War and Peace in the Twelfth Century. The Reign of Stephen Reconsidered', *War and Peace in the Middle Ages*, ed. B.P. McGuire (Copenhagen, 1987), 76–7.

28 Keen, *Laws of War*, 98.

29 Bodleian MS Hatton 82; BL Stowe Charter 622; *Calendar of Inquisitions Miscellaneous*, iii. 109.

30 This necessarily brief summary of ideas to be found in romances is drawn from M.A. Gist, *Love and War in the Middle English Romances* (1947), 137–90.

31 P. Chaplais, 'Some Private Letters of Edward I', *EHR*, 77 (1962), 79–80; D.J. Conlon, 'La Chanson d'Audigier – A scatological parody of the chansons de geste edited from Ms. Bibliothèque nationale, f. fr.

19152', *Nottingham Medieval Studies*, 33 (1989), 21–55.

32 *Facsimile of British Museum Harleian MS 2253*, introduction by N.R. Ker (Early English Text Soc., 1965), ff. 122v–4v.

33 Vale, *Edward III and Chivalry*, 49.

34 *The Song of Carlaverock*, ed. Wright, 74 (I have adjusted Wright's translation); *Pierre de Langtoft*, 401.

35 *Orderic Vitalis*, v. 238–9, 244–5; Barlow, *William Rufus*, 118.

36 *The Historia Novella by William of Malmesbury*, ed. K.R. Potter (1955), 34–5.

37 Walker, *The Lancastrian Affinity*, 55–6.

38 *Scalacronica*, 155.

39 *Anonimalle Chronicle*, 22; Froissart, v. 188; *Scalacronica*, 188.

40 *Chronicles by Sir John Froissart*, trans. Johnes, 448, 452.

41 *English Historical Documents IV, 1327–1485*, ed. A.R. Myers (1969), 1127–9.

42 Crouch, *William Marshal*, 172; *Vita Edwardi Secundi*, 52–3.

43 *Le Bel*, i. 317–18.

44 *Chroniques de Froissart*, vi. 156–7.

45 A.J. Pollard, *John Talbot and the War in France 1427–1453* (1983), 129.

46 *Froissart*, v. 34.

47 *Political Poems and Songs*, ed. Wright, i. 1–25.

48 *Froissart*, iv. 80–81, 83; v. 63.

49 Prestwich, *Edward I*, 56.

50 *CPR 1301–7*, 121, 242; *CCR 1302–7*, 66; *CCR 1313–18*, 71; H. Johnstone, *Edward of Caernarvon, 1284–1307* (Manchester, 1946), 116–17; *Chronicles of the Reigns of Edward I and II*, ed. W. Stubbs (RS, 1882), i. 157, 267; G.W.S. Barrow, *Robert Bruce and the Community of the Realm of Scotland* (1965), 295–6. Giles's death features in the *Vita Edwardi Secundi*, 53; it is interesting that he had been involved along with the putative author, John Walwayn, in an attack on a manor in Suffolk in 1302; *CPR, 1301–7*, 86. His career is dis-

cussed by Barker, *Tournament in England*, 127–8.

51 *Vita Edwardi Secundi*, 53–4.

52 J. Gillingham, 'War and Chivalry in the History of William the Marshal', *Thirteenth-Century England II*, ed. P.R. Coss and S.D. Lloyd (Woodbridge, 1988), 1–13.

53 *Froissart*, v. 159–60.

54 Pollard, *John Talbot*, 129.

55 Wendover, ii. 214; *The Chronicle of Bury St Edmunds*, 144.

56 Baker, 104.

57 *Giraldi Cambrensis Opera*, ed. J.F. Dimock (RS, 1868), vi, 220.

58 Suppe, *Military Institutions on the Welsh Marches: Shropshire, a.d. 1066–1300*, 21–2; see above, 219, for another example of head-hunting in a Welsh context; Prestwich, *Edward I*, 435, 510.

59 *Orderic Vitalis*, ii. 316.

60 Gillingham, '1066 and the Introduction of Chivalry into England', 31–55; M. Strickland, 'Against the Lord's Anointed: aspects of warfare and baronial rebellion in England and Normandy, 1075–1265', *Law and Government in Medieval England and Normandy*, 56–79.

61 Carpenter, *The Minority of Henry III*, 48–9.

62 M.C. Prestwich, 'England and Scotland during the Wars of Independence', *England and Her Neighbours 1066–1453: Essays in Honour of Pierre Chaplais*, ed. M. Jones and M. Vale (1989), 196.

63 S. Painter, *William Marshal, Knight-Errant, Baron, and Regent of England* (1933), 14–16; Turner, *King John*, 139; *Chronicles by Sir John Froissart*, trans. Johnes, 499.

64 Allmand, *Henry V*, 94–5.

65 *Chroniques par Waurin*, ii. 321–2.

66 Girart de Bornelh, quoted by Keen, *Chivalry*, 234.

67 Quoted by Gillingham, 'War and Chivalry in the *History of William the Marshal*', 13.

68 *Gesta Stephani*, 222–3.

69 It is, however, noteworthy

that a journal of Henry's Norman *chevauchée* of 1356 makes no reference to the destruction of territory, though the capture of 2,000 horses is recorded with pleasure: *Avesbury*, 462–5.
70 *Anglo-Scottish Relations 1174–1328: Some Selected Documents*, ed. E.L.G. Stones (1965), 107.
71 *Chron. Guisborough*, 325; Prestwich, *Edward I*, 508.
72 *Avesbury*, 314.
73 *Froissart*, vii. 250.
74 *Froissart*, iii. 145.
75 *The Brut*, ed. F.W.D. Brie (Early English Text Soc., 1906), i, 21.
76 Pollard, *John Talbot*, 126.
77 Vale, *War and Chivalry*, 174.
78 L. Farrago, *Patton: Ordeal and Triumph* (1969 edn), 284.

10 The Logistics of War

1 Van Crefeld, *Supplying War*, provides an excellent account of the logistics of modern warfare.
2 Ibid., 17–19.
3 Ibid., 35.
4 Ibid., 29; Black, *A Military Revolution?*, 29.
5 *Matthaei Parisiensis, Chronica Majora*, ed. H.R. Luard (RS, 1877), iv, 481–4.
6 E 163/4/11, nos 42, 73. Interestingly, another letter, no. 81 in the file, does not mention the role of the Flemings.
7 *The Bruce*, ed. W.W. Skeat (Early English Text Soc., extra series 55, 1874, 1877), 452.
8 *Le Bel*, i. 58–60.
9 *Orderic Vitalis*, vi. 472.
10 E 101/27/28.
11 *Gesta Henrici Quinti*, 48, 58.
12 C. Green and A.B. Whittingham, 'Excavations at Walsingham Priory, Norfolk, 1961', *Archaeological Journal*, 125 (1968), 285, 287.
13 *The Chronicle of Walter of Guisborough*, 325. Medieval men habitually drank impressive quantities; B. Harvey, *Living and Dying in England 1100–1540. The Monastic Experience* (Oxford, 1993), 58, shows that alcoholic drink probably provided a quarter of the energy value of the monastic diet at Westminster Abbey.
14 B.S. Bachrach, 'The Military Administration of the Norman Conquest', *Anglo-Norman Studies*, 8 (1985), 11–15; Bachrach, 'Logistics in Pre-Crusade Europe', *Feeding Mars: Logistics in Western Warfare from the Middle Ages to the Present*, ed. J.A. Lynn (Boulder, Colorado, 1993), 72, 78.
15 SC6/1212/1. Grain was measured by volume, not by weight. There were two gallons to a peck, four pecks to a bushel, and eight bushels to a quarter. A tun would hold about four quarters.
16 M.C. Prestwich, 'Victualling Estimates for English Garrisons in Scotland during the Early Fourteenth Century', *EHR*, lxxxii (1967), 346–53.
17 Prestwich, *War, Politics and Finance*, 121.
18 E 101/13/36, no. 220. It is not clear what was meant by *bacones*; was a *baco* a side of bacon, or the carcass of a bacon pig? It is simplest, if imprecise, to refer to them as 'bacons'.
19 C47/2/31, no. 1.
20 Latimer, 'Henry II's Campaign against the Welsh in 1165', 553–4; Prestwich, *War, Politics and Finance*, 119.
21 *Ralph of Coggeshall, Chronicon Anglicanum*, ed. J. Stevenson (RS, 1875), 154.
22 *Pipe Roll, 8 John*, xviii–xix.
23 *Pipe Roll, 12 John*, xxxii, 149.
24 *Pipe Roll, 13 John*, xiv, 40, 89. I have taken the figures from the text, rather than the introduction.
25 H.M. Cam, *The Hundred and the Hundred Rolls* (1930), 101.
26 The provision of carts was a traditional duty laid upon the monasteries. An order of 1333 implies that it was connected with the king's personal presence on campaign: *Rotuli Scotiae*, i. 232.
27 Prestwich, *War, Politics and Finance*, 119–20; *Edward I*, 181–2, 198–9.
28 Prestwich, *War, Politics and Finance*, 120–21; *Documents Illustrating the Crisis of 1297–8*, ed. Prestwich, 12; E101/6/15.
29 Stevenson, *Historical Documents of Scotland*, ii. 351.
30 *Liber Quotidianus Contrarotulatoris Garderobae*, 119.
31 Prestwich, *War, Politics and Finance*, 124.
32 E 101/13/36.
33 BL Add. Ms 7965, f. 50v.
34 *Liber Quotidianus Contrarotulatoris Garderobae*, 125–6.
35 E 101/10/4.
36 *Rotuli Scotiae*, i. 70–71, 94–5, 102–3, 156–7. This is not a comprehensive list of demands for victuals in this period.
37 E 101/16/19.
38 E 101/19/6.
39 E 101/21/4. Dunstable had been asked to provide more than this: 3,600 quarters of wheat, 4,100 quarters of malt, 200 quarters of beans and peas were requested, with meat, cheese and fish in addition: *CPR 1337–1339*, 75–6.
40 C 47/2/29.
41 E 101/569/9.
42 W.A. Morris, *The Medieval English Sheriff to 1300* (Manchester, 1927), 157; J.C. Holt, *Magna Carta Second Edition* (Cambridge, 1992), 459; *Documents of the Baronial Movement of Reform and Rebellion 1258–1267*, ed. R.F. Treharne and I.J. Sanders (Oxford, 1973), 85–6.
43 Prestwich, *War, Politics and Finance*, 118; Cam, *The Hundred and the Hundred Rolls*, 101–2.
44 For an excellent discussion of purveyance, or prise, see Maddicott, *The English Peasantry and the Demands of the Crown*, 24–34.
45 *A Lincolnshire Assize Roll for 1289*, ed. W.S. Thomson (Lincoln Record Soc., 36, 1944), lii–lxi.
46 J. Lydon, 'The Dublin Purveyors and the Wars in Scotland, 1296–1324', *Keimelia: Studies in Medieval Archaeology*

and History in honour of Tom Delaney, ed. G. MacNiocall and P.F. Wallace (Galway, 1988), 439.

47 *The 1341 Royal Inquest in Lincolnshire*, ed. McLane, nos 57, 65, 149, 173, 743, 1174.

48 E 101/21/38.

49 Prestwich, *War, Politics and Finance*, 135; Maddicott, *The English Peasantry and the Demands of the Crown*, 20–2.

50 Prestwich, *War, Politics and Finance*, 130–32.

51 Ordinances, clause 10.

52 SC 1/39; CDS, iii. nos 1075, 1076.

53 *Anglo-Norman Political Songs*, ed. I.S.T. Aspin (Anglo-Norman Text Society, 1953), 186.

54 E.B. Fryde, *Studies in Medieval Trade and Finance* (1983), 266.

55 G.L. Harriss, *King, Parliament and Public Finance* (Oxford, 1975), 376.

56 CFR 1347–56, 273–7, 288–91. The reduced quantities were: barley 4,400 quarters; oats 1,800 quarters; beans and peas 300 quarters; beef carcasses 2,540; bacons 4,020. The only commodity of which more was ordered in the revised instructions was coal from the north-east.

57 *Rotuli Parliamentorum*, ii. 240, 258.

58 S.J. Burley, 'The Victualling of Calais, 1347–65', *BIHR*, 81 (1958), 53; CCR 1354–60, 223.

59 *Rotuli Parliamentorum*, ii. 269; Given-Wilson, *The Royal Household and the King's Affinity*, 111–12.

60 Harriss, *King, Parliament and Public Finance*, 382, identifies some licences to merchants to export victuals in 1359 as part of the effort to supply the English army in France. This is unlikely; these licences in CPR 1358–61, 312, appear to refer to straightforward commercial dealings.

61 Prestwich, *War, Politics and Finance*, 116–17; Prestwich, *Edward I*, 199; *Rotuli Litterarum Clausarum*, 131b; *Rotuli Scotiae*, i. 125–6, 219–20, 558–9, 778, 786–7.

62 E 101/16/18.

63 Prestwich, *War, Politics and Finance*, 117; *Edward I*, 199; *Rotuli Scotiae*, i. 120, 159, 201.

64 Newhall, *The English Conquest of Normandy*, 247–9, 256–7.

65 *Wars of the English in France*, ed. Stevenson, II, ii. 558–9.

66 Cam, *The Hundred and the Hundred Rolls*, 101.

67 Prestwich, *Edward I*, 180.

68 Ellis, *Original Letters*, 3rd ser., iv, 36.

69 Froissart, v. 224–5.

70 *Gesta Henrici Quinti*, 33, 69, 115.

71 Nicolas, *Agincourt*, appendix, 40; *Wars of the English in France*, ed. Stevenson, II (ii), 597.

11 The Navy

1 Allmand, *Henry V*, 222–3, argues to the contrary, and suggests that 'In a very practical sense "control" of the sea could be effectively achieved by the squadron or flotilla on patrol.' See, however, C.F. Richmond, 'The War at Sea', *The Hundred Years War*, ed. K. Fowler (1971), 98–9.

2 T.J. Runyan, 'Naval Logistics in the Later Middle Ages', *Feeding Mars: Logistics in Western Warfare from the Middle Ages to the Present*, ed. Lynn, 79–100, provides a very useful overview.

3 Prestwich, *War, Politics and Finance*, 138.

4 *The Navy of the Lancastrian Kings: Accounts and Inventories of William Soper, Keeper of the King's Ships, 1422–1427*, ed. S. Rose (Navy Records Soc., 1982), 40–46 provides a good account of the different types of ships in use at that period. See also I. Friel, 'Winds of Change? Ships and the Hundred Years War', *Arms, Armies and Fortifications in the Hundred Years War*, ed. Curry and Hughes, 183–93; R.W. Unger, *The Ship in the Medieval Economy 600–1600* (1980), and, still of some value, R. and R.C.

Anderson, *The Sailing Ship* (1926).

5 E 36/204, f. 108.

6 For evidence of this, see J.T. Tinniswood, 'English Galleys, 1272–1377', *Mariner's Mirror* 35 (1949), 306.

7 *The Crusade of Richard Lion-Heart by Ambroise*, trans. M.J. Hubert, ed. J.L. La Monte (Columbia, 1941), 110; Allmand, *Henry V*, 232; *The Navy of the Lancastrian Kings*, ed. Rose, 44–5, 191; G.S. Laird Clowes, *Sailing Ships, their History and Development* (1932), 42. R.C. Anderson, 'Early Two-Masted and Three-Masted Ships in England', *Mariner's Mirror*, 14 (1928), 84–5, sets out the difficulties in determining the rig of early fifteenth-century ships; was the 'mesan' a mizzenmast, or a fore-mast (*misaine* in modern French)?

8 C. Tipping, 'Cargo Handling of the Medieval Cog', *Mariner's Mirror*, 80 (1994), 12.

9 E 101/20/22.

10 Sumption, *The Hundred Years War*, 406; *Chronicon Henrici Knighton*, ed. J.R. Lumby (RS, 1895), ii. 27–8.

11 Prestwich, *War, Politics and Finance*, 145; *Original Letters*, ed. Ellis, 2nd ser., i. 69; *The Navy of the Lancastrian Kings*, 45; H.I. Chapelle, *The History of the American Sailing Navy: the Ships and their Development* (New York, 1949), plan facing p. 120. Medieval tonnage was calculated as an estimate of the number of tuns of Bordeaux wine a vessel could carry.

12 *Pipe Roll, 14 John*, 57, 75.

13 R.J. Whitwell and C. Johnson, 'The "Newcastle" Galley. A.D. 1294', *Archaeologia Aeliana*, 4th ser., 2 (1926), 145; C. Johnson, 'London Shipbuilding, A.D. 1295', *Antiquaries Journal*, 7 (1927), 426.

14 C. Platt, *Medieval Southampton: the Port and Trading Community*, A.D. 1000–1600 (1973), 61–2.

15 E 101/19/3. The measurements of the sail are given as 25 ells long and 26 cloths wide. These huge dimensions have wor-

ried historians of sailing craft, and attempts have been made to reduce the size of the sail by arguing that the ell must have been two feet, not the usual forty-five inches, in length. See Tinniswood, 'English Galleys, 1272–1377', 301. The accounts for *La Philippe* are summarised by N.H. Nicolas, *History of the English Navy*, ii (1847), appendix ii, and the sail is discussed by R.C. Anderson, 'Wynewes', *Mariner's Mirror*, 14 (1928), 183.

16 J.W. Sherborne, 'The English Navy: Shipping and Manpower', *Past and Present*, 37 (1967), 169.

17 *Pipe Roll, 7 John*, ed. S. Smith (PRS, 1941), xiv–xv.

18 E 159/68, m. 77; R.C. Anderson, 'English Galleys in 1295', *Mariner's Mirror*, 14 (1928), 220–41. There is also evidence that there was a Lynn galley: Prestwich, *War, Politics and Finance*, 139, and it is conceivable that others were built. Letters were sent to Grimsby and Hull, ordering them to hasten construction: E 159/68, m. 79.

19 *Wardrobe Book of William de Norwell*, 363–4; T.J. Runyan 'Ships and Mariners in Medieval England', *Journal of British Studies* 16 (1977), 5; Sherborne, 'The English Navy: Shipping and Manpower', 166; BL Add. MS 24511, p. 63.

20 Allmand, *Henry V*, 220–32.

21 Prestwich, *War, Politics and Finance*, 143–4; Sherborne, 'The English Navy', 167.

22 Prestwich, *War, Politics and Finance*, 146; BL Add. MS 8835, ff. 16.

23 M. Jones, 'Two Exeter Ship Agreements of 1303 and 1310', *Mariner's Mirror*, 53 (1967), 316–7.

24 J.S. Kepler, 'The Effects of the Battle of Sluys upon the Administration of English Naval Impressment, 1340–1343', *Speculum*, 48 (1973), 73–4.

25 Runyan, 'Ships and Mariners', 11–12; Sherborne, 'The English Navy: Shipping and Manpower', 165–6; Sherborne, 'The Battle of La Rochelle and the War

at Sea, 1272–5', *BIHR*, 42 (1969), 20.

26 A. Saul, 'Great Yarmouth and the Hundred Years War in the Fourteenth Century', *BIHR* 52 (1979), 105–15; *Calendar of Inquisitions Miscellaneous*, iii. 14.

27 E 101/391/20; *Histoire des ducs de Normandie*, 185.

28 J.H. Pryor, 'The Transportation of Horses by Sea during the Era of the Crusades', *The Mariner's Mirror*, 68 (1982), 9–27, 103–25, discusses the problem in a Mediterranean context. See E 101/10/29 for an account of the conversion of ships to carry horses. To equip a ship for ten horses needed sixty planks and 250 nails.

29 E 101/10/29.

30 J. le Patourel, *The Norman Empire* (Oxford, 1976), 164–70, 175–8.

31 A.L. Poole, *From Domesday Book to Magna Carta, 1087–1216* (2nd edn, 1955), 307, 309.

32 *Pipe Roll, 8 John*, xvi–xviii; *Rotuli Litterarum Patentium*, 82–3. For William of Wrotham, see F.W. Brooks, 'William de Wrotham and the Office of Keeper of the King's Ports and Galleys', *EHR*, 40 (1925), 570–9.

33 *Pipe Roll, 14 John*, 75–6.

34 BL Add. MS 7966a, ff. 102–3, 130–31.

35 E 101/17/3.

36 *Liber Quotidianus Contrarotulatoris Garderobae*, 273–4.

37 BL Add. MS 7966a, f. 130v.

38 Prestwich, *War, Politics and Finance*, 134; *The War of Saint-Sardos*, ed. Chaplais, 222.

39 F.W. Brooks, *The English Naval Forces, 1199–1272* (1932), 187–8; Prestwich, *War, Politics and Finance*, 142; *The Wardrobe Book of William de Norwell*, ciii, 363; N.H. Nicolas, *A History of the Royal Navy* (1932), ii. 507–10.

40 *Scalacronica*, 186. It has normally been assumed that the payments covered all the horses on the campaign, and that many more horses were brought back from France than went out; see for example Hewitt, *Organisa-*

tion of War, 88. However, it has been convincingly argued by Ayton, *Knights and Warhorses*, 268–70, that these payments relate solely to those horses for which transport was not available in royal or commandeered ships.

41 Prestwich, *War, Politics and Finance*, 142; *Wardrobe Book of William de Norwell*, 363; *The Navy of the Lancastrian Kings*, ed. Rose, 43.

42 Tipping, 'Cargo Handling of the Medieval Cog', 11–12; Prestwich, *War, Politics and Finance*, 142.

43 E 101/25/9; Fowler, *King's Lieutenant*, 50; Runyan, 'Ships and Mariners in Later Medieval England', 4.

44 Sherborne, 'The English Navy', 171–2.

45 E 101/32/39; Newhall, *English Conquest of Normandy*, 32, 196–9, 204.

46 Allmand, *Henry V*, 220–32; Newhall, *English Conquest of Normandy*, 199; Richmond, 'The War at Sea', 114–5.

47 *Wardrobe Book of William de Norwell*, 363.

48 Saul, 'Great Yarmouth and the Hundred Years War in the Fourteenth Century', 114.

49 There is a convenient list of captains and admirals in *Handbook of British Chronology*, ed. E.B. Fryde, D.E. Greenway, S. Porter and I. Roy (1986), 134–41. See also A.E. Prince, 'The Army and Navy', *The English Government at Work*, ed. J.F. Willard and W.A. Morris, i (Cambridge, Mass., 1940), 378–9.

50 Friel, 'Winds of Change?', 186; *The Navy of the Lancastrian Kings*, ed. Rose, 141, 194.

51 Carpenter, *Minority of Henry III*, 43–4; H.L. Cannon, 'The battle of Sandwich and Eustace the Monk', *EHR*, 27 (1912), 649–70; Powicke, *King Henry III and the Lord Edward*, i. 15–16.

52 The battle is fully described by Lucas, *The Low Countries and the Hundred Years War*, 397–401, and by Sumption, *Hundred Years War*, 325–8.

53 Sherborne, 'The Battle of La Rochelle and the War at Sea, 1272–5', *BIHR*, 42 (1969), 17–29.

54 *Histoire militaire de la France*, i, ed. Contamine, 166.

55 Prestwich, *War, Politics and Finance*, 139–40.

56 M. Hughes, 'The Fourteenth-Century French Raids on Hampshire and the Isle of Wight', *AAF*, 121–37.

57 *CCR, 1341–3*, 107–8.

12 Siege Warfare

1 *Gesta Stephani*, 180–83.

2 *Memoriale Walteri de Coventria*, ed. W. Stubbs (RS, 1872–3), ii. 227.

3 Goodman, *The Wars of the Roses*, 181–92, provides an excellent discussion.

4 Frame, 'War and Peace in the Medieval Lordship of Ireland', 123.

5 T.F. Tout, 'The Fair of Lincoln and the "Histoire de Guillaume le Maréchal"', *Collected Papers*, ii. 213.

6 *Gesta Stephani*, 174.

7 *Vita Edwardi Secundi*, 94–5.

8 *The Siege of Carlaverock*, 65–87; *Liber Quotidianus Contrarotulatoris Garderobae*, 257–8, 264, 266–7.

9 R. Rogers, *Latin Siege Warfare in the Twelfth Century* (Oxford, 1992), 243.

10 *Orderic Vitalis*, iii. 288.

11 *The History of the King's Works*, i, ed. R.A. Brown, H.M. Colvin and A.J. Taylor (1963), 59–61; Round, *The King's Sergeants and Officers of State*, 15–16; *Rotuli de Liberate ac de Misis et Praestitis*, 14, 190, 215.

12 A.J. Taylor, 'Master Bertram, *Ingeniator Regis*', *Studies in Medieval History presented to R. Allen Brown* (Woodbridge, 1989), 289–315. One difficulty with this ingenious analysis of Bertram's career is the total absence of any evidence for his activities between 1254 and 1276.

13 A.J. Taylor, *Studies in*

Castles and Castle-Building (1985), 189–94; *The History of the King's Works*, i. 216–17.

14 Taylor, *Studies in Castles and Castle-Building*, 72–3; E 10/ 364/13, f. 59.

15 *Historical Documents of Scotland*, ed. Stephenson, ii. 479–80; BL Add. MS 8835, ff. 21v., 44. Ibid., f. 7, shows that he had already used sulphur for burning Brechin castle.

16 *The History of the King's Works*, i. 222–3; T.F. Tout, 'Firearms in England in the Fourteenth Century', *Collected Papers*, ii. 238–49; J. Hunter, 'Proofs of the Early Use of Gunpowder in the English Army', *Archaeologia*, 32 (1847), 382.

17 *Rotuli Litterarum Clausarum*, ii. 609, 617; E 101/12/16.

18 For a recent discussion, see J. Bradbury, *The Medieval Siege* (Woodbridge, 1992), 241ff.

19 *Orderic Vitalis*, iii. 232; vi, 342; *De Expugnatione Lyxbonensi, The Conquest of Lisbon*, ed. C.W. David (New York, 1936), 134–6, 142–3, 146–7, 158–65.

20 Prestwich, *Edward I*, 493; *Chronicle of Lanercost*, 232.

21 E 101/20/25.

22 P. Vremming Hansen, 'Reconstructing a Medieval Trebuchet', *Military Illustrated – Past and Present* (1990), 9–16; L. Krizek, 'Trebuchet Constructions in Czechoslovakia', *ibid.* (1992), 18–20. I owe these references to Keith Bartlett. The French example stood outside the walls of Chinon in 1991; I have been told of the Kalamazoo weapon by Jeff Anderson, who saw it in operation. These are formidable machines: see below, 289 for the results achieved by the Danish reconstruction. Similar results were obtained in the former Czechoslovakia.

23 E 101/467/73, 7; *Historical Documents of Scotland*, ed. Stevenson, ii. 320.

24 E 101/11/15; E 101/12/25.

25 *Gesta Stephani*, 34, 182; *De Expugnatione Lyxbonensi*, 142.

26 *Pipe Roll, 20 Henry II*, 6, 82.

27 *Pipe Roll, 6 Richard I*, 176, 212, 251; *Pipe Roll, 17 John*, 13. A very useful discussion of the various types of throwing engines is provided by Rogers, *Latin Siege Warfare in the Twelfth Century*, 254–73.

28 *Jordan Fantosme's Chronicle*, 93–4.

29 T.F. Tout, 'The Fair of Lincoln and the "Histoire de Guillaume le Maréchal"', *Collected Papers*, ii. 217–20; *Rotuli Litterarum Clausarum*, ii. 606–7.

30 *Roll of Divers Accounts for the early years of the Reign of Henry III*, 17.

31 Prestwich, *Edward I*, 501–2; *Historical Documents of Scotland*, ed. Stevenson, ii. 465–6, 481, 483–4.

32 *Gesta Stephani*, 140, 222.

33 *Pipe Roll, 6 Richard I*, 175, 212.

34 F.M. Powicke, *King Henry III and the Lord Edward* (Oxford, 1947), i. 64.

35 Barrow, *Robert Bruce*, 228.

36 *The Bruce*, ed. Skeat, 429, 432.

37 *Pipe Roll, 6 Richard I*, 175, 212.

38 BL Add. MS 8835, f. 8v.

39 R.D. Smith, 'Artillery and the Hundred Years War', *AAF*, 151–60; T.F. Tout, 'Firearms in England in the Fourteenth Century', *Collected Papers*, ii. 237–42, 252, 256; *Proceedings and Ordinances of the Privy Council*, ed. N.H. Nicolas, ii. 339–40; *Brut*, ii. 376; *Gesta Henrici Quinti*, 46.

40 Vale, *War and Chivalry*, 132, 138; E.F. Jacob, *The Fifteenth Century 1399–1485* (Oxford, 1961), 532.

41 T.A. Heslop, 'Orford Castle, Nostalgia and Sophisticated Living', *Architectural History*, xxxiv (1991), 36–58; *History of the King's Works*, i. 369–71.

42 Simeon of Durham, *Historia Regum*, ed. Arnold, ii. 273–4; Crouch, *The Beaumont Twins*, 19–20.

43 *Histoire des ducs de Normandie*, 178.

44 *Gesta Stephani*, 152.

45 K. Norgate, *The Minority of*

Henry III (1912), 16; G.A. Holmes, *The Good Parliament* (Oxford, 1975), 44, 130.

46 *Gesta Stephani*, 83, 104.

47 *Giraldi Cambrensis Opera*, vi. 50–51, 63–4.

48 *Lanercost*, 220–21.

49 Barrow, *Robert Bruce*, 275–8.

50 *Gesta Stephani*, 33–43, 49–50, 172.

51 Barrow, *Robert Bruce*, 150.

52 *Historical Documents of Scotland*, ed. Stevenson, ii. 229.

53 *Chronici Rogeri de Wendover*, iii. 278–81; *Roll of Divers Accounts for the Early Years of Henry III*, 52.

54 *Cal Liberate Rolls, 1260–67*, 221–3, 225, 229–33; Cam, *The Hundred and the Hundred Rolls*, 101.

55 BL Add. MS 8835, ff. 8v., 15v.; E 101/364/13, ff. 48, 53v.; E 101/11/15; *Flores Historiarum*, ed. H.R. Luard (RS, 1890), iii. 120; *Pierre de Langtoft, le règne d'Edouard Ier*, 417; Prestwich, *Edward I*, 501–2; A.Z. Freeman, 'Wall-Breakers and River-Bridgers', *Journal of British Studies*, 10 (1970), 12–15. It should be noted that the engine called 'Ludgar' is to be identified with the Warwolf, or *Loup de guerre*.

56 Fowler, *The King's Lieutenant*, 161–4.

57 Allmand, *Henry V*, 122–6.

58 Froissart, 213; *Eulogium Historiae*, iii. 219–20; *Baker*, 141. Baker's account suggests that the fire was started in the foundations of the keep, weakened by the work of miners.

59 The celebrated example is that of Count Geoffrey of Anjou, who was found reading a copy of Vegetius on the art of war in the course of the siege of Montreuil-Bellay: see above, 186.

60 Keen, *The Laws of War*, 119–33.

61 *Chronici Rogeri de Wendover*, iii. 55–6.

62 *CDS*, iv, no. 568.

63 *CDS*, iii, no. 1567.

64 Crouch, *William Marshal*, 16–17.

65 *Jordan Fantosme's Chronicle*, 38–41; *Flores*, iii. 118.

66 *Orderic Vitalis*, iii. 128.

67 *Willelmi Rishanger, Chronica et Annales*, 402.

68 *Orderic Vitalis*, iii. 128.

69 *CDS*, iii, nos 470, 477.

70 *Gesta Henrici Quinti*, 44–5.

13 Battle

1 *Baker*, 141.

2 *Froissart*, vi. 159, 168.

3 *Le Bel*, ii. 105–6.

4 Prestwich, *Edward I*, 481.

5 J. Gillingham, 'William the Bastard at War', *Studies in Medieval History presented to R. Allen Brown*, 143. The reasons for the rarity of medieval battles are well set out by Gillingham, *ibid.*, 145–8.

6 Prestwich, *Edward I*, 223.

7 Fryde, *Tyranny and Fall of Edward II, 1321–1326*, 129.

8 R.F. Frame, 'War and Peace in the Medieval Lordship of Ireland', *The English in Medieval Ireland*, ed. J.F. Lydon (Dublin, 1984), 124.

9 *CDS*, v, no. 809.

10 *Scalacronica*, 185.

11 *Expugnatio Hibernica*, 128–9. The quotation within the quotation is from Terence.

12 Roger of Howden, *Gesta Regis Henrici Secundi*, ii. 6–7.

13 *CCR 1346–9*, 58; Gillingham, 'William the Bastard at War', 147, notes that the only two occasions on which Fulk, count of Anjou referred to God's grace was in the context of victories in battle.

14 *Chronici Rogeri de Wendover*, iii. 61.

15 *CPR 1345–8*, 516–17. For an argument setting out the view that Edward III was seeking battle in 1346, see C.J. Rogers, 'Edward III and the Dialectics of Strategy', *TRHS*, 6th ser., 4 (1994), 83–102. Unfortunately this article appeared too late to be fully taken into account in this book.

16 *Gesta Henrici Quinti*, 61.

17 William of Newburgh, 184–5; *Jordan Fantosme's Chronicle*, 128–34.

18 *Froissart*, iii. 69; the battle is analysed in detail by A.H. Burne, *The Crécy War* (1955), 105–12.

19 William of Newburgh, 108.

20 D.A. Carpenter, *The Battles of Lewes and Evesham 1264/5* (1987), 58–9.

21 *Ibid.*, 26–7; *Political Songs*, ed. Wright, 81.

22 *Gesta Henrici Quinti*, 80.

23 *The Chronicle of Walter of Guisborough*, 326–7.

24 *The Chronicles of Sir John Froissart*, trans. Johnes, 55, 163; Froissart, ii. 177; iii. 168.

25 Roger of Howden, *Gesta Henrici Secundi*, i. 52–3.

26 Froissart, iv. 22.

27 J.R.E. Bliese, 'Aelred of Rievaulx's Rhetoric and Moral at the Battle of the Standard, 1138', *Albion*, xx (1988), 548–56; *Chronicles of Stephen, Henry II and Richard I*, iii. 185–9.

28 Henry of Huntingdon, 268–71.

29 Barrow, *Robert Bruce*, 322.

30 *Le Bel*, ii. 106; *Murimuth, Avesbury*, 68; *Chroniques de Froissart*, iii. 170.

31 *Baker*, 145–6.

32 *Chroniques par Waurin*, ed. W. Hardy (RS, 1868), ii. 203–4.

33 Prestwich, *Edward I*, 43; *Chronicles of Edward I and II*, 75; Frame, 'War and Peace in the Medieval Lordship of Ireland', 132.

34 Above, 232.

35 G.J. White, 'The End of Stephen's Reign', *History*, 75 (1990), 7–10.

36 Roger of Howden, *Gesta Regis Henrici Secundi*, i. 51–3; William of Newburgh, 248.

37 *Chronici Rogeri de Wendover*, ii. 105; R.V. Turner, *King John* (1994), 133–4.

38 *Le Bel*, i. 162–5.

39 Froissart, 186–9.

40 *Anonimalle Chronicle*, 61; J.W. Sherborne, 'John of Gaunt, Edward III's Retinue and the French Campaign of 1369', *Kings and Nobles in the Later Middle Ages*, ed. R.A. Griffiths and J.W. Sherborne (Gloucester, 1986), 47–8.

41 Bradbury, *Medieval Archer*, 39–57, gives a good account of

what is known of tactical dispositions in this period.
42 Bennett, 'Wace and Warfare', *ANW*, 249–50 (the text is
printed here); *Orderic Vitalis*, vi.
348; D. Crouch, *The Beaumont
Twins* (Cambridge, 1986), 22.
43 Richard of Hexham, *Chronicles of the Reigns of Stephen,
Henry II and Richard I*, iii. 163.
44 Ambroise, *Crusade of Richard Lion-Heart*, 254.
45 Carpenter, *Lewes and
Evesham*, 31, 64.
46 Morris, *Welsh Wars of
Edward I*, 256; Prestwich,
Edward I, 223. One account
of the battle makes no mention
of such tactics.
47 *Baker*, 9, explains the English defeat as being partly due to
the failure to position the archers
in the way that became usual during the Hundred Years War.
48 Barrow, *Robert Bruce*, 310.
49 G.H. Orpen, *Ireland under
the Normans 1216–1333*, iv
(1920), 200–6.
50 *Lanercost*, 243–4, has the
fullest account of the battle
of Boroughbridge; accounts of
Hereford's death differ, and I
have followed that in the *Brut*,
ed. F.W.D. Brie (Early English
Text Soc., 1906), i, 219, which is
similar to *Baker*, 14.
51 *Rotuli Scotiae*, i. 208; *Le
Bel*, 53, 65.
52 *Baker*, 51.
53 *Oeuvres de Froissart*, ed.
Kervyn de Lettenhove, xviii, 90;
Froissart, ii. 179.
54 *Baker*, 76–7; *Murimuth,
Avesbury*, 128–9; Burne, *The
Crécy War*, 71–5; T.F. Tout, 'The
Tactics of the Battles of
Boroughbridge and Morlaix',
Collected Papers, ii. 224–5.
55 This problem is discussed at
length by Bradbury, *Medieval Archer*, 95–101, and most recently
by Bennett, 'The Development of
Battle Tactics in the Hundred
Years War', *AAF*, 7, 15.
56 *Le Bel*, ii. 105–6; *Baker*, 82,
83–4. There is no archaeological
evidence for pits dug at Crécy,
but the battlefield at Albjubarotta
(1385) has yielded evidence of
rows of such pits, arranged 200

yards wide, and 100 yards in
depth; see Bennett, *op. cit.*, 13.
57 Sumption, *The Hundred
Years War*, 527–8. There has, of
course, been considerable argument about the cannon at Crécy.
Burne, *The Crécy War*, 192–202,
discusses the problem at length.
See also below, 324.
58 T.F. Tout, 'Some Neglected
Fights between Crécy and
Poitiers', *Collected Papers*, ii.
227–31. The battle of Poitiers is
not easy to reconstruct, though
many attempts have been made.
A full account is provided by
Burne, *The Crécy War*, 275–321,
and see also Bennett, 'The Development of Battle Tactics in the
Hundred Years War', 11–13.
59 *Froissart*, v. 77.
60 *Froissart*, vi. 162–9.
61 C. Philpotts, 'The French
Plan of Battle during the
Agincourt Campaign', *EHR*, 30
(1984), 59–68; *Gesta Henrici
Quinti*, 82. For the stakes, see
above, 136.
62 *Chroniques par Waurin*, iii.
110, 113–15.
63 *Jordan Fantosme's Chronicle*, 48–9.
64 Henry of Huntingdon, 121.
65 *Chronici Rogeri de Wendover*, iii. 70.
66 *Baker*, 83, 151. These drums
would not have been used as a
means to encourage men to
march in step; it was not until the
later fifteenth century that more
substantial drums were used with
that purpose. See Vale, *War and
Chivalry*, 152–3.
67 *Gesta Henrici Quinti*, 86.
68 Barrow, *Bruce*, 323–4.
69 *Baker*, 83, 87–8.
70 *Eulogium Historiarum*, 225.
71 *Baker*, 88; *Froissart*, vi. 163.
72 Bennett, 'La Règle de
Temple as a military manual *or*
how to deliver a cavalry charge',
7–19. Training is discussed by
Verbruggen, *The Art of Warfare*,
28–39.
73 D.C. Douglas, *William the
Conqueror* (1964), 202.
74 S. Morillo, 'Hastings: An
Unusual Battle', *The Haskins Society Journal*, 2 (1990), 95–103,
makes some perceptive remarks.

75 *Gesta Stephani*, 112, 146;
Gervase of Canterbury, i. 125–6;
J.O. Prestwich, 'Military Intelligence under the Norman and
Angevin Kings', 16.
76 *Expugnatio Hibernica*, 83.
77 Gillingham, 'William the
Marshal', 10.
78 Ambroise, *Crusade of Richard Lion-Heart*, 256ff.
79 For these battles, see
Carpenter, *Lewes and Evesham*.
80 My account largely follows
the excellent reconstruction by
Barrow, *Robert Bruce*, 310ff. For
Clifford's flight, however, see
Vita Edwardi Secundi, 51.
81 For Badlesmere, see *Political
Songs*, ed. T. Wright, 263–5;
Baker, 8, suggests that Gloucester
was not displaying his coat of
arms.
82 *Jordan Fantosme's Chronicle*, 132, 134, 138.
83 Nicholson, *Edward III and
the Scots*, 88–9.
84 These heaps are well described in *Gesta Henrici Quinti*,
90.
85 Morillo, 'Hastings', 96.
86 *Baker*, 77.
87 Sumption, *Hundred Years
War*, 528–9; *Anonimalle
Chronicle*, 27.
88 *Gesta Henrici Quinti*, 91.
89 *The Chronicle of Walter
of Guisborough*, 328. Accounts
of the battle are inconsistent;
those given in *Willelmi
Rishanger, Chronica et Annales*,
187–8, 385–6, make no mention
of the infantry, apart from the refusal of the Welsh to attack or
participate in the battle until the
final stages.
90 *Baker*, 151.
91 William of Poitiers, trans. in
R.A. Brown, *The Norman Conquest* (1984), 35.
92 *Froissart*, v. 50–52.
93 *The Chronicle of Walter of
Guisborough*, 302, 328.
94 *Chronicles of Edward I and
II*, 58; on the other hand,
Lanercost, 239, suggests that the
Scots killed 4,000, while 1,000
drowned in the Swale.
95 J.L. Gillespie, 'Cheshiremen
at Blore Heath: a Swan Dive',
People, Politics and Community

in the Later Middle Ages, ed. J. Rosenthal and C. Richmond (Gloucester, 1987), 77–89; *Pierre de Langtoft*, 316–17; *The Chronicle of Walter of Guisborough*, 278; *Le Bel*, ii. 108; *Baker*, 85; *Eulogium Historiae*, iii. 225.

96 *Orderic Vitalis*, vi. 240.

97 Carpenter, *Lewes and Evesham*, 64–5.

98 Prestwich, *Edward I*, 192.

99 Barrow, *Robert Bruce*, 329; *Annales Londonienses*, 231. The *Gesta Edwardi* claims that six score nobles and knights were killed.

100 Keen, *Chivalry*, 222.

101 *Froissart*, iii. 421.

102 *Oeuvres de Froissart*, ed. Kervyn de Lettenhove, xviii, 391–2.

103 *Gesta Henrici Quinti*, 95–7; A.H. Burne, *The Agincourt War* (1956), 93.

104 *Baker*, 89.

105 C. Tyson, 'The Battle of Otterburn: when and where was it fought?', *War and Border Societies in the Middle Ages*, ed. A. Goodman and A. Tuck (1992), 91.

106 E 101/25/10.

107 *Expugnatio Hibernica*, 76–7.

108 *Froissart*, vii. 203, 207.

109 *Gesta Stephani*, 134–5.

110 A. Borg, 'Some Medieval War Memorials', *Medieval Architecture and its Intellectual Context: studies in honour of Peter Kidson*, ed. E. Fernie and P. Crossley (1990), 1–7; *CDS*, iii. no. 875; Carpenter, *Lewes and Evesham*, 61.

14 Conclusion: A Military Revolution?

1 I have developed some of the ideas in this chapter in a volume presented to E.B. Fryde, ed. C.F. Richmond (1996).

2 Roberts, *The Military Revolution, 1560–1660*, reprinted in his *Essays in Swedish History*, 195–225.

3 Parker, *The Military Revolution?*, Black, *A Military Revolution?*, 29–30, 93–6.

4 Parker, *The Military Revolution*, 2–3.

5 L. White Jr, *Medieval Technology and Social Change* (Oxford, 1962). The most recent demolition is provided by DeVries, *Medieval Military Technology*, 95–110, who summarises the debate.

6 See most recently C.J. Rogers, 'The Military Revolutions of the Hundred Years' War', *Journal of Military History*, 57 (1993), 241–78.

7 Abels, *Lordship and Military Obligation in Anglo-Saxon England*, 168; Prestwich, 'War and Finance in the Anglo-Norman State', *ANW*, 59–83; *Pipe Roll, 17 John and Praestita Roll, 14–18 John*, 79; Morris, *The Welsh Wars of Edward I*, 68, 108.

8 Ayton, *Knights and Warhorses*, 12.

9 S. Adams, 'The Gran Armada: 1988 and After', *History*, 76 (1991), 247; Black, *A Military Revolution?*, 6–7; Parker, *The Military Revolution*, 23, 69.

10 Roberts, 'The Military Revolution', 216.

11 Parker, *The Military Revolution*, 75–7; Black, *A Military Revolution?*, 37–8, 42–4; Van Crefeld, *Supplying War*, 17–19.

12 Parker, *The Military Revolution*, 77.

13 The costs were first calculated by J.G. Edwards, 'Edward I's Castle-Building in Wales', *Proceedings of the British Academy*, 32 (1946), 62–3; see also *The History of the King's Works*, i, 406–7.

14 Parker, *The Military Revolution*, 61–4.

15 For a convenient summary of these arguments, see W.A. Speck, 'England in the 1690s. The emergence of the Fiscal–Military State', *The Historian*, 38 (1993), 3–8.

16 J. Gillingham, *Richard the Lionheart* (1978), 303–4; J.C. Holt, 'The Loss of Normandy and Royal Finances', *War and Government in the Middle Ages*, ed. Gillingham and Holt, 92–105; J.E.A. Joliffe, 'The Chamber and the Castle Treasures under King John', *Studies in Medieval History presented to F.M. Powicke*, ed. Hunt, Pantin, Southern, 134.

17 Prestwich, *War, Politics and Finance*, 170, 175; E.B. Fryde, *Studies in Medieval Trade and Finance* (1983), VI, 1142; Tout, *Chapters in Medieval Administrative History*, iv. 144; Sherborne, 'The Costs of English Warfare with France', 140.

18 Figures from W.M. Ormrod, 'The Crown and the English Economy', *Before the Black Death*, ed. B.M.S. Campbell (Manchester, 1991), 153, 161; E.B. Fryde, 'Parliament and the French War', in *Historical Studies of the English Parliament, i, Origins to 1399*, ed. E.B. Fryde and E. Miller (Cambridge, 1970), 245, 247.

19 'Annales Prioratus de Dunstaplia', *Annales Monastici*, ed. H.R. Luard (RS, 1864–9), iii. 258.

20 Customs duties are conveniently discussed by Ormrod, 'The Crown and the English Economy', 167–75.

21 R.W. Kaeuper, *Bankers to the Crown: the Riccardi of Lucca and Edward I* (Princeton, 1973); E.B. Fryde, 'Public Credit, with Special Reference to North-Western Europe', *The Cambridge Economic History of Europe*, iii, ed. M.M. Postan, E.E. Rich, E. Miller (Cambridge, 1963), 454–63; E.B. Fryde, 'Financial Resources of Edward III in the Netherlands, 1337–40', in Fryde, *Studies in Medieval Trade and Finance* (1983), VII. 1146, 1153. It may be that much of the money lent by the Bardi and Peruzzi was recycled, with part of their advances being used to repay them for earlier loans: Edwin S. Hunt, 'A New Look at the Dealings of the Bardi and Peruzzi with Edward III', *Journal of Economic History*, 50 (1990), 149–62, has argued that the real level of Edward III's debt to the companies was much lower than these figures suggest.

22   Parker, *The Military Revolution*, 62–4.
23   Calculated from Prestwich, *War, Politics and Finance*, 175, 208–9.
24   E.B. Fryde, 'Financial Resources of Edward I in the Netherlands, 1294–98: main problems and some comparisons with Edward III in 1337–40', in Fryde, *Studies in Medieval Trade and Finance*, II. 1186. The statement by Harriss, *King, Parliament and Public Finance in Medieval England to 1369*, 242, that almost £28,000 was sent overseas by the exchequer in the five months from July 1338 is mistaken. The correct figure is £26,670 17s 2¹/₂d, and it represents not cash sent abroad, but money charged by the exchequer to the wardrobe, including over £11,000 in repayment of loans. See *The Wardrobe Book of William de Norwell*, 2–7, and Tout, *Chapters in Medieval Administrative History*, iii. 91.
25   Parker, *The Military Revolution*, 64.
26   Allmand, *Henry V*, 398.
27   A. Curry, 'The First English Standing Army? – Military Organisation in Lancastrian Normandy, 1420–1450', *Pedigree, Patronage and Power in Late Medieval England*, ed. C. Ross (Gloucester, 1979), 202, 208.
28   Above, 185.
29   Contamine, *Guerre, état et société à la fin du moyen âge*, 255, 278, 304–5, 314, 333.
30   Black, *A Military Revolution?*, 94.

Bibliography

Printed primary sources

(All works are published in London unless otherwise specified)

Acta Imperii Inedita Seculi XIII, ed. E. Winkelman (Innsbruck, 1888)
Adae Murimuth, Continuatio Chronicarum. Robertus de Avesbury, De Gestis Mirabilis Regis Edwardi Tertii, ed. E.M. Thompson (RS, 1889)
Anglo-Scottish Relations 1174–1328: Some Selected Documents, ed. E.L.G. Stones (1965)
Annales Monastici, i–iv, ed. H.R. Luard (RS, 1864–9)
The Anonimalle Chronicle 1333 to 1381, ed. V.H. Galbraith (Manchester, 1927, revised edn 1970)
Book of Prests 1294–5, ed. E.B. Fryde (Oxford, 1962)
The Bruce, ed. W.W. Skeat (Early English Text Soc., extra series 55, 1874, 1877)
The Book of Fayttes of Arms and of Chyvalrye, ed. A.T.P. Byles (Early English Text Soc., 1932)
The Brut, ed. F.W.D. Brie (Early English Text Soc., 1906, 1908)
Calendar of Close Rolls (1892–)
Calendar of Documents relating to Scotland, i–iv, ed. J. Bain (Edinburgh, 1881–8); v, ed. G.G. Simpson and J.D. Galbraith (Edinburgh, 1986)
Calendar of Inquisitions Miscellaneous, iii (1937)
Calendar of Liberate Rolls (1916–)
Calendar of Patent Rolls (1891–)
Catalogus Baronum, ed. E. Jamison (Rome, 1972)
Chancellor's Roll, 8 Richard I, ed. D.M. Stenton (PRS, ns. 7, 1930)
The Chronicle of Bury St Edmunds, 1212–1301, ed. A. Gransden (1964)
Chronica Rogeri de Houeden, iv, ed. W. Stubbs (RS, 1871)
Chronica Rogeri de Wendover, ed. H. Hewlett, iii (RS, 1889)
The Chronicle of Richard of Devizes, ed. J.T. Appleby (1963)
The Chronicle of Walter of Guisborough, ed. H. Rothwell (Camden Soc., 89, 1957)
Chronicle of William of Rishanger of the Barons' Wars, ed. J.O. Halliwell (Camden Soc., 1840)
Chronicles of England, France, Spain and the Adjoining Countries by Sir John Froissart, trans. T. Johnes (1839)
Chronicles of the Reigns of Edward I and II, ed. W. Stubbs (RS, 1882–3)
Chronicles of the Reigns of Stephen, Henry II and Richard I, ed. W. Stubbs (RS, 1884–9)
Chronicon Galfridi le Baker de Swynebroke, ed. E.M. Thompson (Oxford, 1889)
Chronicon Henrici Knighton, ed. J.R. Lumby (RS, 1895)
Chronicon de Lanercost, ed. J. Stevenson (Maitland Club, Edinburgh, 1839)
Chronique de Jean le Bel, ed. J. Viard and E. Déprez (Paris, 1904)
Chroniques de J. Froissart, ed. S. Luce, 15 vols (Paris, 1869–1975)
Close Rolls, 1261–4 (1936)
The Controversy between Sir Richard Scrope and Sir Robert Grosvenor in the Court of Chivalry, i, ed. N.H. Nicolas (1832)

The Crusade of Richard Lion-Heart by Ambroise, trans. M.J. Hubert, ed. J.L. La Monte (Columbia, 1941)

De Expugnatione Lyxbonensi, The Conquest of Lisbon, ed. C.W. David (New York, 1936)

Diplomatic Documents preserved in the Public Record Office, i, 1101–1272, ed. P. Chaplais (Oxford, 1964)

Documents Illustrating the Crisis of 1297–8 in England, ed. M.C. Prestwich (Camden Soc., 4th ser., 24, 1980)

Documents Illustrative of English History in the Thirteenth and Fourteenth Centuries, ed. H. Cole (1844)

Documents Illustrative of the History of Scotland, ed. J. Stevenson (Edinburgh, 1870)

Documents and Records Illustrating the History of Scotland, ed. F. Palgrave (1837)

Domesday Book, ed. A. Farley (1783)

The Ecclesiastical History of Orderic Vitalis, ed. M. Chibnall, 6 vols (Oxford, 1969–80)

English Historical Documents IV, 1327–1485, ed. A.R. Myers (1969)

Eulogium Historiarum, iii, ed. F.S. Haydon (RS, 1863)

Expugnatio Hibernica: the Conquest of Ireland by Giraldus Cambrensis, ed. A.B. Scott and F.X. Martin (Dublin, 1978)

Facsimile of British Museum Harleian MS 2253, introduction by N.R. Ker (Early English Text Soc., 1965)

Flores Historiarum, iii, ed. H.R. Luard (RS, 1980)

Foedera, Conventiones, Litterae etc., ed. T. Rymer, rev. A. Clarke et al. (1816–69)

Gesta Henrici Quinti, ed. F. Taylor and J.S. Roskell (Oxford, 1975)

Gesta Stephani, ed. K.R. Potter and R.H.C. Davis (Oxford, 1976)

Giraldi Cambrensis Opera, vi, vii, ed. J.F. Dimock (RS, 1867, 1868)

Guillaume de Poitiers, Historie de Guillaume le Conquérant, ed. R. Foreville (Paris, 1952)

Histoire des ducs de Normandie et des rois d'Angleterre, ed. F. Michel (Paris, 1840)

The Historia Novella by William of Malmesbury, ed. K.R. Potter (1955)

Historical Documents of Scotland, i and ii, ed. J. Stephenson (Edinburgh, 1870)

Historical Letters and Papers from Northern Registers, ed. J. Raine (RS, 1873)

The Historical Works of Gervase of Canterbury, ed. W. Stubbs (RS, 1879–80)

The Holkham Picture Bible Book, ed. W.O. Hassall (1954)

'Indentures of Retinue with John of Gaunt, Duke of Lancaster, enrolled in Chancery 1367–1399', ed. N.B. Lewis, *Camden Miscellany 22* (Camden Soc., 4th. ser., 1, 1964)

Jordan Fantosme's Chronicle, ed. R.C. Johnston (Oxford, 1981)

Lestoire des Engles solum la translacion Maistre Geffrei Gaimar, ed. T.D. Hardy (RS, 1888)

Letters and Papers Illustrative of the Wars of the English in France during the reign of Henry VI, II (ii), ed. J. Stevenson (RS, 1864)

Liber Quotidianus Contrarotulatoris Garderobae, ed. J. Topham et al. (Soc. of Antiquaries, 1787)

A Lincolnshire Assize Roll for 1289, ed. W.S. Thomson (Lincoln Record Soc., 36, 1944)

The London Eyre of 1276, ed. M. Weinbaum (London Record Soc., 1976)

Map, Walter, *De Nugis Curialum*, ed. M.R. James (1914)

Matthaei Parisiensis, Chronica Majora, ed. H.R. Luard, iv (RS, 1877)

Memoriale Walteri de Coventria, ed. W. Stubbs (RS, 1872–3)

Le Morte Arthur, ed. P.F. Hissiger (The Hague, 1975)

The Navy of the Lancastrian Kings: Accounts and Inventories of William Soper, Keeper of the King's Ships, 1422–1427, ed. S. Rose (Navy Records Soc., 1982)

Northern Petitions, ed. C.M. Fraser (Surtees Soc., 194, 1981)

Oeuvres de Froissart, ed. Kervyn de Lettenhove (Brussels, 1867–77)

Original Letters, iv, ed. H. Ellis, 3rd ser. (1846)

Parliamentary Writs, ed. F. Palgrave (1827–34)

Patent Rolls, 1225–32 (1903)

Philippe de Commynes. Memoirs, trans. M. Jones (Harmondsworth, 1972)

Pierre de Langtoft, le règne d'Edouard Ier, ed. J.C. Thiolier (Créteil, 1989)

Pipe Roll, 20 Henry II (PRS, 21, 1896)
Pipe Roll, 2 Richard I, ed. D.M. Stenton (PRS, ns 1, 1925)
Pipe Roll, 5 Richard I, ed. D.M. Stenton (PRS, ns 3, 1927)
Pipe Roll, 7 Richard I, ed. D.M. Stenton (PRS, ns 6, 1929)
Pipe Roll, 5 John, ed. D.M. Stenton (PRS, ns xx, 1942)
Pipe Roll, 6 John, ed. D.M. Stenton (PRS, ns xviii, 1940)
Pipe Roll, 9 John, ed. A.M. Kirkus (PRS, ns xxii, 1946)
Pipe Roll, 12 John, ed. C.F. Slade (PRS, ns xxvi, 1951)
Pipe Roll, 16 John, ed. P.M. Barnes (PRS, ns xxxv, 1962)
Pipe Roll, 17 John and Praestita Roll, 14–18 John, ed. R.A. Brown and J.C. Holt (PRS, ns xxxvii, 1964)
Pipe Roll, 4 Henry III, ed. B.E. Harris (PRS, ns 85, 1987)
'A Plea Roll of Edward I's Army in Scotland, 1296', *Miscellany of the Scottish History Society*, xi (1990), ed. C.J. Neville
Political Poems and Songs, ed. T. Wright, i (RS, 1859)
Political Songs, ed. T. Wright (Camden Soc., 1839)
'Private Indentures for Life Service in Peace and War', ed. M. Jones and S. Walker, *Camden Miscellany* 32 (Camden Soc. 5th ser., 3, 1994)
Proceedings and Ordinances of the Privy Council, ed. N.H. Nicolas, ii (1834)
'The Ransom of John II, 1360–70', ed. D.M. Broome, *Camden Miscellany*, xiv (Camden Soc., 1926)
Ralph of Coggeshall, *Chronicon Anglicanum*, ed. J. Stevenson (RS, 1875)
Receipt and Issue Rolls, 26 Henry III, ed. R.C. Stacey (PRS, 1992)
Recueil des Chroniques et anchiennes Istoires de la Grant Bretaigne, a present nomme Engleterre, par Jean de Waurin, ii, ed. W. Hardy (RS, 1868)
The Red Book of the Exchequer, i–iii, ed. H. Hall (RS, 1896)
Regesta Regum Anglo-Normannorum 1066–1154, ii, ed. C. Johnson and H.A. Cronne (Oxford, 1956); iii, ed. H.A. Cronne and R.H.C. Davis (Oxford, 1968)
Register of the Black Prince, iv, A. D. 1351–1365 (1933)
Roger of Howden, *The Chronicle of the Reigns of Henry II and Richard I, known comonly under the name of Benedict of Peterborough*, ed. W. Stubbs (RS, 1867)
Rogeri de Wendover liber qui dicitur Flores Historiarum, ii, ed. H.G. Hewlett (RS, 1887)
Roll of Divers Accounts for the Early Years of Henry III, ed. F.A. Cazel, jr (PRS, ns 44, 1982)
Rotuli de Liberate ac de Misis et Praestitis regnante Johanne, ed. T.D. Hardy (1844)
Rotuli Litterarum Clausarum, ed. T.D. Hardy (1833–4)
Rotuli Litterarum Patentium in Turri Londonensi asservati, ed. T.D. Hardy (1835)
Rotuli Parliamentorum, ed. J. Strachey et al. (1783–1832)
Rotuli Scotiae in Turri Londinensi et in Domo Capitulari Westmonasteriensi asservati, i, ed. D. Macpherson, J. Caley, W. Illingworth and T.H. Horne (1814)
Scalacronica by Sir Thomas Grey of Heton Knight, ed. J. Stevenson (Edinburgh; Maitland Club, 1836)
Scotland in 1298, ed. H. Gough (Paisley, 1888)
Select Cases in the Court of King's Bench, Edward I, iii, ed. G.O. Sayles (Selden Soc., 58, 1939)
Select Cases of Procedure without Writ under Henry III, ed. H.G. Richardson and G.O. Sayles (Selden Soc., 60, 1941)
Select Charters and other Illustrations of English Constitutional History, ed. W. Stubbs, rev. H.W.C. Davis (9th edn, Oxford, 1921)
The Siege of Carlaverock, ed. N.H. Nicolas (1828)
Simeon of Durham, *Symeonis Monachi Opera Omnia*, ed. T. Arnold (RS, 1882–5)
The 1341 Royal Inquest in Lincolnshire, ed. B.W. McLane (Lincoln Record Soc., 78, 1987)
The Treatise of Walter of Milemete, ed. M.R. James (Roxburghe Club, 1913)
La Vie du Prince Noir by Chandos Herald, ed. D.B. Tyson (Tübingen, 1975)
Vita Edwardi Secundi, ed. N. Denholm-Young (1957)
The War of St Sardos (1323–1325), ed. P. Chaplais (Camden Soc., 3rd ser., 87, 1954)

The Wardrobe Book of William de Norwell 12 July 1338 to 27 May 1340, ed. M. Lyon, B. Lyon, H.S. Lucas (Brussels, 1983)
Willelmi Rishanger, Chronica et Annales, ed. H.T. Riley (RS, 1865)

Secondary sources

Abels, R.P., *Lordship and Military Obligation in Anglo-Saxon England* (1990)
Ailes, A., 'The Knight, Heraldry and Armour: The Role of Recognition and the Origins of Heraldry', *Medieval Knighthood*, iv, ed. C. Harper-Bill and R. Harvey (Woodbridge, 1992)
Ainsworth, P.F., *Jean Froissart and the Fabric of History* (Oxford, 1990)
Alban, J.R., 'English Coastal Defence: some Fourteenth-Century Modifications within the System', *Patronage, The Crown and The Provinces in Later Medieval England*, ed. R.A. Griffiths (Gloucester, 1981)
Alban, J.R., and Allmand, C.T., 'Spies and Spying in the Fourteenth Century', *War, Literature and Politics in the Late Middle Ages*, ed. C.T. Allmand (Liverpool, 1976)
Allmand, C.T., *The Hundred Years War* (1988)
———, *Henry V* (1992)
———, (ed.), *War, Literature and Politics in the Late Middle Ages* (Liverpool, 1976)
Anderson, R. and R.C., *The Sailing Ship* (1926)
Anderson, R.C., 'Early Two-Masted and Three-Masted Ships in England', *Mariner's Mirror*, 14 (1928)
———, 'English Galleys in 1295', *Mariner's Mirror*, 14 (1928)
———, 'Wynewes', *Mariner's Mirror*, 14 (1928)
Arthurson, I., 'Espionage and Intelligence from the Wars of the Roses to the Reformation', *Nottingham Medieval Studies*, 35 (1991)
Ayton, A.C., 'The Warhorse and Military Service under Edward III' (Hull Ph.D. thesis, 1990)
———, 'The English Army and the Normandy Campaign of 1346', *England and Normandy in the Middle Ages*, ed. D. Bates and A. Curry (1994)
———, *Knights and Warhorses. Military Service and the English Aristocracy under Edward III* (Woodbridge, 1994)
Bachrach, B.S., 'The Military Administration of the Norman Conquest', *ANS*, 8 (1985)
———, 'Logistics in Pre-Crusade Europe', *Feeding Mars: Logistics in Western Warfare from the Middle Ages to the Present*, ed. J.A. Lynn (Boulder, Colorado, 1993)
Barker, J.R.V., *The Tournament in England 1100–1400* (Woodbridge, 1986)
Barlow, F., *Edward the Confessor* (1970)
———, *William Rufus* (1983)
Barrow, G.W.S., *Robert Bruce and the Community of the Realm of Scotland* (1965)
Bates, D., and Curry, A., *England and Normandy in the Middle Ages* (1994)
Bean, J.M.W., *From Lord to Patron: Lordship in Late Medieval England* (Manchester, 1989)
Beeler, J.H., 'Castles and Strategy in Norman and Early Angevin England', *Speculum*, 31 (1956)
———, *Warfare in England, 1066–1189* (Ithaca, 1966)
Bennett, M., '*La Règle du Temple* as a Military Manual, *or* How to Deliver a Cavalry Charge', *Studies in Medieval History presented to R. Allen Brown*, ed. C. Harper-Bill, C.J. Holdsworth, J.L. Nelson (Woodbridge, 1989)
———, 'Wace and Warfare', *Anglo-Norman Warfare*, ed. Strickland (Woodbridge, 1992)
———, 'The Development of Battle Tactics in the Hundred Years War', *Arms, Armies and Fortifications in the Hundred Years War*, ed. Curry and Hughes (Woodbridge, 1994)
Bennett, M.J., *Community, Class and Careerism: Cheshire and Lancashire Society in the Age of Sir Gawain and the Green Knight* (Cambridge, 1983)
Black, J.M., *A Military Revolution? Military Change and European Society 1550–1800* (1991)
Blair, C., *European Armour* (1958)

Borg, A., 'Some Medieval War Memorials', in *Medieval Architecture and its Intellectual Context: studies in honour of Peter Kidson*, ed. E. Fernie and P. Crossley (1990)

Boulton, D'A.J.D., *The Knights of the Crown. The Monarchical Orders of Knighthood in Later Medieval Europe 1325–1520* (Woodbridge, 1987)

Boussard, J., 'Les mercenaires au xiie siècle: Henri II Plantagenet et les origines de l'armée de métier', *Bibliothèque de l'école des Chartes*, 106 (1945–6)

Boutrouche, R., 'The Devastation of Rural Areas during the Hundred Years War and the Agricultural Recovery of France', *The Recovery of France in the Fifteenth Century*, ed. P.S. Lewis (1971)

Bradbury, J., *The Medieval Archer* (Woodbridge, 1985)

——, 'Battles in England and Normandy, 1066–1154', *Anglo-Norman Warfare*, ed. Strickland (Woodbridge, 1992)

——, *The Medieval Siege* (Woodbridge, 1992)

Bridge, J.C., 'Two Cheshire Soldiers of Fortune of the XIV Century: Sir Hugh Calveley & Sir Robert Knollys', *Journal of the Chester Archaeological Society*, 14 (1908)

Brill, R., 'The English Preparations before the Treaty of Arras: a New Interpretation of Sir John Fastolf's "Report", September, 1435', *Studies in Medieval and Renaissance History* 7 (1970)

Brooks, F.W., 'William de Wrotham and the Office of Keeper of the King's Ports and Galleys', *EHR*, 40 (1925)

——, *The English Naval Forces, 1199–1272* (1932)

Brooks, N.P., 'The Development of Military Obligations in Eighth- and Ninth-Century England', *England before the Conquest*, ed. P. Clemoes and K. Hughes (Cambridge, 1971)

——, and Walker, H.E., 'The Interpretation and Authority of the Bayeux Tapestry', *Proceedings of the Battle Conference 1978*, ed. R.A. Brown (Ipswich, 1979)

Brown, R.A., 'A Note on Kenilworth Castle: the change to Royal Ownership', *Archaeological Journal*, 110 (1953)

——, *Origins of English Feudalism* (1973)

——, *The Norman Conquest* (1984)

——, 'The Battle of Hastings', *Anglo-Norman Warfare*, ed. Strickland (Woodbridge, 1992)

Brown, R.A., Colvin, H.M., Taylor, A.J., *The History of the King's Works*, i (1963)

Brown, S., 'The Mercenary and his Master: Military Service and Monetary Reward in the Eleventh and Twelfth Centuries', *History*, 74 (1989)

Burne, A.H., *The Agincourt War* (1956)

——, *The Crécy War* (1955)

Burton, D.W., 'Requests for Prayers and Royal Propaganda under Edward I', *Thirteenth Century England III*, ed. P.R. Coss and S.D. Lloyd (Woodbridge, 1991)

Cam, H.M., *The Hundred and the Hundred Rolls* (1930)

Cannon, H.L., 'The Battle of Sandwich and Eustace the Monk', *EHR*, 27 (1912)

Carpenter, D.A., 'Was there a Crisis of the Knightly Class in the Thirteenth Century? The Oxfordshire Evidence', *EHR*, 95 (1980)

——, *The Battles of Lewes and Evesham 1264/5* (1987)

——, *The Minority of Henry III* (1990)

Carpenter, D.A., Coss, P.R., Crouch, D., 'Debate: Bastard Feudalism Revised', *Past and Present*, 131 (1991)

Chaplais, P., *Piers Gaveston, Edward II's Adoptive Brother* (Oxford, 1994)

Chibnall, M., 'Mercenaries and the *Familia Regis* under Henry I', *Anglo-Norman Warfare*, ed. Strickland (Woodbridge, 1992), and *History*, 62 (1977)

——, *The Empress Matilda, Queen Consort, Queen Mother and Lady of the English* (Oxford, 1991)

——, 'Military Service in Normandy before 1066', *Anglo-Norman Warfare*, ed. Strickland (Woodbridge, 1992)

Childs, W.R., *Anglo-Castilian Trade in the Later Middle Ages* (Manchester, 1978)

Church, S.D., 'The Knights of the Household of King John: A Question of Numbers', *Thirteenth*

Century England IV. Proceedings of the Newcastle upon Tyne Conference 1991
(Woodbridge, 1992)
——, 'The Earliest English Muster Roll, 18/19 December 1215', *Historical Research*, 67
(1994)
Cockayne, G.E. et al. (ed.), *The Complete Peerage* (1910–57)
Conlon, D.J., 'La Chanson d'Audigier – A scatological parody of the *chansons de geste* edited
from Ms Bibliothèque nationale, f. fr. 19152', *Nottingham Medieval Studies*, 33 (1989)
Contamine, P., *Guerre, état et société à la fin du moyen âge. Etudes sur les armées des rois de
France 1337–1494* (Paris, 1972)
——, *War in the Middle Ages*, trans. M. Jones (Oxford, 1984)
——, ed., *Historie militaire de la France, I – Des origines à 1715* (Paris, 1992)
Contamine, P., Giry-Deloison, C., Keen, M.H. (eds), *Guerre et société en France, en Angleterre
et en Bourgogne, xive–xve siècle* (Villeneuve d'Asq, 1991)
Coss, P.R., 'Sir Geoffrey de Langley and the Crisis of the Knightly Class in Thirteenth Century
England', *Past and Present*, 68 (1975)
——, 'Bastard Feudalism Revised', *Past and Present*, 125 (1989)
——, *Lordship, Knighthood and Locality. A Study in English Society c. 1180–c. 1280*
(Cambridge, 1991)
——, *The Knight in Medieval England 1000–1400* (Stroud, 1993)
Coulson, C.H., 'The Castles of the Anarchy', *The Anarchy of Stephen's Reign*, ed. E. King
(Oxford, 1994)
——, 'Freedom to Crenellate by Licence – An Historical Revision', *Nottingham Medieval
Studies*, 38 (1994)
Critchley, J.S., 'Summonses to Military Service early in the reign of Henry III', *EHR*, 85 (1971)
——, 'The Early History of the Writ of Protection', *BIHR*, 45 (1972)
Crouch, D., *The Beaumont Twins* (Cambridge, 1986)
——, *William Marshal. Court, Career and Chivalry in the Angevin Empire 1147–1219*
(1990)
——, *The Image of Aristocracy in Britain 1000–1300* (1992)
Crouch, D., Carpenter, D.A., Coss, P.R., 'Debate: Bastard Feudalism Revised', *Past and Present*,
131 (1991)
Cruickshank, C.G., *Elizabeth's Army* (2nd edn, Oxford, 1966)
Curry, A., 'The First English Standing Army? – Military Organisation in Lancastrian
Normandy, 1420–1450', *Pedigree, Patronage and Power in Late Medieval England*, ed. C.
Ross (Gloucester, 1979)
——, *The Hundred Years War* (1993)
——, 'English Armies in the Fifteenth Century', *Arms, Armies and Fortifications in the
Hundred Years War*, ed. Curry and Hughes (Woodbridge, 1994)
——, and Hughes, M. (eds), *Arms, Armies and Fortifications in the Hundred Years War*
(Woodbridge, 1994)
Davies, R.R., *Conquest, Coexistence and Change: Wales, 1063–1415* (Oxford, 1987)
Davis, R.H.C., *The Medieval Warhorse* (1989)
Denholm-Young, N., 'Feudal Society in the Thirteenth Century: the Knights', in his *Collected
Papers on Medieval Subjects* (Oxford, 1946)
——, *History and Heraldry 1254 to 1310* (Oxford, 1965)
DeVries, K., *Medieval Military Technology* (Peterborough, Ontario, 1992)
Dixon, P., *Aydon Castle* (1988)
——, 'From Hall to Tower: The Change in Seigneurial Houses on the Anglo-Scottish Border
after c. 1250', *Thirteenth Century IV*, ed. P.R. Coss and S.D. Lloyd (Woodbridge, 1992)
Douglas, D.C., *William the Conqueror* (1964)
Eales, R.G., 'Royal Power and Castles in Norman England', *The Ideals and Practice of Medieval
Knighthood*, iii, ed. C. Harper-Bill and R. Harvey (1990)
Edwards, J.G., 'The Treason of Thomas Turberville, 1295', *Studies in Medieval History pre-
sented to F.M. Powicke*, ed. R.W. Hunt, W.A. Pantin, R.W. Southern (Oxford, 1948)

Fernie, E., and Crossley, P. (eds), *Medieval Architecture and its Intellectual Context: studies in honour of Peter Kidson* (1990)

Fleming, D.F., 'Landholding by *Milites* in Domesday Book: a Revision', *ANS*, 13 (1990)

Fowler, K.A., *The King's Lieutenant, Henry of Grosmont, First Duke of Lancaster 1310–1361* (1969)

———, 'News from the Front in the XIVth Century', *Guerre et société en France, en Angleterre et en Bourgogne xive–xve siècle*, ed. P. Contamine, C. Giry-Deloison, M.H. Keen (Villeneuve d'Ascq, 1991)

Frame, R.F., 'War and Peace in the Medieval Lordship of Ireland', *The English in Medieval Ireland*, ed. J.F. Lydon (Dublin, 1984)

———, 'Military Service in Ireland', *Medieval Frontier Societies*, ed. R.A. Bartlett and A. MacKay (Oxford, 1989)

Freeman, A.Z., 'Wall-Breakers and River-Bridgers', *Journal of British Studies*, 10 (1970)

Friel, I., 'Winds of Change? Ships and the Hundred Years War', *AAF*

Fryde, E.B., 'Public Credit, with Special Reference to North-Western Europe', *The Cambridge Economic History of Europe* iii, ed. M.M. Postan, E.E. Rich, E. Miller (Cambridge, 1963)

———, *Studies in Medieval Trade and Finance* (1983)

———, 'Magnate Debts to Edward I and Edward III', *National Library of Wales Journal*, 27 (1992)

Fryde, N., *The Tyranny and Fall of Edward II* (Cambridge, 1979)

Garnett, G., and Hudson, J., *Law and Government in Medieval England and Normandy* (Cambridge, 1994)

Géraud, H., 'Les Routiers au douzième siècle', *Bibliothèque de l'école des Chartes*, 3 (1841–2)

Gillingham, J., *Richard the Lionheart* (1978)

———, 'The Introduction of Knight Service into England', *ANS*, 5 (1982)

———, 'Richard I and the Science of War in the Middle Ages', *War and Government in the Middle Ages*, ed. J. Gillingham and J.C. Holt (Woodbridge, 1984)

———, 'War and Chivalry in the History of William the Marshal', *Anglo-Norman Warfare*, ed. Strickland, and *Thirteenth Century England II*, ed. P.R. Coss and S.D. Lloyd (Woodbridge, 1988)

———, 'William the Bastard at War', *Studies in Medieval History presented to R. Allen Brown*, ed. C. Harper-Bill, C.J. Holdsworth, J.L. Nelson (Woodbridge, 1989)

———, '1066 and the Introduction of Chivalry into England', *Law and Government in Medieval England and Normandy: Essays in honour of Sir James Holt*, ed. G. Garnett and J. Hudson (Cambridge, 1994)

———, and Holt, J.C., *War and Government in the Middle Ages* (Woodbridge, 1984)

Gillespie, J.L., 'Cheshiremen at Blore Heath: a Swan Dive', *People, Politics and Community in the Later Middle Ages*, ed. J. Rosenthal and C. Richmond (Gloucester, 1987)

Gist, M.A., *Love and War in the Middle English Romances* (1947)

Given-Wilson, C.J., *The Royal Household and the King's Affinity: Service, Politics and Finance in England 1360–1413* (1986)

Golding, B., *Conquest and Colonisation. The Normans in Britain 1066–1100* (1994)

Goodman, A., 'The Military Subcontracts of Sir Hugh Hastings, 1380', *EHR*, 95 (1980)

———, 'Responses to Requests in Yorkshire for Military Service under Henry V', *Northern History*, 17 (1981)

———, *The Wars of the Roses: Military Activity and English Society, 1452–97* (1981)

———, *John of Gaunt. The Exercise of Princely Power in Fourteenth-Century Europe* (1992)

———, and Tuck, A., *War and Border Societies in the Middle Ages* (1992)

Graham-Campbell, J., 'Anglo-Scandinavian Equestrian Equipment in Eleventh Century England', *ANS*, xiv (1992)

Green, C., and Whittingham, A.B., 'Excavations at Walsingham Priory, Norfolk, 1961', *Archaeological Journal*, 125 (1968)

Grose, F., *Military Antiquities respecting a History of the English Army* (1801)

Hansen, V.P., 'Reconstructing a Medieval Trebuchet', *Military Illustrated –Past and Present*

(1990)

Hardy, R., *Longbow* (revised edn, 1982)

Harvey, S., 'The Knight and the Knight's Fee in England', *Past and Present*, 49 (1970)

Heslop, T.A., 'Orford Castle, nostalgia and sophisticated living', *Architectural History*, 34 (1991)

Hewitt, H.J., *The Black Prince's Expedition 1355–1357* (Manchester, 1958)

——, *The Organisation of War under Edward III* (Manchester, 1966)

——, 'The Organisation of War', *The Hundred Years War*, ed. K. Fowler (1971)

——, *The Horse in Medieval England* (1983)

Holdsworth, C.J., 'War and Peace in the Twelfth Century. The Reign of Stephen Reconsidered', *War and Peace in the Middle Ages*, ed. B.P. McGuire (Copenhagen, 1987)

Hollister, C.W., *Anglo-Saxon Military Institutions* (Oxford, 1962)

——, *The Military Organisation of Norman England* (Oxford, 1965)

Holmes, G.A., *The Good Parliament* (Oxford, 1975)

Holt, J.C., *The Northerners* (Oxford, 1961)

——, 'The Loss of Normandy and Royal Finances', *War and Government in the Middle Ages*, ed. Gillingham and Holt (Woodbridge, 1984)

——, 'The Introduction of Knight-Service in England', *Anglo-Norman Warfare*, ed. Strickland, and *ANS*, 6 (1983)

Huizinga, J., *The Waning of the Middle Ages* (1924)

Hunt, E.S., 'A New Look at the Dealings of the Bardi and Peruzzi with Edward III', *Journal of Economic History*, 50 (1990)

Hunter, J., 'Proofs of the Early Use of Gunpowder in the English Army', *Archaelogia*, 32 (1847)

Hyland, A., *The Medieval Warhorse from Byzantium to the Crusades* (Gloucester, 1994)

Jacob, E.F., *The Fifteenth Century 1399–1485* (Oxford, 1961)

Jefferson, L., 'MS Arundel 48 and the Earliest Statutes of the Order of the Garter', *EHR*, 109 (1994)

Johnson, C., 'London Shipbuilding, AD 1295', *Antiquaries Journal*, 7 (1927)

Johnstone, H., *Edward of Caernarvon, 1284–1307* (Manchester, 1946)

Joliffe, J.E.A., 'The Chamber and the Castle Treasures under King John', *Studies in Medieval History presented to F.M. Powicke*, ed. R.W. Hunt, W.A. Pantin, R.W. Southern (Oxford, 1948)

Jones, M., 'Two Exeter Ship Agreements of 1303 and 1310', *Mariner's Mirror*, 53 (1967)

——, *Ducal Brittany, 1364–1399* (Oxford, 1970)

——, 'An Indenture between Robert, Lord Mohaut, and Sir John de Bracebridge for life service in peace and war, 1310', *Journal of the Society of Archivists*, 4 (1972)

——, 'John Beaufort, duke of Somerset and the French expedition of 1443', *Patronage, the Crown and the Provinces in Later Medieval England*, ed. R.A. Griffiths (Gloucester, 1981)

——, 'War and Fourteenth-Century France', *Arms, Armies and Fortifications in the Hundred Years War*, ed. Curry and Hughes (Woodbridge, 1994)

Kapelle, W.E., *The Norman Conquest of the North* (1979)

Keen, M., *The Laws of War in the Middle Ages* (1965)

——, *Chivalry* (1988)

Keefe, T.K., *Feudal Assessments and the Political Community under Henry II and his Sons* (Berkeley and Los Angeles, 1983)

Kepler, J.S., 'The Effects of the Battle of Sluys upon the Administration of English Naval Impressment, 1340–1343', *Speculum*, 48 (1973)

Krizek, L., 'Trebuchet Constructions in Czechoslovakia', *Military Illustrated –Past and Present* (1992)

Laird Clowes, G.S., *Sailing Ships, their History and Development* (1932)

de Larrea Rojas, J.A.F., *Guerra y sociedad en Navarra durante la Edad Media* (Bilbao, 1992)

Latimer, P., 'Henry II's Campaign against the Welsh in 1165', *Welsh History Review*, 14 (1989)

Le Patourel, J., *The Norman Empire* (Oxford, 1976)

Lewis, A., 'Roger Leyburn and the Pacification of England, 1265–7', *EHR*, 54 (1939)

Lewis, N.B., 'An Early Indenture of Military Service, 27 July 1287', *BIHR*, 13 (1935)
——, 'The Last Medieval Summons of the English Feudal Levy, 13 June 1385', *EHR*, 73 (1958)
——, 'Recruitment and Organisation of a Contract Army. May to November 1337', *BIHR*, 37 (1964)
Lloyd, S.D., 'The Lord Edward's Crusade, 1270–2: its setting and significance', *War and Government in the Middle Ages*, ed. Gillingham and Holt (Woodbridge, 1984)
——, *English Society and the Crusade 1216–1307* (Oxford, 1988)
Lomas, R.A., *North-East England in the Middle Ages* (Edinburgh, 1992)
Lucas, H.S., *The Low Countries and the Hundred Years War* (Ann Arbor, 1929)
Lydon, J., 'The Dublin Purveyors and the Wars in Scotland, 1296–1324', *Keimelia: Studies in Medieval Archaeology and History in honour of Tom Delaney*, ed. G. MacNiocall and P.F. Wallace (Galway, 1988)
Lyon, B.D., 'The Feudal Antecedents of the Indenture System', *Speculum*, 29 (1954)
——, *From Fief to Indenture* (Cambridge, Mass., 1957)
McFarlane, K.B., 'A Business Partnership in War and Administration, 1421–45', *EHR*, 78 (1963)
——, 'An Indenture of Agreement between two English Knights of Mutual Aid and Counsel in Peace and War, 5 December 1298', *BIHR*, 38 (1965)
——, *The Nobility of Later Medieval England* (1973)
McKisack, M., *The Fourteenth Century 1307–1399* (Oxford, 1959)
McNamee, C., 'Buying Off Robert Bruce: An Account of Monies paid to the Scots by Cumberland Communities in 1313–14', *Transactions of the Cumberland and Westmorland Antiquarian and Archaeological Society*, 92 (1992)
Maddicott, J.R., *Thomas of Lancaster* (Oxford, 1970)
——, *The English Peasantry and the Demands of the Crown 1294–1341 (Past and Present Supplement 1, 1975)*
Marks, R., 'Sir Geoffrey Luttrell and some Companions: Images of Chivalry c. 1320–50', *Wiener Jahrbuch für Kunstgeschichte*, 46–7 (1993–4)
Mason, J.F.A., 'Barons and their Officials in the Later Eleventh Century', *ANS*, 13 (1990)
Massey, R., 'The Land Settlement in Lancastrian Normandy', *Property and Politics: Essays in Later Medieval English History*, ed. A.J. Pollard (Gloucester, 1984)
Mathew, G., 'Ideals of Knighthood in Late-Fourteenth-Century England', *Studies in Medieval History presented to F.M. Powicke*, ed. R.W. Hunt, W.A. Pantin, R.W. Southern (Oxford, 1948)
Matthew, D., *The Norman Kingdom of Sicily* (1992)
Mitchell, S.K., *Studies in Taxation under John and Henry III* (Oxford, 1914)
Morgan, P., *War and Society in Medieval Cheshire, 1277–1403* (Chetham Soc., 3rd ser., 34, 1987)
Morillo, S., 'Hastings: An Unusual Battle', *The Haskins Society Journal*, 2 (1990)
——, *Warfare under the Anglo-Norman Kings, 1066–1135* (Woodbridge, 1994)
Morris, J.E., *The Welsh Wars of Edward I* (Oxford, 1901)
——, 'Mounted Infantry in Medieval Warfare', *TRHS*, 3rd ser. viii (1914)
Nicolas, N.H., *A History of the Battle of Agincourt* (1832)
——, *A History of the Royal Navy* (1847)
Newhall, R.A., *The English Conquest of Normandy 1416–1424* (New Haven, 1924)
——, *Muster and Review* (Harvard, 1940)
Norgate, K., *The Minority of Henry III* (1912)
Oakeshott, R.E., *The Archaeology of Weapons* (1960)
——, *The Sword in the Age of Chivalry* (1981)
Oman, C., *A History of the Art of War in the Middle Ages*, ii (revised edn, 1924)
Ormrod, W.M., 'The Crown and the English Economy', *Before the Black Death*, ed. B.M.S. Campbell (Manchester, 1991)
Orpen, G.H., *Ireland under the Normans 1216–1333*, iv (1920)

Painter, S., *King John* (Baltimore, 1949)

——, *William Marshal, Knight Errant, Baron, and Regent of England* (repr. 1971)

Palliser, D.M., 'Domesday Book and the "Harrying of the North"', *Northern History*, 29 (1993)

Palmer, J.J.N., 'The Last Summons of the Feudal Army in England', *EHR*, 83 (1968)

Parker, G., *The Military Revolution: Military Innovation and the Rise of the West, 1500–1800* (Cambridge, 1988)

Patourel, J. le, *The Norman Empire* (Oxford, 1976)

Peirce, I., 'The Knight, his Arms and Armour in the Eleventh and Twelfth Centuries', *The Ideals and Practice of Medieval Knighthood*, ed. C. Harper-Bill and R. Harvey (Woodbridge, 1986)

——, 'The Development of the Medieval Sword', *The Ideals and Practice of Medieval Knighthood*, 3 (1990)

——, 'The Knight, his Arms and his Armour c. 1150–1250', *ANS*, xv (1992)

Perroy, E., 'Gras profits et rançons pendant la guerre de Cent Ans; l'affaire du comte de Denia', *Mélanges d'histoire du Moyen Age dédiés à la mémoire de Louis Halphen* (Paris, 1951)

Phillips, J.R.S., *Aymer de Valence, Earl of Pembroke 1307–1324* (Oxford, 1972)

Philpotts, C., 'The French Plan of Battle during the Agincourt Campaign', *EHR*, 30 (1984)

Platt, C., *Medieval Southampton. The Port and Trading Community, AD 1000–1600* (1973)

Pollard, A.J., *John Talbot and the War in France 1427–1453* (1983)

Pollock, F., and Maitland, F.W., *The History of English Law* (2nd edn, Cambridge, 1898)

Poole, A.L., *The Obligations of Society in the XII and XIII Centuries* (Oxford, 1946)

——, 'Richard the First's Alliances with the German Princes in 1194', *Studies in Medieval History presented to F.M. Powicke*, ed. R.W. Hunt, W.A. Pantin, R.W. Southern (Oxford, 1948)

Pounds, N.J.G., *The Medieval Castle in England and Wales* (Cambridge, 1990)

Powicke, F.M., *King Henry III and the Lord Edward*, i (Oxford, 1947)

——, *The Loss of Normandy* (2nd edn, Manchester, 1960)

Powicke, M., 'Lancastrian Captains', in *Essays in Medieval History presented to Bertie Wilkinson*, ed. T.A. Sandquist and M.R. Powicke (Toronto, 1969)

——, *Military Obligation in Medieval England* (Oxford, 1962)

Prestwich, J.O., 'War and Finance in the Anglo-Norman State', *Anglo-Norman Warfare*, ed. Strickland (Woodbridge, 1992), and *TRHS*, 5th ser. 4 (1955)

——, 'The Military Household of the Norman Kings', *Anglo-Norman Warfare*, ed. Strickland, and *EHR*, 96 (1981)

——, 'Richard Coeur de Lion: *Rex Bellicosus*', *Richard Coeur de Lion in History and Myth*, ed. J.L. Nelson (1992)

——, 'Military Intelligence under the Norman and Angevin Kings', *Law and Government in Medieval England and Normandy*, ed. G. Garnett and J. Hudson (Cambridge, 1994)

Prestwich, M.C., 'Victualling Estimates for English Garrisons in Scotland during the Early Fourteenth Century', *EHR*, lxxxii (1967)

——, *War, Politics and Finance under Edward I* (1972)

——, 'An Indenture between Ralph, Lord Basset of Drayton, and Philip de Chetwynd, 4 March 1319', *Transactions of the Stafford Historical and Civic Society* (1971–3)

——, *The Three Edwards: War and State in England, 1272–1377* (1980)

——, 'English Castles in the reign of Edward II', *Journal of Medieval History*, 8 (1982)

——, 'English Armies in the Early Stages of the Hundred Years War', *BIHR*, 56 (1983)

——, 'Cavalry Service in Early Fourteenth Century England', *War and Government in the Middle Ages*, ed. Gillingham and Holt (Woodbridge, 1984)

——, 'Royal Patronage under Edward I', *Thirteenth Century England I*, ed. P. Coss and S.D. Lloyd (Woodbridge, 1986)

——, 'Colonial Scotland: the English in Scotland under Edward I', *Scotland and England 1286–1815*, ed. R.A. Mason (Edinburgh, 1987)

——, *Edward I* (1988)

——, 'England and Scotland during the Wars of Independence', *England and Her Neighbours 1066–1453: Essays in Honour of Pierre Chaplais*, ed. M. Jones and M. Vale (1989)

Prince, A.E., 'The Strength of English Armies in the Reign of Edward III', *EHR*, 46 (1931)

——, 'The Indenture System under Edward III', *Historical Essays presented to James Tait*, ed. J.G. Edwards, V.H. Galbraith, E.F. Jacob (Manchester, 1933)

——, 'The Army and Navy', *The English Government at Work, 1327–1336*, ed. J.F. Willard and W.A. Morris, i (Cambridge, Mass, 1940)

Pryor, J.H., 'The Transportation of Horses by Sea during the Era of the Crusades', *The Mariner's Mirror*, 68 (1982)

Quick, J., 'The Number and Distribution of Knights in Thirteenth Century England: The Evidence of the Grand Assize Lists', *Thirteenth Century England I*, ed. P. Coss and S.D. Lloyd (Woodbridge, 1986)

Reynolds, S., *Fiefs and Vassals* (Oxford, 1994)

Richardson, H.G., and Sayles, G.O., *The Governance of Medieval England* (1963)

Richmond, C.F., 'The War at Sea', *The Hundred Years War*, ed. K. Fowler (1971)

Roberts, M., *The Military Revolution, 1560–1660*, reprinted in *Essays in Swedish History* (1967)

Rogers, C.J., 'The Military Revolutions of the Hundred Years War', *Journal of Military History*, 57 (1993)

——, 'Edward III and the Dialectics of Strategy', *TRHS*, 6th ser., 4 (1994)

Rogers, R., *Latin Siege Warfare in the Twelfth Century* (Oxford, 1992)

Roskell, J.S., Clark, L., and Rawcliffe, C., *The History of Parliament. The House of Commons, 1386–1421* (Stroud, 1992)

Round, J.H., *Feudal England* (1895)

——, *The King's Sergeants and Officers of State* (1911)

Runyan, T.J., 'Ships and Mariners in Later Medieval England', *Journal of British Studies*, 16 (1977)

Russell, F.H., *The Just War in the Middle Ages* (1975)

Sanders, I.J., *Feudal Military Service in England* (Oxford, 1956)

Saul, A., 'Great Yarmouth and the Hundred Years War in the Fourteenth Century', *BIHR*, 52 (1979)

Saul, N., *Knights and Esquires: The Gloucestershire Gentry in the Fourteenth Century* (Oxford, 1981)

Scammell, J., 'Robert I and the North of England', *EHR*, 73 (1958)

——, 'The Formation of the English Social Structure: Freedom, Knights and Gentry, 1066–1300', *Speculum*, 68 (1993)

Sherborne, J.W., 'Indentured Retinues and English Expeditions', *EHR*, 79 (1964)

——, 'The English Navy: Shipping and Manpower', *Past and Present*, 37 (1967)

——, 'The Battle of La Rochelle and the War at Sea, 1272–5', *BIHR*, 42 (1969)

——, 'The Cost of English Warfare with France in the Later Fourteenth Century', *BIHR*, 50 (1977)

——, 'John of Gaunt, Edward III's Retinue and the French Campaign of 1369', *Kings and Nobles in the Later Middle Ages*, ed. R.A. Griffiths and J. Sherborne (Gloucester, 1986)

Shrader, C.R., 'A Handlist of Extant Manuscripts containing the *De Re Militari* of Flavius Vegetius Renatus', *Scriptorium*, 33 (1979)

Smith, R.D., 'Artillery and the Hundred Years War', *AAF*

Stacey, R.C., *Politics, Policy and Finance under Henry III, 1216–1245* (Oxford, 1987)

Stenton, F.M., *The First Century of English Feudalism, 1066–1166* (Oxford, 1932)

Strickland, M., 'Securing the North: Invasion and the Strategy of Defence in twelfth-century Anglo-Scottish Warfare', *Anglo-Norman Warfare*, ed. Strickland (Woodbridge, 1992)

——, 'Against the Lord's Anointed: aspects of warfare and baronial rebellion in England and Normandy, 1075–1265', *Law and Government in Medieval England and Normandy: Essays in Honour of Sir James Holt*, ed. G. Garnett and J. Hudson (Cambridge, 1994)

——, ed., *Anglo-Norman Warfare* (Woodbridge, 1992)

Sumption, J., *The Hundred Years War: Trial by Battle* (1990)

Suppe, F.C., *Military Institutions on the Welsh Marches: Shropshire, a.d. 1066–1300* (Woodbridge, 1994)

Sutherland, D.W., 'Peytevin *v.* La Lynde', *Law Quarterly Review*, 83 (1967)

Taylor, A.J., 'Master Bertram, *Ingeniator Regis*', *Studies in Medieval History presented to R. Allen Brown* (Woodbridge, 1989)

Thompson, K., 'Robert of Bellême Reconsidered', *ANS*, 13 (1990)

Timbal, P.-C., *La Guerre de cent ans vue à travers les registres du parlement (1337–1369)* (Paris, 1961)

Tinniswood, J.T., 'English Galleys, 1272–1377', *Mariner's Mirror*, 35 (1949)

Tipping, C., 'Cargo Handling of the Medieval Cog', *Mariner's Mirror*, 80 (1994)

Tout, T.F., *Chapters in the Administrative History of Mediaeval England*, 6 vols (Manchester, 1920–33)

———, 'The Fair of Lincoln and the "Histoire de Guillaume le Maréchal"', *Collected Papers*, ii (1934)

———, 'Firearms in England in the Fourteenth Century', *Collected Papers*, ii (1934)

———, 'Some Neglected Fights between Crécy and Poitiers', *Collected Papers*, ii (1934)

———, 'The Tactics of the Battles of Boroughbridge and Morlaix', *Collected Papers*, ii (1934)

Tuck, J.A., 'War and Society in the Medieval North', *Northern History*, 21 (1985)

Turner, R.V., *King John* (1994)

Tyerman, C., *England and the Crusades 1095–1588* (Chicago, 1988)

Tyson, C., 'The Battle of Otterbourne. When and where was it fought?', *War and Border Societies in the Middle Ages*, ed. A. Goodman and A. Tuck (1992)

Unger, R.W., *The Ship in the Medieval Economy 600–1600* (1980)

Vale, J., *Edward III and Chivalry: Chivalric Society and its Context 1270–1350* (Woodbridge, 1983)

Vale, M.G.A., *English Gascony, 1399–1453* (Oxford, 1970)

———, 'Sir John Fastolf's "Report" of 1435: a New Interpretation Reconsidered', *Nottingham Medieval Studies*, 17 (1973)

———, *War and Chivalry: Warfare and Chivalric Culture in England, France and Burgundy at the End of the Middle Ages* (1981)

———, *The Angevin Legacy and the Hundred Years War 1250–1340* (Oxford, 1990)

Van Crefeld, M., *Supplying War* (Cambridge, 1977)

Verbruggen, J.F., *The Art of Warfare in Western Europe during the Middle Ages* (Amsterdam, 1977)

Vincent, N., 'A Roll of Knights Summoned to Campaign in 1213', *Historical Research*, 66 (1993)

Walker, R.F., 'Hubert de Burgh and Wales, 1218–1232', *EHR*, 87 (1972)

Walker, S., 'Profit and Loss in the Hundred Years War: the subcontracts of Sir John Strother, 1374', *BIHR*, 58 (1985)

———, *The Lancastrian Affinity 1361–1399* (Oxford, 1990)

Waugh, S.L., 'Tenure to Contract: Lordship and Clientage in Thirteenth-Century England', *EHR*, 101 (1986)

Whitwell, R.J. and Johnson, C., 'The "Newcastle" Galley. A.D. 1294', *Archaeologia Aeliana*, 4th ser., 2 (1926)

Wright, S.M., *The Derbyshire Gentry in the Fifteenth Century* (Derbyshire Record Soc., viii, 1983)

Wrottesley, G., *Crécy and Calais* (1898)

Index

Entries in **bold** type refer to illustrations. Individuals are normally referred to by their surname, where known.